COMMODITY CHAINS
AND GLOBAL CAPITALISM

COMMODITY CHAINS
AND
GLOBAL CAPITALISM

EDITED BY
Gary Gereffi and
Miguel Korzeniewicz

Westport, Connecticut
London

Library of Congress Cataloging-in-Publication Data

Commodity chains and global capitalism / edited by Gary Gereffi and
   Miguel Korzeniewicz.
       p.   cm.
    Includes bibliographical references and index.
    ISBN 0–275–94573–1 (alk. paper)
    1. Commercial products.   2. International division of labor.
3. Manufactures.   4. Offshore assembly industry.   5. International
business enterprises—Management.   6. Competition, International.
I. Gereffi, Gary.   II. Korzeniewicz, Miguel.
HF1040.7.C66   1994
338.4′767—dc20   93–7082

British Library Cataloguing in Publication Data is available.

A hardcover edition of *Commodity Chains and Global Capitalism* is available from the
Greenwood Press imprint of Greenwood Publishing Group, Inc. (ISBN: 0–313–28914–X).

Library of Congress Catalog Card Number: 93–7082
ISBN: 0–275–94573–1

First published in 1994

Praeger Publishers, 88 Post Road West, Westport, CT 06881
An imprint of Greenwood Publishing Group, Inc.

Printed in the United States of America

The paper used in this book complies with the
Permanent Paper Standard issued by the National
Information Standards Organization (Z39.48–1984).

10 9 8 7 6 5 4 3 2 1

Contents

Illustrations

FIGURES

TABLES

MAPS

Acknowledgments

All the papers assembled in this volume were presented at the Sixteenth Annual Conference on the Political Economy of the World-System, held at Duke University on April 16–18, 1992. We would like to thank all the participants, including those not represented here, for making the conference a lively and intellectually stimulating event.

Organized under the auspices of the Political Economy of the World-System section of the American Sociological Association, the conference's local costs were generously supported by the Duke University Department of Sociology through funding provided by the Howard E. Jensen Trust and by the Office of the Provost at Duke. In addition, the publication of the paperback edition of this volume was made possible by grants from the Howard E. Jensen Trust, as well as from the Duke University Center for International Studies. Special thanks are given to Alan Kerckhoff and Kenneth Land of Duke's Sociology Department for their support of this initiative.

Numerous people were involved in facilitating the conference as well as the publication of this volume. Judith Dillon has coordinated the administrative support of all phases of this project with an uncommon degree of wit and charm. During the conference, she was assisted by a variety of sociology graduate students, including Phillip Atkison, Insook Chang, and Deborah Gross, along with Jay Chen, Lu-Lin Cheng, Stephanie Fonda, Kevin Kresse, and Brigitte Neary. The Department of Sociology at the University of New Mexico provided both financial and administrative assistance to Miguel Korzeniewicz, while Victoria Carty contributed to our efforts with logistical and research inputs. Amby

Rice, working at Duke University, has greatly improved the look of this volume by designing many of the figures and tables used in various chapters. Martha Dimes Toher has our thanks for the often underappreciated task (except by scholars) of preparing the index.

1

Introduction: Global Commodity Chains

Gary Gereffi, Miguel Korzeniewicz,
and Roberto P. Korzeniewicz

Industrialization on a world scale has undergone significant shifts during the past two decades. The capacity to produce and export manufactured goods is being dispersed to an ever expanding network of peripheral and core nations alike. Economic globalization has been accompanied by flexible specialization, or the appearance of new, technologically dynamic forms of organization that usually are characterized by low equipment dedication, high product differentiation, and short production runs. In today's global factory, the production of a single commodity often spans many countries, with each nation performing tasks in which it has a cost advantage. The components of the Ford Escort, for example, are made and assembled in fifteen countries across three continents. Capitalism today thus entails the detailed disaggregation of stages of production and consumption across national boundaries, under the organizational structure of densely networked firms or enterprises (see Dicken, 1992; Porter, 1990; Reich, 1991). Crucial concepts in comparative sociology, such as national development and industrialization, are increasingly perceived as problematic in facilitating an understanding of these emerging patterns of social and economic organization.

But how novel are these emerging phenomena and world-economic patterns? Do they indeed signal the emergence of a new international division of labor? In order to successfully address these questions, we must find a theoretical approach that is analytically sensitive to historical change in order to evaluate and distinguish cyclical patterns from new trends. This framework must capture both the spatial features of these transformations across the world-economy, and the relationships that link these processes together. To contribute to such a theory, and as a means of understanding the changing spatial organization of production and consumption in the contemporary world-economy, the articles in this book critically explore and elaborate the global commodity chains (GCCs) approach, which reformulates the basic conceptual categories needed to analyze new patterns of global organization and change.

A commodity chain has been defined by Hopkins and Wallerstein (1986: 159) as "a network of labor and production processes whose end result is a finished commodity." A GCC consists of sets of interorganizational networks clustered around one commodity or product, linking households, enterprises, and states to one another within the world-economy. These networks are situationally specific, socially constructed, and locally integrated, underscoring the social embeddedness of economic organization. As indicated by Hopkins and Wallerstein (chapter 2 in this volume), "the greatest virtue of a commodity chain is its emphasis on process" (p.50).

Specific processes or segments within a commodity chain can be represented as boxes or nodes, linked together in networks. Each successive node within a commodity chain involves the acquisition and/or organization of inputs (e.g., raw materials or semifinished products), labor power (and its provisioning), transportation, distribution (via markets or transfers), and consumption. The analysis of a commodity chain shows how production, distribution, and consumption are shaped by the social relations (including organizations) that characterize the sequential stages of input acquisition, manufacturing, distribution, marketing, and consumption.

The GCCs approach promotes a nuanced analysis of world-economic spatial inequalities in terms of differential access to markets and resources. Our GCC framework allows us to pose questions about contemporary development issues that are not easily handled by previous paradigms, and permits us to more adequately forge the macro-micro links between processes that are generally assumed to be discretely contained within global, national, and local units of analysis. The paradigm that GCCs embody is a network-centered and historical approach that probes above and below the level of the nation-state to better analyze structure and change in the world-economy.

COMPETITION, INNOVATION AND COMMODITY CHAINS

Bringing a new focus to world-systems theory, the articles in this book share an emphasis on competition and innovation as crucial world-economic components of historical shifts in the organization of global commodity chains. For example, Hopkins and Wallerstein (chapter 2) tell us that monopoly and competition are key to understanding the distribution of wealth among the nodes in a commodity chain. Within a commodity chain, a relatively greater share of wealth generally accrues to core-like nodes than to peripheral ones. This is because competitive pressures are less pronounced in core-like nodes than in peripheral ones. Enterprises and states in the core, according to this argument, gain a competitive edge through innovations that transfer competitive pressures to peripheral areas of the world-economy.

To provide historical evidence for these propositions, Özveren and Pelizzon contribute to chapter 2 by analyzing (respectively) the organization of shipbuilding and wheat production. In shipbuilding, the type of networks linking labor, enterprises, and states were crucial in shaping competition. Dutch shipyards initially gained a competitive edge by exploiting lower costs (e.g., in raw materials and labor). Likewise, in the semiperipheral colonies of North America the availability of land acted as a magnet for labor, enhancing the competitive position of shipbuilders. Spain underwent an economic decline, but England remained an important competitor, partly because of navy orders. Later, the Dutch shipyards lost ground to their rivals in the Thames and colonial America. For the English shipyards, access to colonial raw materials lowered costs, while the growing importance of oceanic trade for the country increased demand. For the American shipyards, easy access to raw materials (timber) allowed them to overcome the constraint of higher labor costs. As a result of effective competition, shipbuilders in the core constantly faced the peripheralization of certain production processes, and responded by generating innovations designed to provide a new competitive edge (e.g., the introduction of steamships in the nineteenth century).

Innovation was not limited to manufacturing processes. Pelizzon (chapter 2) analyzes the characteristics of the wheat commodity chain to show that marketing emerged as a distinct set of activities only in core areas. In the periphery, landlords and merchants tended to be the same individuals. Core and peripheral areas were also distinct in their infrastructure, with the core being characterized by faster and more effective transportation. Finally, consumption showed distinct patterns in core and peripheral areas: wheat bread, for example, tended to be consumed only by the wealthy in core zones and the highest magnates of the periphery, while the poor in core zones and the well-off in the periphery consumed rye bread.

Differences between nodes located in core and peripheral areas also are explored by Appelbaum, Smith, and Christerson (chapter 9), who argue that the crucial distinction between poor and rich countries is in the relative value of the commodities produced in each area—rather than a simple expression of varying degrees of processing (for a similar point, see chapter 4 by R. P. Korzeniewicz and Martin; chapter 7 by Raynolds; and chapter 15 by Wilson and Zambrano). The authors examine whether high-value products (e.g., wool suits) tend to be characterized by greater spatial concentration than low-value goods (e.g., synthetic blouses). Their results show that high-value commodities indeed exhibit a greater degree of clustering in fewer nations. This research suggests that the growth of manufacturing in peripheral and semiperipheral areas has been fueled not only by high labor costs in the core, but as part of an entrepreneurial strategy designed to enhance industrial flexibility and overcome protectionist barriers preventing the free flow of commodities. Access to GCCs, the timing and place of entry, and upgrading are sources of power for firms that hope to be internationally competitive. Constant upgrading becomes a driving objective in the organizational strategy of enterprises.

Patterns of competition and innovation are crucial to understanding the organization and transformation of GCCs. The relative distribution of wealth within a commodity chain often has been portrayed in the social sciences as reflective of levels in a hierarchy of production. Within this hierarchy, less wealth was assumed to accrue to nodes involving the production of raw materials, and to increase proportionally as movement proceeded to manufacturing, distribution, and so forth. But traditional "extractive" activities such as agriculture and mining are giving rise to new export-oriented and technology-intensive forms of production with considerable industrial value-added at the local level (see Raynolds, chapter 7; Wilson and Zambrano, chapter 15). Similarly, many of today's most profitable "service" industries are intimately tied to manufacturing activities that demolish the myth of a postindustrial society (Cohen and Zysman, 1987). In many developing nations, relatively labor-intensive services (like software programming, bank and airline data processing, and inexpensive medical services) may become a more important growth area than manufacturing. These cross-sectoral linkages can best be seen and appreciated using a GCC framework that does not limit itself to conventional "industry" boundaries. In fact, Hopkins and Wallerstein (chapter 2) indicate that the concept of GCCs ultimately challenges the hierarchical distinction between raw material production, industry, and services. All activities transform, all involve "human skilled judgment." Within a commodity chain, profitability shifts from node to node according to competitive pressures, and "industry" is not always a motor of development. The GCCs approach explains the distribution of wealth within a chain as an outcome of the relative intensity of competition within different nodes.

This emphasis on the important role of competition and innovation in shaping the distribution of wealth within global commodity chains brings a new focus to world-systems theory. To some extent, this is part of an interdisciplinary phenomenon in the social sciences. Recent changes in world markets and political structures have made international competitiveness a fashionable buzzword as well as a burgeoning topic in comparative research. But within world-systems theory, this new concern does not merely follow intellectual fashion: it is a consequence of ongoing debates about the role of entrepreneurial strategies, Schumpeterian innovations, and patterns of competition in shaping the global division of labor.[1]

COMMODITY CHAINS AS COMPETITION EMBEDDED IN TIME AND SPACE

Is the world-economy characterized by a new division of labor? Focusing primarily on the twentieth century, Schoenberger (chapter 3) tends to answer yes. Her contribution tells us that competition, time, and space are closely interrelated. Competition is geographically embedded, and commodity chains highlight this dimension. Earlier in the twentieth century, product stability (or stable markets) provided spatial freedom to enterprises by allowing the development of mass production methods. With stable product configuration and consistent flow, internationalized production was facilitated: "in short, control over time allows an unusual form of control over space." Batch production, on the other hand, emphasizes the constant development of products, and over recent decades this has entailed a new organization of time and space built around product differentiation. In this sense, "time has become part of the firm's competitive strategy in the market." Thus, "standardized mass production . . . allowed a truly extraordinary and extensive spatial division of labor. The development process was wholly divorced from actual production, and discrete elements of the manufacturing system could be hived off and settled in far-flung corners of the globe, the whole knit together by the steady flow of slowly changing, standardized product through the pipeline. Flexible mass production is less likely to assume this spatial form." The new system that characterizes the global division of labor, because of the very organization of markets and consumption in the contemporary world, "is much less flexible spatially."

Whereas Schoenberger emphasizes the qualitative nature of these transformations, Hopkins and Wallerstein (chapter 2) suggest that concentration and decentralization, or shifts in the zonal location of nodes (e.g., from core to periphery), are associated with cyclical rhythms of the world-economy. Already in the seventeenth and eighteenth centuries, as Hopkins and Wallerstein tell us, commodity chains "traversed many frontiers and tended to reach throughout most areas within the effective boundaries of the capitalist world-economy in that era." During periods of world-economic contraction, or B-phases, falling demand leads to a narrowing of the number of production units and product specialization lessens. Periods of expansion, or A-phases, are characterized by growing vertical integration, for enterprises seek to reduce the number of market transactions to lower costs. In other words, A-phases provide incentives to lower transaction costs (and hence lead to growing vertical integration), while B-phases provide incentives to reduce labor costs (leading to declining vertical integration and an increase of subcontracting). Current transformations in the world-economy, we may assume, are rooted in these historical cycles.

These arguments on cyclical rhythms suggest that organizational strategies are shaped by patterns of competition that vary across chains and within nodes. Fitting well with this overall proposition, most contributions to this volume emphasize the heterogeneity of organizational arrangements characterizing nodes and networks within commodity chains. For example, Özveren (chapter 2) suggests that technological innovation in shipbuilding was concentrated in the larger shipyards, but these latter units were often shifting production to smaller enterprises characterized by more intense competition and greater capital risks. For a much later period, Taplin (chapter 10) highlights the heterogeneity of entrepreneurial strategies in the apparel commodity chain in the United States. In an effort to enhance profits, enterprises must seek an effective balance between domestic subcontracting, overseas production, and rationalized manufacturing. Competitiveness is based (for some firms more than others) not only on cost but speed of delivery, availability of an infrastructure, control, and risk. In the United States, production for fashion-oriented enterprises tends to be small-batch and centered in New York City and Los Angeles; for enterprises engaged in standardized production, the area of choice for U.S. manufacturing is the Southeast region of the country.[2] Given this emphasis on heterogeneity, most authors in this volume seek to identify patterns of competition and organization within GCCs.

THE ORGANIZATION OF COMMODITY CHAINS AND INTERNATIONAL COMPETITIVENESS

The GCCs approach has significant links to the broader literature on international competitiveness. For example, there are a number of similarities between GCCs and Michael Porter's value chain approach: "a firm's value chain is an interdependent system or network of activities, connected by linkages. Linkages occur when the way in which one activity is performed affects the cost or effectiveness of other activities" (Porter, 1990: 41). As in our GCCs, Porter's value chains show the benefits that firms derive in breaking the production process into discrete segments to help them look for innovative organizational and managerial practices to improve their productivity and profit. Porter (1987: 29) argues that the appropriate focus in studying competitiveness is the industry (or, in our terms, the commodity chain) because this is "the arena in which competitive advantage is won or lost." And perhaps the most important aspect of this perspective for our purposes is Porter's (1987: 30) assertion that competitive success in a global industry requires a firm to manage the linkages in a GCC in an integrated or systemic fashion.

From this point of view, there are two primary factors that explain shifts in the geographical location and organization of manufacturing in GCCs. One is the search for low-wage labor, and the other is the pursuit of organizational flexibility. These two factors alone cannot account, however, for dynamic trends in international competitiveness. Cheap labor is what Porter calls a "lower-order" competitive advantage, since it is an inherently unstable basis on which to build a global strategy. More significant factors driving the international competitiveness of firms are the "higher-order" advantages such as proprietary technology, product differentiation, brand reputation, customer relationships, and constant industrial upgrading (Porter, 1990: 49–51). These assets allow enterprises to exercise a greater degree of organizational flexibility and thus to create as well as respond to new opportunities in the global economy.

While Porter's approach helps pinpoint the mechanisms that generate dynamic competitive advantages, the GCC framework allows us to specify more precisely, both in space and across time, the organizational features and changes in the transnational production systems undergirding the competitive strategies of firms and states. Gereffi (chapter 5) argues that commodity chains have three main dimensions: an input-output structure (a set of products and services linked together in a sequence of value-adding economic activities); a territoriality (spatial dispersion or concentration of enterprises in production and distribution networks); and a governance structure (authority and power relationships). As Chandler (1977) has described for the United States in the late nineteenth and early twentieth centuries, commodity chains were internalized within the organizational boundaries of vertically integrated corporations. In such cases, the governance structure became the ''visible hand'' of corporate management. However, as commodity chains have become more globalized in the second half of the twentieth century, some links that were internal to the modern corporation are being externalized, thereby becoming the tasks of a network of independent firms. Under these circumstances, the governance structure, which is essential to the coordination of transnational production systems, is no longer synonymous with a corporate hierarchy.

Gereffi (chapter 5) argues that governance structures for the networked GCCs that have emerged in the last two decades can usefully be conceptualized as falling into two types: producer-driven and buyer-driven commodity chains. The difference between these two types of commodity chains resides in the location of their key barriers to entry. Producer-driven commodity chains are those in which large, usually transnational, corporations play the central roles in coordinating production networks (including backward and forward linkages). This is most characteristic of capital- and technology-intensive commodities such as automobiles, aircraft, semiconductors, and electrical machinery.

Buyer-driven commodity chains, on the other hand, are those in which large retailers, brand-named merchandisers, and trading companies play the central role in shaping decentralized production networks in a variety of exporting countries, frequently located in the periphery. This pattern of industrialization is typical in relatively labor-intensive consumer goods such as garments, footwear, toys, and housewares. The main functions of the core enterprises in these networks are to undertake the high-value activities, such as design and marketing, and to coordinate the other relationships, thus assuring that all the network transactions mesh smoothly. An important trend in global manufacturing appears to be a movement from producer-driven to buyer-driven commodity chains.

The GCC approach thus is linked to the concerns raised by network analysis in sociology. The relational terminology and methodology used by network analysts are highly appropriate for our GCC framework. In general, the term ''network'' may be defined as ''a set of units (or nodes) of some kind and the relations of specific types that occur among them'' (Alba, 1982: 42). The form of the network refers to the overall configuration of relations in the network or its parts. These properties, applied to the analysis of commodity chains, include the ''length'' of a chain, the ''density'' of interactions in a particular segment, and the ''depth'' or number of levels that occur at different stages of a GCC.

An example of a "dense" production network is found in the garment industry, where large numbers of local subcontractors often supply a single manufacturer (Rothstein, 1989). The Japanese automobile industry and the U.S. defense industry are examples of "deep" production networks, with each final assembly firm cultivating ties with numerous layers of component suppliers in a pyramidal fashion (Hill, 1989). The power of network analysis lies in the potential explanatory contribution of the various structural properties of a network.[3]

We can draw on the rich vocabulary of network analysis to compare GCCs diachronically as well as synchronically. If we are correct in asserting, for example, that recent changes in the world-economy involve the development of longer, more decentralized, and more flexible commodity chains (in contrast to commodity chains that tended to be internalized within large corporations located primarily in core countries), then the formal properties of GCCs such as length, centrality, density, depth, and size should be measured with some degree of precision. Similarly, it is important to study changes in the organization of the same GCC over time. There has been a tendency for the GCCs in most industries to become internationally more dispersed during the past two decades, with increased production in low-wage areas. However, this "new international division of labor" hides increased levels of product specialization within individual nations, and tends to minimize the extent of industrial upgrading that is occurring within the NICs that are moving to high-value-added, more profitable products within specific industries. Further development of the tools of network analysis will be essential to map these diachronic changes, including the growth and contraction of particular GCCs. The contribution by R. P. Korzeniewicz and Martin (chapter 4) suggests concrete methodological procedures that can be undertaken to advance in this direction.

But how do we know where GCCs start and where they end? What criteria should we use in determining which GCCs to study? For instance, a manufacturing plant might be a central unit in the production network of a GCC, but this node may also serve as the end-point of the raw material supply network and as the starting point for the export network. Pushed to an extreme, we would need a Leontieff-type input-output matrix of the entire world-economy just to do a totally comprehensive GCC analysis of an automobile with its 15,000 individual parts. We are thus best advised to design categories in which GCCs can be appropriately grouped or clustered to meaningfully test specific hypotheses, and draw boundaries that capture those segments of GCCs that are functionally linked, not well understood, and for which good data can be obtained.

For example, if we wish to explore the hypothesis that the spatial dispersion of GCCs to peripheral nations in the world-system is directly related to the labor-intensity of the commodities being produced, then we might group GCCs into the categories of labor-intensive consumer nondurable goods (e.g., garments and footwear), versus the more capital- and technology-intensive consumer durable products (e.g., automobiles and computers) and capital goods (e.g., machinery).

Or alternatively, we might want to show from a world-systems perspective that the degree of value-added in a GCC declines as we move from core to semi-peripheral to peripheral production sites (controlling for the possible effects of different technologies). Again, the contribution by R. P. Korzeniewicz and Martin (chapter 4) provides useful methodological guidelines for designing studies along these lines. Ultimately, the choice of which GCCs to study is a theoretical matter.

LINKING THE MICRO AND MACRO DIMENSIONS OF COMMODITY CHAINS

A GCC approach can both draw upon and contribute to the literature that focuses on development issues by analyzing the trajectory of individual enterprises and commodities. In fact, several of the contributions to this volume emphasize the importance of looking at organizational strategies and competitive relations between firms to understand the dynamics of commodity chains (see, for example, chapter 5 by Gereffi, chapter 7 by Raynolds, chapter 12 by M. Korzeniewicz, and chapter 14 by Kim and Lee). To the extent that it allows a focus on enterprises (either individually or within the production network of particular commodities), the analysis of GCCs provides a bridge between the macro-historical concerns that have usually characterized the world-systems literature, and the micro-organizational and state-centered issues that have stimulated recent studies in international political economy.

By analyzing patterns of competition among specific enterprises, the GCC approach can explore issues such as the role of ethnicity as a variable shaping the structure of commodity chains. For example, Chen (chapter 8) suggests that the structure of investments in Mainland China by enterprises in Hong Kong and Taiwan was significantly shaped by preexisting ties based on kinship. Likewise, Raynolds (chapter 7) argues that ethnic identification between Asian producers in the Dominican Republic and Asian wholesalers in the United States allowed for the creation and maintenance of trade networks that were essential to exports of fresh vegetables. Within global commodity chains, kinship and ethnic identity appear as crucial social resources that can be deployed by enterprises in their efforts to gain or sustain a competitive edge.

Several of the articles emphasize the importance of state action as a variable shaping the organization of enterprises within commodity chains. Chen (chapter 8) indicates that state policies were central to the development and growing integration of the commodity chain networks linking Mainland China, Taiwan, and Hong Kong in a new spatial division of labor. Foreign investments in China's labor-intensive industries can be explained in part by the role of rising labor costs and growing competitive pressures in core and semiperipheral areas, as well as an entrepreneurial effort to penetrate the Mainland market. To explain the *timing* of these transformations, however, Chen emphasizes a state-centered argument that focuses on China's policies. Likewise, Lee and Cason (chapter

11) suggest that variation and heterogeneity in industrial upgrading in the semi-periphery are explained by state policy, business strategy, and geographical variables. Eschewing simple generalizations about patterns of development in Asia and Latin America, Lee and Cason argue that there are greater similarities between Mexico and South Korea than between Mexico and Brazil. Finally, Wilson and Zambrano (chapter 15) show that crack cocaine has involved the development of flexible production systems linked to new markets. In a sense, according to the authors, Colombian drug organizations can be understood as multinational corporations geared toward the U.S. market. Less state regulation is to be found within this commodity chain, but the authors suggest that state policies nevertheless significantly affect the organization of this commodity chain at each of its networks and nodes.

LINKING PERIPHERAL AND CORE NODES: SERVICES, DISTRIBUTION, AND CONSUMPTION

The chapters in this volume indicate that to analyze processes of competition and innovation within a commodity chain, it is often necessary to focus on activities other than production. Gereffi (chapter 5) suggests that globalization involves functional integration, and this requires administrative coordination or governance. Governance structures can be either centralized or decentralized. Centralized coordination tends to be producer-driven (e.g., coordination by a transnational auto company of its many subsidiaries and subcontractors), while decentralized coordination prevails in buyer-driven commodity chains (e.g., those organized by retailers or brand-name companies). In this particular case, overseas sourcing became an innovation that allowed some retailing firms to gain a competitive edge in an increasingly complex consumer market. As in other cases, innovation itself increased the share of wealth captured by certain nodes (marketing) within a commodity chain, while decreasing the share of the "peripheralized" nodes (manufacturing). Hence Gereffi suggests that GCCs are characterized by change over time in the type of agents that characterize different nodes. An understanding of these agents can ultimately be produced only by a historical and comparative analysis.

Services are a frequently neglected component in the analysis of economic globalization. Rabach and Kim (chapter 6) indicate that services are crucial in linking the nodes of a commodity chain together. Drawing on Gereffi's analytical distinction between producer-driven and buyer-driven types of commodity chains, the authors suggest that producer-driven chains contain both systemic and subsystemic niches. The systemic niches tend to be closely integrated with established markets and are characterized by high capital investments. Although these niches have initial periods of strong competition, they can develop into a "winner takes all" type of situation (e.g., VHS versus Beta in the market for video players) that is followed by limited competitive challenges. The subsystemic core niches, on the other hand, are flexible but dependent on the technological and marketing paradigms generated by the systemic niches. In buyer-driven chains, on the other hand, "the 'state of the art' remains subsystemic," and there are no qualitative or paradigmatic technological shifts of the type that prevail in the systemic niches of producer-driven chains.

Rabach and Kim suggest that the organization of services is crucial to GCCs because "they *integrate* and *coordinate* the atomized and globalized production processes." Services shape what is produced (e.g., design, research and development), how it is produced (e.g., choice of technology, organization of production), spatial coordination (e.g., production transfers, or what Gereffi in chapter 5 refers to as "triangular manufacturing"), other facilitating activities (e.g., insurance, finance), and the distribution of commodities. Services involve the organization of information, and control over this information generally entails a commanding position over the wealth produced within a commodity chain. The competitive edge here is provided by the rate of increase of knowledge rather than the total stock of knowledge.

Discussion of recent transformations in the organization of production and consumption is often carried out as if the emerging changes are simply functional requirements or outcomes of postindustrial or post-Fordist social arrangements. By emphasizing the multiplicity of organizational arrangements, however, the GCC approach identifies these transformations as an outcome of the complex and diverse strategic choices pursued by households, states, and enterprises. Wilson and Zambrano (chapter 15), for example, suggest that coca cultivation is one mechanism through which peasant households have responded to falling commodity prices in Latin America, while selling drugs constitutes in part a response of the urban poor in the United States to the prevalence of low-paid jobs. Distribution networks are also diversified, as Wilson and Zambrano show in the cocaine commodity chain.

Raynolds (chapter 7) challenges the concepts of Fordism and post-Fordism as analytical categories. Although agriculture was characterized by mass production during the 1950s and 1960s, flexible production has become more pronounced over the last two decades. As a result, agriculture involves a heterogeneous combination of firms, types of ownership, size, and relative access to markets. Large enterprises tend to gain a competitive advantage because of their market power, but small enterprises retain a competitive edge from their greater flexibility in organizing production. Large enterprises are less rigid than generally assumed: size enables them to implement large-scale innovations. On the other hand, small firms are less flexible than usually assumed: restricted assets and markets make them particularly vulnerable to cycles. Raynolds convincingly suggests that a commodity-based approach can provide a more nuanced analysis of organizational structures and strategies in agriculture. Similar to other contributions to this volume, she emphasizes the active relationships (e.g., competition, innovation) through which agents (e.g., enterprises, states) generate new patterns of organization.

Finally, the contributions by M. Korzeniewicz (chapter 12) and Goldfrank (chapter 13) emphasize the importance of consumption patterns to understanding the basic dynamics of a commodity chain. In the case of athletic footwear, as indicated by M. Korzeniewicz, the success of the Nike Corporation can be largely traced to the firm's success in extending effective control to the distribution, marketing, and advertising nodes of this commodity chain. An important corollary of the transfer of manufacturing to peripheral nations is that the distribution and marketing segments of GCCs have become increasingly profitable. The wealth that accrues to brand-name companies and retailers in core countries generally is much higher when production is done overseas rather than domestically, because of savings in labor costs and the greater flexibility of sellers in filling specialized niches of consumer demand.

Goldfrank's contribution analyzes the hitherto neglected portions of the commodity chain in Chilean fruit. Focusing on distribution, promotion, and particularly final consumption, he argues that a new "produce-stand ethic" of health and fitness consciousness among affluent consumers in North America is joined with wholesalers' and produce multinationals' efforts to provide year-round supplies of formerly seasonal fresh fruits and vegetables to drive an expanding set of commodity chains involving counterseasonal production in the southern hemisphere. Like M. Korzeniewicz in his treatment of athletic shoes, Goldfrank places great emphasis on the changing culture of the core.

These arguments suggest that one theoretically relevant category is largely implicit but not sufficiently developed in this volume: households. Low labor costs in peripheral nations, and the development of new consumer markets in core nations, are discussed as important variables shaping ongoing transformations in GCCs. But neither of these variables can be fully addressed without a more substantial discussion of the organization and composition of households, and the changing relationship of households to enterprises and states. At stake is not merely the issue of households as a source of labor (waged or unwaged, expensive or cheap). In the modern world-economy the organization and composition of households embodies the construction of consumption as well as processes of status group formation (constructed around dimensions such as gender sterotypes, age, and female and male participation in the labor force). Households are a principal site in the construction of identities (e.g., gender, race, class, ethnicity, sexuality), and a GCCs approach must further elaborate this category to avoid missing a crucial analytical link.

CONCLUSION

A GCCs approach ultimately allows us to critically evaluate theoretical concepts that have hitherto prevailed in the comparative study of development, and that are deeply embedded in conventional analyses and vocabulary. Two such concepts, national development and industrialization, have become increasingly problematic in facilitating an understanding of emerging patterns of social and economic organization. Conventional approaches within the sociology of development tend to assume that development and industrialization are positively linked. Furthermore, although they differ in many of their main tenets and hypotheses, modernization and dependency theorists have shared the assumption that nation-states constitute the primary locus of capital accumulation, industrial growth, and state policies fostering integrated national development. All these assumptions are debatable, and some have suggested that any study of the distribution of wealth in the world-economy must necessarily avoid treating industrialization as synonymous with development (Arrighi and Drangel, 1986; see also Block, 1990). Global commodity chains allow us to focus on the creation and distribution of global wealth as embodied in a multidimensional, multistage sequence of activities, rather than as an outcome of industrialization alone. In this sense a GCCs approach provides the theoretical and methodological basis needed for a more systematic analysis of micro and macro processes within a new political economy of the world-system.

NOTES

The authors would like to thank Ann E. Forsythe and Thomas Janoski for their helpful comments. Some of the arguments in this introduction were originally contained in a paper presented by Gary Gereffi and Miguel Korzeniewicz at a conference on "The New Compass of the Comparativist: Methodological Advances in Comparative Political Economy," April 26–27, 1991, Duke University, Durham, NC.

1. Within world-systems theory, the contributions of Giovanni Arrighi were particularly important in promoting this analytical shift. See, for example, Arrighi and Drangel (1986) and Arrighi (1990).

2. Perhaps the differences between New York, Los Angeles, and the U.S. Southeast are related to the possibility of adapting different-sized business to regulated and unregulated labor markets and their environments.

3. Alba (1982) outlines two broad approaches to network analysis: "relational methods are based on the direct and indirect connections that exist between units in a network, while positional methods are based on similarities in their patterns of relations to others" (Alba, 1982: 52). While relational methods typically identify networks in terms of their internal structure and focus on the "pathways" in networks, the positional method identifies nodes that are defined in terms of their structural equivalence or similarity.

REFERENCES

Alba, Richard D. 1982. "Taking Stock of Network Analysis: A Decade's Results." *Research in the Sociology of Organizations* 1: 39–74.

Arrighi, Giovanni. 1990. "The Developmentalist Illusion: A Reconceptualization of the Semiperiphery." In *Semiperipheral States in the World Economy*, edited by William G. Martin, pp. 11–12. Westport, CT: Greenwood Press.

Arrighi, Giovanni, and Drangel, Jessica. 1986. "The Stratification of the World-Economy: An Exploration of the Semiperipheral Zone." *Review* 10, 1 (Summer): 9–74.

Block, Fred. 1990. *Postindustrial Possibilities: A Critique of Economic Discourse*. Berkeley: University of California Press.

Chandler, Alfred D., Jr. 1977. *The Visible Hand*. Cambridge, MA: Harvard University Press.

Cohen, Stephen S., and Zysman, John. 1987. *Manufacturing Matters: The Myth of the Post-Industrial Economy*. New York: Basic Books.

Dicken, Peter. 1992. *Global Shift: The Internationalization of Economic Activity*. 2d ed. New York: Guilford Publications.

Hill, Richard C. 1989. "Comparing Transnational Production Systems: The Automobile Industry in the USA and Japan." *International Journal of Urban and Regional Research* 13, 3 (Sept.): 462–80.

Hopkins, Terence K., and Wallerstein, Immanuel. 1986. "Commodity Chains in the World-Economy Prior to 1800." *Review* 10, 1: 157–70.

Porter, Michael E. 1987. "Changing Patterns of International Competition." In *The Competitive Challenge: Strategies for Industrial Innovation and Renewal*, edited by David J. Teece, pp. 27–57. Cambridge, MA: Ballinger.

———. 1990. *The Competitive Advantage of Nations*. New York: Free Press.

Reich, Robert B. 1991. *The Work of Nations: Preparing Ourselves for 21st-Century Capitalism*. New York: Alfred A. Knopf.

Rothstein, Richard. 1989. *Keeping Jobs in Fashion: Alternatives to the Euthanasia of the U.S. Apparel Industry*. Washington, D.C.: Economic Policy Institute.

PART I

Historical and Spatial Patterns of Commodity Chains in the World-System

2

Commodity Chains in the Capitalist World-Economy Prior to 1800

2.1
COMMODITY CHAINS: CONSTRUCT AND RESEARCH
Terence K. Hopkins and Immanuel Wallerstein

By commodity chain we mean "a network of labor and production processes whose end result is a finished commodity" (Hopkins and Wallerstein, 1986: 159). All firms or other units of production receive inputs and send outputs. Their transformation of the inputs that results in outputs locates them within a commodity chain (or quite often within multiple commodity chains). In terms of the structure of the capitalist world-economy, commodity chains may be thought of as the warp and woof of its system of social production. By tracing the networks of these commodity chains, one can track the ongoing division and integration of labor processes and thus monitor the constant development and transformation of the world-economy's production system.

The major direction of interzonal movements along the commodity chains is from a peripheral product to a core product. This is reflected in the widespread (and simplified) assumption that peripheral zones produce the raw materials and core zones the industrial products. We know that this bare-bones imagery is much too simple. Nonetheless, and however complex we make our analysis of the workings of the world-economy, it remains true that the principal interzonal movements along the commodity chains are in the direction periphery-to-core. It is also true, however, that the various commodity chains have differing proportions of their constituent production processes located in countries of predominantly core-like or predominantly peripheral production processes, or in semiperipheral countries that have roughly equal mixes of such production processes. Furthermore, we know that a historically given commodity chain may be so reconstructed that a larger or lesser proportion of its constituent production processes are located in one zone or the other. We shall argue that such consequential shifts in proportions—and hence of the complex axial division of labor—are linked to the cyclical rhythms of the world-economy.

We call the separable processes constituting a commodity chain "boxes." A box is thus a particular, quite specific production process. The first thing to note about a box is that its boundaries are socially defined, and thus may be redefined. Boxes may be consolidated (where there were two, there comes to be one) or subdivided (where there was one, there come to be two). These redefinitions are effected through technological changes and/or social organizational changes. (A further complication is that there may well not be a common pattern throughout the world-economy. It is quite possible that what is organized in one place as two or more separate boxes is organized in another as a single box.)

Focusing on any single box, one can pose a series of questions about the social organization of its constituent units. The first and in some ways the most important question is the degree to which the box is relatively monopolized by a small number of units of production, which is the same as asking the degree to which it is core-like and therefore a locus of a high rate of profit (often misleadingly called the "value-added"). One of the most important processes of the capitalist world-economy is the trend toward demonopolization of any highly profitable box, which is then often countered by technological changes and/or redefinitions of the organizational boundaries of the box by production units seeking to restore a high level of profit. Alternatively, big capital may shift its investment to other boxes (or of course to other chains) in search of increased profit.

A second question one can ask about a given box is the degree of geographic spread of the units of production filling that box. A core-like box is likely to have its units located in a very few countries. A peripheral box will tend to have units in a large number of countries (unless there are ecological reasons that limit the location of the production activity). It follows that as boxes are historically shifted from being core-like (relatively monopolized and highly profitable) to being peripheral (competitive and yielding a low rate of profit), their units tend to become located in more and more countries. There are also cyclical effects. Insofar as B-phases entail less demand for the world production of a given box, that usually results in the number of units of production being reduced, often resulting in turn in a narrowing of the geographic spread of the remaining units of production.

A third question one can ask about any box is the number of different commodity chains in which that box is located. There are obvious protections for the producers within any box in being linked to a diversity of kinds of outlets (other boxes) for their product. Hence the structure of production within a given box or its boundaries tend to be altered if that results in increased diversity. It is probable that such lessening of product specialization occurs more frequently in B-periods than in A-periods.

A fourth question one can ask about any box is the kind of property-like arrangements associated with the units of production in that box. There are many different possible arrangements. In one, the producers are all petty owners. In a second, they are part of a larger entity (whether this entity is private or parastatal), sometimes merely one of its component parts, but sometimes a (quasi-) autonomous division. In a third, the units are managed by nonowners who have a concession or a lease or some other equivalent arrangement that gives them administrative control and usufruct against certain fees or other transfers of money (or produce). And there are others. It is not at all necessary that all units of a given box have the same property arrangements. (This fact is sometimes used as the basis of a comparison of efficiencies on the doubtful assumption that property-like arrangements are alone causally relevant.) It can also be asked whether the comparative efficiencies differ between A- and B-periods.

And fifth, one can ask what modes of labor control are to be found in the box. These can range from many forms of wage employment to various forms of tenancy and other kinds of nonwage arrangements to varieties of coerced labor. Generally speaking, coerced labor tends to be found only in peripheral boxes. Sometimes the units of a given box may exhibit different forms of labor control, and quite regularly different boxes in a commodity chain have different characteristic modes of labor control.

Finally, we can look at the linkages joining the boxes. The sale of outputs and the purchase of inputs is only one form. To the extent that (the units in) two or more boxes are part of the same firm, we talk of vertical integration. We know that the degree of vertical integration tends to be cyclical, its increases usually coming in A-periods and its declines in B-periods, whereas concentration (reduced numbers of units within a box) follows an inverse pattern (up in B-periods, down in A-periods). Vertical integration by definition removes commodity-chain linkages from the sphere of market-like transactions (particularly significant when such linkages cross national boundaries), whereas the return of boxes to separate ownership normally reintroduces sale-purchase relations, which may of course be characterized by different modes of pricing (competitively formed, negotiated, administered, and so forth).

Cyclical shifts are thus one of the key considerations in the construction of commodity chains. They are basically the direct reflection of the organizing contradictions of the capitalist development of productive forces. For example, two system-imposed concerns of entrepreneurs—the reduction of transaction costs and the reduction of labor costs—commonly require quite opposite changes in social organization and geographical location. In general, transaction costs are reduced through the vertical integration and geographical convergence of boxes of a chain (both worldwide concentration and local urbanization). Labor costs, however, are generally reduced through subcontracting (adding boxes, the opposite of vertical integration) and geographical dispersal of the chain's boxes (both worldwide, and locally ruralization). So far, it would seem, reduction of transaction costs has taken priority over the reduction of labor costs in A-periods, while in B-periods the converse has been true.

Our research has proceeded using this framework. We obviously found it impossible to pursue all these themes simultaneously. We have therefore engaged in a pilot research. We have chosen to (re)construct two commodity chains—shipbuilding and grain flour. We have chosen to construct them for the early period of historical capitalism, specifically between 1590 and 1790. During this period, shipbuilding was a leading manufacturing activity. And the supply of grain flour was a principal political concern of states and their large urban centers. In both cases we seek to examine the geographic scope and social complexity of the commodity chains.

We have tried to determine the identification of the boxes for each chain during this period, and the descriptive anatomy of each box and each linkage. We have sought to describe these boxes as they were at each of eight specific moments—1590, 1620, 1650, 1672, 1700, 1733, 1770, and 1790. These years were chosen in the light of our reading of the historical literature describing A- and B-periods for the (European) world-economy over these two centuries. Thus we think we are dealing with Kondratieff cycles, 1590–1620 being a B-phase, and alternating thereafter (Research Working Group, 1979: 499). The basic plan of research is twofold: one, to depict the changes in the form of the commodity chains and, two, to see whether and to what extent the structures of the boxes change in accord with the cyclical rhythms of the world-economy. In the process we hope to assess the degree of geographical convergence and dispersion of these chains. We have found of course, as we suspected from the outset, that the commodity chains for these two products, which were so central to the workings of the world-economy in the seventeenth and eighteenth centuries, traversed many frontiers and tended to reach throughout most areas within the effective boundaries of the capitalist world-economy in that era.

REFERENCES

Hopkins, Terence K., and Wallerstein, Immanuel. 1986. "Commodity Chains in the World-Economy Prior to 1800." *Review* 10, 1:157–70.
Research Working Group on Cyclical Rhythms and Secular Trends. 1979. "Cyclical Rhythms and Secular Trends of the Capitalist World-Economy: Some Premises, Hypotheses, and Questions." *Review* 2, 4:483–500.

2.2
THE SHIPBUILDING COMMODITY CHAIN, 1590–1790
Eyüp Özveren

The study of world shipbuilding between 1590 and 1790 starts from the shipyards, whose output was destined for navies and the merchant marine in general, and the joint stock companies in particular. Shipyards were sites of production where construction, assemblage, and outfitting operations were carried out by a sizable work force. The production processes in the shipyard depended on the supply of timber, iron, flax and hemp, and pitch and tar, which came from spatially and operationally distinct production activities. The timber was used for hulls and masts, the flax and hemp for sails and cordage, and iron for anchors, nails, and tools. Pitch and tar were applied to the hulls and cordage to make them more durable. These subchains extended far beyond the vicinity of shipyards and had many different relations of production, such as wage, guild, slave, convict, part-time peasant, serf labor (See Figure 2.1). During the period under study, ships constituted a very important industrial item insofar as they signified and reinforced economic and technological superiority in the capitalist world-economy during a logistic of contraction in which intracore rivalry had, by necessity, intensified.

The period 1590–1790 was circumscribed by two outstanding eras of technological breakthrough in ship design. The main trend was the continual diffusion of, and improvement upon, the technical advances already initiated in the long sixteenth century. If the primarily English ship-of-the-line was an immensely improved derivative of the Spanish galleon, the legendary Dutch *fluyt* was the culmination of a long evolution of the full-rigged ship as first developed in the ocean-looking shipyards located on the fringes of the Mediterranean world. Toward the nineteenth century, the approaching heyday of steam-operated steel ships appeared on the horizon.

The most significant feature of shipbuilding in these two centuries was the generalization of specialization between warships and cargo ships, a distinction first introduced by the Venetians in the long sixteenth century. In the seventeenth century, the average size of warships steadily increased, but that of ocean-going merchant ships remained around 200 tons, although the East India companies used larger ships of up to 600 tons or more. On the whole, ships of larger size, whether intended for naval purposes or for the East India trade, were built in the larger shipyards. The concern with quality controls, and the constant availability of sizable work crews and storage facilities, accounted for this. Many of the larger ships were built in docks, which tended to be concentrated in the relatively larger shipyards because of the costs of construction. The larger shipyards were complex industrial units of their day, combining in themselves not only shipbuilding and maintenance activities, but also a significant number of related production processes that helped to prepare the necessary inputs. While the larger shipyards produced a minority of the total tonnage, they became the engine of growth for the entire commodity chain by the pressures they exerted on the labor market, by the technological and organizational advances they encouraged, and by the global networks of provisioning they nurtured. Smaller vessels were built on the ground and then slipped into water wherever appropriate. Small private shipyards specializing in their construction were owned and run by shipwrights. These could not have generated technological advance, as their owners lacked the financial means to experiment with major design changes that

Figure 2.1
Shipbuilding Commodity Chain

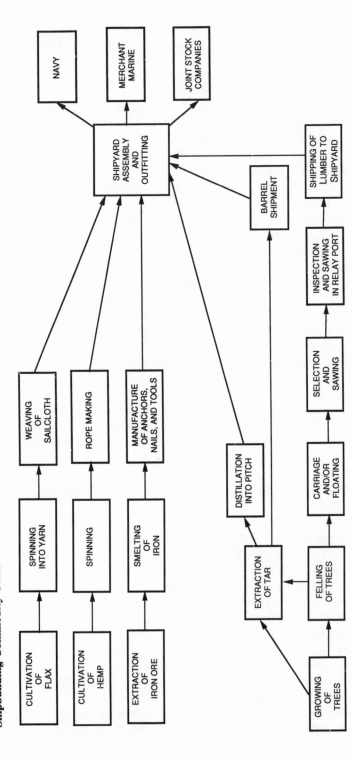

involved great risks in proportion to their small capital. This was largely responsible for the overall slowness of technical advance, as well as for the concentration of major innovations in the larger sites of production that could count on subsidies of various kinds.

It would be wrong to conclude that the naval shipyards of this period were mere extravagant replicas of the once glorious Venetian arsenal. Throughout the seventeenth century, under the cost-reducing pressures of the capitalist world-economy, the average size of the larger shipyards decreased on a world scale, a trend which would gradually be reversed in the eighteenth century. Be that as it may, the cost calculus and the constant concern with economizing the use of factors of production gained ground in these larger shipyards. The model they found for this purpose was none other than that of the smaller private shipyards. It is in this sense that a reciprocal relationship between the two different-sized sites of production was constantly reproduced to the advantage of the entire commodity chain.

Timber was the most essential shipbuilding material throughout this period. If we leave aside the demand originating from the construction industry, shipbuilding constituted the largest single consumer of timber resources. Even after the invention of steam-run steel ships at the end of the eighteenth century, wooden ships still had a century of unprecedented growth lying ahead of them. Hence ships have until recently implied wood by definition, and the location of shipyards was determined by proximity and seaborne access to timber resources. It may seem paradoxical that the factor that exerted the strongest influence in determining the major sites of shipbuilding was at the same time the most important object of long-distance trade for the provisioning of shipyards. Once the shipyards came into being, they became pooling centers for skilled labor, organized trade, and infrastructural construction. These elements helped to conserve a shipyard after the depletion of hinterland resources of timber. The existence of quality differentials among the produce of various timber zones, as well as the specialized utilization of various types of timber for the different parts of ships, necessitated long-distance trade. The indispensability of the timber trade led to concern with the control of distant supplies, the use of ships in the transportation of timber, and eventually comparative cost advantages. As most timber transport was by water, those who built and owned cargo ships were at an advantage in procuring cheap timber for themselves on a regular basis.

The subchain that gave timber as its end product went from growing and felling trees, to floating and transporting them, to selecting for use as masts or other pieces, to sawing and shipping lumber to the shipyards. The greatest innovation of the two centuries was in sawmill technology. The machines that characterized this technology consisted of reciprocating saws set up in wooden frames and driven by wind and/or water power. While adjustments and improvements of the equipment continually took place, a second major leap in the technology did not occur until the mid-eighteenth century, when the first circular saw was invented. The tendency toward the diffusion of sawmills originated in part from the need to reduce costs by reducing the mass of wood to be transported, as well as by giving it a proper shape for easy placement in the cargo ships. There was also the need to retain the quality of the timber over time. In the period preceding the spread of sawmills, most hand-sawn timber had been rafted and floated down rivers to the ports where it was loaded onto the ships. As a consequence, the wood was subject to losing its color and becoming grayish, a fact much resented by the purchasers.

Of course, trees were used not only for timber but also, with or without felling, for the purpose of extracting tar, which, when needed, was distilled into pitch. The demand for pitch and tar rose in constant proportion to the scarcity or increasing prices of timber. This was because the application of tar to hulls extended the average life of ships. The connection between tar and timber went further insofar as tar-producing zones geographically lay in the outer perimeter of timber-processing zones and had a tendency to be converted to timber production whenever favorable market circumstances prevailed. As long as transportation costs of timber from these inland locations to exporting ports remained uneconomic, it was more advantageous for entrepreneurs to concentrate on tar production. Throughout the two centuries much of the land that initially produced tar was gradually taken over by the more profitable timber-related activities. Not all tar required distillation into pitch before use. Quality tar could be applied to ships and cordage directly, whereas lower-quality produce had to be distilled to make up for its shortcoming. This distillation was usually carried out in the receiving ports in the proximity of shipyards.

Shipbuilding necessitated the regular consumption of two natural fibers originating from flax and hemp. Flax was used for sailcloth, whereas hemp was used for cordage. The full transition from oar ships to sail ships, the steady increase of the sail area, and the use of heavier anchors resulted in a growing demand for quality flax and hemp. Not only did the processing of flax and hemp resemble each other from the viewpoint of cultivation, spinning, and weaving, but also, in instances of dire need, hemp was used as a substitute for flax in the making of sailcloth. The production of flax and hemp extended the commodity chain back into the heart of the agricultural sector, often in overseas lands where appropriate climatic conditions prevailed. Peasant households were extensively involved in expanding the output. Ropes and sailcloth were sometimes produced in peripheral zones and traded to the shipbuilding sites. On the whole, however, unprocessed inputs were delivered to larger shipyards, where they were transformed into rope and sailcloth by wage-laborers in specialized workshops. Peripherally produced rope and sailcloth, unless it was of excellent quality, found its way to private shipyards that built for the merchant marine. Ropemaking was likely to be concentrated in larger shipyards because of the need for space for ropewalks. Some significant amount of sailcloth making took place in shipbuilding and/or seafaring ports. Female labor available in such ports was used for the weaving and repair of sailcloth.

Between 1590 and 1790, metallic inputs played only a minor role in shipbuilding. Iron came to replace copper as the major metallic input, and the significant transformation of the techniques of iron production affected the making of nails, anchors, and tools. The concentration of capital and labor in iron-related activities was also much higher than in other shipbuilding-related production processes. In the end, progress along the iron-related subchain was detrimental to the development of steamships. However, the massive changes in this subchain were not shipbuilding-derived, as the bulk of iron output was directed toward other uses. In the course of the nineteenth century, the timber and iron subchains would trade their places in terms of overall relevance for the shipbuilding commodity chain. This subchain extended from extraction of iron ore to smelting and then to the manufacture of anchors, nails, and tools. While one could economize on the use of iron nails by using wooden substitutes, iron anchors were indispensable, representing the minimum amount of iron needed to have an operable ship. The unavailability of iron ore meant a serious bottleneck for the Portuguese shipyards in Goa and Brazil as well as for the Spanish shipyards in Cuba, which counted on the import of anchors and nails, as well as tools from the Old World. Nor was it coincidence that the shipbuilders of the North American colonies gave priority to the orders of New England merchants who could provide the metallic inputs via Britain.

THE CHANGING PATTERNS OF THE CHAIN

Around 1590, the shift of the center of gravity of world shipbuilding from the Mediterranean world to northwest Europe was well under way. The output of Venetian, Iberian, and French shipyards had shrunk considerably, although, in terms of shipping tonnage, Iberian powers still matched the rising United Provinces (Usher, 1967: 212). The decline of Mediterranean shipbuilding was due both to the depletion of regional timber resources and the high operation costs of large-scale shipyards relying on well-paid guild labor. The exemplary Venetian arsenal was noted for its scale, turnover rate, and the way it combined shipbuilding and raw material processing activities, employing 1,000–2,000 workmen at a time, with a tendency to substitute well-supervised day labor for contracts and piecework (Lane 1934: 17). The arsenal moved from being a site of production to being one of repair, and the relative share of carpenters in the work force declined to the advantage of caulkers and oarmakers. Ragusa duplicated, on a reduced scale, the physical layout of the arsenal but not its ownership relations, as its work force consisted of independent and privately engaged artisans who occasionally commissioned Venetian masters to improve their craftmanship.

Things looked otherwise in the north. English shipbuilding started to grow along the east coast by building ships of heavier burden for the chartered companies. More importantly, the Dutch shipyards developed the *fluyt*, the most economic cargo ship of its time, especially suited for the Baltic trade. Few English shipbuilding locales had guilds, while the Dutch guilds were not as much an obstacle to change as those of their Mediterranean counterparts. In 1590 a process of making masts in several sections was also invented by the Dutch. Last but not least, the major breakthrough in sawing came about by the invention of sawmilling in the United Provinces about 1590. In the eastern Baltic, native merchants delivered by rafts vast timber supplies from the estates owned by noblemen to Dutch-dominated ports like Gdansk. In a parallel fashion, Dutch merchants had a strong grip over the Baltic tar originating from the Prussian ports. A novel form of business cooperation, the *rederij*, which combined capitals of various Dutch merchants for the purpose of building, chartering, or freighting a ship, gave a further impetus to the demand for ships.

During the hardship of the 1620s, the Dutch suffered much less than their rivals. As *fluyts* were launched in ever increasing numbers, in addition to Amsterdam, the Zaan shipyards prospered. Major Indies companies had started their own shipyards. The rise of Dutch shipping and shipbuilding had its negative consequences elsewhere. The Spanish West Indies trade shrunk as the Dutch entered the scene. The same was true of the English Baltic trade, which fell prey to the Dutch. The English shipyards cut their losses by specializing in building vessels for the coastal and oceanic trade in which England enjoyed a comparative advantage. As tar production in Norway declined, the English shipyards came to depend on the Amsterdam tar market more than ever. The English started to experiment with shipbuilding in their timber-rich North American colonies. The first sawmills were erected by immigrant craftsmen in the colonies noted for their virgin forests. The prime center of shipbuilding in the Americas was Havana, where an increasing proportion of the Spanish fleet was being built. As for the Portuguese, the comparative advantage of building *naos* in India was clear. Even so, the royal dockyard in Lisbon, reminiscent of the now defunct Venetian arsenal, continued to employ some 1,500 men (Boxer, 1969: 210). The Dutch did everything to expand and protect their domestic sawmilling. Unlike the deforested English, they could afford to have sawmills in timber-receiving ports because the distances involved were less, and because some of their timber arrived through the Rhine. Most important of all, the Dutch shipbuilding centers regularly received large quantities of timber, which found a ready market. Richelieu's plans to strengthen the merchant marine included the settlement in France, along with their families, of some 400 Dutch and Flemish mariners, shipwrights, and artisans (Charliat, 1931b: 19).

By the mid-seventeenth century, the Dutch dominance of the Baltic trade was virtually complete, primarily because of the lower freight rates made possible by lower shipbuilding costs in the United Provinces. With the rise of Zaan, the tendency for wages to rise because of guild pressure was also overcome, and the "fossilization" of the money wage of shipwrights achieved. The Dutch launched 250–350 new ships on an annual basis, receiving additional orders from France, Italy, Spain, Denmark, and Sweden (Houtte, 1977: 174). Had it not been for the orders of the navy, the English shipyards would have suffered greater hardship. The advance in technology (drydocks) and naval design provided an infrastructural basis for private shipbuilding. Shipbuilding continued to expand in the North American colonies. The colonies encouraged this expansion by granting free land for shipyards, thus attracting skilled shipwrights from England. This provided a competitive edge to colonial shipwrights over their England-based rivals, who had to pay high rents in the Thames estuary. Meanwhile, regular supplies of New England masts were now being shipped to English naval shipyards, lessening dependence on the Dutch-dominated Baltic. This became all the more important as royal forests were virtually depleted. Given the demand for quality timber, privately owned estates undertook replantation schemes. Money wages of dockyard employees stagnated and remained the same until 1788, to be supplemented only by a nonpecuniary right to chips. The English shipyards also avoided the Baltic by obtaining Russian flax through Archangel, thanks to English factors located there, who were also instrumental in establishing sawmills. Far away in Brazil, the Portuguese surmounted the problem of lack of skilled labor by bringing shipwrights from the Old World, and managed to benefit from the availability of Negro slaves and white convicts for menial tasks.

Shipping tonnage in 1670 is estimated to have been 568,000 tons for the United Provinces, 94,000 tons for England, and 80,000 tons for France (Vogel, 1915: 331). A significant portion of the tonnage of the latter countries was also Dutch-built. Zaan was the leading center, where the wharfs had doubled since 1650 (Feyter, 1982: 140). The overall operation costs of Dutch shipyards were reduced by using wind-driven mills and large cranes. The central role of Amsterdam in the distribution of Baltic tar started to decline as of 1673 for the English, even though English tar imports continued to come from the eastern Baltic. This was the result of enforcement of the Navigation Acts, which promoted English shipping. As for anchors and nails, a noticeable decline occurred in areas specializing in their production. Ironmongers' and Blacksmiths' Companies of London were alarmed by the influx of Swedish iron. The Thames shipyards specializing in the Levant and Indies trades performed better than their East Anglian counterparts. The colonies improved their standing. To upgrade their facilities, colonies started to offer fifteen-year monopoly rights to shipbuilders who built drydocks. French shipbuilding entered a period of growth under Colbert's ambitious program. His exemplary arsenals, whether intended for the navy or for the trading companies, contracted skilled foreign craftsmen. The double dock in Rochefort was the biggest installation of its kind in the world (Merino, 1985: 39). While the *Compagnie du Nord* attempted to procure naval supplies in the Baltic, native forests were being inspected and reorganized. In a similar way, the forests of French Canada were being inspected and organized for felling. France was a producer and exporter of flax. Brittany supplied French, English, and to a lesser degree Dutch shipbuilding with quality sailcloth. The English were the main customers of French merchants, who controlled the produce, as the Dutch insisted on buying flax and processing it themselves.

By 1700, total English tonnage had risen to some 500,000 tons, although

Dutch tonnage was still some 900,000 tons (Baasch, 1927: 107). In addition to absence of guilds, the Zaan shipbuilding now was distinguished for speculative building and its advanced economies of scale. However, the gap between the Dutch and English shipbuilding was rapidly being closed as the rising northeast region of England began to produce cargo vessels of high quality at low cost. Colonial shipbuilding continued to expand as well. Whereas New England supplied the English shipyards with the largest hard-to-find masts, masts of smaller size were delivered from the Baltic. The spread of sawmilling in Norway made their produce more attractive for the English. The Dutch, in order to protect their domestic sawmilling, refused to import sawn timber. The reorientation of Norwegian timber from the United Provinces to England meant a shift of control of timber trade from Dutch to Norwegian merchants. The ownership of forests rested in the hands of small proprietors, whose output was traded by numerous merchants relying on the credit advances of English merchant houses of London. To the east of Norway, timber production took place on a larger scale in Sweden than in Finland, where the crown reclaimed much of the forests from small proprietors. Amsterdam had lost its grip over tar trade, as tar-processing activities shifted from the south to the north of the Baltic. Just as the Swedish tar monopoly was consolidated, London assumed Amsterdam's former role and became the entrepôt for reexport to French and even to Mediterranean ports. The best Swedish tar was now directed to England, while lesser-quality produce ended up in the Dutch ports, which also started to import Russian tar through Archangel. The English attempted to encourage tar production in colonial America in order to counter the Swedish monopoly.

English iron production was now relocated to the northeast. A modern, highly concentrated ironworks complex was established by private enterprise in New Castle in 1682. It employed some skilled continental workmen for manufacturing anchors and nails from imported Swedish iron (Darby, 1973: 369–70). Because of the Navigation Acts the Dutch could no longer deliver Swedish iron to English ports; hence native Swedes benefited and displaced foreign factors in their ports. Swedish ironworks were relatively concentrated and bore the imprint of continental techniques and craftsmen. Louis de Geer, a leading industrialist, was an immigrant from the Netherlands who recruited Walloons as workers (Montelius, 1966: 2–3). Even so, ironworks continued to use part-time peasant labor in order to keep the wages down at a time when they had displaced English iron in its own market. The only iron manufacture that figured significantly among Sweden's exports was ships' anchors, much of which found its way to English shipyards. Having established their sailcloth manufactures, the English declined to buy woven cloth and insisted on importing flax from Brittany. English efforts to introduce flax culture proved more successful in Ireland than in the colonies. Colonial shipyards relied heavily on England for the resupply of sailcloth and cordage.

By the 1730s Dutch shipbuilding had become a phantom of what it once was. The Zaan industry was defunct. The government helped to keep the shipyards of Amsterdam and Rotterdam in operation. An Englishman was appointed as director of the Admiralty. After 1730, large quantities of cheap Russian sailcloth arrived and heralded the demise of Dutch sailcloth making. In England shipyards located in the northeast succeeded in emulating Dutch designs. The brig and the snow noted for their cheap cost of operation and large cargo capacity came into prominence. The massive emergence of North America helped the English undermine Dutch supremacy in the shipbuilding commodity chain by starting from elementary operations such as provisioning inputs. In the process, the radius of the zone from which naval supplies were procured had undergone a considerable expansion. A further consequence of this process was the pull to concentrate shipbuilding activities in the vicinity of these supplies. As the Thames shipyards advanced their position at the expense of their Dutch counterparts on the one front, they could but cede to their colonial rivals on the other. They had little room for maneuver. Since they could not come up with more core-like techniques of production, they were condemned to observe the spread of assemblage outward.

It is no surprise that one-sixth of the English ships were by then American-built. Colonial timber resources were being exploited as sawmills replaced the two-man saw team. The shift of South Carolina from tar to pitch was less than well received in England, since a sizable wage-earning population was employed in distilling tar into pitch in ports like Glasgow. Of course, such activities were less concentrated in the colonies and relied on the exploitation of slave labor. England improved her position in the Baltic, as the mast trade of St. Petersburg was now in the hands of English merchant houses, even when intended for Dutch or French consumption. Some 10,000 Tartars with 3,000–4,000 horses delivered the timber of Kazan to the banks of the Volga River for further rafting. Sawmilling spread rapidly in the eastern Baltic, often with the inflow of foreign masters. The sawmill in Narva, an exceptionally concentrated enterprise, employed masterbuilders, 30 sawyers, 18 itinerant workers employed for wages, and several foremen (Åstrom, 1975: 6). At a time when they were more dependent on Swedish iron than ever before, the English benefited from the rise of the Russian iron industry in the Urals region, where private firms owned by a few leading families controlled production by using serf labor. As Russia did not have a merchant marine, English merchants monopolized their iron trade and turned London into an entrepôt for iron purchases by third parties.

The fortunes of French shipping and shipbuilding also tended to improve. The French merchant marine now exceeded its Dutch rival and approached the size of the English. The French sailcloth industry recovered because of rising domestic demand. The Spanish, who had lost their continental ambitions, turned to protecting their overseas empire, and for this reason sought to build an armada equivalent in size to that of the French. The upturn of the world-economy in the eighteenth century, which brought about the advance of French and colonial American shipbuilding, also led to a general recovery in the shipyards of numerous other countries. Nonetheless, despite the increase of their capacity and output, France and the American colonies could not approach the production level of the leading zones.

By 1770, if Amsterdam still had 20 wharfs in operation, Rotterdam was in decline. Dutch sailcloth fabrication went down from 60,000 pieces in 1730 to 28,000 pieces by 1770, largely because of Russian exports. The same was true of Dutch rope manufactures. English shipping tonnage continued to rise. It was not so much the shift of control over the Baltic trade that determined English ascendance, but rather the growing importance of oceanic trade in which the English had a comparative advantage. By 1774, one-third of English ships were American-built (Davis, 1962: 68). There was increasing pressure for wage raises from the naval dockyard employees, who argued that they were paid less than their counterparts in the privately owned shipyards. As capacity utilization increased, the demand for higher wages gained precedence over job security. The relocation of tar production from South to North Carolina reversed the tendency to upgrade colonial production from tar to pitch. As of mid-century, British subjects opened up Russian territory to timber trade. Oak came from as far away as the forests of central Russia by way of rivers. Around this time, Brittany was the leading locale of French shipbuilding, Bordeaux ranked second, and the Mediterranean ports a distant third (Le Goff and Meyer, 1971: 180). The Atlantic coast monopolized 51 percent of new construction and 60 percent of new tonnage. The need for the purchase of foreign vessels was eliminated. As for the Spanish, the costs of production of Havana amounted to less than one-half of the costs of production in the mainland. This was due not only to the lower timber price, but also to lower labor costs because of the use of slaves.

Around 1790, Great Britain (no longer including what was now the United States) had 26 percent of world shipping tonnage, France 21 percent, and the Dutch only 12 percent (Romano, 1962: 578). The loss of the colonies, however, boosted domestic shipbuilding in England. There was a pronounced tendency for the relocation of shipyards from London to outports. The Thames shipyards responded by reconsolidating their monopoly over the East India and Levant trades. Independence deprived American shipping of the benefits of the Navigation Acts. The main advantage of U.S. ships was their low cost of construction, which could be traced primarily to low timber costs, since labor cost more in the United States than in Europe. In the presence of large favorable nonlabor cost differentials, expensive labor alone did not stimulate concentration and mechanization. After losing her colonies, England attempted to expand tar production in Scotland. Attempts to develop "coal tar" intensified. Coal tar was suitable for application to hulls but not to ropes. Where the English shipyards lost, lay the gain of North American shipyards. Southern tar now found its way to shipyards in the northern United States, which built for native merchants. Short of flax and hemp, the northern shipyards turned to the Baltic for sailcloth and cordage imported by New England merchants.

CONCLUSIONS

Ample, albeit partial, evidence for cyclical fluctuations in vertical integration and concentration has been shown at the local, regional, and global levels. Needless to say, for a strategic commodity such as ships the production of which is constrained by natural endowments, the secular trend overtakes the cyclical rhythms, and patterns of ownership and the organization of production and trade are far less open to short-term variation. Hence, in order to assess the effect of the Kondratieffs on the shipbuilding commodity chain, indirect analysis is in order. Of all the shipbuilding materials, hemp alone had no alternate use; furthermore, it originated almost entirely from the Baltic during the period under study. In the light of this, the cyclical behavior of the quantity of hemp passing through the Sund may be assumed to correlate with the pulse of world shipbuilding. The hemp trade expanded from 1590 through the 1620s, decreased in the 1650s, and stagnated in 1673, only to expand hesitantly toward the 1730s. An unprecedented phase of expansion followed as of the 1730s. The Sund records also employ a second aggregated category, "flax and hemp." This cluster experienced a slight decrease from 1595 until the 1620s. A sustained expansion from 1625 to mid-century gave way to a continued decline, which reached its low point by 1673. The quantity traded at this date equaled that of 1565. From 1673 to 1701, despite short-term interruptions, the trade underwent expansion. A period of stagnation followed, lasting from 1701 to the 1730s. As of then the trade in "flax and hemp" underwent an unprecedented growth, which was sustained until the end of the eighteenth century.

In the light of our findings, we may speak of a tendency to lessen product specialization in the B-periods caused by decreasing demand. For example, it is no coincidence that during these periods same or similar ships are equipped differently in order to serve a variety of purposes. This phenomenon is associated with a reduction in the number of units of production as well as a consolidation of the boxes that constitute the commodity chain. Reduced in number and possibly consolidated as they may be, the remaining units of production tend to spread geographically during the very same B-phases. Precisely because the imperative of labor cost reduction outweighs the reduction of transaction costs during the B-phases, there is a pronounced tendency toward the geographical lengthening of the commodity chain. To put it differently, B-phases are characterized by a commodity chain containing fewer boxes, which are nevertheless geographically more dispersed and locally "ruralized." In-depth studies of shipbuilding activities in Venice, Spain, the United Provinces, and England illustrate the workings of this mechanism in the face of downturns.

In juxtaposition to the B-phases, the A-phases followed upon the introduction of new technologies and organizational innovations, which often stimulated product differentiation and specialization at a time of rising demand. The consequences were severalfold. The number of boxes increased. However, the increasing number of boxes were concentrated in location, "urbanized" so to speak, and moreover, vertically integrated, to the extent possible, under a particular business enterprise. This spatial and organizational concentration of production processes created economies of scale and scope, and new monopolistic advantages for firms that could relocate their capital outlay among the different boxes as circumstances dictated. More often than not, the firms profited more from the monopolizing linkages between the boxes rather than monopolizing the boxes per se. This pattern gave them an advantage in the subsequent B-phase, when significant segments of the production were subcontracted. Hence, as long as the firms could exercise capital mobility and monopoly of the connections between the various production processes, vertical integration remained more the exception than the rule, although it occurred from time to time. The strong merchant houses of Amsterdam and London all worked with this kind of perspective.

During the sixteenth and seventeenth centuries the presence of shipbuilding activities in a particular locale could be read as a sign of core-like status. Largely because of the lack of technological breakthroughs between 1590 and 1790, shipyard activities had a tendency to be emulated and hence spread geographically. What accounts for the relative slowness of this process was the difficulties potential candidates experienced in establishing control over zones of procurement of naval supplies. When the English succeeded in breaking Dutch hegemony in Baltic trade by expanding their colonial raw material output, they undermined the extra-shipyard strength of Dutch shipbuilding. The subsequent spread of shipyards brought about the overall downgrading of shipbuilding activity. It is no coincidence that, as the English moved to replace the Dutch in the leadership of the world-economy, their shipbuilding underwent a far less impressive advance than had been the case with the Dutch during their ascendance. Only after the inventions and innovations leading to the construction of steamships would shipbuilding, once again, be upgraded as an activity, recentralized in space and restored to its former status as a marker of core-ness in the course of the nineteenth century. Although shipbuilding zones exerted a pulling effect on subsidiary activities, peripheral zones that produced raw materials constantly tried to upgrade their operations by instituting some processing activities. Whenever and to the extent they were successful, they contributed to the peripheralization of these activities and concomitant innovations by core zones in response to their challenge. In the final analysis, what defined core zones was not the absence of peripheral activities characterized by high labor and low capital intensities, but the exclusive and self-perpetuating presence of organizational and innovational practices that counteracted the tendency toward the spread of production processes in the world-economy to the disadvantage of the core zones.

REFERENCES

Adler, Gerhard von. 1929. *Englands Versorgung mit Schiffsbaumaterialen aus englischen und amerikanischen Quellen vornehmlich im 17. Jahrhundert* Stuttgart: Verlag von W. Kohlhammer.

Albion, Robert Greenhalgh. 1926. *Forests and Sea Power: The Timber Problem of the Royal Navy, 1652–1862*. Cambridge, MA: Harvard University Press.

Åstrom, Sven-Erik. 1975. "Technology and Timber Exports from the Gulf of Finland, 1661–1740." *Scandinavian Economic History Review* 23, 1:1–14.

Baasch, Ernst. 1927. *Holländische Wirtschaftsgeschichte*. Jena: G. Fisher.

Bamford, Paul Walden. 1956. *Forests and French Sea Power, 1660–1789*. Toronto: University of Toronto Press.

Barbour, Violet. 1950. *Capitalism in Amsterdam in the Seventeenth Century*. Baltimore: Johns Hopkins University Press.

———. 1930. "Dutch and English Merchant Shipping in the Seventeenth Century." *Economic History Review*, 2nd ser., 2, 2:261–90.

Boethius, B. 1958. "Swedish Iron and Steel, 1600–1955." *Scandinavian Economic History Review* 6, 2:144–75.

Boxer, C.R. 1969. *The Portuguese Seaborne Empire, 1415–1825*. New York: Alfred A. Knopf.

Charliat, P. J. 1931a. "La Flotte de commerce français sous l'Ancien Régime (1610–1789)." *Communications et mémoires* 10:197–219. Paris: Académie de Marine.

———. 1931b. *Trois siècles d'économie maritime française*. Paris: Librairie des sciences politiques et sociales.

Darby, H.C., ed. 1973. *A New Historical Geography of England*. Cambridge: Cambridge University Press.

Davis, Ralph. 1962. *The Rise of English Shipping Industry in the Seventeenth and Eighteenth Centuries*. London: Macmillan.

De Vries, Jan. 1982. "An Inquiry into the Behavior of Wages in the Dutch Republic and the Southern Netherlands from 1580 to 1800." In *Dutch Capitalism and World Capitalism*, edited by Maurice Aymard, pp. 37–61. Cambridge: Cambridge University Press.

Feyter, C.A. de. 1982. *Industrial Policy and Shipbuilding: Changing Economic Structures in the Low Countries, 1600–1980*. Utrecht: HES Publishers.

Galdacano, Gervasio de Artinano y de. 1920. *La Arquitectura naval española*. Madrid: Editada en Madrid por el Autor.

Goldenberg, Joseph A. 1976. *Shipbuilding in Colonial America*. Charlottesville: University Press of Virginia.

Guiard, Teofilo. 1968. *La Industria naval vizcaina*. Bilbao: Biblioteca Vascongada Villar.

Hautala, Kustaa. 1963. *European and American Tar in the English Market during the Eighteenth and Early Nineteenth Centuries*. Helsinki: Tiedeakatemia.

Henriot, Ernest. 1955. *Geschichte des Schiffsbaus*. Leipzig Jena: Urania Verlag.

Houtte, J. A. van. 1977. *An Economic History of the Low Countries 800–1800*. New York: St. Martin's Press.

Lane, Frederic C. 1934. *Venetian Ships and Shipbuilders of the Renaissance*. Baltimore: Johns Hopkins University Press.

Latham, Bryan. 1957. *Timber: Its Development and Distribution*. London: Harrap.

Le Goff, J. J. A., and Meyer, Jean. 1971. "Les Constructions navales en France pendant la seconde moitié du XVIIIe siècle." *Annales E.S.C.* 26, 1:173–85.

Lindblad, J. Thomas. 1982. *Sweden's Trade with the Dutch Republic, 1738–1795*. Assen: Van Gorcum.

Lower, Arthur R.M. 1973. *Great Britain's Woodyard: British America and the Timber Trade, 1763–1867*. Montreal: McGill-Queen's University Press.

McNeill, John R. 1985. *Atlantic Empires of France and Spain.* Chapel Hill: University of North Carolina Press.

Merino, Jose P. 1985. "Graving Docks in France and Spain before 1800." *Mariner's Mirror* 71, 1:35–58.

Montelius, S. 1966. "Recruitment and Conditions of Life of Swedish Ironworkers during the Eighteenth and Nineteenth Centuries." *Scandinavian Economic History Review* 14, 1:1–17.

Parker, W. H. 1968. *An Historical Geography of Russia.* London: University of London Press.

Richardson, H. E. 1947. "Wages of Shipwrights in H.M. Dockyards, 1496–1788." *Mariner's Mirror* 33, 4:265–74.

Romano, Ruggiero. 1962. "Per una valutazione della flotta mercatile Europea alla fine del secolo XVIII." *Studi in Onore di Amintore Fanfani.* 5:573–91. Milano: Dott. A. Giuffrè Ed.

Symcox, Geoffrey. 1974. *The Crisis of French Sea Power, 1688–1697.* The Hague: Martinus Nijhoff.

Unger, Richard W. 1978. *Dutch Shipbuilding Before 1800.* Amsterdam: Van Gorcum.

Usher, Abbott Payson. 1967. "Spanish Ships and Shipping in the Sixteenth and Seventeenth Centuries." *Facts and Factors in Economic History*, pp. 189–213. New York: Russell & Russell.

Vogel, Walther. 1915. "Zur Grösse der europäischen Handelsflotten im 15., 16. und 17. Jahrhundert: ein historischstatistischer Versuch." *Forschugen zur Geschichte des Mittelalters und der Neuzeit, Festschrift Dieter Schafer zum Geburtstag dargebracht von seinen Schülern*, pp. 268–333. Jena: Verlag Gustav Fischer.

2.3
THE GRAIN FLOUR COMMODITY CHAIN, 1590–1790
Sheila Pelizzon

The production of and trade in grain was still a, if not the, primary economic activity in this period. In contrast to shipbuilding, however, grain was a low-priced consumer commodity having little elasticity of demand. Grain was used not only for food but as a raw material for brewing and starch industries, but we have excluded these end products to concentrate on grain flour. The supply of grain flour to the urban centers was at that time a central concern of state and municipal authorities. And long-distance trade in grain provided a large percentage of the urban supply (DeVries, 1974: 172). This section is in fact dealing with the commodity chain of grain flour to urban centers, presuming always of course that part of this supply is coming from producers within a 25-kilometer radius and part from producers much farther away (see Figure 2.2).

There were several trends general to the period under study: an increasing tendency for white (wheat) bread to be consumed; a tendency for landlords to eliminate peasant farming in favor of large-scale agriculture oriented toward provisioning of urban markets; the growth of secondary towns which served as relay points, processing centers for milling and malting, and market towns, often

Figure 2.2
Grain Flour Commodity Chain

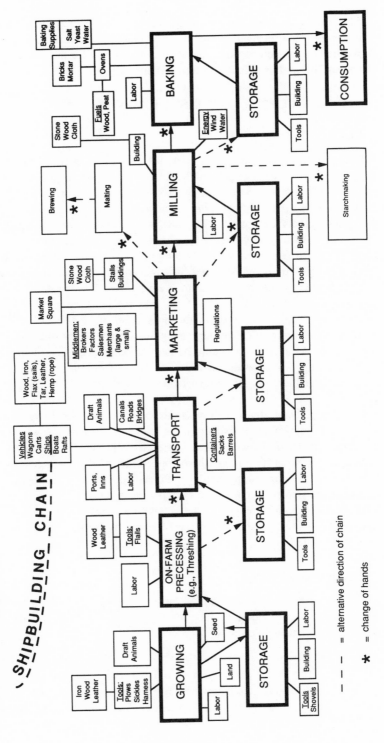

at the expense of traditional markets geared to more local provisioning; improvements in transport and preservation techniques such that cereal grains were increasingly marketed as flour; and a shift in primacy for the chain from Mediterranean to North Sea/Baltic to trans-Atlantic trade.

FROM PRODUCTION TO CONSUMPTION

Growing

In core zones (the United Provinces, [U.P.], France north of the Loire, and England), there were three predominant land-tenure patterns and forms of labor arrangements. Large estates of about 100 hectares (ha.) or more, which were owned by urban patricians or religious houses and which existed to grow grain for urban markets (Jacquart, 1974: 168), were worked with peasant labor who lived some distance away, receiving wages in kind (Bois, 1984: 114). Freehold farms, or farms rented on relatively long leases, of about 40 ha. in size, were worked by the farmer himself and his family, with the aid of tools and draft animals owned by the farmer, and practicing mixed farming with marketing of surpluses. The smallholding of 5–6 ha. was the most common type of farm. Where such farms were given to the production of high-value crops such as horticulture, dairy farming, or the raising of industrial crops (the U.P.) or vines (France), an adequate living could be had. In other cases, the owner practiced mixed farming, which produced a meager living. Draft animals might not exist on such a smallholding, but human labor replaced what was lacking (Jacquart, 1974: 168–69).

In semiperipheral zones such as southern France, smallholdings were interspersed with plots held on sharecropping leases. Tools on these were primitive; carts, ploughs, harrows were either rented from the landlord or replaced with human labor. In northern Italy, sharecropped farms were the general rule.

In peripheral zones (e.g., Sicily or Poland) all freehold disappeared in the course of the sixteenth century, to be replaced in the seventeenth by latifundia estates raising grain for export. Highly coercive forms of labor control such as re-enserfment (without the conferring of rights in the land), or debt-bondage were practiced on these.

On-Farm Processing

This consisted of threshing. Small farmers threshed their grain immediately at harvest in order to feed their families and pay rents and tithes. Large farmers waited for advantageous prices.

Marketing

Core economic zones had many more types of buyers, sellers, and middlemen, and many more types of buying and selling locations than did other zones.

Market activities on the rural end of the chain in core zones might take place in the local market, on small farms, in regional markets, at the granary of a landlord, or at an inn. Buyers and sellers might be itinerant grain traders scouring the countryside for small quantities of grain to buy, large-scale grain buyers, millers, bakers, carters, boatmen, purchasing agents of city-based merchants. However, those buying for long-distance trade preferred to do their buying outside of the official market in order to strike the best deals regarding quantity, price, and quality.

At the city of destination, the grain might be sold, warehoused, or transported further. City authorities usually designated marketplaces where, ideally, sellers came, displayed their wares, named their prices, sold their goods, and left in as short a time as possible. These and other regulations were intended to keep prices low.

In the peripheral zone there were very few traders or middlemen. In Poland landlords eliminated their middlemen and marketed grain themselves in Gdansk. In Sicily, muleteers tended to take over from landlords the transporting of grain to the *caricatori* on the coast.

Transportation

While water has been generally acknowledged as the cheaper form of transportation for goods of high bulk and low value, road transport was relatively faster, and in the quiet part of the agricultural year peasant labor for hauling was readily available (Braudel, 1982: 352–53).

Again in core zones there were more types of transporters and better transportation technology than was found in the other two zones. There were small carriers whose business consisted of a few horses and carts. Large firms specializing in transport began appearing in the seventeenth century. In the U.P., freighting was a well-organized, highly specialized activity.

When country people brought their own grains to city markets, they often walked if the distance involved was within about 8 kilometers. From further away a small-time grain merchant would transport grain on the backs of a string of packhorses or by cart. Large-scale grain merchants employed haulers and transported grains in carts and wagons. These were pulled by oxen or horses, depending on the distance involved. During very long overland journeys, the grain was relayed through inns for separate laps of the trip.

Less varied forms of transport obtained in other zones. South of the Loire, in a region extending to the Pyrenees, carts and mules were used for transport, with carts predominating. In southeastern France, however, mules predominated. This constituted land transport of the semiperipheral zone. In the peripheral zone (Spain, southern Italy, and Sicily) the pack mule predominated as the form of land transport.

There is a much less clear relation between types of water transportation and economic zones. The transportation of grain by river was used where navigable rivers existed—quite extensively in France, the U.P., England, and Poland. Canal building took place when and where profitable. Very long-distance transportation of grain involved ocean voyages—from Gdansk to the ports of Holland and Zeeland and from there to the Mediterranean; the trans-Atlantic transport of grain; and from Sicily to the mainland. Sophistication of water transport technologies ranged all the way from the *fluyt* to rafts.

Storage

Consumers might store grain on the stalk, as threshed grain, or as flour. Commercially, the preference was for storage of unmilled grain as a precaution against spoilage. Warehouses were located near roadways or waterways to await transport. Otherwise grain could be stored on the landlord's farm, in inns, in peasant's houses, or in monasteries. Seventeenth-century city authorities often looked with disfavor on urban warehousing, but this changed. In eighteenth-century Paris, hospitals, educational institutions, and military barracks were often locations of storage for grain and flour.

Commercial storage involved not only the labor of loading and unloading but also stirring the grain to prevent rotting or spontaneous combustion. In Amsterdam "rowers" were employed for just this purpose. The importance of commercial storage was that the stored grain could be used as a surety against which money could be borrowed and credit extended, as a way of ensuring profits through influencing certain market prices, and as hoarding against future price rises. Storage, of course, occurred at other points in the chain as well.

Milling

People in country villages milled their grain at the local mill, which the miller might own or lease from a landlord. Where people in urban areas had bought grain rather than flour, they had their grain milled in the city or in its outskirts. Usually millers worked alone or with one hired helper to aid in grinding and bolting, and in the maintainance of the mill and millstones. In the eighteenth century millers also raised wheat and sold baked bread, although they did less repair of the mill.

Baking

Baking arrangements seemed to vary less with economic zone than in terms of whether it was done in rural or urban loci. Rural people either baked at home or used the village oven, which might belong to the landlord. In the cities, bread was baked in the homes of those rich enough to have an oven, or in bakeshops for those rich enough to buy from these. The urban poor bought loaves that were baked in the suburbs and sold in one of the city's open markets.

Consumption

There was a hierarchy of grain consumption. The urban wealthy of the core zones ate the greatest quantity of white (wheat) bread. The urban poor ate a bread having a greater quantity of rye. Rural people in core zones ate rye bread, as did semiperipheral urban populations. In Poland rye was the bread of the local nobles. Wheat bread appeared on the tables only of the highest magnates (Braudel, 1981: 128). In hard times, consumers of wheat ate rye; consumers of rye ate oats or barley; consumers of oats or barley went to acorns, chestnuts, or bread made with flour from pulses (Slicher von Bath, 1977: 123).

THE CHANGING PATTERNS OF THE CHAIN

1590–1620

A shortage of grain occurred in 1590 in northern Italy. The Dutch, who had the advantage of cheap freighting technology (Barbour, 1954: 250), and the English started to transport Baltic, mainly Polish, grain to Lisbon (Collins, 1984: 240) and Leghorn, from which ports they reexported it to eastern Spanish ports, aided by Marseillais shippers (Braudel and Romano, 1951: 44). The Genoese were displaced as carriers of Baltic grain (Samsonowicz, 1973: 542). The Sicilian export trade in wheat collapsed. After 1610 a recovery began—a building of new towns and a tightening of labor conditions. Wheat was produced for Sicilian towns, carried to them overland or to Messina via a coasting trade (Davies, 1983: 384), or exported sporadically (Aymard, 1983: 179). Dutch-transported grain that was not immediately exported to the Mediterranean or carried to rural markets was warehoused in Amsterdam (Barbour, 1950: 17).

Baltic grain fed the population of Genoa. Venice increasingly relied on its hinterland (Pullan, 1965: 155), as did Naples (Coniglio, 1955: 77). Madrid increasingly used Baltic grain (Malvezin, 1892: 190). Milan relied as ever on Lombardy, even exporting grain to Switzerland. Marseilles relied on the Rhone valley (Parry, 1967: 156). London depended on Kent, and Paris on the area north of the city and on part of Normandy. But even these cities' provisioning authorities relied on Baltic grain in times of emergency.

It was their system of warehousing and technical improvements in freighting that allowed the Dutch to cut labor costs in a B-phase, and thus to capture the lion's share of the long-distance trade in grain and establish monopoly control over Europe's surplus grain.

1620–1650

Farmers in the region of Bordeaux began to drain marshes to plant wheat because of increased prices. In order to supply growing urban populations, the supply areas for London expanded to a radius of about 100 kilometers, and for Paris to the Loire valley, Brittany, and Normandy (Usher, 1913: 85–86).

The Dutch ceased to carry grain from the Baltic to the Mediterranean and the Iberian peninsula. The economic crisis in Italy, illegal sales to the Spanish army in Flanders, and tripled grain prices from 1620 to 1621 accounted for this. After 1630 the Dutch again supplied the Portuguese, but indirectly, the grain being changed to English ships in Bordeaux (Israel, 1982: 90, 286–87). This represented a reduction in risk and costs of doing business for the Dutch rather than loss of a long-distance route.

Traders from Marseilles supplied Spain, Portugal, and Provence with grain from the Levant and North Africa. Marseilles traders sent some of the city's French wheat to the Genoese riviera (Frèche, 1974: 750). Milan imported rye through Genoa and exported rice toward Lyons (Sella, 1979: 144).

The English began to import Russian grain from Archangel in their own ships, but Dutch shippers soon replaced them. This grain was brought into the North Sea ports and carried to London via a coasting trade (Ohberg, 1955: 152).

1650–1672

England replaced Poland as the main provider of cereals to the Dutch. This resulted in tightening labor conditions for Polish peasantry (Wallerstein, 1980: 138–39). This shift was initiated by the English government in order to undercut the Dutch monopoly in shipping and warehousing of surplus grain. However, the Dutch may not have minded too much, as they were reducing their own dependence on Baltic grain as a result of oversupply in the world-economy.

Population growth rates evened out and southern Europe became more self-sufficient in wheat for local markets because of the introduction of maize and buckwheat into peasant diets in southern France and northern Italy. In Spain a general expansion of grain production took place, particularly in Galicia and the Basque country (Le Roy Ladurie and Goy, 1982: 131–32, 152). This meant falls in prices and rates of profit for long-distance grain trading to the Mediterranean in this B-phase. The supply zone for London now expanded to Cornwall, Berwick, and Wales. This grain was not only intended to feed the expanding London population, but was exported through London to Spain (Chalklin, 1978: 172).

Two-thirds to three-fourths of the grain coming into Paris arrived by water, imported into the city by large-scale, registered grain traders (Bernard, 1970: 237; Mousnier, 1978: 196). Around 1666 Marseilles became a free port and as such was the center of a Mediterranean coasting trade extending from the pillars of Hercules to the Levant. Storage was permitted (Tavernier, 1973: 55–62). In 1664 the Compagnie des Indes Occidentales was founded in Bordeaux. This stimulated a river trade up the Garonne, which brought products essential to the colonies, such as grain and flour, into the city from the area along the Garonne

(Boutruche, 1966: 477). This trade in grain did not replace the provisioning as the principal purpose of bringing grain into the city (Usher, 1913: 30–31).

1672–1700

In Landes, the Acquitanian basin, and the area around Bordeaux, landlords made a switch to cereal production after 1696, as the demand for grain rose. Labor for this enterprise was provided by seasonal migrants from the Pyrenees and the Massif Central. These grew their own food—maize, buckwheat, and millet.

After the opening of the Midi canal in 1681, grain from Languedoc was shipped toward Narbonne by water rather than by road. There it was warehoused against high prices in Provence, Italy, or Roussillon. The opening of the canal meant that grain from the Haut Languedoc went toward Bordeaux as well as toward Narbonne. Toulouse became a regional market town to which grain was brought from the surrounding countryside and smaller market towns for resale and shipment on the canal. This left the Haut Languedoc grain poor in time of crisis (Frèche, 1974: 753).

In Sicily wild fluctuations in prices and harvests led to abandonment of land by peasants. In 1683 the city authorities of Palermo gained monopoly rights to provide cheap bread for the poor at fixed prices and weights. As a result the population of Palermo swelled (Mack Smith, 1968: 2: 274).

A consequence of the decline of the Polish grain trade was the alteration of farming and internal transport patterns in the U.P. Grain transported by barge no longer left Amsterdam for rural areas daily. Grain was grown in the Dutch countryside and carried to Amsterdam from rural areas twice a week (De Vries, 1974: 17). Grain was also transported into the U.P. from the Spanish Netherlands. The Dutch sought grain in Polish Prussia and in Denmark. Dutch grain exports to Portugal were maintained (Sée, 1926: 223).

The English government withdrew its regulation of grain prices in favor of establishing bounties to encourage exports (De Vries, 1976: 83). From 1697 this export trade centered on barley malt, which was shipped to Holland for the Dutch brewing industries, with rye, wheat, and oatmeal shipped in small quantities (Ormrod, 1975: 39). Those merchants provisioning London began to ship their cereals first to Amsterdam to collect the bounty, warehouse in Amsterdam, and reimport to London markets when prices were highest (Westerfield, 1968: 163). The English exported English grain to Portugal (Hanson, 1981: 202).

We see in this period an increase in the geographic spread of the "growing" box in the area around Bordeaux, the U.P., and presumably England as well, in response to the increased demands in an A-phase. Further we see that the English were able to locate their growing, processing, and transport boxes in two chains: the industrial supply chain to Dutch brewing, and the cereal grain supply to Lisbon. Further, the beginning of the activity described by Westerfield suggests that it was now the English that had the technological improvements in transportation and communications. The building of the Midi canal suggests investment in a trade route deemed profitable because of A-phase demand.

1700–1733

In southern France sharecropping arrangements underwent a change. Large landlords rented out many farms, but the takers were now townspeople who sublet to peasants on one-year leases, or on conditions of *maître-valetage*, which meant they could have no part of the harvest but were paid in coin or in kind. The Bas-Quercy began to specialize in growing a type of grain preferred by French colonists in the Antilles. There was a tendency to prefer grain to be shipped in barrels as flour that had been ''half-sifted'' as a preservation technique (Enjalbert, 1950: 29).

The trans-Atlantic trade grew in importance both from the standpoint of provisioning the settlers and in terms of the needs of Bordeaux. Between 1700 and 1715 wheat was also brought into Bordeaux from Brittany, the U.P., England, Scotland, and Hamburg. After 1710 ships from Bordeaux went to the Baltic for grain in replacement of the Dutch, who were excluded from selling goods in France (Huetz de Lemps, 1975: 96).

English grain exports to Holland consisted largely of barley malt that had been ''blown up'' in order to allow the exporter to collect the maximum possible bounty (Ormrod, 1975: 39–40). English cereal grains intended for consumption as bread and flour tended to be grown in the west of England (John, 1976: 50). These were shipped through London and went directly to Lisbon or Oporto. Grain grown in New York, Pennsylvania, and Maryland was exported by Philadelphia merchants to London or Bristol, and thence by the English to Oporto or Lisbon. Once in Lisbon or Oporto, the masters of the carrying vessels sold the grain wherever the best price could be had. Millers often made large purchases, which they ground into flour and reexported to Brazil. Some imported grain was consumed locally, and some was relayed to other parts of the Iberian peninsula (Fisher, 1971: 17–18).

Wheat was the only grain coming into Paris at this time, increasingly marketed as flour. As flour spoiled if wet, there began to be a demand to cover the Halles market (Kaplan, 1984: 117). Flour was transported via a land route by estate agents, *blatiers*, or (within the limits of the supply zone) by farmers. This zone expanded to 10 kilometers around Paris. Grain was still transported via river by the large-scale, registered grain merchants of the Rue de la Mortellerie (Cahen, 1922: 163).

The establishment of an Office of Abundance in 1723 hampered the role of Marseilles as an entrepôt for the Mediterranean grain trade. When the amounts of grain in the Office's warehouses fell below a certain level, exports were forbidden (Masson, 1967: 458).

In this period we see attempts to lower labor costs in response to a B-phase.

Also we see the geographic lengthening of the trans-Atlantic and the London-Portugal chains (really a North America-London-Lisbon-Brazil chain in its longest form).

1733–1770

At this time there was a tendency for landlords to reconsolidate large estates by renewed attacks on peasants. In England this took the form of parliamentary intervention to renew efforts toward enclosure (Yelling, 1977; Mingay, 1962; 309–21). In France a combination of royal decrees and tax incentives to landlords tended to produce the same effect. In Sicily changes in leasing arrangements produced the same effects (Sée, 1926; 43). In the U.P. changes in leasing arrangements produced the same effects (Mack Smith, 1968: 2:278–79). In Spain a system of subleasing led to the expropriation of poor peasants and the consolidation of landholdings by their wealthy neighbors (Herr, 1958: 107).

The importation of wheat via Rouen and Le Havre from Brittany and the Bordelais was supplemented in 1769 by wheat from England, the U.P., and North America (Dardel, 1963: 259). A covered Halles market with a storage area was completed in 1767. The Rue de la Mortellerie grain merchants were finally driven out of business (Kaplan, 1984: 124). All kinds of people began trading in grain on various scales (Cahen, 1922: 170–71). *Forain* bakers now brought white bread into the city (Cahen, 1926: 463). Some of these were millers who began to farm and sell bread. Milling became an entirely suburban activity. Technological improvements in milling meant that more flour could be gotten out of the wheat berry (Kaplan, 1984: 254). Technological rearrangement of the milling box, plus the increased availability of storage, was rendering the monopolistic, large-scale grain merchants obsolete.

Lisbon became a grain entrepôt for the Iberian peninsula, controlled by English exporters based in London, and English importers based in Lisbon, who were in business on their own account and acted as factors for London-based grain exporters. There was a high degree of concentration of grain trade among English exporters (Fisher, 1971: 67). After 1767 England became a net importer of grain from the American colonies. London declined as an export center to the advantage of Liverpool and Bristol, which were import centers for North American grain (Thomas and McCloskey, 1981: 92). The Baltic trade revived (Ormrod, 1975: 38). Here we see a shortening of the supply chain.

Grain from Italy, Spain, North Africa, the Levant, and the Archipelago was brought into Marseilles. Marseillais merchants became grain suppliers of Mediterranean coastal cities from Cadiz to Genoa, and to the Caribbean islands and Portugal (Masson, 1967: 464).

1770–1790

Flour bound for the French colonies in the Caribbean left Bordeaux in ever increasing quantities. The grain used in this trade came not only from France, but also from Poland. The colonial traffic was handled by French ships. Commerce between Bordeaux and European destinations was handled by ships of other nationalities (Butel, 1980: 39, 49, 61).

Russia and the United States now became two of the main suppliers of wheat to Marseilles (Masson, 1967: 464; Tavernier, 1973: 62). Russian ships supplied even Sicily with wheat. Sicily went out of the picture again as a wheat exporter (Mack Smith, 1968: 309–12). Once again in a B-phase we see the chains lengthen geographically.

CONCLUSION

There appears to be a tendency for the chains to lengthen geographically in B-phases. Chains lengthened in the periods 1590–1620, 1650–1672, 1700–1773, and 1770–1790. Chains generally do not lengthen geographically in A-phases, although they may remain the same as they were established in the previous B-phase. A possible exception might be the Archangel-to-Hull chain started in 1630. However, arguably the Dutch were not increasing the number of miles traveled with this chain over the number of miles involved in the Gdansk-Leghorn chain of the previous period. What was probably happening was the replacement of a geographically very long chain with two smaller ones.

Certain changes in the structures of the boxes may be seen in accord with the changing rhythms of the world-economy. Growing is a peripheral (i.e., relatively low-profit) box because growing is found in all geographic regions in the study. There has been a long-term tendency to consolidate and enlarge landholdings over time. Yet in peripheral areas such as Sicily and Poland, such consolidation (monopolization) appears to have taken place in response to B-phases (such as the periods after 1590 and 1650), as landlords attempted to shore up their rates of profit and eliminate competition in the face of diminished markets. In core areas, the opposite appears true: increased monopolization appears to have happened in response to A-phases and increased demand and higher prices. This seems especially evident in the period after 1733.

One of the reasons English grain growers may have been so successful in making growing profitable between 1700 and 1733 was that in England grain production was connected to the industrial barley-malt-beer brewing chain as well as to the grain flour chain. Thus the lessening of product specialization gave English grain production a diversity of outlets that protected the profits of producers in a B-phase.

Another change in box structure, this time more in accordance with the tendency of boxes to become repeatedly demonopolized, was the decreasing degree of monopolization of long-distance haulage. It went from an activity engaged in by core states' merchants to an activity increasingly shared in by transporters from semiperipheral areas. Thus long-distance transport went from a core-like activity to a semiperipheral activity. Although there appears to have been increasingly more monopolization in peripheral areas, simultaneously there was less specialization of occupation, as it was the landlords in Poland and the *massari* in Sicily who exercised the monopoly over transport. Our period started out with the Dutch establishing a quasi-monopoly of long-distance (especially ocean-going) transport. With the breakdown of the Dutch monopoly, English and French shipping participated increasingly in this box with the growth of trans-Atlantic trade, and eventually this box included transporters from semiperipheral areas like Russia and British North America. Peripheral areas either participated in ocean-going trade as a coasting trade (Sicily) or did so out of necessity, bringing grain to the buyer as an alternative to not selling it at all (Poland). The cost of doing business went up without the carrying trade proving very profitable.

Demonopolization also occurred in long-distance land trade. By the mid-eighteenth century, the quasi-monopoly of the big grain merchants had given way to transport by many small sellers. This was no doubt facilitated in the 1733 A-phase by technological changes in the milling box.

REFERENCES

Aymard, Maurice. 1983. "L'Approvisionnement des villes de la Méditerranée occidentale (XVI-XVIIIe siècles)." *Flaran 5*: 165–85. Bordeaux: Conseil Général de Gers.

Barbour, Violet. 1950. *Capitalism in Amsterdam in the Seventeenth Century*. Baltimore: Johns Hopkins University Press.

———. 1954. "Dutch and English Merchant Shipping in the Seventeenth Century." In *Essays in Economic History*, edited by E.M. Carus-Wilson, 1: 227–53. London: Edward Arnold Publishers.

Bernard, L. 1970. *The Emerging City, Paris in the Age of Louis XIV*. Durham, NC: Duke University Press.

Bois, Guy. 1984. *The Crisis of Feudalism: Economy and Society in Eastern Normandy c. 1300–1500*. New York: Cambridge University Press.

Boutruche, Robert, ed. 1966. *Bordeaux de 1453 à 1715*. Bordeaux: Fédération Historique du Sud-Est.

Braudel, Fernand. 1981. *The Structures of Everyday Life*. New York: Harper & Row.

———. 1982. *The Wheels of Commerce*. New York: Harper & Row.

Braudel, Fernand, and Romano, Ruggiero. 1951. *Navires et Marchandises à l'entrée du port de Livourne, 1547–1611*. Paris: Librairie Armand Colin.

Butel, Paul. 1980. *La Vie quotidienne à Bordeaux au XVIII siècle*. Paris: Hachette Littérature.

Cahen, Léon. 1922. "L'Approvisionnement de Paris en grains au début du XVIII siècle." *Bulletin de la Société d'Histoire Moderne*.

———. 1926. "L'Approvisionnement en pain de Paris au XVIIIe siècle et la question de la boulangerie." *Revue d'histoire économique et sociale* 14: 456–72.

Chalklin, Christopher W. 1978. *Seventeenth-Century Kent: A Social and Economic History*. Rochester: John Hellewell Publishers.

Collins, James B. 1984. "The Role of Atlantic France in the Baltic Trade: Dutch Traders and Polish Grain at Nantes, 1625–1675." *Journal of European Economic History* 13, 2:239–89.

Coniglio, Giuseppe. 1955. *Il Viceregno di Napoli nel secolo XVII*. Roma: Ed. di Storia e Letteratura.

Dardel, Pierre. 1963. *Navires et marchandises dans les ports de Rouen et du Havre au XVIIIe siècle*. Paris: SEVPEN.

Davies, Timothy. 1983. "Changes in the Structure of the Wheat Trade in Seventeenth-Century Sicily and the Building of New Villages." *Journal of European Economic History* 12, 2:371–405.

De Vries, Jan. 1976. *The Economy of Europe in an Age of Crisis, 1600–1750*. New York: Cambridge University Press.

————. 1974. *The Dutch Rural Economy in the Golden Age, 1500–1700*. New Haven, CT: Yale University Press.

Enjalbert, Henri. 1950. "Le Commerce de Bordeaux et la vie économique dans le bassin acquitain au XVIIe siècle." *Annales du Midi* 62, 9:21–35.

Fisher, Harold Edward Stephen. 1971. *The Portugal Trade: A Study of Anglo-Portuguese Commerce*. London: Methuen.

Frèche, Georges. 1974. *Toulouse et la région Midi-Pyrénées au siècle des lumières (vers 1670–1789)*. Paris: Cujas.

Hanson, Carl A. 1981. *Economy and Society in Baroque Portugal, 1668–1703*. Minneapolis: University of Minnesota Press.

Herr, Richard. 1958. *The Eighteenth-Century Revolution in Spain*. Princeton, NJ: Princeton University Press.

Huetz de Lemps, Christian. 1975. *Géographie du commerce de Bordeaux à la fin du règne de Louis XIV*. Paris: Mouton.

Israel, Jonathan Irvine. 1982. *The Dutch Republic and the Hispanic World, 1606–1661*. Oxford: Clarendon Press.

Jacquart, Joan. 1974. "French Agriculture in the Seventeenth Century." In *Essays in Economic History, 1500–1800*, edited by P. Earle, pp. 165–84. Oxford: Clarendon Press.

John, A. H. 1976. "English Agricultural Improvement and Grain Exports 1660–1765." In *Trade Government and Economy in Pre-Industrial England*, edited by D. C. Coleman and A. H. John, pp. 45–67. London: Weidenfeld & Nicolson.

Jones, Ernest L. 1981. "Agriculture, 1700–80." In *The Economic History of Britain*, edited by R. Floud and D. McCloskey, 1: 66–86. New York: Cambridge University Press.

Kaplan, Steven. 1984. *Provisioning Paris: Merchants and Millers in the Grain and Flour Trade During the Eighteenth Century*. Ithaca, NY: Cornell University Press.

Le Roy Ladurie, Emmanuel, and Goy, Joseph. 1982. *Tithe and Agrarian History from the Fourteenth to the Nineteenth Centuries*. Cambridge: Cambridge University Press.

Mack Smith, David. 1968. *A History of Sicily*. Vol. 1, *Medieval Sicily 800–1713*. Vol. 2, *Modern Sicily*. New York: Viking Press.

Malvezin, Theophile. 1892. *Histoire du commerce de Bordeaux depuis les origines jusqu'à nos jours*. 3 vols. Bordeaux.

Masson, Paul. 1967. *Histoire du commerce français dans le Levant au XVIII siècle*. New York: Burt Franklin.

Mingay, G. E. 1962. "The Agricultural Depression, 1730–1750." In *Essays in Economic History*, edited by E. M. Carus-Wilson, 2: 309–26. London: Edward Arnold Publishers.

Mousnier, Roland. 1978. *Paris, capitale au temps de Richelieu et de Mazarin*, Paris: A. Pedone.

Ohberg, A. 1955. "Russia and the World Market in the Seventeenth Century." *Scandinavian Economic History Review* 3, 2:123–62.

Ormrod, David. 1975. "Dutch Commercial and Industrial Decline and British Growth in the Late Seventeenth and Early Eighteenth Centuries." In *Failed Transitions to Modern Industrial Society: Renaissance Italy and Seventeenth-Century Holland*, edited by F. Krantz and P. Hohenburg, pp. 36–43. Montreal: Interuniversity Centre for European Studies.

Parry, J. H. 1967. "Transport and Trade Routes." In *The Economy of Expanding Europe in the Sixteenth and Seventeenth Centuries*, edited by E. E. Rich and C.H. Wilson, pp. 155–219. Cambridge Economic History of Europe, vol. 4 Cambridge: Cambridge University Press.

Pullan, Brian S. 1965. "Wage Earners and the Venetian Economy 1550–1650." In *Crisis and Change in the Venetian Economy*, edited by B. Pullan, pp. 407–26. London: Methuen.

Samsonowicz, Henryk. 1973. "Relations commerciales entre la Baltique et la Méditérranée aux XVIe et XVIIe siècles, Gdansk et l'Italie." In *Histoire économique du monde méditérranéen 1450–1650: Mélanges en l'honneur de Fernand Braudel*, pp. 537–46. Toulouse: Privat Editeur.

Sée, Henri. 1926. "L'Activité commerciale de la Hollande à la fin du XVIIe siècle." *Revue d'histoire économique et sociale* 14, 26: 200–53.

Sella, Domenico. 1979. *Crisis and Continuity. The Economy of Spanish Lombardy in the Seventeenth Century*. Cambridge, MA: Harvard University Press.

Slicher van Bath, B.H. 1977. "Agriculture in the Vital Revolution." In *Cambridge Economic History of Europe*, edited by E. E. Rich and C. H. Wilson, 5: 42–132. Cambridge: Cambridge University Press.

Tavernier, Félix. 1973. *La Vie quotidienne à Marseille de Louis XIV à Louis-Philippe*. Paris: Hachette Littérature.

Thomas, R.P., and McCloskey, D.N. 1981. "Overseas Trade and Empire 1700–1860." In *The Economic History of Britain since 1700*. Vol. 1, *1700–1860*, edited by R.C. Floud and D.N. McCloskey, pp. 87–102. New York: Cambridge University Press.

Usher, Abbot Payson. 1913. *The History of the Grain Trade in France, 1400–1710*. Cambridge: Harvard University Press.

Wallerstein, Immanuel. 1980. *The Modern World-System*. Vol. 2, *Mercantilism and the Consolidation of the European World-Economy, 1600–1750*. New York: Academic Press.

Westerfield, Ray Bert. 1968. *Middlemen in English Business, Particularly Between 1660 and 1760*. New York: A. M. Kelley, New Haven, CT: Connecticut Academy of Arts and Sciences (orig. 1915).

Yelling, James A. 1977. *Common Field and Enclosure in England, 1450–1850*. Hamden, CT: Archon Books.

2.4
CONCLUSIONS ABOUT COMMODITY CHAINS
Terence K. Hopkins and Immanuel Wallerstein

What conclusions may we tentatively draw? We think it is quite clear that for these two fundamental processes of the capitalist world-economy in the seventeenth and eighteenth centuries, the commodity chains were geographically extensive, complex, and in constant recomposition. We think it is equally clear that it would be imprudent to assume that production decisions were made by anyone without some awareness of the existence of such chains, at least to the degree of appreciating that there were alternative possible sources of inputs and alternative possible outlets of outputs. Large producers probably were aware of boxes further upstream and downstream than small producers.

Governments seem to have been clearly aware of the insertion of "their" producers within these larger chains, and to have taken action in consequence of this awareness. If governments, national or local, were often protectionist in policy, they don't seem to have been particularly "nationalist" (or "localist") if this would hurt their interests and the profit-making possibilities of their producers.

The shipbuilding commodity chain illustrates well the process by which monopolization and demonopolization worked. The existing Mediterranean centers, long having cornered a large share of the total production, underwent a decline just as our story begins. One factor clearly noted was the high labor costs because of the strength of the guilds in the Venetian arsenal, as well as the increasing costs of production because of the exhaustion of inputs produced within reasonable distance.

The United Provinces in effect seized its chance (and England tried as well), offering lower labor costs, cheaper inputs, as well as an important technological advance (the *fluyt*). Zaan was able to build on these three elements to gain a relative monopoly not only on the shipbuilding but also downstream on the merchant marine carrying trade and upstream on key inputs (such as hemp, tar, timber).

The high profitability of the Amsterdam operation led to increasing competition from the English and the French, and then in a lesser way from the Spanish, who in turn had recourse to their colonies as sites of construction. It took a century, but all this pressure eroded the Dutch monopolistic advantage. Given, however, the absence of technological advances in shipbuilding, the advantage did not really shift to an alternative core locus, but instead there was the rise of semiperipheral loci and a reduction in the overall profitability of the operations, not to be overcome until the nineteenth-century emergence of the steamship. It is important to observe also the wide variety of modes of labor control not only in such peripheral activities as timber harvesting, and the production of hemp, tar, pitch, and iron (from independent producers to serfs), but in the more "industrial" end of the chain (slaves in construction in the Havana shipyards).

The grain flour chain similarly shows the establishment and decline of a Dutch relative monopoly on long-distance trade. The grain flour trade also strikingly demonstrates the constant geographical reshuffling of the links in the chain. It seems quite clear that the large cities, in their quest for a stable, low-cost supply of cereal grains, so necessary for their survival, were constantly willing (or constantly forced) to restructure the commodity chains. One might have thought that so basic a phenomenon as bread supply was located in a sort of secular unchanging pattern in early modern times. Quite the contrary. The grain flour chain seemed astonishingly responsive to every fluctuation in the world-economy. And its extensiveness is quite startling, moving from one end of the capitalist world-economy (as it was then bounded) to the other.

We do not pretend to have drawn a definitive picture of even these two commodity chains. Our methods are still primitive, and the collected data are recalcitrant to analysis, since they consist largely of monographic studies and articles that are very partial in time-space scope and narrow in focus.

Why should we be interested in reconstructing commodity chains? The crucial element for us is that it is a chain, and allows us to get beyond the observation of particular production processes in particular times and places in themselves. Once we place the various processes (what we have named the boxes) in their chain or chains, we can evaluate the significance of the choice of property arrangements, labor control, and mode of linkage with boxes upstream and downstream.

In a capitalist world-economy, the alternatives in each of these choices are quite many, and a choice can be evaluated in terms of the degree to which it results in increased capital accumulation at two levels. One is the capital accumulation resulting from the chain as a whole. This dictated our selection of chains to study: they were both major loci of accumulation in the period under analysis. In addition, they both had crucial geopolitical significance: assuring the control of the sea traffic, and assuring the political stability of large urban populations. One way to extend this work on commodity chains would be to develop a mode of evaluating the entire network of commodity chains at successive points in time, so as to locate shifts in which chains are the major loci of capital accumulation. (The work on so-called leading industries could be reformulated in terms of such a network of chains.)

But there is a second, less self-evident but even more important mode of analysis of the role of commodity chains in capital accumulation. If one thinks of the entire chain as having a total amount of surplus value that has been appropriated, what is the division of this surplus value among the boxes of the chain? This is the kind of issue that lay behind the debate on unequal exchange.

We may presume, and our own research seems to suggest, that capital investment is shifted from one part of the chain to other parts as the possibilities of relative monopolization within boxes shift. When storage of grains in Amsterdam played a large part in the world distribution, this was clearly a good place to invest. When storage became more diversified geographically, it may have become more useful to invest in other parts of the chain. The important lesson to be drawn is that there is no box that is automatically the high-profit box. No doubt there is some tendency for the most upstream boxes ("raw materials") to be peripheral (competitive and low-profit) but even this is not necessarily the case (as in the period of a relative Swedish monopoly in quality iron ore production).

What the commodity chain construct makes evident is that the Colin Clark trinity of primary, secondary, and tertiary sectors is descriptive and not terribly helpful. Each box in the chain transforms something and is therefore "industrial." Each box, or almost every box, involves some human skilled judgment of the type we usually call "services." In any case, since the level of profitability shifts from one to another box over time, there is no long-term fixed priority for the "secondary" sector as a motor of capitalist development.

The greatest virtue of a commodity chain approach is its emphasis on process. Not only do commodities move extensively through chains, but the chains are scarcely static for a moment. The capitalist world-economy reveals itself via this kind of radiography as a fast-moving network of relations that nonetheless constantly reproduces a basic order that permits the endless accumulation of capital, or at least has thus far reproduced this basic order.

3

Competition, Time, and Space in Industrial Change

Erica Schoenberger

We have learned a lot about how production works, technically and socially, and how it changes over time. To find out about these things, we have tended, not surprisingly, to look first into the production process itself: the division of labor, technological change, industrial organization, capital-labor relations, the experience of work, and the ways different social groups and parts of the globe are integrated into the production system.

The analysis of commodity chains is centrally concerned with these issues while emphasizing the geographical embeddedness of production systems (Gereffi, 1991, 1992). It links up, in this way, with the work of geographers who have sought to show how the production of space and spatial relations operates within the contradictory tendencies of capitalism (see Harvey, 1982; Massey, 1984; Scott, 1988; Smith, 1984; Storper and Walker, 1989). For the most part, this research also takes the organization of production and of work as its starting point.

What I want to do here is change the starting point and look at the categories of competition, time, and space as interrelated theoretical and historical problems whose analysis can tell us something about the evolution of the production system.

A number of related claims are implicit in this statement. First is that how competition works, and the competitive strategies available to firms, are different in different historical circumstances. Second is that control over time and space is always and centrally a problem for the firm, but that its specific character also varies, with changing repercussions for the character of production and competition. Third is that how the problems of competition, time, and space are constituted and resolved at different times is interconnected. Fourth is that while the character of the production system shapes the specific historical content of these categories, we must expect that this process goes two ways. In other words, how competition takes place, and how the problems of time and space are worked out, also feed back upon the constitution of the production system.

To fully argue the case would go well outside the bounds of a single chapter. This is, then, an exercise in building historical and analytical content into the categories of time, space, and competition and their relationship to production. The method is to recount two episodes in the history of industrial change. In each case, the problems of competition, time, and space are different and are related to the constitution of the production system in a different way. The first concerns the consolidation of the system of mass production in the early and mid-twentieth century, and the second is an attempt at writing the history of current industrial transformations.

EPISODE ONE: MASS PRODUCTION
OF THE AUTOMOBILE

In his recent book about Chicago, *Nature's Metropolis*, environmental historian William Cronon provides one of the more eloquent descriptions available of how the product of an individual's labor is abstracted and transformed into a nearly pure flow of value across time and space (Cronon, 1991). The commodity in question is grain. The original distribution system, which carried the grain from the plains to coastal markets, was organized around the transport of grain in sacks, linking individual producers to individual buyers. The key institutional innovation that transformed this system was the creation of the Chicago Board of Trade in 1848, which established standardized grades of corn and wheat. This accomplished three things. It allowed the mixing of the individual farmer's output into homogenized (although stratified) collective output. Second, it permitted the transformation of the technology of distribution. Instead of storing and moving piles of sacks, the homogenized output could flow like liquid in and out of grain elevators, railroad cars, and barges, thus vastly reducing the time and labor effort involved in the process. Third, it allowed the development of futures markets, which rationalized the flow of grain across time and space. This enormous innovation secured Chicago's dominance in the North American grain trade against a number of traditional rivals.

Corn, of course, is quite different from cars. Yet Henry Ford's innovation in the mass production of automobiles had as its aim, realized to an extraordinary degree, the transformation of the production of complex mechanical goods into something approximating the liquid flow of grain through Chicago. Ford's actual model may have been the disassembly lines of Chicago meatpackers, but the analogy to grain in some ways provides more useful guidance.

Continuous Flow Production of Mechanical Goods:
Gains and Limits

Prior to the innovation of the moving assembly line in 1913, Ford had already taken a number of steps to convert production to a highly systematized operation emphasizing above all continuity and speed. Machine tools, formerly grouped by type, were arrayed according to sequential operations on particular parts, with nonmachining tasks (such as heating) integrated into the sequence. Gravity slides were already being used to move parts between machines. This arrangement allowed substantial savings on factory space and forced the smooth flow of work lest parts start to pile up in the aisles.

In 1909 the decision was taken to produce only the Model T, which allowed a massive shift to dedicated machine tools. Innovations in machine tool design permitted consistently accurate work at high volumes, something that would be crucial to true mass production. The flow of materials from start to finish was further regulated by detailed scheduling and long-term supply relations (with the supplier holding the inventory). Parts were carried to individual work stations as they were needed (Hounshell, 1984: 221–36).

The Ford system had already reached such a state of smoothness of flow that one expert observer was able to remark: "It is impossible to give an adequate description of the general assembly of the Ford automobiles, as this could only be done with a modern moving-picture machine" (quoted in Hounshell, 1984:236). Yet the implementation of the moving assembly line would thoroughly revolutionize production, allowing unimaginable savings in time. Within a year, assembly time of the flywheel magneto dropped from 20 person-minutes to 5 minutes; of the engine from 594 to 226 minutes; and of the chassis from 12.5 hours to 93 minutes. Not only were the times incomparably faster, they were also consistent and predictable (Hounshell, 1984:248–55).

What I would like to emphasize here is not only the reductions in production time, which were stunning, but the ability to regulate the flow of production. Production time here is both speeded up and *managed* in a way previously unknown. The manufacture and assembly of thousands of individual parts had been made to resemble the unimpeded and undifferentiated flow of grain in a continuous stream through Chicago.

This system worked wonderfully well for over a decade, producing 15 million Model Ts. Or, to put this another way, the system worked well so long as it produced only Model Ts. But the innovations of Alfred Sloan at GM, involving market segmentation and the annual model change, made the Model T obsolete in the very market that it had created. Ford's market share slumped precipitously, and it was forced to introduce the Model A in response. The changeover, hastily done and badly planned, threw Ford's carefully calibrated production system into chaos. The lesson from this experience was that planning for change was as important as production planning. In effect, change needed to be regulated as smoothly as production (Hounshell, 1984:267-301).

One needs to be careful about how much change could be tolerated by the system, even with good planning. Sloanism implied a very different competitive strategy from Fordism. Ford's strategy had been to maximize output of a basic, standard, and largely unchanging product at the lowest possible price. He rigorously eschewed advertising. Sloan advertised with a vengeance, highlighting product change and product differentiation. And he won. As Hounshell notes, Sloanism replaced Fordism even at Ford (Hounshell, 1984:263-67).

Yet there were still considerable constraints on the amount of change that could be tolerated in the industry. Advertising was key to GM's strategy for a reason: it had to sell the *idea* of change in order to induce constant turnover in the market even though the key elements of what constituted a car remained essentially the same for years on end. Much of the announced change was superficial, bearing largely on the external styling, and its impact on production was confined to final assembly (Friedman, 1983; Altshuler et al., 1984).

Thus the car as product was a much more stable entity over time than the ebb and flow of fins and chrome would suggest. Some of this stability was enforced by the technology and economics of production. Deep changes in the product, however well planned, would render too much fixed capital ''prematurely'' obsolete. These investments still had to be amortized over huge volumes of output, which meant over fairly long periods of time. Gradual obsolescence could be planned and accommodated, but not constant wholesale transformations of the product. Rather than Sloanism replacing Fordism, it may be more accurate to describe the system as Fordism-Sloanism.

There was, in any case, a second factor that rigorously enforced product stability over time. If production of automobiles had been almost magically transformed into a continuous-flow process, this was decidedly not the case in product design and development. The development process for new cars or major subsystems was a lengthy and extremely expensive process in its own right. These dollar costs also had to be amortized over large volumes of product. But time in the development process could not be managed as it was in production.

A third feature should be drawn into the picture. If product stability was enforced by the economics of production and the unmanageability of time in development, it was also *permitted* by the character of competition in the industry. In effect, the stability of the competitive environment and the way competition was managed helped to sustain Fordism-Sloanism.

The key to this was the maintenance of a stable oligopoly. The overtaking of Ford by GM in the 1920s was the last great upset in the industry until the advent of Japanese competition in the 1970s. The hundreds of firms that had vied for market share in the early days of the industry were progressively winnowed down to the Big Three. The surviving firms were in this way protected against both uncontrolled price competition and, crucially, uncontrolled product proliferation, which would have forced them to accelerate the introduction of new or significantly renovated products. It was this protection that allowed them to pursue a strategy of incremental product change and gradual obsolescence of their fixed capital stock (see Aglietta, 1979). In this way, too, the turnover time of capital was *managed* and *controlled*—it became a strategic device rather than an abstract compulsion. This is no small achievement, as it goes some way to resolving a deep tension in capitalism between the pressure to constantly revolutionize production and the need to valorize prior investments (Harvey, 1982).

Competition in this environment, then, was channeled away from cutthroat pricing and unmanageable product change. It centered instead on the familiar devices of advertising, brand-name identification, distribution, and financing. This provided an essential buffer to the production system, allowing the smooth flow of throughput to proceed relatively undisturbed. The unmanageability of product development did not, in this context, pose a serious problem.

Managed Time and Spatial Control

The managed continuity of flow in production in turn allows for an extraordinary degree of spatial freedom. There are two basic prerequisites for this. The first is that the product configuration remain relatively stable over time, and the second is that the regularity and consistency of the flow can be more or less guaranteed. As we have seen, Fordism-Sloanism, in the context of a stable competitive environment, allowed both of these prerequisites to be met. This in turn provides the basis for the establishment of a highly internationalized production system. In short, control over time allows an unusual form of control over space.

The automobile industry internationalized very early. Ford began investing in the British market shortly following World War I, for example (Lewchuk, 1987). The pattern of investment of the two great competitors was different, Ford generally preferring to start up its own facilities while GM often bought existing producers overseas (e.g., Vauxhall in Britain or Opel in Germany). However, there are some notable general tendencies.

The first is that final assembly was decentralized first and farthest, both within the United States and abroad. To this day, components manufacture is much more spatially centralized than assembly (Altshuler et al., 1984).

Second, this spatial expansion had as its principal aim, probably right through the mid-1960s, market access and market control rather than cost reduction. This is true even of much of the investment that went to developing countries during this period. Investments in developing-country markets such as India, Brazil, Argentina, or Mexico were driven mainly by extremely high protectionist barriers associated with import substitution policies. In general, these markets were not sufficiently large to sustain optimum volume production, so costs tended to be high in any case (see Holmes, 1983; Nofal, 1983). Nor were they large enough to allow for fully integrated or wholly self-contained production. Thus the system as a whole functioned on the basis of long-distance—sometimes extremely long-distance—supply lines.

The ability to organize such a spatially extensive production system is directly related to the ability to manage or regulate time in production in the ways described above. Key to this is that the nature of the product changes only slowly and that production flows in a generally undifferentiated stream through the system. No individual part X produced in place A needs to be in place B, perhaps thousands of miles away, at any particular time. What is required is a homogeneous and continuous flow of Xs through the pipeline, which, in this case, takes the form of trucks, railroad cars, boats, and, not insignificantly, buffer inventories. And as we have seen, what allowed the flow to maintain this particular character was the controlled nature of competition in the industry.

It is useful to recall that this system worked quite well for some fifty years until it was shaken to its core by the challenge from Japanese producers. This challenge posed to the system exactly the two problems it was particularly ill-equipped to meet: serious price competition and a proliferation of new and significantly differentiated products on the market. The Japanese firms were able to do this for a number of reasons. They had developed different ways of organizing the flow of work and of using labor on the shop floor to enormously compress the time it took to manufacture and assemble a car. Partly in response to conditions in their own market, they had devised ways of producing a wider array of products on the line without efficiency losses. And they had substantially reduced the time involved in designing and developing new or renovated products (see Cusumano, 1985; Altshuler et al., 1984; Abernathy, Clark, and Kantrow, 1984).

The initial response of the American firms centered on the issue of price competitiveness. What they sought to do was redeploy their already internationalized production infrastructure in a new way in order to reduce costs, particularly labor costs. Thus was born the era of the "world car." This envisaged a hugely complex international flow of parts and assembled cars, connecting up all of the outposts of the production empire (Dicken, 1986). Along the way, production was savagely rationalized in the core automobile manufacturing region around Detroit. Some of it, following the Canada-U.S. Auto Pact in 1965, was pushed northward (Holmes, 1988); the networks in Europe were rearranged with some southward drift into lower-cost EC countries such as Spain and Portugal; and Latin America, especially Mexico, was integrated more fully and directly into the flow (Gereffi, 1991).

The flaw in this scenario is that it didn't respond to the second part of the challenge posed by Japan—the proliferation and rapid renovation of product lines. The competitive environment would no longer sustain the time-space strategy that the American firms had, in many ways remarkably, pioneered. It was a strategy that had enabled the extraordinary dominance of American products in domestic and foreign markets for roughly two generations. But this control over space hinged fundamentally on a certain kind of control over time that was no longer valid. What this upheaval in the meaning of control over time and space might mean is the subject of the next section.

EPISODE TWO: THE NEW COMPETITION AND THE RECALIBRATION OF TIME AND SPACE

As we have seen, the ability to manage time in production, characteristic of mass-production techniques, allowed an unusual form of mastery over space. In effect, distance appeared to be a solved problem for the system, apparently fulfilling Marx's famous dictum concerning the annihilation of space by time. This was a world in which it was plausible for an American firm to develop automobile engines in Detroit, make them in Australia, and ship them to Europe for assembly into the final product.

This world has been irrevocably altered by the advent of powerful new competitors on the scene and the consequent transformation in the nature of competition in global markets. This has further entailed a redefinition of the meaning of control over time and a recalibration of the relationship between time and space. What Harvey refers to as a new round of "time-space compression" has had, in my view, the unusual effect of reposing the problem of space for the system (Harvey, 1989). In other words, the once-solved problem of distance has become unsolved again, and this despite the fact that the techniques and costs of transportation and communications have steadily improved. The old time-space strategy has become invalid, and a new one is being worked out in its place.

Given the work-in-process character of this transition, it is useful to offer a stylized version of what seems to be taking place. This version does not apply to every firm in every segment of every industry, although it can be seen to be emerging in a startling array of quite different sectors. This includes certain important segments of the apparel industry (Taplin, 1991; also chapters 5, 9, and 10 in this volume), computers (Saxenian, 1990b), semiconductors (Saxenian, 1990a; Schoenberger, 1986), automobiles (Holmes, 1987, 1988, 1989; Schoenberger, 1987), and chemicals (MIT Commission on Industrial Productivity, 1989). While it is perfectly true that a variety of industry segments continue to operate on traditional principles (Gertler, 1988), if for no other reason than the barriers to rapid adjustment of fixed capital stock (Clark, 1991; Mair, 1991), what follows is based on the assertion that a significant reorientation is taking place that will embrace a progressively larger proportion of the manufacturing industry.

Time as Competitive Strategy

The great upheaval in the international competitive environment dating to the 1970s has undermined the basis for gradualism in the renovation and expansion of product lines. Accordingly, the great difference between now and the period of high Fordism-Sloanism is the necessity to compress drastically the time it takes to move a product through the cycle from design and development to scaled-up manufacturing. This further requires that the manufacturing base be capable of rapidly and smoothly adjusting to continually changing product configurations. Finally, the cycle from manufacture of a given product or component to its delivery also has to be accelerated and made more reliable.

What has happened, in essence, is that time has become part of the firm's competitive strategy in the market. In other words, firms compete in significant measure on their ability to compress time in all the dimensions just described. The firm that can bring new products to market faster or turn around an order more quickly and reliably gains a significant advantage—in effect, it is selling speed (and reliable service) as well as the physical product itself (see Stalk and Hout, 1990; Smith and Reinertsen, 1991).[1] And, as competition proceeds on this basis, the necessity of continually compressing time is continually reinforced. Under these circumstances, Ford's achievement in regulating time in production in a way that was detached from a development process that could not be so regulated is invalidated. The key arena in which control over time must now be exerted is in product development, and manufacturing has, in consequence, to be adapted to that tempo.

The pressures for accelerated product development are being met in a variety of ways, none mutually exclusive. Simplifying and standardizing components that can be mixed and matched in a variety of configurations is one approach. Some kinds of functional variability can be introduced via software rather than through modifications of hardware. Strategic alliances and technical collaborations can spread the costs and risks of major development projects while generating time economies through task specialization (see Schoenberger, 1986, 1989; Sabel, Kern, and Herrigel, 1989; Saxenian, 1990a; Cooke, 1988).[2]

Design automation techniques, of course, figure importantly here as well. But perhaps the most significant shift is the reorganization of the development process implicit in simultaneous engineering. Instead of moving through a fixed and unidirectional sequence of phases, each carried out in a separate part of the organization, all of the phases—product design, product engineering, prototype development and test, and manufacturing engineering—are accomplished simultaneously and collectively. This eliminates certain obvious kinds of delays, as when a product design turns out to be unmanufacturable and has to be backed up the sequence, and it eliminates a lot of wasted time as those responsible for downstream phases wait for the earlier work to be accomplished (cf. Brooks, 1982; *Chemical and Engineering News*, 1985; *Financial Times*, 9/30/91).

One of the more interesting side effects of this reorganization is the need to assemble shifting groups of development people on a continuous basis. Note that this specifically includes inputs from manufacturing proper. Long-distance computer networks notwithstanding, this kind of intense, continuous exchange of information relies on constant, face-to-face interaction (Saxenian, 1990a, 1990b; Waxman, Saunders and Carter, 1989; Smith and Reinertsen, 1991; Stalk and Hout, 1990). The erstwhile splendid isolation of the product development process from the production system, and of the various parts of the development function from one another, is no longer tenable. Where once it was considered a positive gain to separate development organizationally and geographically from the rest of the firm, there is now considerable hand-wringing over the possibility that people on different floors of the same building will be inhibited from interacting sufficiently.

This entire transformation is driven by the need to get new or renovated products to the market as fast as possible. And, as the life span of specific products in the market erodes, it is necessary to do this all the time. In effect, time has surfaced as a strategic variable to be deployed directly as a competitive weapon, and in this manifestation it directly affects how the production system operates.

Consider, for example, how the much-vaunted just-in-time system (JIT) fits into this scenario. It is by now universally seen as wholly superior to the just-in-case (JIC) approach characteristic of Fordism-Sloanism, which is viewed as something of a misguided historical aberration, typically American in its undisciplined wastefulness. Yet it is not at all obvious that JIT would be a superior form of production organization in the context of standardized mass production.

JIC involved producing to forecasted demand and relied on smoothing the flow of production through buffer inventories. On the downside were the overhead costs of carrying the inventories and the possibility of producing large quantities of defective parts before the error was noticed and corrected (although it would not seem inherently impossible to ally quality controls with production for stock). JIT, which is based on producing to actual or current demand, certainly reduces the inventory problem, but at the price of rendering the production system more fragile in the face of external shocks. Disruption of components production at a supplier or branch plant or a transit strike could shut down an entire production process indefinitely.[3] Further, while workers are never idle in this system, individual machines often are, so the inventory savings are partially offset by the carrying charges on unproductive equipment (McMillan, 1984).

What makes JIT necessary, despite its riskiness, is the shift to destandardized or flexible mass production in which, at any given time, a wide variety of product types is being produced, and their character or configuration also changes rapidly and continually over time. In short, the proliferation of significantly differentiated product types, and their rapid replacement by new product generations, require that the production system adapt to constant change. That capability is what JIT provides. JIC clearly doesn't, but then it wasn't necessary at the time.

This kind of production strategy is far less tolerant of distance than high Fordism-Sloanism in a number of ways. And, though geographers typically focus on the costs of transportation over great distance, this is really a problem of time, reliability, and coordination rather than the dollar costs of transport. Standardized mass production, as we have seen, allowed a truly extraordinary and extensive spatial division of labor. The development process was wholly divorced from actual production, and discrete elements of the manufacturing system could be hived off and settled in far-flung corners of the globe, the whole knit together by the steady flow of slowly changing, standardized product through the pipeline. Flexible mass production is less likely to assume this spatial form.

By way of a stylized illustration, imagine in the first system an undifferentiated stream of X parts produced in place A being matched up with an undifferentiated stream of Y parts produced in place B. So long as the costs of transportation constitute an acceptably small share of total costs, distance is not a problem. It is the continuity of the flow over space that counts, and this continuity is guaranteed by the stability and homogeneity of the product.

In the second system, the X and Y parts all have a specific, differentiated identity. X_1 must be paired up with Y_1, X_2 with Y_2, and so on. Moreover, X_1 has to arrive in place B at exactly the moment that Y_1 has been produced. Now imagine that A and B are thousands of miles apart, with transport by truck, rail, and ship, crossing two borders and several time zones. Imagine further that you are producing to current demand with a promised delivery date in place C. Add perhaps that in the current market environment, being able to guarantee a specific and early delivery date yields an advantage against your competition. If you can't reliably make your delivery dates, you can't sell your product. These constraints apply both to final consumption goods (cf. Taplin, 1991; Gereffi, 1992) and to industrial markets where your output enters into the production process of another firm. Indeed, this is an accurate description of the constraints imposed by JIT, which requires guaranteed reliability of supply.

This is why Toyota, which invented JIT, built Toyota City. The system in its most advanced form is extremely sensitive to logistical breakdowns, which means that it is less able to accommodate the spatial extensiveness that is, by contrast, rather well tolerated by standardized mass production. It is no exaggeration to say that all auto producers are now trying to be like Toyota in the key dimensions of fielding a differentiated and rapidly changing product line on the basis of a tight JIT organization. That they can only move to this very gradually is a function of the legacy of existing fixed capital investments (Mair, 1991).

In short, this system, driven by the need to compress time in product change and to smoothly produce a highly differentiated output mix, is much less flexible spatially. Development has to be more closely integrated with manufacturing, and the various pieces of the manufacturing empire have to be more closely integrated and coordinated with one another.

Yet at the same time, there is reason to suppose that all of this has to be more closely integrated with differentiated geographical markets, and here lies an interesting source of tension. Considered purely as a production strategy, at the limit every firm (along with its important suppliers) should have its own city. Yet in order to remain effectively engaged in international markets, given political obstacles and the need to respond rapidly to the specific (changing) character of demand in these markets, they also need to produce internationally (Schoenberger, 1990). But if a GM or an IBM in the past could have proliferated branch plants in a huge number of individual country markets, this strategy seems less valid in the current environment.

Instead, what seems likely is a gradual move to reconcentrating production in the most important market regions of the globe, with one highly integrated production complex serving a number of country markets.[4] Note that, if the most important market regions are assumed to be the EC, North America, and East Asia, this still allows for a considerable amount of spatial diversity. Mexico, for example, can certainly be a major production site for the North American market.

If the hallmark of the 1970s and 1980s, for American industry, seemed to many to be the shift of production away from rich markets to cheap export platforms, the tendencies I have described here would represent a significant reversal. The logic of a progressive decentralization of production to low-cost, nonunionized labor markets in a steadily growing assortment of peripheral countries appeared to be impeccable. But it depended crucially on the principles of managed time characteristic of standardized mass production and its consequent spatial flexibility. When these principles are overturned, the spatial flexibility is lost.

Recent UN statistics on foreign direct investments (FDI) confirm the diminishing allure of cheap-labor locations in the Third World to multinational corporations from the United States, Japan, and Europe. FDI grew at an astonishing pace from 1983 to 1989, at an average of 29 percent per year greatly outpacing overall economic growth (7.8 percent per year) and the growth rate of exports (9.4 percent per year). Although the absolute amounts of investment in developing countries grew, their share of the total fell from 25 to 18 percent over this period. Of this, three-quarters went to only ten countries.[5] By contrast, the United States became the principal destination of this kind of investment, absorbing about half of the annual flows in the same period (cited in *Financial Times*, 7/22/91, 7/29/91).

Obviously, new investment is still being directed to a rather restricted set of less developed countries. But it is equally clear that the priorities of multinational corporations are shifting toward the richest and/or fastest-growing market areas of the globe, despite high wages and a high degree of labor regulation in many of these areas. How the former East Bloc countries will be drawn into this picture is still unclear, but there is a strong possibility that, once the necessary institutional supports are in place, they will function as a "proximate semi-periphery" to the EC, replacing less developed regions within the EC proper as a location for investment. The competition for this kind of export capital promises to become fierce.

Serving as the site for low-waged, low-skilled employment in foreign-owned branch plants was hardly the path to a golden future under any circumstances. Yet if even this "option" is diminishing over time, this recasts the problem of development and growth in the core and the periphery alike.

Our expectation for some time has been that one of the key mechanisms mediating the core-periphery relationship would continue to be the progressive dispersal of manufacturing employment from the advanced industrial areas to the developing areas via the multinational corporation (Hymer, 1979; Frobel, Heinrichs, and Kreye, 1980; Bluestone and Harrison, 1982; Hopkins and Wallerstein et al., 1982; Chase-Dunn, 1989). The pressures for spatial reconcentration of production outlined here suggest at the least that we need to reconsider these expectations and the political strategies that follow from them. Even the apparent benefit to the core regions of this spatial reallocation is questionable since the viability of this move hinges in part on advanced automation, which greatly reduces direct labor inputs for any given level of output. If production is being reconcentrated geographically, this is not true in the same degree for jobs, many of which are simply being eliminated (Schoenberger, 1989).

Uneven geographic development is an old story under capitalism, and it might not seem worthwhile to retell it. Yet, within the general dynamics of capitalism, the organizing principles of geographical unevenness at any given time have considerable historical specificity. This means that we do need to retell the story because it changes with each recounting. In this period, the new pattern of competition is leading to a recalibration of the meaning of time and space in the production system. As a consequence, the probable fates of large areas of the globe stand to be significantly altered.

CONCLUSION

In each of these episodes, the interplay between competition, time, and space has taken different forms. In the first, the resolution of a specific temporal problem in production is dependent on the nature of competition. In other words, the stability of a particular competitive environment sustains the ability of firms to organize production in a particular way. Moreover, the specific temporal strategy involved creates the basis for an historically unprecedented spatial flexibility and extensiveness of the production system.

In the second episode, the problems of competition, time, and space are reconstituted in a new way for the firm. The leading temporal problem shifts into a new arena, and the production system has to be adapted as a consequence. The transformation of the competitive environment and the new temporal strategy have the further effect of re-creating distance as a problem in the production system. In short, new constraints are imposed on the spatial flexibility that had been won in the previous period. As a result, an apparently plausible production strategy, involving the progressive displacement of production to ever cheaper areas of the globe, is undermined.

What I have wanted to show particularly is, first, that time and space are strategic problems for the firm whose character changes over time and whose resolution influences the character of the production system. Second, the specific ways in which these problems manifest themselves or are resolved are conditioned by the nature of competition in an industry. Third, the resolution of the problems of time and space can only be provisional; although their specific manifestation changes over time, the problems are permanent ones for the system.

The value of this approach, I hope, lies in enlarging the range of questions we bring to the investigation of the structure and dynamics of production systems. This is especially important in an era of rapid and in many ways tumultuous social and economic change. In such a period, it is crucial that we be able to use our analytical categories to look some way into the future, to anticipate the stresses and tensions that will be produced along with a new industrial landscape. If the struggle for control over time and space is a permanent feature of capitalism, the particular form that it takes now will directly affect the fates of all regions in the global economy for some time into the future in quite particular and possibly unexpected ways. The stakes in understanding how this struggle is being waged are correspondingly high.

NOTES

This paper draws on research originally supported by the National Science Foundation. This support is gratefully acknowledged. I also wish to thank Gary Gereffi and Miguel Korzeniewicz for their very helpful comments.

1. Smith and Reinertsen (1991) offer numerical examples suggesting that, in rapidly changing markets, a delay of just six months in bringing a new product to market can reduce its lifetime profit yield by one-third.

2. It is worth noting that these strategic alliances may also help to stabilize firms' competitive environments to some degree by aligning the technological trajectories of the partners.

3. The head of a British auto parts supplier characterized the state of affairs as follows: "If we were to have a [labor] dispute, Ford would be shut down in a couple of days and Rover a day after that. That's the legacy of Just-in-Time manufacturing" (quoted in *Financial Times*, 12/30/91). As the article goes on to point out, this fragility, which is a consequence of the new principles of time management, is directly contributing to widespread efforts to develop more cooperative relations on the shopfloor.

4. Sabel (1989) and Storper (1992) provide evidence that sectorally integrated and specialized regions are emerging as the fundamental territorial unit of production and trade.

5. The countries are China, Hong Kong, Malaysia, Singapore, Thailand, Argentina, Brazil, Colombia, Mexico, and Egypt. Note, however, that these statistics do not take into account direct investment from certain newly industrialized countries such as Hong Kong or Taiwan to less developed nations (e.g., China, Malaysia, etc.).

REFERENCES

Aglietta, Michel. 1979. *A Theory of Capitalist Regulation*. London: New Left Books.
Abernathy, William J.; Clark, Kim B.; and Kantrow, Alan H. 1984. *Industrial Renaissance: Producing a Competitive Future for America*. New York: Basic Books.
Altshuler, Alan; Anderson, Martin; Jones, Daniel T.; Roos, Daniel; and Womack, James P. 1984, *The Future of the Automobile*, Cambridge, MA: MIT Press.
Bluestone, Barry, and Harrison, Bennett. 1982. *The Deindustrialization of America*. New York: Basic Books.

Brooks, Frederick P., Jr. 1982. *The Mythical Man-Month: Essays on Software Engineering*. Reading, MA: Addison-Wesley.

Chase-Dunn, Christopher. 1989. *Global Formation: Structures of the World-Economy*. Oxford: Basil Blackwell.

Chemical and Engineering News. 1985. "Role and Education of Engineers Face Change in Wake of Computers." July 22.

Clark, Gordon L. 1991. "Industrial Restructuring and Regional Adjustment: Costs and Prices, Competitive Strategies and Regions." Monash-Melbourne Joint Project on Comparative Australian-Asian Development, Monash University Development Studies Center. Working Paper 91–6.

Cooke, Philip. 1988. "Flexible Integration, Scope Economies and Strategic Alliances: Social and Spatial Mediations." *Environment and Planning D: Society and Space* 6:281–300.

Cronon, William, 1991. *Nature's Metropolis: Chicago and the Great West*. New York: W. W. Norton.

Cusumano, Michael. 1985. *The Japanese Automobile Industry: Technology and Management at Nissan and Toyota*. Cambridge, MA: Harvard University Press.

Dicken, Peter. 1986. *Global Shift: Industrial Change in a Turbulent World*. London: Harper & Row.

Financial Times. 7/22/91. "UN Says Companies Fuel World Growth." p. 14.

Financial Times. 7/29/91. "UN Tracks the Cash in a New World Order." p. 13.

Financial Times. 9/30/91. "Digger Demolishes Divisions." p. 12.

Financial Times. 12/30/91. "Breaking Barriers between 'Us and Them.' " p. 7.

Friedman, David. 1983. "Beyond the Age of Ford: The Strategic Basis of the Japanese Success in Automobiles." In *American Industry in International Competition*, edited by John Zysman and Laura Tyson, pp. 350–90. Ithaca, NY: Cornell University Press.

Frobel, Folker; Heinrichs, Jurgen; and Kreye, Otto. 1980. *The New International Division of Labor*. Cambridge: Cambridge University Press.

Gereffi, Gary. 1991. "The 'Old' and 'New' Maquiladora Industries in Mexico: What Is Their Contribution to National Development and North American Integration?" *Nuestra economía* 2, 8 (May–August): 39–63.

———. 1992. "Transnational Production Systems and Third World Development: New Trends and Issues for the 1990s." Paper presented at a conference on "The New International Context of Development," University of Wisconsin, Madison, April 24–25.

Gertler, Meric S. 1988. "The Limits to Flexibility: Comments on the Post-Fordist Vision of Production and its Geography." *Transactions/Institute of British Geographers* 13(4):419–32.

Harvey, David. 1982. *The Limits to Capital*. Oxford: Basil Blackwell.

———. 1989. *The Condition of Post-Modernity*. Oxford: Basil Blackwell.

Holmes, John. 1983. "Industrial Reorganization, Capital Restructuring and Locational Change: An Analysis of the Canadian Automobile Industry in the 1960s." *Economic Geography* 59, 3:251–71.

———. 1987. "The Crisis of Fordism and the Restructuring of the Canadian Automobile Industry." In *Frontyard Backyard: The Americas in the Global Crisis*, edited by John Holmes and Colin Leys, pp. 95–129. Toronto: Between the Lines.

———. 1988. "Industrial Restructuring in a Period of Crisis: An Analysis of the Canadian Automobile Industry, 1973–1983." *Antipode* 20:19–51.

———. 1989. "New Production Technologies, Labor and the North American Auto Industry." In *Labour, Environment and Industrial Change*, edited by G. J. R. Linge and G. A. van der Knaap, pp. 87–106. London: Routledge.

Hopkins, Terence; Wallerstein, Immanuel; and associates. 1982. "Patterns of Development of the Modern World-System." In *World-Systems Analysis: Theory and Methodology*, edited by Terence Hopkins and Immanuel Wallerstein. Beverly Hills, CA: Sage Publications.

Hounshell, David. 1984. *From the American System to Mass Production, 1800–1932*. Baltimore: Johns Hopkins University Press.

Hymer, Steven. 1979. *The Multinational Corporation: A Radical Approach*. Cambridge: Cambridge University Press.

Lewchuk, Wayne. 1987. *American Technology and the British Vehicle Industry*. Cambridge: Cambridge University Press.

Mair, Andrew. 1991. "Just-in-Time Manufacturing and the Spatial Structure of the Automobile Industry: In Theory, in Japan, in North America and in Western Europe." Unpublished MS. Department of Geography, University of Durham, UK.

Massey, Doreen. 1984. *Spatial Divisions of Labor: Social Structures and the Geography of Production*. New York: Methuen.

McMillan, C. 1984. *The Japanese Industrial System*. New York: Walter de Gruyter.

MIT Commission on Industrial Productivity. 1989. "The Transformation of the US Chemical Industry." In *The Working Papers of the MIT Commission on Industrial Productivity*. 1: 1–103. Cambridge, MA: MIT Press.

Nofal, M. Beatriz. 1983. "Dynamics of the Motor Vehicle Industry in Argentina." Ph.D. dissertation, Department of Geography and Environmental Engineering, Johns Hopkins University.

Sabel, Charles F. 1989. "The Re-emergence of Regional Economies." In *Reversing Industrial Decline*, edited by Paul Hirst and Jonathan Zeitlin, pp. 17–70. Oxford: Berg Press.

Sabel, Charles F.; Kern, Horst; and Herrigel, Gary. 1989. "Collaborative Manufacturing." Unpublished MS. Department of Political Science, MIT.

Saxenian, Annalee. 1990a. "Regional Networks and the Resurgence of Silicon Valley." *California Management Review* 33:89–112.

———. 1990b. "The Origins and Dynamics of Production Networks in Silicon Valley." Paper prepared for the Networks of Innovators Conference, Montreal, May 1–3.

Schoenberger, Erica. 1986. "Competition, Competitive Strategy, and Industrial Change: The Case of Electronic Components." *Economic Geography* 62, 4 (Oct.):321–33.

———. 1987. "Technological and Organizational Change in Automobile Production: Spatial Implications." *Regional Studies* 21, 3: 199–214.

———. 1989. "Some Dilemmas of Automation: Strategic and Operational Aspects of Technological Change in Production." *Economic Geography* 65, 4:232–47.

———. 1990. "US Manufacturing Investments in Western Europe: Markets, Corporate Strategy and Competitive Environment." *Annals of the American Association of Geographers* 80, 3:379–93.

Scott, Allen J. 1988. *New Industrial Spaces: Flexible Production Organization and Regional Development in North America and Western Europe*. London: Pion.

Smith, Neil. 1984. *Uneven Development*. Oxford: Basil Blackwell.

Smith, Preston G., and Reinertsen, Donald G. 1991. *Developing Products in Half the Time*. New York: Van Nostrand.

Stalk, George, and Hout, Thomas. 1990. *Competing Against Time: How Time-Based Competition is Reshaping Global Markets*. New York: The Free Press.

Storper, Michael, 1992. "The Limits to Globalization: Technology Districts and International Trade." Forthcoming in *Economic Geography*.

Storper, Michael, and Walker, Richard. 1989. *The Capitalist Imperative*. Oxford: Basil Blackwell.

Taplin, Ian. 1991. "Rethinking Flexibility: The Case of the Apparel Industry." Unpublished MS., Department of Sociology, Wake Forest University.

Waxman, Ronald; Saunders, Larry; and Carter, Harold. 1989. "VHDL Links Design, Test, Maintenance." *IEEE Spectrum*, May, pp. 40–44.

4

The Global Distribution of Commodity Chains

Roberto P. Korzeniewicz and William Martin

Over the course of the last fifteen years, our understanding of the world-economy has been enriched by studies using diverse conceptual and research strategies, ranging from dense narrative histories drawing on qualitative sources, to empirical studies focused on large sets of quantitative data. While this research has provided a sounder footing for the world-systems approach, considerable debate and controversy continue to surround some of the most basic questions and concepts in our field. How do we demarcate the distribution and integration of production processes on a world-economic scale? Is this global distribution and integration of production processes related to the existence of world-economic zones? If so, how and to what degree are these processes accompanied by an unequal distribution of rewards among the various zones of the world-economy?

This chapter addresses these issues and debates with three distinctive contributions. First, we present original data on long-term patterns of the global distribution of wealth in order to provide a more systematic classification of the boundaries, membership, and degree of polarization across the zones of the world-economy. Second, this step permits us to explore the relationship between long-term trends in zonal structures and the location of, and linkages between, production processes across time. Relating these two arenas of work allows us to address not only current research strategies, but central claims regarding transformations in the spatial distribution of linked production processes and their relationship to polarization across the zones of the world-economy over long periods of time. Third, and most importantly for the analysis of commodity chains, we introduce a more systematic procedure to evaluate the zonal distribution of commodity production using a global and longitudinal approach.

WHAT IS LINKED BY COMMODITY CHAINS?

Central to any investigation of the world-economy is a conception of the global division of labor. The concept of "commodity chains" was introduced to address a fundamental problem in world-system studies: How do we depict and investigate the relationships that sustain and reproduce core-peripheral relations over time and space? Studies during the 1970s embarked on this task by attempting to establish zonal boundaries and inequalities by comparing national differentials in income, wages, or capital investment (e.g., Rubinson, 1976; Bornschier, Chase-Dunn, and Rubinson, 1978). Other scholars investigated networks of production by identifying patterns of commodity production and especially trade (e.g., Snyder and Kick, 1979; Nemeth and Smith, 1985). While all these studies have partially advanced our understanding of trends in the global division of labor, they generally presumed that either factors of production or readily visible flows of commodities (e.g., raw materials, manufactures) between nations equaled core-peripheral relationships and, therefore, served to identify the states that composed each of the zones of the world-economy. In this section we examine the conceptual limits of these approaches. We suggest that a new strategy is needed to examine cycles and trends in the relationship between positions in the global distribution of labor and the spatial distribution and integration of production processes. This new strategy is designed to simultaneously reveal the zonal structures embedded in the global distribution of wealth while examining commodity chains as relational processes formative of core-peripheral relations.

In fact, this was part of the original agenda behind the concept of commodity chains. As Hopkins and Wallerstein summarized in the mid-1980s,

The predominant current procedure is to trace primarily the economic flows between states (that is, across frontiers) such as trade, migration or capital investment. . . . Such efforts do not, however, and for the most part cannot, show the totality of the flows or movements that reveal the real division, and thus integration, of labor in complex production processes. . . . It should be noted, moreover, that the concept of a commodity chain does not *presume* either a geographically dispersed division of labor or the interrelation or separation of states via commodity movements (Hopkins and Wallerstein, 1986: 160, emphasis in original).

In short, the concept of commodity chains sought to provide a relational construct for investigating the structure of the world-economy. As constructed, the concept was agnostic even about the nation-state units of analysis that had come to provide (largely for reasons of readily available databases) the primary categories within the world-systems approach.

Both the advantages and the limitations of the concept can be readily illustrated from existing studies. Research by the Fernand Braudel Center's Research Working Group on Commodity Chains has sought to demonstrate that a worldwide division of labor was the organizing force behind commodity production in early modern (sixteenth- to seventeenth-century) Europe (e.g., Hopkins and Wallerstein, 1986, as well as chapter 2 in this volume). More common has been the concept's utility in depicting the trans-zonal networks of labor and production processes that result in a finished commodity and its eventual consumption, as in Gereffi and Korzeniewicz's study (1990) of the differentiation and changing locations of footwear production over the last two decades. Such studies mark a significant advance in tracing relational production networks at any one point in time, as well as revealing the zonal shifts involved over time in the location of the production activities required to produce a single commodity. Both studies also address critical debates. The Fernand Braudel Center Group is able to contest developmentalist accounts of capitalism's birth as an incrementalist process contained within nation-states, while the second study illuminates the relational processes that have sustained the advance of "newly industrializing countries" and the current reorganization of commodity production across the global division of labor.

But if the study of commodity chains allows us to escape developmentalist assumptions, it also remains a construct with distinct constraints for the exploration of the global division of labor. We note here its main limitations. A focus on single commodities over brief periods of time will often distort the observation of core-peripheral relations by relying on an intuitive typology of production processes. For example, it has often been assumed that certain commodities or production processes inherently command greater wealth than others: manufacturing as opposed to raw materials, or advanced capital goods as opposed to nondurable consumer goods. Most typologies of global production processes are built on the "commodity hierarchies" that result from such (explicit or implicit) assumptions. But in the absence of alternative indicators of the global distribution of production, the assumptions and typologies themselves generally have not been empirically tested. Moreover, historical research on such topics as the production of cereals from the sixteenth century onward suggests that over long periods of time certain commodity nodes may shift from core to periphery, and then back from periphery to core. Finally, it remains to be seen if the study of commodity chains can isolate the processes that generate polarization across either the particular chain in question, or—even more precariously by inference—the world-economy as a whole.

Any claims derived from commodity chain analysis regarding the structure of the global division of labor would require the accumulation of a very large set of commodity chains. Such research would have to capture both core and peripheral nodes of commodity chains, and not simply the shift of the production of select commodities from core to peripheral areas (as is often the case when product life cycles of commodities produced in core areas, and subsequently devolved toward peripheral areas, are presented as commodity chains). Even with a plethora of commodity chains in hand we will still confront several difficulties: the logic by which parts are aggregated to a whole (e.g., the degree to which any particular chain[s] can be claimed to replicate the operations of the whole world-economy); the manner by which zones of the world-economy are related to the spatial configuration of a commodity chain (and even the question of whether commodity chains necessarily cross national or zonal boundaries); and the extent to which commodity chains reveal not simply an integrated division of labor over time but the unequal distribution of rewards and wealth among their nodes. These observations suffice to highlight the complexity inherent in the concept of commodity chains.

We set aside here the question of the logic of assembling a global division of labor from commodity chains. The goals of this chapter are more modest. We seek to outline a possible methodology for evaluating the zonal distribution of commodity chains. Our next section reviews new data on the changes in the global distribution of wealth among the core, semiperiphery, and periphery of the world-economy since the 1930s, and identifies the composition of each of these zones over time. In turn, we use these data on the composition of world-economic zones to propose a new indicator that allow us to examine components of commodity chains in relation to zonal locations, wealth, and inequality. This indicator allows for further methodological and empirical observations on the analysis of recent transformations in the spatial distribution of commodity chains within the world-economy.

THE ZONAL BOUNDARIES OF THE WORLD-ECONOMY

As noted above, zones of the world-economy are frequently identified from the analysis of trade networks (or even commodity chains) through typologies of commodities. The problem with this procedure—even when used for the analysis of short time periods—is that the commodity typologies or hierarchies used to define these zones are themselves generally untested, rendering this approach prone to teleological explanations.

But we can resort to an alternative methodological procedure. To the extent that the production processes constitutive of commodity chains operate to generate uneven rewards, world-systems theory would predict that the global distribution of wealth is unequal among the core and peripheral nodes on any complete set of commodity chains. If commodity chains do depict relations that form and sustain an integrated division of labor (and wealth), the outcome of all commodity chains should be directly observable in the global distribution of income (or "wealth" if income is summed over time).

We can hence attempt to specify long-term patterns in the unequal rewards that accrue to world-economic zones by using available longitudinal data on national income. Here we follow the method laid forth by Arrighi and Drangel (1986), which provided basic procedures to analyze the distribution of global income and membership in particular zones. The use of GNP per capita as an indicator has generated controversy both within and outside world-systems theory.[1] Even among those who otherwise sympathize with a world-systems approach, there are some who argue that GNP per capita is not a *relational* indicator (see, for example, Snyder and Kick, 1979: 1098). But we use GNP per capita as an indicator of the *relative distribution* of aggregate rewards that are themselves assumed to be indicative of the distribution of core and peripheral activities among nations in the world-economy.[2] As such, the indicator is intended as a *relational* measure that can be used in a *long-term* analysis to analyze the trimodal distribution of wealth in the world-economy, and to determine the overall trajectory and composition of world-economic zones. The same indicator has indeed been used under different theoretical and methodological assumptions to measure levels of economic "development" or standards of living, but these assumptions will continue to differ from a world-systems approach that focuses on the inequalities that characterize the spatial distribution of commodity chains.

Our basic procedure is to analyze the distribution of global GNP by charting national population (as a percentage of total population) by the log of GNP per capita in current dollars (details on this methodology are provided in the Appendix). While Arrighi and Drangel's study (1986) addressed the definition of the semiperipheral zone, and was limited to observations clustered around nine points in time, our current analysis extends the analysis to far more time-points (34) and countries (up to 134).[3] Our presentation here is concerned primarily with establishing zonal boundaries, so we will not elaborate substantially on a broader set of issues addressed by the data (such as trends in inequality, or the shifting membership of the zones).

We will first simply note that the trimodal character of the zonal structure of the world-economy is confirmed even over the much longer period and number of observations we have examined. The data for the latest year is provided in Figure 4.1. As can be seen from the 1990 example, we have established boundaries for core, semiperipheral, and peripheral zones. Where appropriate, low-frequency intervals between the three main zones have been demarcated as the "perimeter of the periphery" and the "perimeter of the core" (for a fuller discussion of these procedures, see Arrighi and Drangel, 1986, as well as the Appendix). This first, simple conclusion of trimodal stability is itself an important one, for most versions of both modernization and dependency theory predict a bimodal distribution, and even some cases of world-systems analysis assert that there exists an even distribution, or simple continuum, across the zones of the world-economy (e.g., Chase-Dunn, 1990).

Long-term trends in the modes and weight of the core, semiperiphery, and periphery are indicated in Figures 4.2 and 4.3. Figure 4.2 presents long-term trends in the midpoint, or mode, of each of the three zones, while Figure 4.3 indicates the cumulative population of each zone over time.

Regarding the strictly core-peripheral relationship, Figures 4.2 and 4.3 demonstrate that over at least the last half-century the gap (or the difference of the

Figure 4.1
Percentage of Total Population by Log GNP per Capita of the Country of Residence, 1990

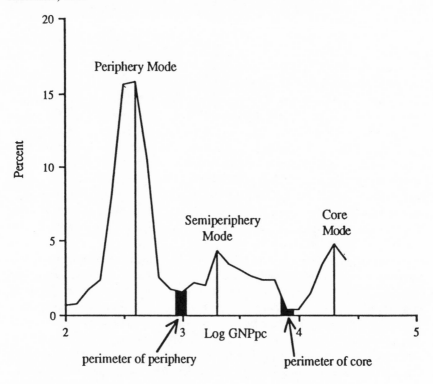

Figure 4.2
Trends in Modal GNP per Capita by Zone (Three-year Moving Average after 1962)

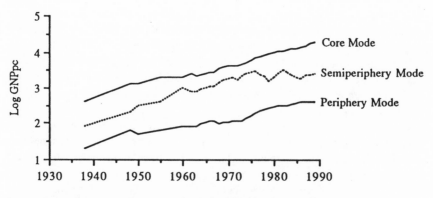

Note: Separate data sources for 1938/1948; 1950; 1955–90; see Appendix.

Figure 4.3
Trends in the Relative Size of the Three Zones (Smoothed Data)

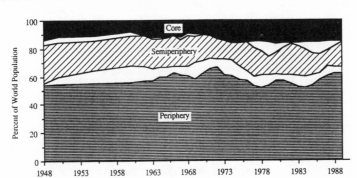

logs of their modal per capita GNP) has considerably increased. Particularly striking is the disparity in the current period of hegemonic crisis and global stagnation: notwithstanding momentary increases in the oil and commodity booms of the mid- and late 1970s, the core-periphery gap has reached levels higher than in any time over our whole period.[4] If we were to plot the annual observations for the last five years (they are smoothed by a three-year moving average in Figure 4.2), an even more striking and accelerating gap would be apparent. The net outcome is thus simply stated: the gap between the modal rewards of the core and periphery has sharply increased over at least the last half-century.

Focusing on the semiperipheral zone presents more startling conclusions, subject as the zone is to widely divergent interpretations amid all the discussion of "newly industrializing countries" and the "new international division of labor." As suggested by our data, there is no support for arguments that the lot of the semiperipheral zone has benefited from such phenomena. Contrary to dependency expectations of advance during B-phases, the point of greatest closure of the gap was during the previous A-phase (i.e., 1945/50 to the early 1970s).[5] Since that moment the gap between the core and semiperipheral zones has appreciably widened, and if the trends for the last few years continue to hold, is sharply accelerating. If there is a "new international division of labor" and a group of "newly industrializing countries," they have had remarkably little impact on the global distribution of wealth.

This is not to argue that states have not moved across the zonal boundaries of the world-economy. Indeed, as Arrighi and Drangel (1986) argued, significant cases are to be found; this topic alone could entail a discussion of considerable length that we will not enter in this article. What our procedures so far permit us to do, however, is to locate individual states and their production processes and commodity chain nodes within a zonal structure defined by the wealth generated by participation in the world-economy.

Our study also provides a far more complete assessment of the composition

Figure 4.4
Hypothetical Commodity Chain

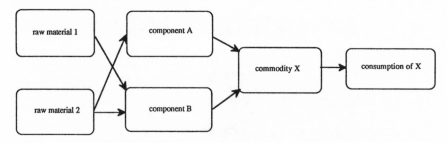

of the zones than has previously been available. Overall, our findings suggest that there has been considerable stability in the composition of the zones over time. This does not mean that transitions were absent: there were quite a number of these transitions, particularly during the 1950s. Since the late 1960s, however, the membership of the zones has become considerably more stable. Beyond these empirical findings, the new data are important because they provide us with an alternative indicator to assess the spatial distribution of production processes.

THE SPATIAL DISTRIBUTION OF COMMODITY CHAINS: A PRELIMINARY ASSESSMENT

This section of the chapter reports preliminary results of a study that will eventually identify the spatial distribution of production processes involving a larger sample of commodities. As an initial step, our study has used the classification developed in the previous section to evaluate how the production of six commodities (crude steel, motor vehicles, tires, cotton fiber, cotton yarn, and wheat) was distributed among the core, semiperipheral and peripheral zones of the world-economy. Eventually, by comparing and contrasting trends among a wider range of commodities (raw materials, capital goods, durable and nondurable consumer goods) and breaking down constituent aspects of the production process, our research will provide a more detailed matrix of major shifts in commodity chains over the twentieth century.

The problem addressed in this section is straightforward. Within a hypothetical commodity chain (see Figure 4.4), we find both nodes and linkages involving distinct production processes, transportation, processing, consumption. Studies on commodity chains will generally focus on the nature of the global division of labor that characterizes these processes (for example, production of raw materials in the periphery, final processing in the core), as well as on the transformations experienced by these commodity chains over time (for example, the shift of assembly operations from core to peripheral nations). Our task in this section is to propose an instrument that can be used to evaluate these issues in a more systematic manner.

This exercise addresses a critical shortcoming of existing work on the global division of labor, including many studies of commodity chains. Simply stated, most typologies of commodities are based on common-sense observations regarding the distribution of production processes in the world-economy. For example, it is widely assumed that growing manufacturing production in the core, as well as specialization of the periphery in agriculture and/or the production of raw materials, constituted the global division of labor that characterized the world-economy through most of the nineteenth and twentieth centuries. The "new international division of labor," according to the same line of interpretation, represents a breakdown of this earlier pattern, with a pronounced shift of manufacturing activities to peripheral nations. Yet most studies along these lines are often based on untested hierarchies of commodity types, generalizations developed on the basis of a small number of national trajectories, and/or an intuitive classification of states (and often too few states) into the categories of core, periphery, and, less frequently, semiperiphery.

Rather than assume the existence and character of a hierarchy of production processes in the world-economy, we have reclassified cross-national data for our six commodities (as measured in volume by United Nations data) according to their distribution among the three world-economic zones identified in the earlier section. This allows us to evaluate whether it is the case that manufactured and unprocessed commodities have followed the patterns depicted by "new international division of labor" theorists. In addition, we can examine global production patterns in relation to global zonal membership—something rarely achieved, especially by studies focusing simply on trade relationships.

This procedure provides only a rough and approximate indicator of the spatial distribution of commodity processes. Even within a single commodity, particularly using data on volume, we are often likely to find great heterogeneity in the nature of both production processes and output. Cotton yarn, for example, can be produced in capital-intensive factories or craft household production, but aggregate data on the volume of commodity production (such as those used in this article) will reveal few of these differences. Similarly, automobiles produced under certain conditions will command higher market prices than others, but our data reveal little about the relative value of a Volvo as compared to a LADA. Our initial work here does, however, lay the basis for more extended research on the complexity of commodity chains and specific production processes, thus providing a new perspective on fundamental assumptions of world-systems theory.

For each of our six commodities, we have used the classification of nations according to world-economic zones to establish the shares of overall production accounted by core, semiperipheral, and peripheral areas of the world-economy between 1970 and 1987. Thus we use the term "core production" to refer to all production taking place in nations that fall under the "core" category according to the zonal classification presented in the previous section. The same consideration applies to the notions of "semiperipheral" and "peripheral" pro-

Figure 4.5
Zonal Distribution of Motor Vehicle Production (Thousands of Units), 1970–1987

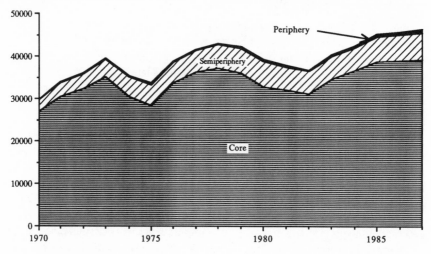

Source: See Appendix.

duction (greater details on our sources and procedures are provided in the Appendix). Figures 4.5 through 4.10 provide a breakdown of production of our six commodities among the three zones of the world-economy between 1970 and 1987. As indicated, the six commodities were characterized by distinct patterns.

In comparative terms, motor vehicle production (see Figure 4.5) has been highly concentrated in core areas of the world-economy throughout the period under consideration (for an overview of recent changes in automobile production, see Dicken, 1992: ch. 9, as well as Law, 1991). By 1970, semiperipheral nations gradually came to account for about a tenth of world vehicle production. Peripheral areas of the world-economy have consistently accounted for only a marginal share of overall final production. Of the six commodities analyzed in this article, motor vehicles have involved the smallest share of production by peripheral nations. During the 1970–1987 period, the spatial distribution of final motor vehicle production was characterized by considerable stability; the data fail to provide strong evidence of a substantial shift in final production from the core to other areas in the world-economy, particularly the periphery. By itself, this is a significant finding, for it challenges some of the expectations held by subscribers to the notion of the "new international division of labor."

In tires and crude steel production, two of the basic backward linkages in a motor vehicle commodity chain, semiperipheral nations accounted for a greater share of overall output by the 1970s (see Figures 4.6 and 4.7). Peripheral nations also accounted for a growing (albeit rather small) share of overall production after the 1970s. In the case of tire production, the share of semiperipheral and

Figure 4.6
Zonal Distribution of Tire Production (Thousands of Units), 1970–1987

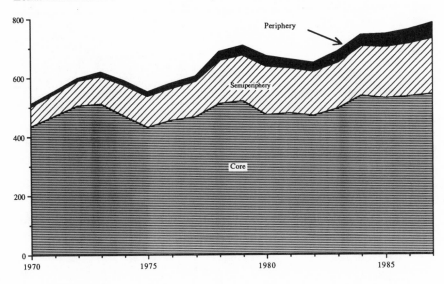

Source: See Appendix.

Figure 4.7
Zonal Distribution of Crude Steel Production (Thousand Tons), 1970–1987

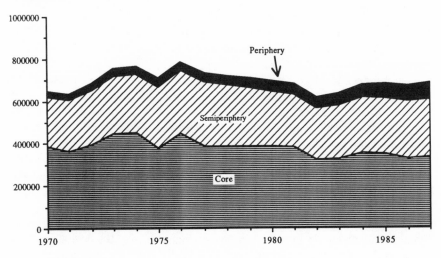

Source: See Appendix.

Figure 4.8
Zonal Distribution of Cotton Fiber Production (Thousand Metric Tons), 1970–1987

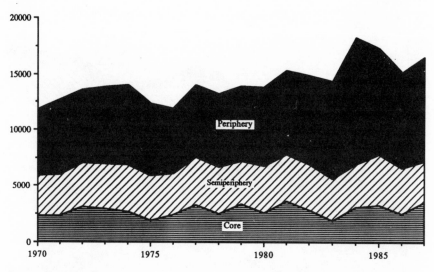

Source: See Appendix.

peripheral nations grew at a more rapid pace than the share accounted for by core nations in the world-economy. By 1987, however, most tire output still continued to be centered in the core. In the case of crude steel production, on the other hand, the share of core nations declined more rapidly in a context of falling overall production. By 1987, semiperipheral and peripheral production had jointly come to account for a slight majority of overall production (for an overview of recent changes in the spatial location of crude steel production, see Hogan, 1991).

The production of cotton fiber and yarn has shown a different pattern (see Figures 4.8 and 4.9). In both commodities, peripheral areas already accounted for the majority of overall production by the early 1970s, and this share continued to grow throughout the period under consideration (for an overview of some of these changes, see Dicken, 1992: ch. 8). In the case of these two commodities, through the 1960s and 1970s, the share of production accounted for by the semiperiphery and core areas of the world-economy has declined either in relative (cotton fiber) or absolute terms (cotton yarn). Finally, the share of peripheral areas has also increased in wheat production (see Figure 4.10).

This exercise allows us to introduce a methodological innovation beyond its empirical findings. As presented in the preceding figures, the data allow some interesting comparisons, but provide little in the way of determining how to evaluate the extent to which a given commodity (and the production processes

Figure 4.9
Zonal Distribution of Cotton Yarn Production (Thousand Metric Tons), 1970–1982

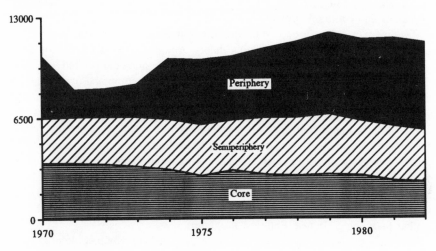

Source: See Appendix.

Figure 4.10
Zonal Distribution of Wheat Production (Thousand Metric Tons), 1970–1987

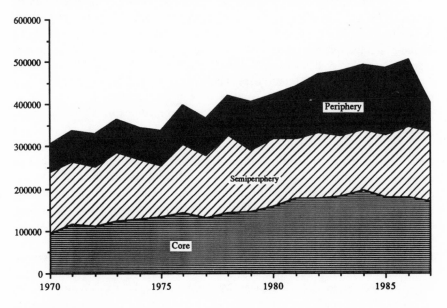

Source: See Appendix.

involved) should be considered "core-like" or "peripheral-like." In other words: to what extent does a given commodity or node in a production process appear to be associated with zones that control relatively larger or smaller shares of global wealth? What trends can be discerned over both the short and the long term? This type of assessment is central to the analysis of global production processes and commodity chains.

Two indexes can be used to analyze the zonal distribution of world-economic production processes. World-systems theory argues that most production processes can be characterized as being either "core" (allowing a relatively high command over wealth) or "peripheral" (allowing little command over wealth). The first index should therefore measure the extent to which a given commodity or production process is "core" or "peripheral." For each of our six commodities, we have hence built a "coreness" index by dividing core production by the sum of core and peripheral production. According to this index, a commodity that is produced almost exclusively in the core would approximate a value of 1.00, while a commodity that is produced almost exclusively in the periphery would approximate a value of zero. As predicted by most world-systems analysts, most commodities should cluster either at the high or the low end of this index (rather than being aligned along a continuum).

The second index is designed to evaluate the extent to which commodities or production processes are located in the semiperiphery of the world-economy. We use a separate index to measure "semiperipherality" because world-systems theory often argues that this zone is characterized by a "mix" of core and peripheral activities—rather than by distinct "semiperipheral" production processes (for example, Arrighi and Drangel, 1986). By using a separate index to measure semiperipherality, we can empirically test this theoretical proposition. For each of our six commodities, we have built a "semiperipherality" index by dividing semiperipheral production by overall production. According to this index, a commodity that is heavily produced in the semiperiphery should approximate a value of 1.00, and there should be a value of zero when the semiperiphery accounts for little of overall production. As predicted by most world-systems analysts, there should be virtually no commodities in which the semiperiphery accounts for a majority of production.

Combined, these two indexes allow for a more systematic evaluation of the zonal distribution of production processes. These indexes can be used, for example, to *compare* the zonal distribution of different commodities at any one point in time. The indexes can be also used to evaluate changes *through time* in the zonal distribution of commodities/production processes. These uses of the two indexes are illustrated by Figure 4.11. In this figure we have plotted the world-economic location of each of our six commodities according to the "coreness" and "semiperipherality" indexes. Movement along the x axis represents the extent to which production of a commodity is centered in the core (high values) or the periphery (low values). Movement along the y axis represents the extent to which production of a commodity is centered in the semiperiphery

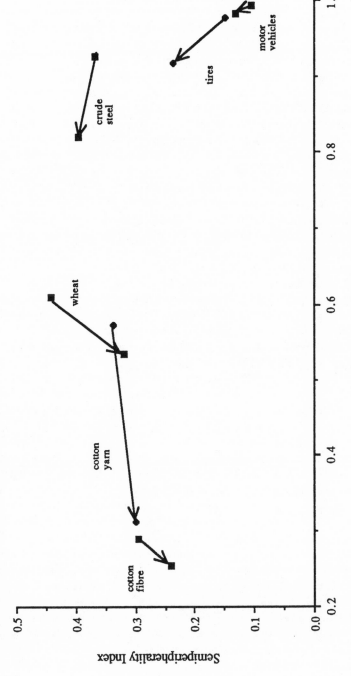

Figure 4.11
Zonal Shifts in Selected Commodities, 1970–1987

Coreness Index

Semiperipherality Index

Note: For the case of cotton yarn, the shift occurs between 1970 and 1982.

(high values) as opposed to either periphery or core (low values). The arrows indicate, for each of the six commodities, the world-economic locational shift that has taken place between 1970 and 1987.

Our indexes serve to raise several immediate observations. Allowing us to compare the spatial distribution of different commodities at discrete points in time, Figure 4.11 suggests an identical *ranking* in the relative "coreness" of the six commodities for both 1970 and 1987: moving from "most core" to "most peripheral," we find motor vehicles, tires, crude steel, wheat, cotton yarn, and cotton fiber. The indexes also serve to contrast the relative "semi-peripherality" of the production of the six commodities (for example, among the three commodities most heavily concentrated in the core, we find the same ranking in relative "semiperipherality" for both 1970 and 1987). Consistent with the expectations of world-systems theory, for no commodity does the semi-periphery account for a majority of production.

Used in a similar manner for a larger sample, the indexes can be used to ascertain the world-economic location of different commodities, so as to assess the validity of existing assumptions regarding the zonal distribution of global production. For example, many studies in the sociology of development intuitively rank agricultural production as a more peripheral activity than manufacturing. But our indexes suggest that by the 1970s and 1980s, wheat production was more heavily centered in core and semiperipheral areas of the world-economy than cotton yarn production (see Figure 4.11). In this fashion, the indexes can be used to provide a more systematic evaluation of the hierarchies of production processes and commodities that are often assumed in studies focusing on development and/or the global division of labor.

The indexes also provide a means to trace and compare changes over time in the zonal distribution of commodity production. For example, in the case of motor vehicle production, Figure 4.11 reveals considerable stability for the 1970–1987 period, as compared to the other five commodities examined in our research. Some cases (such as crude steel and, particularly, cotton yarn) show a more rapid pace of peripheralization than other commodities. While production has shifted rapidly into the semiperiphery in some cases (e.g., tires), it has moved away from the semiperiphery in others (e.g., wheat). Consistent with world-systems theory, Figure 4.11 suggests that peripheralization of production may be characterized by a shift to the semiperiphery in its early stages, followed by a shift away from the semiperiphery after a certain threshold.

More specifically, focusing on the character of commodity chains, the indexes constitute an essential indicator to evaluate the characteristics of the nodes involved in linkages and production processes. From raw materials to consumption, the indexes will provide a means of evaluating for specific commodity chains whether their organization involves a hierarchy of nodes and linkages, as well as allowing us to trace within these chains the spatial characteristics of longitudinal change. A graphic example of how these indexes may be used to analyze the structure of commodity chains is provided in Figure 4.12. As indicated in

Figure 4.12
Construction of Zonal Distribution of Hypothetical Commodity Chain

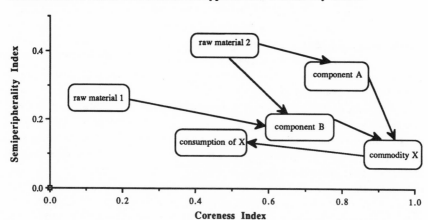

the figure, the indexes can provide an accessible mechanism for evaluating the spatial location of the nodes of a commodity chain. In the figure, linkages between nodes involve movement between zones, so that the structure of a commodity chain is rendered more clearly as a set of world-economic relationships. In an aggregate, longitudinal study of key commodity chains, this type of exercise will yield a more precise understanding of the timing and scope of shifts in the zonal distribution of the global division of labor.

CONCLUSION

One of the most resilient notions shaping the study of economic development has been that industrialization constitutes an engine of growth and the primary source of wealth in the global economy. Even within the world-systems approach, analysts have too often relied on this assumption to characterize the nature of uneven development in the world-economy. According to this inherent model, peripheral nations are those whose participation in the global economy is limited to producing those commodities found in the lower ranks in the hierarchy of industrialization. As commodities become more processed, rising in the ranks of the manufacturing hierarchy, so does their production and marketing become increasingly dominated by wealthy nations. The uneven exchange of these commodities between nations, according to the model, constitutes the very essence of global inequality. For this reason, national trade in these commodities has often been used as the fundamental indicator of world-economic zones.

This chapter challenges these assumptions. Analyzing the zonal composition of the world-economy by measuring the relative distribution of wealth, our findings suggest a stable trimodal distribution of the world population among core, periphery, and semiperipheral zones, rather than a sliding continuum between core and periphery. The relative distance or gap between core and periphery is, moreover, clearly increasing over the last half-century, particularly since the transition to a period of global stagnation in the mid-1970s. This finding sharply contrasts with both the expectations of dependency theory (which has asserted that B-phases are periods of widespread advance for noncore states) and the conclusion, largely drawn from selective case studies of "newly industrializing countries," that "development," at least in terms of an expanding semiperipheral zone, has been a widespread phenomenon of the last fifteen years.

One of the key advantages of this method of locating states by their share of global income is that it provides an independent classification of zonal membership that may then be used to analyze shifting patterns of commodity production, trade, and investment. In this instance we have used the classification for an exploratory examination of the relationship between the world distribution of wealth and the spatial distribution of commodity chains. The commodities analyzed in this article have shown distinct patterns in their spatial location. Our indexes suggested significant variations in the rate of "peripheralization" that has characterized the six commodities over time. The shift of production toward the periphery was characterized by simultaneous movement toward the semiperiphery in its early stages, but away from the semiperiphery after an apparent threshold. Our future research will evaluate whether these same findings apply to a larger sample of commodities over a longer period of time.

Within world-systems theory, the "coreness" and "semiperipherality" indexes developed in this article provide a means of estimating whether commodity production indeed tends to be characterized by significant polarization between "core" and "peripheral" production (as opposed to a continuum in the relative "coreness" of production processes, or the presence of production processes centered almost exclusively in the semiperiphery). In a longitudinal study, these indicators can be used to evaluate whether production processes tend to become peripheralized over time, as well as to ascertain the timing and rate of change. Advances in these areas will further strengthen our understanding of commodity chains, while providing a substantial contribution to the continuing development of world-systems theory.

APPENDIX: ON CALCULATING ZONAL MODES, BOUNDARIES, AND "ORGANIC MEMBERS"

In order to allow for comparative arguments and illustrations, our procedures to determine core, semiperipheral, and peripheral zones followed closely those employed by Arrighi and Drangel (1986) for the determination of zonal modes and boundaries. Given our much larger number of observations (34 annual observations and up to 134 countries versus Arrighi and Drangel's nine annual observations and a maximum of 105 countries), our sources and calculation of organic zonal members could expand beyond their procedures in some key respects. We thus sketch below the central elements of our sources, our calculation of modes and boundaries, our classification of "organic" members of the zones, and our procedures for calculating the zonal distribution of commodity production.

SOURCES

For 1938 and 1948 we utilized Woytinsky and Woytinsky (1953); Morawetz (1977; estimates based on World Bank sources) for 1950; and World Bank (various sources) for 1955–1990. In the last case, our primary source was the diskette version of *World Tables Update 1991*, followed by data held on World Bank computer tapes, World Bank (1984) for 1955 and 1960, and for 1990, data provided by *World Atlas 1991*. These sources provided GNP per capita in U.S. dollars; in some instances it was necessary to convert GNP in local dollars to U.S. dollars (1955, 1960, 1962–1969). Data on exchange rates were derived from the same World Bank sources with the exception of a few cases in 1955, which relied upon a United Nations (1957) source. A few additional population estimates were drawn from United Nations (1979).

The coverage of each source varied, ranging from the 57 countries provided by Woytinsky and Woytinsky to the World Bank data that covered up to 134 countries. We always took all the nations provided by each source, since our aim was to achieve as complete a global distribution of income as possible. A few large countries were missing from several sources, particularly the Soviet Union and China. For China (missing from 1948, 1955, and 1960) we provided our own estimates based in part on Arrighi's calculations. Data for the USSR are the subject of considerable debate, as is indicated by U.S. dollar estimates of GNP per capita for 1989, which range from $1,780 (World Bank, IMF, OECD, and EBRD, 1990a: 9) to $9,230 (United States, CIA, 1990: 31 [errata update page], using purchasing power equivalents). For the USSR over time we utilized Marer's (1985) estimates for 1964–1979 (derived from World Bank data), and then extended these backward and forward through estimations of Soviet growth rates provided in CIA calculations (1988, 1990, 1991). The resulting time series falls within the middle range of competing estimates for the 1980s; the results probably overestimate the long-term weight and value of the USSR GNP per capita figures. As Rosenfelde (1991: 604) notes, however, no satisfactory alternative time series have been constructed. For the purposes of our research, even lower estimates of Soviet GNP would not affect overall zonal distributions to any significant degree over long periods of time because of the size of the respective zones and the relational gap between the Soviet Union and states located in core and peripheral zones.

It should be noted that the GNP per capita for any individual state, for any single year, has no significance other than by relation to the GNP per capita of other nations. Furthermore, it must be remembered that we are interested in GNP as an indicator of command over global economic resources, and not of the well-being of a nation's citizens. For this latter purpose but not, in our view, to estimate command over world-economic resources—other indicators might well be used.

CALCULATING MODES AND BOUNDARIES

Procedures to estimate modes and boundaries closely followed those of Arrighi and Drangel (1986: 62–64). In order to single out the three maxima designated as peripheral, semiperipheral, and core modes, we first took the midpoints of the intervals with the highest frequency in the lower and upper ranges of logged GNP per capita and designated them as the peripheral and core modes. The semiperipheral mode was then defined as the midpoint of highest frequency in the range, three intervals to the left of the core mode and three intervals to the right of the peripheral mode. This three-interval rule was used in order to ensure (with a one-interval margin) that no country would enter into the determination of the two different modes via the three-interval moving average used to smooth frequencies across all intervals (see Figure 4.1 for an example).

These procedures were slightly abrogated by Arrighi and Drangel in two of their nine observations (1960, 1970). Out of our 34 time-point observations, we were posed with two similar cases. In 1974, using the strict three-interval rule, the semiperipheral mode would be 2.9 (rather than the more obvious 3.5, which is too close to the core mode of 3.7). This seemed excessively formalistic, especially by comparison to modes for the decades before and after 1974. We thus used 3.5 as the semiperipheral mode. In 1984 the maximum peak between the peripheral and core modes (even with the three-interval rule) was 2.9 (rather than the more obvious, and just slightly lower, peak of 3.3). Again, by comparison to years before and after, we chose to use 3.3 as the semiperipheral mode.

The boundaries between the zones (perimeter of perimeter and perimeter of core) were calculated following the Arrighi and Drangel rules, which were:

(a) If the distribution had only one local minimum between the two modes, the interval representing that minimum was taken as the boundary separating the two zones, provided that the states falling in the interval had not entered (via the three-interval moving average) in the determination of one or both of the two modes.
(b) If the distribution had only one local minimum between the two modes, but the states falling in the corresponding interval had entered in the determination of both the modes, the distribution would have been considered nontrimodal and discarded.
(c) If the distribution had only one local minimum between the two modes and the states falling in the corresponding interval had entered in the determination of one of the two modes, the interval was included in the zone, and the boundary was defined by a line rather than an interval.
(d) If the distribution had more than one local minimum between the two modes (as happened in most instances), we discarded the minima that had frequencies higher than either of the two modes. If we were left with only one minimum, we set the boundaries following the procedure set out above. If we were still left with more than one minimum,

we took the two minima with the lowest frequency and defined the perimeters of the zones as consisting of all the intervals enclosed by (but excluding) the intervals corresponding to the two minima.

We abrogated these rules in the one instance (1970) where the proximity of the semiperipheral and core modes would have excluded this case from consideration. This allowed us to use 1970 in the calculation of the three-year moving average of our zonal boundaries, which mitigated the centrality of 1970 as a pivotal year (as was posed for Arrighi and Drangel given their more limited 1965–1970–1975 observations). This provided the basic data to construct Figure 4.2.

Once the boundaries were determined, states were classified by zone according to their GNP per capita position. In order to obtain the relative size of the zones, the percentage of the world population comprised by the countries in each zone was then calculated; this provided the data for Figure 4.3.

ESTIMATING ORGANIC MEMBERS OF THE ZONES FOR USE WITH COMMODITY PRODUCTION DATA

For the five-year periods 1970–1974, 1975–1979, 1980–1984, and 1985–1989, we defined organic members by first averaging their logged GNP per capita position over the five years involved. The resulting figure was then placed within core-semiperipheral-peripheral averages for the respective five-year period; these were estimated by taking the annual boundaries as defined above. For each of the five-year periods in our sample, we constructed the core as including *both* the perimeter of the core and core, the periphery as including *both* the perimeter of the periphery and the periphery, and the semiperiphery as the zone between the perimeter of the core and the perimeter of the periphery. We classified as organic members of a zone (for the 1970–1989 period) those nations that in most observations (for the five-year periods) appeared within that same zone. A total of 109 nations met this previous condition. For those few cases (nine nations) that involved an even number of observations in two separate zones, we chose to classify the nations according to their last observed location. These nine cases could be deleted from our sample with no significant change in the results reported. There were no cases of nations that were observed to shift among all three zones for the period under consideration.

Thus the term "core production" refers to all production taking place in nations that fall under the "core" category according to the zonal classification presented above. For our six commodities, these nations include Australia, Austria, Belgium, Canada, Denmark, Finland, France, Hong Kong, Ireland, Israel, Italy, Japan, Luxembourg, Netherlands, New Zealand, Norway, Saudi Arabia, Spain, Sweden, Switzerland, United Kingdom, United States, and West Germany.

The term "semiperipheral production" refers to all production taking place in nations that fall under the "semiperiphery" category according to the zonal classification presented in this section. For our six commodities, these nations include Albania, Algeria, Argentina, Brazil, Bulgaria, Chile, Cuba, Cyprus, Czechoslovakia, East Germany, Greece, Hungary, Iran, Iraq, Jordan, Lebanon, Malaysia, Mexico, North Korea, Panama, Poland, Portugal, Romania, South Africa, South Korea, Taiwan, USSR, Uruguay, Venezuela, and Yugoslavia.

The term "peripheral production" refers to all production taking place in nations that fall under the "periphery" category according to the zonal classification presented in this section. For our six commodities, these nations include Afghanistan, Angola, Bangladesh, Benin, Bhutan, Bolivia, Botswana, Burkina Faso, Burma, Burundi, Cameroon, Central African Republic, Chad, China, Colombia, Dominican Republic, Ecuador, Egypt, El Salvador, Ethiopia, Ghana, Guatemala, Guinea Bissau, Haiti, Honduras, India, Indonesia, Ivory Coast, Jamaica, Kampuchea, Kenya, Laos, Lesotho, Madagascar, Malawi, Mali, Mongolia, Morocco, Mozambique, Namibia, Nicaragua, Niger, Nigeria, Pakistan, Paraguay, Peru, Philippines, Rwanda, Senegal, Somalia, Sri Lanka, Sudan, Swaziland, Syria, Tanzania, Thailand, Togo, Tunisia, Turkey, Uganda, Vietnam, Yemen, Zaire, Zambia and Zimbabwe.

ESTIMATING PRODUCTION AND POPULATION FOR USE WITH COMMODITY DATA

Production data for each of our six commodities (motor vehicles, tires, crude steel, cotton yarn, cotton fiber, and wheat) were drawn primarily from the *Statistical Yearbook* of the United Nations (multiple volumes). The data on motor vehicle production measure "the manufacture of vehicles either wholly or mainly from domestically produced parts. Vehicles shipped in 'knocked down' form from assembly abroad are included," and the data used in our study include both commercial vehicles and passenger cars (United Nations, 1978: 353, and annual yearbooks of the Motor Vehicle Manufacturers Association of the United States). Data on tires "refer to the production of rubber tires for passenger cars and commercial vehicles . . . data do not cover tires for vehicles operating off the road, motorcycles, bicycles and animal-drawn road vehicles. Data also exclude the production of inner tubes" (United Nations, 1988: 509). The data on crude steel cover, "as far as possible, the total production of crude steel, both ingots and steel for castings, whether obtained from pig-iron or scrap" (United Nations, 1978: 335). Data on cotton yarn "refer to pure cotton yarn including yarn from cotton waste and mixed yarn in which cotton or cotton waste is the predominant material by weight, containing less than 10 per cent by weight of silk, noil or other waste silk or any combination thereof" (United Nations, 1983: 669). The data on cotton yarn cover only the 1970–1982 period.

NOTES

Research for this article was made possible by Faculty Development Grants from Albion College. We would like to thank Gary Gereffi and Miguel E. Korzeniewicz for substantial comments on earlier versions of this article, and Dawn Owens for her valuable work on the GNP data.

1. We draw here from Korzeniewicz (1992).

2. In a subsequent article, Arrighi points out that "wealth is long-term income. If the claims of world-systems analysis have any validity at all, observation of the distribution of incomes among the various political jurisdictions of the capitalist world-economy over relatively long periods of time should reveal the existence of three separate standards of wealth . . . '' (1990: p. 18).

3. We note two limitations of our sources. First, we rely on data presented by state boundaries rather than, for example, measures of income inequality disaggregated below the state level and then summed to a global distribution. This asserts (for we cannot in this limited space carry forward the argument) that state boundaries and actions do matter in determining over long periods of time whether core or peripheral nodes/activities are located within the boundaries of any particular state. It must be further noted that no data exist over any period of time that would allow any estimation of income distribution within states (although Taylor's 1988 estimate for more recent years using alternative measures of inequality did indeed support Arrighi and Drangel's 1986 argument). We are not measuring, using GNP per capita, any level or standard of living. The aim is quite different: to approximate the distribution of command over world-economic resources rather than any standard of living or value-driven estimation of the quality of life. For these reasons alternative measures of GNP, such as purchasing power parities, are invalid for our purposes as they fail to measure direct command in the world market.

4. We have left logged per capita GNP in current dollars to reduce (at least for presentation here) the effects of deflating all national GNPs by the U.S. GNP deflator (as done by Arrighi and Drangel, 1986).

5. We previously raised this hypothesis in Arrighi, Korzeniewicz, and Martin (1986).

REFERENCES

Arrighi, Giovanni. 1990. "The Developmentalist Illusion." In *Semiperipheral States in the World-Economy*, edited by William G. Martin, pp. 11–42. Westport, CT: Greenwood Press.

Arrighi, Giovanni, and Drangel, Jessica. 1986. "The Stratification of the World-Economy: An Exploration of the Semiperipheral Zone." *Review* 10, 1 (Summer): 9–74.

Arrighi, Giovanni; Korzeniewicz, Roberto P. and Martin, William. 1986. "Three Crises, Three Zones: Core-Periphery Relations in the Long Twentieth Century." *Cahier du GIS Economie Mondiale, Tiers Monde Développment* 6 (Mar.): 125–62.

Bornschier, Volker; Chase-Dunn, Christopher; and Rubinson, Richard. 1978. "Cross-national Evidence of the Effects of Foreign Investment and Aid on Economic Growth and Inequality." *American Sociological Review* 84, 3: 651–83.

Chase-Dunn, Christopher. 1990. *Global Formation*. Cambridge, MA: Basil Blackwell.

Dicken, Peter. 1992. *Global Shift*. New York: The Guilford Press.

Gereffi, Gary, and Korzeniewicz, Miguel. 1990. "Commodity Chains and Footwear Exports in the Semiperiphery." In *Semiperipheral States in the World-Economy*, edited by William G. Martin pp. 45–68. Westport, CT: Greenwood Press.

Hogan, Willam T. 1991. *Global Steel in the 1990s*. Lexington, MA: Lexington Books.

Hopkins, Terence K., and Wallerstein, Immanuel. 1986. "Commodity Chains in the World-Economy Prior to 1800." *Review* 10, 1 (Summer): 157–70.

Korzeniewicz, Roberto P. 1992. "Democratic Transitions and the Semiperiphery of the World-Economy." *Sociological Forum* 7, 4: 1–32.

Kurtzweg, Laurie Rogers. 1990. *Measures of Soviet gross national product in 1982 prices: a study prepared for the use of the Joint Economic Committee, Congress of the United States.* Washington, D.C.: Government Printing Office, 1990.

Law, Christopher M. 1991. *Restructuring the Global Automobile Industry.* London: Routledge.

Marer, Paul. 1985. *Dollar GNPs of the U.S.S.R. and Eastern Europe.* Baltimore: Johns Hopkins University Press.

Morawetz, David. 1977. *Twenty-Five Years of Economic Development, 1950–1974.* Baltimore: Johns Hopkins University Press.

Nemeth, Roger, and Smith, David. 1985. "International Trade and World-system Structure: A Multiple Network Analysis." *Review* 8: 517–60.

Nolan, Patrick. 1983. "Status in the World System, Income Inequality, and Economic Growth," *American Journal of Sociology* 89:410–409.

Peacock, Walter; Hoover, Greg, and Killian, Charles. 1988. "Divergence and Convergence in International Development: A Decomposition Analysis of Inequality in the World System," *American Sociological Review* 53, 6:838–52.

Rosenfelde, Steven. 1991. "The Illusion of Material Progress: The Analytics of Soviet Economic Growth Revisited," *Soviet Studies* 43, 4:597–611.

Rubinson, Richard. 1976. "The World-Economy and the Distribution of Income Within States: A Cross-National Study." *American Sociological Review* 41: 638–59.

Snyder, D. and Kick, E. 1979. "Structural Position in the World-System and Economic Growth, 1955–1970." *American Journal of Sociology* 84, 5 (Oct.): 1096–1126.

Taylor, Peter J. 1988. "Alternative Geography, A Supportive Note on Arrighi and Drangel." *Review* 11, 4 (Fall): 569–79.

United Nations. 1953–1989. *Statistical Yearbook.* New York: United Nations.

———. 1979. *Demographic Yearbook: Historical Supplement.* New York: United Nations.

United States. Central Intelligence Agency. Directorate of Intelligence. 1988. *Revisiting Soviet Economic Performance under Glasnost: Implications for CIA estimates.* Washington, D.C.: Document Expediting Office, Library of Congress.

———. 1990. *Handbook of Statistics.* Washington, D.C.: CIA.

———. 1991. *Handbook of Statistics.* Washington, D.C.: CIA.

World Bank. 1984. *World Tables.* Washington, D.C.: World Bank.

———. Department of International Economics. 1988. *World Tables of Economic and Social Indicators 1950–87.* [Computer File]. Washington, D.C.: World Bank, International Economics Department. Ann Arbor, MI: Inter-university Consortium for Political and Social Research [distributor], 1990.

———. 1990. *World Development Report 1990.* New York: Oxford University Press.

———. 1991a. *World Tables Update* (diskette). Washington, D.C.: World Bank.

———. 1991b. *World Atlas 1991.* Washington, D.C.: World Bank.

World Bank, IMF, OECD, EBRD. 1990a. *The Economy of the USSR: Summary and Recommendations.* Washington, D.C.: World Bank.

World Bank, IMF, OECD, EBRD, 1990b. *The Economy of the USSR*. 3 vols. Washington, D.C.: World Bank.

Woytinsky, W. S., and Woytinsky, E. S. 1953. *World Population and Production: Trends and Outlook*. New York: Twentieth Century Fund.

PART II

The Organization of Commodity Chains

5

The Organization of Buyer-Driven Global Commodity Chains: How U.S. Retailers Shape Overseas Production Networks

Gary Gereffi

Global industrialization is the result of an integrated system of production and trade. Open international trade has encouraged nations to specialize in different branches of manufacturing and even in different stages of production within a specific industry. This process, fueled by the explosion of new products and new technologies since World War II, has led to the emergence of a global manufacturing system in which production capacity is dispersed to an unprecedented number of developing as well as industrialized countries (Harris, 1987; Gereffi, 1989b). The revolution in transportation and communications technology has permitted manufacturers and retailers alike to establish international production and trade networks that cover vast geographical distances. While considerable attention has been given to the involvement of industrial capital in international contracting, the key role played by commercial capital (i.e., large retailers and brand-named companies that buy but don't make the goods they sell) in the expansion of manufactured exports from developing countries has been relatively ignored.

This chapter will show how these "big buyers" have shaped the production networks established in the world's most dynamic exporting countries, especially the newly industrialized countries (NICs) of East Asia. The argument proceeds in several stages. First, a distinction is made between producer-driven and buyer-driven commodity chains, which represent alternative modes of organizing international industries. These commodity chains, though primarily controlled by private economic agents, also are influenced by state policies in both the producing (exporting) and consuming (importing) countries.

Second, the main organizational features of buyer-driven commodity chains are identified, using the apparel industry as a case study. The apparel commodity chain contains two very different segments. The companies that make and sell standardized clothing have production patterns and sourcing strategies that contrast with firms in the fashion segment of the industry, which has been the most actively committed to global sourcing. Recent changes within the retail sector of the United States are analyzed in this chapter to identify the emergence of new types of big buyers and to show why they have distinct strategies of global sourcing.

Third, the locational patterns of global sourcing in apparel are charted, with an emphasis on the production frontiers favored by different kinds of U.S. buyers. Several of the primary mechanisms used by big buyers to source products from overseas are outlined in order to demonstrate how transnational production systems are sustained and altered by American retailers and branded apparel companies. Data sources include in-depth interviews with managers of overseas buying offices, trading companies, manufacturers, and retailers in East Asia and the United States, plus relevant secondary materials at the firm, industry, and country levels.[1]

PRODUCER-DRIVEN VERSUS BUYER-DRIVEN COMMODITY CHAINS

Global commodity chains (GCCs) are rooted in production systems that give rise to particular patterns of coordinated trade. A "production system" links the economic activities of firms to technological and organizational networks that permit companies to develop, manufacture, and distribute specific commodities. In the transnational production systems that characterize global capitalism, economic activity is not only *international* in scope; it also is *global* in its organization (Ross and Trachte, 1990; Dicken, 1992). While "internationalization" refers simply to the geographical spread of economic activities across national boundaries, "globalization" implies a degree of functional integration between these internationally dispersed activities. The requisite administrative coordination is carried out by diverse corporate actors in centralized as well as decentralized economic structures.

Large firms in globalized production systems simultaneously participate in many different countries, not in an isolated or segmented fashion but as part of their global production and distribution strategies. The GCC perspective highlights the need to look not only at the geographical spread of transnational production arrangements, but also at their organizational scope (i.e., the linkages between various economic agents—raw material suppliers, factories, traders, and retailers) in order to understand their sources of stability and change (see Gereffi and Korzeniewicz, 1990).

Global commodity chains have three main dimensions: (1) an input-output structure (i.e., a set of products and services linked together in a sequence of value-adding economic activities); (2) a territoriality (i.e., spatial dispersion or concentration of production and distribution networks, comprised of enterprises of different sizes and types); and (3) a governance structure (i.e., authority and power relationships that determine how financial, material, and human resources are allocated and flow within a chain).

The governance structure of GCCs, which is essential to the coordination of transnational production systems, has received relatively little attention in the literature (an exception is Storper and Harrison, 1991). Two distinct types of governance structures for GCCs have emerged in the past two decades, which for the sake of simplicity are called ''producer-driven'' and ''buyer-driven'' commodity chains (see Figure 5.1).

Producer-driven commodity chains refer to those industries in which transnational corporations (TNCs) or other large integrated industrial enterprises play the central role in controlling the production system (including its backward and forward linkages). This is most characteristic of capital- and technology-intensive industries like automobiles, computers, aircraft, and electrical machinery. The geographical spread of these industries is transnational, but the number of countries in the commodity chain and their levels of development are varied. International subcontracting of components is common, especially for the most labor-intensive production processes, as are strategic alliances between international rivals. What distinguishes ''producer-driven'' production systems is the control exercised by the administrative headquarters of the TNCs.

Hill (1989) analyzes a producer-driven commodity chain in his comparative study of how Japanese and U.S. car companies organize manufacturing in multilayered production systems that involve thousands of firms (including parents, subsidiaries, and subcontractors). Doner (1991) extended this framework to highlight the complex forces that drive Japanese automakers to create regional production schemes for the supply of auto parts in a half-dozen nations in East and Southeast Asia. Henderson (1989), in his study of the internationalization of the U.S. semiconductor industry, also supports the notion that producer-driven commodity chains have established an East Asian division of labor.

Buyer-driven commodity chains refer to those industries in which large retailers, brand-named merchandisers, and trading companies play the pivotal role in setting up decentralized production networks in a variety of exporting countries, typically located in the Third World. This pattern of trade-led industrialization has become common in labor-intensive, consumer-goods industries such as garments, footwear, toys, consumer electronics, housewares, and a wide range of hand-crafted items (e.g., furniture, ornaments). International contract manufacturing again is prevalent, but production is generally carried out by independent Third World factories that make finished goods (rather than components or parts) under original equipment manufacturer (OEM) arrangements. The specifications are supplied by the buyers and branded companies that design the goods.

Figure 5.1
**The Organization of Producer-Driven and Buyer-Driven Global Commodity
Chains**

1) **Producer-driven Commodity Chains**
   (Industries such as automobiles, computers, aircraft, and electrical machinery)

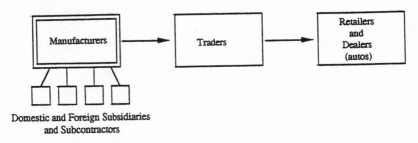

Domestic and Foreign Subsidiaries
and Subcontractors

2) **Buyer-driven Commodity Chains**
   (Industries such as garments, footwear, toys, and housewares)

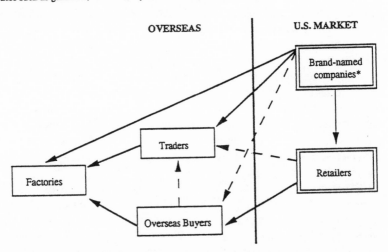

*These design-oriented, national brand companies, such as Nike, Reebok, Liz Claiborne, and Mattel
Toys, typically own no factories. Some, like The Gap and The Limited, have their own retail
outlets that only sell private label products.

Note: Solid arrows are primary relationships; dashed arrows are secondary relationships.

One of the main characteristics of firms that fit the buyer-driven model, including athletic footwear companies like Nike, Reebok, and L.A. Gear (Donaghu and Barff, 1990) and fashion-oriented clothing companies like The Limited, The Gap, and Liz Claiborne (Lardner, 1988), is that frequently these businesses do not own any production facilities. They are not "manufacturers" because they have no factories.[2] Rather, these companies are "merchandisers" that design and/or market, but do not make, the branded products they sell. These firms rely on complex tiered networks of contractors that perform almost all their specialized tasks. Branded merchandisers may farm out part or all of their product development activities, manufacturing, packaging, shipping, and even accounts receivables to different agents around the world.

The main job of the core company in buyer-driven commodity chains is to manage these production and trade networks and make sure all the pieces of the business come together as an integrated whole. Profits in buyer-driven chains thus derive not from scale economies and technological advances as in producer-driven chains, but rather from unique combinations of high-value research, design, sales, marketing, and financial services that allow the buyers and branded merchandisers to act as strategic brokers in linking overseas factories and traders with evolving product niches in their main consumer markets (see Rabach and Kim, chapter 6 in this volume; also Reich, 1991).

The distinction between producer-driven and buyer-driven commodity chains bears on the debate concerning mass production and flexible specialization systems of industrial organization (Piore and Sabel, 1984). Mass production is clearly a producer-driven model (in our terms), while flexible specialization has been spawned, in part, by the growing importance of segmented demand and more discriminating buyers in developed country markets. One of the main differences between the GCC and flexible specialization perspectives is that Piore and Sabel deal primarily with the organization of production in *domestic* economies and local industrial districts, while the notion of producer-driven and buyer-driven commodity chains focuses on the organizational properties of *global* industries. Furthermore, a buyer-driven commodity chain approach would explain the emergence of flexibly specialized forms of production in terms of changes in the structure of retailing, which in turn reflect demographic shifts and new organizational imperatives. Finally, while some of the early discussions of flexible specialization implied that it is a "superior" manufacturing system that might eventually displace or subordinate mass production, buyer-driven and supplier-driven commodity chains are viewed as contrasting (but not mutually exclusive) poles in a spectrum of industrial organization possibilities.

Our analysis of buyer-driven commodity chains will focus on the main companies that coordinate these economic networks: large U.S. retailers. Whereas in producer-driven forms of capitalist industrialization, production patterns shape the character of demand, in buyer-driven commodity chains the organization of consumption is a major determinant of where and how global manufacturing takes place. The economic agents of supply and demand do not operate in a political vacuum, however. They, in turn, respond to political pressures from the state.

THE ROLE OF STATE POLICIES IN GLOBAL COMMODITY CHAINS

National development strategies play an important role in forging new production relationships in the global manufacturing system (Gereffi and Wyman, 1990). Conventional economic wisdom claims that Third World nations have followed one of two alternative development strategies: (1) the relatively large, resource-rich economies in Latin America (e.g., Brazil, Mexico, and Argentina), South Asia (e.g., India and Bangladesh), and Eastern Europe have pursued import-substituting industrialization (ISI) in which industrial production was geared to the needs of sizable domestic markets; and (2) the smaller, resource-poor nations like the East Asian NICs adopted the export-oriented industrialization (EOI) approach that depends on global markets to stimulate the rapid growth of manufactured exports. Although the historical analysis of these transitions tends to have been oversimplified, today it is abundantly clear that most economies have opted for an expansion of manufactured or nontraditional exports to earn needed foreign exchange and raise local standards of living. The East Asian NICs best exemplify the gains from this path of development.

An important affinity exists between the ISI and EOI strategies of national development and the structure of commodity chains. Import substitution occurs in the same kinds of capital- and technology-intensive industries represented by producer-driven commodity chains (e.g., steel, aluminum, petrochemicals, machinery, automobiles, and computers). In addition, the main economic agents in both cases are TNCs and state-owned enterprises. Export-oriented industrialization, on the other hand, is channeled through buyer-driven commodity chains where production in labor-intensive industries is concentrated in small to medium-sized, private domestic firms located mainly in the Third World. Historically, the export-oriented development strategy of the East Asian NICs and buyer-driven commodity chains emerged together in the early 1970s, suggesting a close connection between the success of EOI and the development of new forms of organizational integration in buyer-driven industrial networks.

State policy plays a major role in GCCs. In EOI, governments are primarily facilitators; they are condition-creating and tend not to become directly involved in production. Governments try to generate the infrastructural support needed to make export-oriented industries work: modern transportation facilities and communications networks; bonded areas, like export-processing zones (including China's Special Economic Zones); subsidies for raw materials; customs drawbacks for imported inputs that are used in export production; adaptive financial institutions and easy credit (e.g., to facilitate the obtaining of letters of credit by small firms); etc. In ISI, on the other hand, governments play a much more interventionist role. They use the full array of industrial policy instruments (such as local content requirements, joint ventures with domestic partners, and export-promotion schemes), while the state often gets involved in production activities, especially in upstream industries.

In short, the role of the state at the point of production tends to be facilitative in buyer-driven commodity chains and more interventionist in producer-driven chains. However, there is an important caveat for buyer-driven chains. Since these are export-oriented industries, state policies in the consuming or importing countries (like the United States) also are highly significant. This is where the impact of protectionist measures such as quotas, tariffs, and voluntary export restraints comes in to shape the location of production in buyer-driven chains. If one compares the global sourcing of apparel (where quotas are prevalent) and footwear (no quotas),[3] one sees that far more countries are involved in the production and export networks for clothes than for shoes. This is basically a quota effect, whereby the array of Third World apparel export bases continually is being expanded to bypass the import ceilings mandated by quotas against previously successful apparel exporters. Therefore the globalization of export production has been fostered by two distinct sets of state policies: Third World efforts to promote EOI, coupled with protectionism in developed country markets.

THE APPAREL COMMODITY CHAIN

The textile and apparel industries are the first stage in the industrialization process of most countries. This fact, coupled with the prevalence of developed country protectionist policies in this sector, has led to the unparalleled diversity of garment exporters in the Third World. The apparel industry thus is an ideal case for exploring the organization and dynamics of buyer-driven commodity chains. The apparel commodity chain is bifurcated along two main dimensions: (1) textile versus garment manufacturers; and (2) standardized versus fashion-oriented segments in the industry (see Taplin, chapter 10 in this volume, for a diagram incorporating both of these dimensions). A complete analysis also must take account of how backward and forward linkages are utilized in the apparel commodity chain to protect the profitability of leading firms.

Textile Versus Garment Producers

Textile manufacturers and garment producers inhabit different economic worlds. Textile companies are frequently large, capital-intensive firms with integrated spinning and weaving facilities. The major textile manufacturers "finish" woven fabrics into a variety of end products, including sheets, towels, and pillowcases. While the U.S. fiber industry is composed of TNCs that make synthetic as well as natural fibers, fabric producers are more diverse in size, including numerous small businesses along with industrial giants like Burlington Mills.

The apparel industry, on the other hand, is the most fragmented part of the textile complex, characterized by many small, labor-intensive factories. Two primary determinants explain shifts in the geographical location and organization of manufacturing in the apparel sector: the search for low-wage labor and the pursuit of organizational flexibility. Although apparel manufacturing depends on low wages to remain competitive, this fact alone cannot account for dynamic trends in international competitiveness. Cheap labor is what Michael Porter calls a "lower-order" competitive advantage, since it is an inherently unstable basis on which to build a global strategy. More significant factors for the international competitiveness of firms are the "higher-order" advantages such as proprietary technology, product differentiation, brand reputation, customer relationships, and constant industrial upgrading (Porter, 1990: 49-51). These assets allow enterprises to exercise a greater degree of organizational flexibility and thus to create as well as respond to new opportunities in the global economy.

Standardized Versus Fashion Segments

A second major divide in the apparel commodity chain is between the producers of standardized and fashion-oriented garments. In the United States, the majority of the 35,000 firms in the textile/apparel complex are small clothing manufacturers (Mody and Wheeler, 1987). For standardized apparel (such as jeans, men's underwear, brassieres, and fleece outerwear), large firms using dedicated or single-purpose machines have emerged. Companies that make standardized clothing include the giants of the American apparel industry, like Levi Strauss and Sara Lee (both $4 billion companies), VF Corporation (a $2.6 billion company with popular brands such as Lee and Wrangler jeans and Jantzen sportswear), and Fruit of the Loom (a $1.6 billion firm that is the largest domestic producer of underwear for the U.S. market). These big firms tend to be closely linked with U.S. textile suppliers, and they manufacture many of their clothes within the United States or they ship U.S.-made parts offshore for sewing.[4]

The fashion-oriented segment of the garment industry encompasses those products that change according to retail buying seasons. Many of today's leading apparel firms like Liz Claiborne have six or more different buying seasons every year (Lardner, 1988). These companies confront far greater demands for variation in styling and materials, and they tend to utilize numerous overseas factories because of their need for low wages and organizational flexibility in this labor-intensive and volatile segment of the apparel industry.

It is the fashion-oriented segment of the apparel commodity chain that is most actively involved in global sourcing. In 1990, imports accounted for 51 percent of U.S. consumer expenditures on apparel. Of the $75 billion spent on U.S. apparel imports (in a total U.S. market of $148 billion), $25 billion corresponded to the foreign-port value of imported clothing, $14 billion to landing, distribution, and other costs, and $36 billion to the retailers' average markup of 48 percent on imported goods (AAMA, 1991: 3). The consumer's retail price thus amounts to three times the overseas factory cost for imported clothing. Meanwhile, the wholesale value of domestic apparel production totaling $73 billion in 1990 was $39 billion, with another $34 billion going to the retailers' net markup of 46 percent. In other words, the global sourcing of apparel by major retailers and brand-named companies is big business in the United States and it is growing bigger every year. This is why the organization of global sourcing merits close attention.

The Impact of Backward and Forward Linkages

The severe cost pressures endemic in the labor-intensive segments of the garment industry highlight the interdependence between different economic agents in buyer-driven commodity chains. Throughout the 1980s, U.S. garment companies were demanding lower prices and faster delivery from their overseas (principally Asian) suppliers, as well as their largely immigrant core and secondary contractors in New York City and Los Angeles, who in turn squeezed their workers for longer hours and lower wages (Rothstein, 1989). But the intensity of these pressures has varied over time. Why do the garment manufacturers pressure their contractors more at some times than at others? In a related vein, how can we explain differences in the level and location of profits in this industry over time?

The answers to these questions lie in an analysis of the apparel industry's backward and forward linkages. Garment manufacturers are being squeezed from both ends of the apparel commodity chain. Textile firms in the United States have become larger and more concentrated as they turned to highly automated production processes. This allowed them to place greater demands on the domestic garment manufacturers for large orders, high prices for inputs, and favorable payment schedules (Waldinger, 1986). One response has been for U.S. garment companies to find more competitive overseas suppliers of textiles and fabrics. Since this option is constrained by quotas that limit the extent of U.S. textile imports, many apparel makers had little choice but to accede to the demands of their main domestic textile suppliers.

At the other end of the apparel commodity chain, U.S. retailers went through a merger movement of their own (Bluestone et al., 1981). A number of prominent retail companies have gone into bankruptcy, been bought out, or face serious economic difficulties.[5] Those "big buyers" that remain are becoming larger, more tightly integrated organizationally and technologically, and frequently more specialized. This has put increasing pressure on merchandise manufacturers to lower their prices and improve their performance.[6] The result is that garment firms again are squeezed, with negative consequences (e.g., lower purchase prices, increased uncertainty) for their domestic and overseas contractors and the affiliated workers who actually make the clothes.

These illustrations show the importance of considering the full array of backward and forward linkages in the production process, as the GCC framework does, rather than limiting our notion of transnational production systems to manufacturing alone. Industrial organization economics tells us that profitability is greatest in the more concentrated segments of an industry characterized by high barriers to the entry of new firms. Producer-driven commodity chains are capital- and technology-intensive. Thus manufacturers making advanced products like aircraft, automobiles, and computer systems are the key economic agents in these chains not only in terms of their earnings, but also in their ability to exert control over backward linkages with raw material and component suppliers, as well as forward linkages into retailing.

Buyer-driven commodity chains, on the other hand, which characterize many of today's light consumer goods industries like garments, footwear, and toys, tend to be labor-intensive at the manufacturing stage. This leads to very competitive and globally decentralized factory systems. However, these same industries are also design- and marketing-intensive, which means that there are high barriers to entry at the level of brand-named companies and retailers that invest considerable sums in product development, advertising, and computerized store networks to create and sell these products. Therefore, whereas producer-driven commodity chains are controlled by core firms at the point of production, control over buyer-driven commodity chains is exercised at the point of consumption.

In summary, our GCC approach is *historical* since the relative strength of different economic agents in the commodity chain (raw material and component suppliers, manufacturers, traders, and retailers) changes over time; it also is *comparative* because the structural arrangements of commodity chains vary across industrial sectors as well as geographical areas. Finally, contemporary GCCs have two very different kinds of governance structures: one imposed by core manufacturers in producer-driven commodity chains, and the other provided by major retailers and brand-named companies in the buyer-driven production networks. These have distinct implications for national development strategies and the consequences of different modes of incorporation into the world-economy.

THE RETAIL REVOLUTION IN THE UNITED STATES

In order to gain a better understanding of the dynamics of the governance structure in buyer-driven commodity chains, we need to take a closer look at the U.S. retail sector, whose big buyers have fueled much of the growth in consumer goods exports in the world economy. Changes in America's consumption patterns are one of the main factors that have given rise to flexible specialization in global manufacturing.

For the past two decades, a "retail revolution" has been under way in the United States that is changing the face of the American marketplace. A comprehensive study of U.S. department stores showed that the structure of the industry became more oligopolistic during the 1960s and 1970s as giant department stores swallowed up many once-prominent independent retailers (Bluestone et al., 1981). The growth of large firms at the expense of small retail outlets was encouraged by several forces, including economies of scale, the advanced technology[7] and mass advertising available to retail giants, government regulation, and the financial backing of large corporate parent firms. Ironically, despite the department store industry's transformation into an oligopoly, the price competition between giant retailers became more intense, not less (Bluestone et al., 1981: 2).[8]

In the 1980s, the department store in turn came under siege. In their heyday, department stores were quintessential middle-class American institutions.[9] These retailers offered a broad selection of general merchandise for "family shopping," with "the mother as 'generalist' buying for other family members" (Legomsky, 1986: R62).[10] While this format typically met the needs of the suburban married couple with two children and one income, by 1990 less than 10 percent of American households fit that description. Today the generalist strategy no longer works. The one shopper of yesterday has become many different shoppers, with each member of the family constituting a separate buying unit (Sack, 1989).

The breakup of the American mass market into distinct, if overlapping, retail constituencies has created a competitive squeeze on the traditional department stores and mass merchandisers,[11] who are caught between a wide variety of specialty stores, on the one hand, and large-volume discount chains, on the other.[12] The former, who tailor themselves to the upscale shopper, offer customers an engaging ambience, strong fashion statements, and good service;[13] the latter, who aim for the lower income buyer, emphasize low prices, convenience, and no-frills merchandising.

Tables 5.1 and 5.2 show the varied performance levels of some of the major U.S. retail chains in the 1980s and 1990s. In 1990, both Wal-Mart and Kmart surpassed Sears as the largest U.S. retailers in terms of sales (see Table 5.1). Wal-Mart, Kmart, and Target (a division of Dayton Hudson) now control over 70 percent of the booming discount store business in the United States. Wal-Mart and the leading specialty stores also have far better earnings than the department stores and mass merchandise chains. The 10-year compounded growth rates in net income for Wal-Mart (34.5 percent) and the two leading specialty retailers in apparel, The Gap (34.6 percent) and The Limited (33.5 percent),[14] are the highest of any of the stores listed. In addition, the specialty stores tend to have the top rate of return on revenues of any U.S. retailers between 1987 and 1991 (see Table 5.2).

Wal-Mart appears to be in a much stronger position for future growth than its leading challenger, Kmart. In 1990 Wal-Mart cleared $2 billion before taxes compared to Kmart's $1 billion on basically the same volume of sales (Saporito, 1991: 54). The performance of companies like Kmart,[15] J.C. Penney, and Woolworth have been hindered by their major corporate restructurings over the past several years. Although the specialty stores are considerably smaller than other

Table 5.1
Sales of Leading U.S. Retailers, 1987–1992 (Billions of Dollars)

	1987	1988	1989	1990	1991	1992
Discounters						
Wal-Mart	16.0	20.6	25.8	32.6	43.9	55.5
Kmart	25.6	27.3	29.5	32.1	34.6	37.7
Mass Merchandisers						
Sears	28.1	30.3	31.6	32.0	31.4	32.0
Dayton Hudson	10.7	12.2	13.6	14.7	16.1	17.9
Woolworth	7.1	8.1	8.8	9.8	9.9	10.0
Department Stores						
J.C. Penney	16.4	15.9	17.1	17.4	17.3	19.1
May Department Stores	10.3	8.4	9.4	10.1	10.6	11.2
Specialty Stores						
Melville	5.9	6.8	7.6	8.7	9.9	10.4
The Limited	3.5	4.1	4.6	5.3	6.1	6.9
The Gap	1.1	1.3	1.6	1.9	2.5	3.0
Toys "R" Us	3.3	4.0	4.8	5.5	6.1	7.2

Source: Standard and Poor's Industry Surveys, "Retailing: Current Analysis," April 20, 1989, p. R79; May 2, 1991, p. R80; May 13, 1993, p. R80; and company annual reports.

types of U.S. retailers, the former have the highest ratio of sales per retail square footage of any U.S. retail establishments and they have a reputation for more fashionable and higher quality merchandise.

Unlike the earlier "retail revolution" when department stores became oligopolies, the current surge of specialty and discount formats is less a function of the evolution of retail institutions than of overriding demographic and life style changes in American society. "The fragmentation of the American marketplace . . . reflects the expanding ranks of single-person households, the greater proportion of two-income families, and the sharp rise in the number of working women" (Legomsky, 1986: R62).[16] Furthermore, there has been a widening of the gap between the rich and the poor in the United States.[17] The retail sector has mirrored this dichotomy—stores have either gone upscale or low-price, with middle-income consumers pulled in both directions.

This segmentation of the American market creates numerous opportunities for specialized retail formats. Just as the era of mass production is giving way to flexible manufacturing in the productive sphere, the renowned American mass market is becoming more customized and personalized. This has paved the way for increased trans-Atlantic competition by European and other foreign-based retailers, such as Benetton in Italy and Laura Ashley in the United Kingdom. According to Lester Thurow, professor of economics and management at the Massachusetts Institute of Technology, "The American economy died about 10 years ago, and has been replaced by a world economy. . . . [American retailers] are going to face an international challenge" (Legomsky, 1986: R61).

Table 5.2
Net Income and Return on Revenues of Leading U.S. Retailers, 1987–1991

Company	Net Income[a] (millions of dollars)					Compound Growth Rate (%)			Return on Revenues[b] (%)		
	1987	1988	1989	1990	1991	1-yr.	5-yr.	10-yr.	1987	1989	1991
Discounters											
Wal-Mart	628	837	1076	1291	1608	24.6	29.0	34.5	3.9	4.2	3.7
Kmart	692	803	323	756	859	13.6	8.5	14.6	2.7	1.1	2.5
Mass Merchandisers											
Sears	1649	1032	1446	829	1279	43.4	-1.1	7.0	3.4	2.7	2.2
Dayton Hudson[c]	228	287	410	410	301	-26.6	3.4	6.6	2.1	3.0	1.9
Woolworth	251	288	329	317	-53	NM	NM	NM	3.5	3.7	NM
Department Stores											
J.C. Penney	608	807	802	577	264	-54.2	-13.0	-3.8	3.8	4.7	1.5
May Department Stores[d]	444	503	515	500	515	3.0	6.2	15.1	4.2	5.4	4.9
Specialty Stores											
Melville[e]	285	354	398	385	347	-10.0	7.8	9.8	4.8	5.3	3.5
The Limited[f]	235	245	347	398	403	1.2	12.1	33.5	6.7	7.3	6.4
The Gap[f]	70	74	98	144	230	59.1	27.5	34.6	6.6	6.2	9.1
Toys "R" Us[g]	204	268	321	326	340	4.2	17.4	21.4	6.5	6.7	5.5

Source: Standard and Poor's Industry Surveys, "Retailing: Comparative Company Analysis," May 13, 1993, pp. R104-R107.

[a] "Net income" refers to profits derived from all sources after deduction of expenses, taxes, and fixed charges, but before any discounted operations, extraordinary items, and dividend payments (preferred and common).

[b] Net income divided by operating revenues.

[c] Dayton Hudson stores include: Target, Mervyn's, Marshall Field's, and Hudson.

[d] May Department Stores Company includes: Lord and Taylor, Filene's, Hecht's, Foley's, Kaufmann's, Robinson-May, Famous-Barr, and Meier & Frank, among others. May also owns the discount footwear chain of Payless ShoeSource stores.

[e] Shoes   [f] Garments   [g] Toys   NM=not meaningful

Department stores and other mass merchandisers in the United States have tried to develop effective counterstrategies to these trends. Some retailers like J.C. Penney have sought to upgrade their status from mass merchandiser to department store by adding higher-priced apparel, and to increase profitability by emphasizing higher-margin merchandise that has a faster turn-around time (Sack, 1989: R80). Other firms have begun to diversify their appeal by establishing their own specialty retail outlets (like the Foot Locker stores, which are owned by Woolworth Corporation).[18] On the international front, retailers and manufacturers alike are acquiring large importers to shore up their position in global sourcing networks,[19] while unique organizational forms such as member-owned retail buying groups are being used in overseas procurement.[20]

In summary, the transformation of the retail sector in the United States has remained fast-paced throughout the 1980s and 1990s. This reflects not only the changing demography and purchasing power of American society, but as we will see in the next sections, it also proves to be a significant determinant of production patterns within the global economy.

THE ECONOMIC AGENTS IN BUYER-DRIVEN COMMODITY CHAINS

Big buyers are embedded in GCCs through the export and distribution networks they establish with overseas factories and trading companies. In order to understand the structure and dynamics of this relationship, we must first identify the economic agents in buyer-driven commodity chains (retailers, traders, overseas buyers, and factories), and then look at the impact of the main coordinating group (large retailers) on global production patterns.

Retailers

The organization of consumption in the United States is stratified by retail chains that target distinct income groups in the population. There are several types of retailers: large-volume, low-priced discount stores; mass merchandisers; department stores; and "fashion" or upper-end specialized retailers that deal exclusively with national brand-named products. These stores vary in their mixes of nationally branded, store-branded, and unbranded products.[21] The different categories of retailers also establish distinctive relationships with importers and overseas manufacturers. As one moves down this list of retailers, the quality and price of the goods sold increase, and the requirements for their international contractors become more stringent.

Traders

Trading companies have evolved from the global juggernauts that spanned the British, Dutch, and Japanese empires in centuries past to the highly specialized organizations that exist today. As recently as twenty-five years ago, there were no direct buying offices set up by U.S. retailers in Asia.[22] Originally, American retailers bought from importers on a "landed" basis—that is, the importer cleared the goods through U.S. customs.[23] In the late 1970s, importing began to be done on a "first-cost" basis. The buyer opened a letter of credit directly to the factory and paid the importer (or buying agent) a commission to get the goods to the export port. The buyer handled the shipping and distribution in the United States.

Before retailers established direct buying offices overseas, importers were the key intermediaries between retailers and their foreign contractors. There still is a broad array of specialized importers that deal in particular industries[24] or even in specific product niches within an industry.[25] While the importers handle production logistics and often help to develop new product lines, the leading apparel companies control the marketing end of the apparel commodity chain through their exclusive designs and brand-named products.[26]

Overseas Buyers

There is a symbiotic relationship between the overseas buying offices of major retail chains and the role played by importers and exporters. The direct buying offices of major retailers purchase a wide assortment of products, typically grouped into "soft goods" (like garments and shoes) and "hard goods" (such as lighting fixtures, kitchenware, appliances, furniture, and toys). Obviously, it is difficult for these buyers to develop an intimate knowledge of the supplier networks and product characteristics of such a diverse array of items. As a result, retail chains depend heavily on the specialized importers and trading companies that continuously develop new product lines with the local manufacturers and that provide retailers with valuable information about the hot items and sales trends of their competitors.

In general, the U.S.-based buyers for American retailers tend to work with importers and trading companies in the fashion-oriented and new-product end of consumer-goods industries, while their overseas buying offices purchase the more standardized, popular, or large-volume items directly from the factories in order to eliminate the importer's commission. Large retailers usually have their own product development groups and buying offices in the United States for their most popular or distinctive items.

Factories

The factories that produce the consumer products that flow through buyer-driven commodity chains are involved in contract manufacturing relationships with the buyers who place the orders. Contract manufacturing (or specification contracting) refers to the production of finished consumer goods by local firms, where the output is distributed and marketed abroad by trading companies, branded merchandisers, retail chains, or their agents.[27] This is the major export niche filled by the East Asian NICs in the world economy.

In 1980, for example, Hong Kong, Taiwan, and South Korea accounted for 72 percent of all finished consumer goods exported by the Third World to OECD countries, other Asian nations supplied another 19 percent, while just 7 percent came from Latin America and the Caribbean. The United States was the leading market for these consumer products with 46 percent of the total (Keesing, 1983: 338–39). East Asian factories, which have handled the bulk of the specification contracting orders from U.S. retailers, tend to be locally owned and vary greatly in size—from the giant plants in South Korea to the myriad small family firms that account for a large proportion of the exports from Taiwan and Hong Kong.[28]

LOCATIONAL PATTERNS OF GLOBAL SOURCING

Big retailers and brand-named merchandisers have different strategies of global sourcing, which in large part are dictated by the client bases they serve (see Figure 5.2 and Table 5.3). Fashion-oriented retailers that cater to an exclusive clientele for "designer" products get their expensive, nationally branded goods from an inner ring of premium-quality, high-value-added exporting countries (e.g., Italy, France, Japan). Department stores and specialty chains that emphasize "private label" (or store brand) products as well as national brands source from the most established Third World exporters (such as the East Asian NICs, Brazil, Mexico, and India), while the mass merchandisers that sell lower-priced store brands buy from more remote tiers of medium- to low-cost, mid-quality exporters (low-end producers in the NICs, plus China and the Southeast Asian countries of Thailand, Malaysia, the Philippines, and Indonesia). Large-volume discount stores that sell the most inexpensive products import from the outer rings of low-cost suppliers of standardized goods (e.g., China, Indonesia, Bangladesh, Sri Lanka, Mauritius, the Dominican Republic, Guatemala). Finally, smaller importers serve as industry "scouts." They operate on the fringes of the international production frontier and help develop potential new sources of supply for global commodity chains (e.g., Vietnam, Myanmar, Saipan).

Several qualifications need to be mentioned concerning the schematic, purposefully oversimplified locational patterns identified in Figure 5.2 and Table 5.3. These production frontiers represent general trends that can vary by industry, by specific products, and by time period. More detailed analyses that trace the global sourcing of particular products over time are required to explore the factors that lead to shifts in these linkages. Two examples will illustrate the complexity of these arrangements.

The first example focuses on large-volume discount stores such as Kmart and Wal-Mart. According to Table 5.3, they should source primarily from the three outer rings of the production frontiers, but our direct research indicates that these discounters also are prominent buyers in the second ring of East Asian NICs. Why? The reason is twofold. Apparel factories in relatively high-wage countries

Figure 5.2
Production Frontiers for Global Sourcing by U.S. Retailers: The Apparel Industry

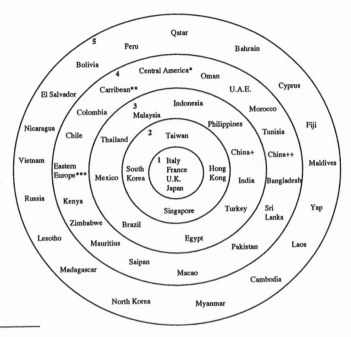

+ Southern China
++ Interior provinces of China
* Guatemala, Honduras, Costa Rica
** Dominican Republic, Jamaica, Haiti
*** Poland, Hungary, Czechoslovakia, Bulgaria

like Taiwan and South Korea work with anywhere from five to twenty clients (buyers) in a year. Although Kmart and Wal-Mart pay much less than department stores and specialty retailers like Macy's or Liz Claiborne, the factories use these discounters' large-volume orders to smooth out their production schedules so they don't have gaps or downtime. The other side of the equation is the discounter's vantage point. Kmart and Wal-Mart tend to source their most expensive, complicated items in the second-ring countries (e.g., infant's wear with a lot of embroidery). Thus they are using the more expensive and skilled workers in the NICs to produce relatively high-quality merchandise.

A second illustration deals with the upper-end retailers. Large apparel retailers like The Limited and The Gap, and brand-named companies like Phillips-Van Heusen and Levi Strauss, tend to source heavily in the second and third rings of Figure 5.2, but they also buy from countries located in the fourth and even the fifth rings. The reason they are positioned in the outer reaches of the production frontiers is that these companies engage in "price averaging" across their different manufacturing sites. A company like Phillips-Van Heusen, the

Table 5.3
Types of Retailers and Main Global Sourcing Areas

Type of Retailer	Representative Firms	Main Global Sourcing Areas[a]	Characteristics of Buyer's Orders
Fashion-oriented Companies	Armani, Donna Karan, Polo/Ralph Lauren, Hugo Boss, Gucci	First and second rings	Expensive "designer" products requiring high levels of craftmanship; orders are in small lots
Department Stores, Specialty Stores, and Brand-named Companies	Bloomingdale's, Saks Fifth Avenue, Neiman-Marcus, Macy's, Nordstrom, The Gap, The Limited, Liz Claiborne, Calvin Klein	Second, third, and fourth rings	Top quality, high-priced goods sold under a variety of national brands and private labels (i.e., store brands); medium to large-sized orders, often coordinated by department store buying groups (such as May Department Stores Company and Federated Department Stores)
Mass Merchandisers	Sears Roebuck, Montgomery Ward, J.C. Penney, Woolworth	Second, third, and fourth rings	Good quality, medium-priced goods predominantly sold under private labels; large orders
Discount Chains	Wal-Mart, Kmart, Target	Third, fourth, and fifth rings	Low-priced, store-brand products; giant orders
Small Importers		Fourth and fifth rings	Pilot purchases and special items; sourcing done for retailers by small importers who act as "industry scouts" in searching out new sources of supply; orders are relatively small at first, but have the potential to grow rapidly if the suppliers are reliable

[a]For the countries in each of these rings, see Figure 5.2.

number-one seller of men's dress shirts in the United States, is confident that its quality control procedures will allow it to produce identical dress shirts in its factories in the United States, Taiwan, Sri Lanka, or El Salvador. This also permits these companies to keep some of their production in, or close to, the United States for quick response to unexpectedly high demand for popular items as well as to gain the goodwill of the American consuming public.

Figure 5.2 highlights some methodological difficulties raised by the commodity chains perspective. Nation-states are not the ideal unit of analysis for establishing global sourcing patterns, since individual countries are tied to the world-economy through a variety of export roles (Gereffi, 1989a, 1992). Production actually takes place in specific regions or industrial districts *within countries* that have very different social and economic characteristics (Porter, 1990). Where commodity chains "touch down" in a country is an important determinant of the kind of production relationships that are established with retailers. Thus there can be several forms of international sourcing within a single nation.[29]

In the People's Republic of China, for example, Guangdong Province has very substantial investments from Hong Kong and Taiwan, while Fujian Province has a natural geographical and cultural affinity for Taiwanese investors. These two provinces in China are part of a Greater China Economic Region that includes Hong Kong and Taiwan (see Chen, chapter 8 in this volume). Thus China falls within both the third and the fourth rings of Figure 5.2: the quality and price of the products made in southern China (third ring) in affiliation with its East Asian NIC partners tend to be higher than for the goods produced in the interior provinces of China (fourth ring), where state enterprises are more prevalent.

Despite these qualifications, several generalizations can be made about the production frontiers identified in Figure 5.2. As one moves from the inner to the outer rings, the following changes are apparent: the cost of production decreases; manufacturing sophistication decreases; and the lead time needed for deliveries increases. Therefore there is a strong tendency for the high-quality, multiple-season "fashion" companies, as well as the more upscale department stores and specialty stores, to source their production from the three inner rings, while the price-conscious mass merchandisers and discount chains are willing to tolerate the lower quality and longer lead times that characterize production in the two outer rings. The "industry scout" role played by certain importers is particularly important for this latter set of buyers, since these importers are willing to take the time needed to bring the new, low-cost production sites located in the fourth and fifth rings into global sourcing networks.

TRIANGLE MANUFACTURING IN GLOBAL COMMODITY CHAINS

How do the countries in the inner rings of our global sourcing chart deal with the maturing of their export industries? What mechanisms are utilized to ensure a smooth transition to higher-value-added activities? One of the most important adjustment mechanisms for maturing export industries in East Asia is the process of triangle manufacturing, which came into being in the 1970s and 1980s.

The essence of triangle manufacturing is that U.S. (or other overseas) buyers place their orders with the NIC manufacturers they have sourced from in the past (e.g., Hong Kong or Taiwanese apparel firms), who in turn shift some or all of the requested production to affiliated offshore factories in one or more low-wage countries (e.g., China, Indonesia, or Vietnam). These offshore factories may or may not have equity investments by the East Asian NIC manufacturers: they can be wholly owned subsidiaries, joint-venture partners, or simply independent overseas contractors. The triangle is completed when the finished goods are shipped directly to the overseas buyer, under the import quotas issued to the exporting nation. Payments to the non-NIC factory usually flow through the NIC intermediary firm.[30]

Triangle manufacturing thus changes the status of the NIC manufacturer from a primary production contractor for the U.S. buyers to a "middleman" in the buyer-driven commodity chain. The key asset possessed by the East Asian NIC manufacturers is their longstanding link to the foreign buyers, which is based on the trust developed over the years in numerous successful export transactions. Since the buyer has no direct production experience, he prefers to rely on the East Asian NIC manufacturers he has done business with in the past to assure that the buyer's standards in terms of price, quality, and delivery schedules will be met by new contractors in other Third World locales. As the volume of orders in new production sites like China, Indonesia, or Sri Lanka increases, the pressure grows for the U.S. buyers to eventually bypass their East Asian NIC intermediaries and deal directly with the factories that fill their large orders.

The process of third-party production began in Japan in the late 1960s, which relocated numerous plants and foreign orders to the East Asian NICs (often through Japanese trading companies or *sogo shosha*).[31] Today, the East Asian NICs, in turn, are transferring many of their factories and orders to China and a variety of Southeast Asian countries. Initially, triangle manufacturing was the result of U.S. import quotas that were imposed on Hong Kong, Taiwan, South Korea, and Singapore in the 1970s. These quotas led to the search for new quota-free production sites in the region. Then in the late 1980s the move to other Asian and eventually Caribbean factories occurred because of domestic changes—increased labor costs, labor scarcity, and currency appreciations—in the East Asian NICs. The shift toward triangle manufacturing has been responsible for bringing many new countries into these production and export networks, including Sri Lanka, Vietnam, Laos, Mauritius, small Pacific islands (like Saipan and Yap), Central America, and Caribbean nations.

The importance of triangle manufacturing from a commodity chains perspective is threefold. First, it indicates that there are repetitive cycles as the production base for an industry moves from one part of the world to another. An important hypothesis here is that the "window of opportunity" for each new production base (Japan—East Asian NICs—Southeast Asian countries—China—Vietnam—

the Caribbean) is growing progressively shorter as more new entrants are brought into these global sourcing networks. The reasons include the fact that quotas on new exporting countries in apparel are being applied more quickly by the United States,[32] and technology transfer from the East Asian NICs is becoming more efficient.

The second implication of triangle manufacturing is for social embeddedness. Each of the East Asian NICs has a different set of preferred countries where they set up their new factories. Hong Kong and Taiwan have been the main investors in China (Hong Kong has taken a leading role in Chinese production of quota items like apparel made from cotton and synthetic fibers, while Taiwan is a leader for nonquota items like footwear,[33] as well as leather and silk apparel); South Korea has been especially prominent in Indonesia, Guatemala, the Dominican Republic, and now North Korea; and Singapore is a major investor in Southeast Asian sites like Malaysia and Indonesia. These production networks are explained in part by social and cultural networks (e.g., ethnic or familial ties, common languange), as well as by unique features of a country's historical legacy (e.g., Hong Kong's British colonial ties gave it an inside track on investments in Jamaica).

A final implication of the GCC framework is that triangle manufacturing has allowed the East Asian NICs to move beyond OEM production. Most of the leading Hong Kong apparel manufacturers have embarked on an ambitious program of forward integration from apparel manufacturing into retailing. Almost all of the major Hong Kong apparel manufacturers now have their own brand names and retail chains for the clothing they make. These retail outlets began selling in the Hong Kong market, but now there are Hong Kong–owned stores throughout East Asia (including China), North America, and Europe.[34] These cycles of change for East Asian manufacturers suggest the need for more elaborated product life cycle theories of Third World industrial transformation.

CONCLUSIONS

The role of the main economic agents in buyer-driven commodity chains is far from static. The sources of change are rooted in economic and political factors, plus the shifting organizational patterns of the distinct segments of GCCs. Several trends are particularly noteworthy. First, there has been an increased concentration of buying power in the leading U.S. retail chains. This has been the result of spectacular growth strategies by a few companies (especially the large-volume discount stores like Wal-Mart in the 1980s and Kmart in the 1970s), slumping performance by several established retail leaders (such as Sears Roebuck and Montgomery Ward), and many bankruptcies in the small- and large-firm retail sector.

Second, at the same time as there has been a consolidation in the buying power of major retail chains, there has been a proliferation of overseas factories (especially in Asia) in most consumer-goods industries. In several notable cases, like garments and shoes, there is currently a substantial excess production capacity worldwide that will lead to numerous plant closings or consolidations in major exporting countries, such as the People's Republic of China. This combination of concentrated buying power in the retail/wholesale sector and excess capacity in overseas factories has permitted the big buyers in GCCs to simultaneously lower the prices they are paying for goods and dictate more stringent performance standards for their vendors (e.g., more buying seasons, faster delivery times, and better quality) in order to increase their profits.

Third, big buyers are acutely sensitive to political factors that can affect global supply networks and they currently are in a position to alter overseas production patterns accordingly. For example, during the recent debate in the United States about renewing the People's Republic of China's most-favored-nation (MFN) status, several large retailers and importers decided to diversify or curtail their purchases from China.[35] This led overseas suppliers to scramble to set up production facilities in nations perceived to relatively "safe" in terms of domestic political stability (such as Indonesia, Thailand, and Malaysia). In quota-restricted industries like garments, retailers and importers also have taken the lead in encouraging production in countries that have favorable quota arrangements with their main export markets in North America and Europe. In other words, quotas drive overseas investment decisions and thus help shape global commodity chains.

Fourth, the recent recession in the world economy has placed a premium on low-priced goods in developed-country markets. This has strengthened the position of the large-volume discount chains in the retail sector and led retailers and manufacturers alike to look for new ways to cut costs. This further enhances the impact of retailers on overseas production networks.

One trend we might look for in the future is the establishment of consolidated factory groups (perhaps involving linkages between manufacturers and trading companies) to counter the increased leverage of the large buying groups. These could be coordinated by manufacturers in the East Asian NICs, who continue to be the nexus for many of the orders placed by U.S. big buyers. Exporters in the East Asian nations have accounted for much of the technology transfer to lower-cost production sites, they have access to export networks through their established contacts with the U.S. buyers, and they still handle much of the quality control, financing, and shipping needed to get goods to their destination markets in a timely fashion.

Finally, despite the fact that the East Asian NICs have managed to move beyond OEM production through forward as well as backward integration in the apparel commodity chain, the implications of triangle manufacturing for downstream exporters in Southeast Asia, Latin America, and Africa are not so promising. Genuine development in these countries is likely to be truncated by the vulnerabilities implied by their export-processing role in global sourcing networks. The main assets that Third World exporters possess in buyer-driven commodity chains are low-cost labor and abundant quotas. These are notoriously unstable sources of competitive advantage, however.

Few countries in the world have been able to generate the backward and forward linkages, technological infrastructure, and high levels of local value-added of the East Asian NICs. Even the obvious job creation and foreign exchange benefits of export-oriented industrialization for Third World nations can become liabilities when foreign buyers or their East Asian intermediaries decide because of short-term economic or political considerations to move elsewhere. Triangle manufacturing is most advantageous to the overseas buyers and intermediaries in buyer-driven commodity chains. The long-run benefits for Third World countries occur only if exporting becomes the first step in a process of domestically integrated development.

NOTES

The research for this paper was funded by grants from the Chiang Ching-Kuo Foundation for International Scholarly Exchange (United States), based in Taiwan, as well as the University Research Council at Duke University. I gratefully acknowledge these sources of support. I also appreciate the research assistance of Jeffrey Weiss at Duke, and the detailed comments provided by Phyllis Albertson, Bradford Barham, Miguel Korzeniewicz, Stephen Maire, and Karen J. Sack on earlier drafts of this paper.

1. The linkages between big buyers and their strategies of global sourcing were derived from numerous interviews carried out by the author in East Asia and the United States. A wide variety of trading companies, direct buying offices, and factories in Taiwan, Hong Kong, South Korea, and the People's Republic of China were visited in August–October 1991 and September–December 1992. Interviews also were conducted in the headquarters of major U.S. retailers and apparel firms in New York City and Los Angeles during the summers of 1991 and 1992.

2. The absence of factories also characterizes a growing number of U.S. semiconductor houses that order customized as well as standard chips from outside contractors (Weber, 1991).

3. Orderly marketing agreements were imposed by the United States on footwear exporters in Taiwan and South Korea in 1977, but these were rescinded in 1981.

4. This used to be known as 807-production in the Caribbean and the Far East, and *maquiladora* assembly in Mexico. Now there is a new U.S. tariff classification system called the Harmonized Tariff Schedule that replaces the 807 section with a 9802 tariff code. The basic idea in this system is to allow a garment that has been assembled offshore using U.S-made and -cut parts to be assessed a tariff only on the value added by offshore labor.

5. The much publicized bankruptcy of R. H. Macy & Company in 1992 is a recent example of the competitive problems that have affected the traditional department store (Strom, 1992).

6. Garment manufacturers have been required to add more buying seasons, offer a greater variety of clothes, agree to mandatory buy-back arrangements for unsold merchandise, provide retailer advertising allowances, and so on.

7. These new technologies include: electronic data interchange (EDI), which is a system for communicating to the retailer what is selling well and what needs to be replenished; computerized point-of-service inventory control; merchandising processing systems that monitor cash flows from order placement to shipping to billing and payment; and electronic mail hook-ups for every online store in worldwide networks of retail outlets.

8. Enhanced price competition is compatible with oligopoly because the economies of scale and scope of large-volume discount chains lead to high concentration levels in the retail sector, at the same time as the discounters stimulate considerable price competition because of their low-income customer base.

9. Many department stores carry familiar household names: Macy's, Bloomingdale's, Jordan Marsh, Mervyn's, Nordstrom, Dillard, Filene's, Kaufmann's, Saks Fifth Avenue. Numerous American retail chains today are owned by holding companies, such as the May Department Stores Company, Federated Department Stores, and Dayton Hudson. In Europe, where consumers were more inclined to shuttle from store to store for their individual apparel and accessory needs, the department store never developed into the prominent retailing institution that it has in the mass market of the United States.

10. General merchandise retailers provide a broad selection of "soft goods" (including apparel and home furnishings) and "hard goods" (appliances, hardware, auto, and garden supplies, etc.).

11. The best-known mass merchandising chains are Sears Roebuck & Co., Montgomery Ward, and Woolworth Corporation. These stores are a notch below the department stores in the quality of their merchandise and their prices, but they offer more service and brand-name variety than the large-volume discount retailers. In terms of their overall position in American retailing, though, department stores and mass merchandisers face similar competitive environments.

12. The three most prominent discount chains today are Wal-Mart, Kmart, and Target. Discount chains may focus on a specific product, such as shoes (Payless ShoeSource, Pic 'n Pay, and the 550-store Fayva Shoes retail chain owned by Morse Shoe). Historically, discount retail chains differed from department stores because the former carried broader assortments of hard goods (e.g., auto accessories, gardening equipment, housewares) and they relied heavily on self-service.

13. Department stores have tried to simulate a specialty-store ambience through the creation of "store-within-a-store" boutiques, each accommodating a particular company (like Liz Claiborne or Calvin Klein) or a distinct set of fashion tastes. Similarly, Woolworth Corporation has shed its mass merchandising image by incorporating dozens of specialty formats in its portfolio of 6,500 U.S. stores, including Foot Locker, Champs Sports, Afterthoughts accessories, and The San Francisco Music Box Co. Specialty stores now account for about half of Woolworth's annual revenue, up from 29 percent in 1983 (Miller, 1993).

14. The Gap, one of the most popular and profitable specialty clothing chains in American retailing today, only sells clothes under its own private label. In 1991 The Gap surpassed Liz Claiborne Inc. to become the second-largest clothes brand in the United States after Levi Strauss (Mitchell, 1992). The Limited is another major force in specialty apparel. It is regarded as the world's largest retailer of women's clothing. The Limited is composed of 17 divisions (such as Victoria's Secret, Lerner, Lane Bryant, and Structure), more than 4,100 stores, 75,000 employees, and 1991 sales of $6.3 billion.

15. Kmart's net income in 1990 recovered to $756 million, after its nosedive to $323 million in 1989. One of the areas where Kmart has been lagging, however, is its electronic

data interchange (EDI) systems. In 1990 it embarked on a six-year store modernization program. Kmart management hopes that point-of-sale systems, a satellite network, and automated replenishment combined with just-in-time merchandise delivery will improve the performance of its 2,400 general merchandise stores. Kmart also has 2,000 specialty retail stores, including Waldenbooks, Pay Less Drug Stores, and PACE Membership Warehouse.

16. At the end of 1985, nearly 60 percent of mothers with children under eighteen were working, according to Labor Department figures, up nearly 5 percent from one year earlier.

17. Between 1977 and 1989, the richest 1 percent of American families reaped 60 percent of the growth in after-tax income of all families and an even heftier three-forrths of the gain in pretax income, while the pretax income of the bottom 40 percent of American families declined (Nasar, 1992). Similarly, a detailed study on family income prepared by the House Ways and Means Committee of the U.S. Congress found that from 1979 to 1987 the standard of living for the poorest fifth of the American population fell by 9 percent, while the living standard of the top fifth rose by 19 percent (Harrison and Bluestone, 1990: xi).

18. The eighteen-year-old Foot Locker chain, with 1,500 U.S. stores and $1.6 billion in annual sales, has generated an entire family of spin-offs, including Kids Foot Locker, Lady Foot Locker, and now World Foot Locker. Woolworth, which already garners 40 percent of its sales in foreign countries, plans to add 1,000 Foot Locker stores in Western Europe by the end of the decade (Miller, 1993).

19. For example, Payless ShoeSource International, the largest U.S. footwear importer, is owned by May Department Stores; and Meldisco, a division of Melville Corporation, handles the international purchasing of shoes for Kmart. Pagoda Trading Co., the second-biggest U.S. shoe importer, was acquired three years ago by Brown Shoe Co., the largest U.S. footwear manufacturer.

20. Associated Merchandising Corporation (AMC) is the world's largest retail buying group. It consolidates the overseas purchasing requirements of 40 member department stores, and it sources products from nearly 70 countries through its extensive network of buying offices in Asia, Europe, and Latin America.

21. Many brand-named companies like Liz Claiborne and Nike don't allow their products to be sold by discount stores or mass merchandisers, which has prompted the proliferation of "private label" merchandise (i.e., store brands).

22. Sears Roebuck, Montgomery Ward, and Macy's were the first U.S. companies to establish direct buying offices in Hong Kong in the 1960s. However, the really big direct orders came when Kmart and J.C. Penney set up their Hong Kong buying offices in 1970; within the next couple of years, these sprawling merchandisers had additional offices in Taiwan, South Korea, and Singapore. By the mid-1970s, many other retailers such as May Department Stores, Associated Merchandising Corporation, and Woolworth jumped on the direct buying bandwagon in the Far East.

23. The early importers with offices in the Far East were Japanese and American companies like Mitsubishi/CITC (a Japanese-U.S. joint venture), C. Itoh, Manow, and Mercury.

24. For example, Payless ShoeSource International, Pagoda, and E.S. Originals are large importers that deal exclusively in footwear.

25. There are different importers for women's shoes versus men's shoes, dress shoes

versus casual footwear, women's dresses versus men's suits, adult versus children's clothes, and so on.

26. Nike, Reebok, and L.A. Gear are the major brand-named companies in athletic footwear, while Armani, Polo/Ralph Lauren, and Donna Karan are premium labels in clothes. However, all of these companies have diversified their presence in the apparel market and put their labels on a wide range of clothes, shoes, and accessories (handbags, hats, scarves, belts, wallets, etc.).

27. "Contract manufacturing" is more accurate than the commonly used terms "international subcontracting" or "commercial subcontracting" (Holmes, 1986) to describe what the East Asian NICs have excelled at. Contract manufacturing refers to the production of finished goods according to full specifications issued by the buyer, while "subcontracting" actually means the production of components or the carrying out of specific labor processes (e.g., stitching) for a factory that makes the finished item. Asian contract manufacturers (also known as contractors or vendors) have extended their production networks to encompass domestic as well as international subcontractors.

28. Taiwan and Hong Kong have multilayered domestic subcontracting networks, including large firms that produce key intermediate inputs (like plastics and textiles), medium-sized factories that do final product assembly, and many small factories and household enterprises that make a wide variety of components.

29. In Mexico, for instance, there is a vast difference between the *maquiladora* export plants along the Mexico-U.S. border that are engaged in labor-intensive garment and electronics assembly, and the new capital- and technology-intensive firms in the automobile and computer industries that are located further inland in Mexico's northern states. These latter factories use relatively advanced technologies to produce high-quality exports, including components and subassemblies like automotive engines. They pay better wages, hire larger percentages of skilled male workers, and use more domestic inputs than the traditional *maquiladora* plants that combine minimum wages with piecework and hire mostly unskilled women (Gereffi, 1991).

30. Typically this entails back-to-back letters of credit: the overseas buyer issues a letter of credit to the NIC intermediary, who then addresses a second letter of credit to the exporting factory.

31. The industries that Japan transferred to the East Asian NICs are popularly known as the "three Ds": dirty, difficult, and dangerous.

32. This may change if a new General Agreement on Tariffs and Trade is signed.

33. After controls were relaxed on Taiwanese investments in the People's Republic of China in the late 1980s, around 500 footwear factories were moved from Taiwan to China in less than two years. Although China recently passed Taiwan as the leading footwear exporter to the United States (in terms of pairs of shoes), it is estimated that nearly one-half of China's shoe exports come from Taiwanese owned or managed firms recently transferred to the mainland (author interviews with footwear industry experts in Taiwan).

34. A good example of this is the Fang Brothers, one of the principal suppliers for Liz Claiborne, who now have several different private-label retail chains (Episode, Excursion, Jessica, and Jean Pierre) in a variety of countries including the United States.

35. During an October 1991 interview in the Hong Kong office of one of the largest U.S. footwear importers, I was told that the American headquarters of the company ordered 25 percent of the importer's purchases from the People's Republic of China to

be shifted to Indonesia within one year to avoid the supply disruptions that would occur if China's MFN status were denied.

REFERENCES

American Apparel Manufacturers Association (AAMA). 1991. *FOCUS: 1991.* Washington, D.C.: AAMA.

Bluestone, Barry; Hanna, Patricia; Kuhn, Sarah; and Moore, Laura. 1981. *The Retail Revolution: Market Transformation, Investment, and Labor in the Modern Department Store.* Boston: Auburn House Publishing Company.

Dicken, Peter. 1992. *Global Shift: The Internationalization of Economic Activity.* 2d ed. New York: Guilford Publications.

Donaghu, Michael T., and Barff, Richard. 1990. "Nike Just Did It: International Subcontracting and Flexibility in Athletic Footwear Production." *Regional Studies* 24, 6: 537-52.

Doner, Richard F. 1991. *Driving a Bargain: Automobile Industrialization and Japanese Firms in Southeast Asia.* Berkeley: University of California Press.

Gereffi, Gary. 1989a. "Rethinking Development Theory: Insights from East Asia and Latin America." *Sociological Forum* 4, 4 (Fall): 505–33.

———. 1989b. "Development Strategies and the Global Factory." *Annals of the American Academy of Political and Social Science* 505 (Sept.): 92–104.

———. 1991. "The 'Old' and 'New' Maquiladora Industries in Mexico: What Is Their Contribution to National Development and North American Integration?" *Nuestra economía* 2, 8 (May–August): 39–63.

———. 1992. "New Realities of Industrial Development in East Asia and Latin America: Global, Regional, and National Trends." In *States and Development in the Asian Pacific Rim*, edited by Richard P. Appelbaum and Jeffrey Henderson, pp. 85–112. Newbury Park, CA: Sage Publications.

Gereffi, Gary, and Korzeniewicz, Miguel. 1990. "Commodity Chains and Footwear Exports in the Semiperiphery." In *Semiperipheral States in the World-Economy*, edited by William G. Martin, pp. 45–68. Westport, CT: Greenwood Press.

Gereffi, Gary, and Wyman, Donald, eds. 1990. *Manufacturing Miracles: Paths of Industrialization in Latin America and East Asia.* Princeton, NJ: Princeton University Press.

Harris, Nigel. 1987. *The End of the Third World.* New York: Penguin Books.

Harrison, Bennett, and Bluestone, Barry. 1990. *The Great U-Turn: Corporate Restructuring and the Polarizing of America.* New York: Basic Books.

Henderson, Jeffrey. 1989. *The Globalisation of High Technology Production: Society, Space and Semiconductors in the Restructuring of the Modern World.* New York: Routledge.

Hill, Richard Child. 1989. "Comparing Transnational Production Systems: The Automobile Industry in the USA and Japan." *International Journal of Urban and Regional Research* 13, 3 (Sept.): 462–80.

Holmes, John. 1986. "The Organizational and Locational Structure of Production Subcontracting." In *Production, Work, and Territory: The Geographical Anatomy of Industrial Capitalism*, edited by Allen J. Scott and Michael Storper, pp. 80–106. Boston: Allen & Unwin.

Keesing, Donald B. 1983. "Linking Up to Distant Markets: South to North Exports of Manufactured Consumer Goods." *American Economic Review* 73: 338–42.

Lardner, James. 1988. "The Sweater Trade—I," *The New Yorker*, January 11, pp. 39-73.

Legomsky, Joanne. 1986. "The Europeanization of American Retailing." *Standard & Poor's Industry Surveys*, April 3, pp. R61–R65.

Miller, Annetta. 1993. "A Dinosaur No More: Woolworth Corp. Leaves Dime Stores Far Behind." *Newsweek*, January 4, pp. 54–55.

Mitchell, Russell. 1992. "The Gap: Can the Nation's Hottest Retailer Stay on Top?" *Business Week*, March 9, pp. 58–64.

Mody, Ashoka, and Wheeler, David. 1987. "Towards a Vanishing Middle: Competition in the World Garment Industry." *World Development* 15, 10/11: 1269–84.

Nasar, Sylvia. 1992. "The 1980's: A Very Good Time for the Very Rich." *New York Times*, March 5, p. 1A.

Piore, Michael J., and Sabel, Charles F. 1984. *The Second Industrial Divide*. New York: Basic Books.

Porter, Michael E. 1990. *The Competitive Advantage of Nations*. New York: Free Press.

Reich, Robert B. 1991. *The Work of Nations*. New York: Alfred A. Knopf.

Ross, Robert J. S., and Trachte, Kent C. 1990. *Global Capitalism: The New Leviathan*. Albany: State University of New York Press.

Rothstein, Richard. 1989. *Keeping Jobs in Fashion: Alternatives to the Euthanasia of the U.S. Apparel Industry*. Washington, D.C.: Economic Policy Institute.

Sack, Karen J. 1989. "Department Stores: Avoiding the Way of the Dinosaur." *Standard & Poor's Industry Surveys*, April 20, pp. R77–R82.

Saporito, Bill. 1991. "Is Wal-Mart Unstoppable?" *Fortune*, May 6, pp. 50–59.

Storper, Michael, and Harrison, Bennett. 1991. "Flexibility, Hierarchy and Regional Development: The Changing Structure of Industrial Production Systems and Their Forms of Governance in the 1990s." *Research Policy* 20, 5 (Oct.): 407–22.

Strom, Stephanie. 1992. "Department Stores' Fate: Bankruptcies Like Macy's Overshadowing Strong Consumer Loyalty, Experts Assert." *New York Times*, February 3, p. C1.

Waldinger, Roger. 1986. *Through the Eye of the Needle: Immigrants and Enterprise in New York's Garment Trades*. New York: New York University Press.

Weber, Samuel. 1991. "A New Endangered Species: Mulling a Fabless Future." *Electronics* 64, 7 (July): 36–38.

6

Where Is the Chain in Commodity Chains? The Service Sector Nexus

Eileen Rabach and Eun Mee Kim

A significant feature of the current restructuring of capitalism is the extensive atomization of production. This atomization, which is a basic property of capitalism, has accelerated because of tremendous advances made in telecommunications, transportation, and the development of Third World nations during the late twentieth century. Concomitant to the atomization of production has been the globalization of production. Both of these processes necessitate an increasingly important role for services to play in GCCs. Global commodity chain (GCC)[1] research has illustrated how production nodes and activities have multiplied and have spread throughout the world.

Services represent the missing link in global commodity chain research on the restructuring of capitalist production. Service activities not only provide linkages between the segments of production within a GCC and linkages between overlapping GCCs, but they also bind together the spheres of production and circulation. Services have come to play a critical role in GCCs because they not only provide geographical and transactional connections, but they *integrate* and *coordinate* the atomized and globalized production process. Without the integrating and coordinating function fulfilled by services, GCCs would not be viable in today's highly competitive economic environment.

In this chapter we focus on services as a point of entry for the analysis of GCCs. There are three purposes in this chapter. The first is to clearly define the concept "services" and to further distinguish categories of services that are critical for a better understanding of GCCs. The second is to discuss the function of services in GCCs and their significance in "core niches." And lastly, we discuss how the service activities in core niches "drive" or coordinate the two types of GCCs, namely "producer-driven" (PDC) and "buyer-driven" (BDC) chains. Here, we develop concepts, "systemic" and "subsystemic" core niches, to further elaborate the nature of control apparent in PDCs.

SERVICES

Services and GCCs in a Broader Economic Context

Global commodity chain research represents an important leap forward in efforts aimed at disentangling the maze of international production processes and transactions that characterize international capitalism. An ever increasing number of discrete economic activities is required to produce a given final output or commodity (Dunning, 1991: 2). The empirical studies utilizing the GCC model have considerably advanced our understanding of the accelerating rate and globalized nature of the atomization of commodity production. However, these studies have focused primarily on industry-specific GCCs (Gereffi and Korzeniewicz, 1990; see also Lee and Cason, chapter 11 in this volume).

GCC research has not yet examined the commodity chain in terms of the linkages or nodes where services predominate. Rather, the commodity "chain" has been conceptualized as a cumulative chronology in which production is analyzed as a succession of inputs and outputs. As a result, the production processes within each "box" (a box represents a stage or portion of a stage of commodity production) is quite detailed, as is the flowchart of directional arrows connecting inputs and outputs. However, little account has been taken of what coordinates and drives the respective GCCs. Without a dynamic perspective that differentiates the significance of a range of activities, including services, GCCs are reduced to a mechanical configuration with little theoretical depth or synergism.

Missing in studies thus far is the notion that the fragmentation of the production process has heightened the importance of services in GCCs. The increased fragmentation of production has often been seen as the result of the heterogeneous and mushrooming capabilities of the service sector.[2] In turn, each increase in the number of production processes generates an even greater increase in the number of transactions. Furthermore, because of the globalization of production "an increasing proportion of those transactions is of a cross-border nature" (Dunning, 1991: 3). This rise in the transactional intensity and internationalization of production requires a very high level of coordination achieved by service activities. Thus service activities can no longer be considered to provide merely auxiliary linkages in GCCs, but are integral to the coordination and operation of GCCs.

The rise in transactional intensity, referred to as "roundaboutness" by economists (Grubel and Walker, 1989: 19), vertically disintegrates the production process into highly specialized activities that are increasingly absorbed by a fragmenting service sector: "pre-production activities such as R&D and design; post-production work such as packaging, selling and advertising; administrative functions including accounting, hiring, training and planning; and financial activities such as banking, securities trading, and insurance" (Storper and Walker, 1989: 195). This dialectical process feeds back on itself as these services continuously facilitate the further atomization of the production process.

Routinized service activities that were once vertically integrated into larger economic units (such as transnational corporations [TNCs]) are being increasingly spun off, subcontracted, and sourced out to specialized and autonomous firms.[3] IBM, AT&T, GE, and Shell Oil, for example, have all recently unloaded routinized service functions such as accounting, legal services, advertisement, and billing and payroll (Dumaine, 1992).

The astonishing fact is that despite the dramatic proliferation of production processes and service activities, the international economy is not "freer" in any sense. Rather, this fragmentation is accompanied by a marked consolidation and centralization of the number of economic agents exerting a dominant influence over the governance of GCCs because of their command over high-end services.

In order to study the significance and impact of services on GCCs, a shift in the customary focus and methodology characterizing GCC research is imperative. The fact is that, notwithstanding the assumptions of neoclassical economics, services are simply not goods.[4] To track their production and distribution as other GCC studies have done for single commodities such as automobiles or entire industries such as textile or fruit would be to lose the great significance of services to GCCs in general. This is because services encompass a countless range of activities that are, in a sense, grafted over the entire process of production.

A brief methodology of the service sector will lay the groundwork necessary for our analysis of its many roles in PDCs and BDCs.

Service Nomenclature

Services have become recognized as an increasingly significant part of the process of capital accumulation. During the 1980s, high-end services and finances "were the fastest growing sectors in the economies of their countries in the 1980s" (Sassen, 1991: 11) and were essential to economic globalization. Although services are complementary to and integral to the process of production, they are distinct from activities at the point of production. The numerous attempts to adequately define and categorize services, however, are frequently contradictory.[5] Table 6.1 highlights some of the main categories of services.

Labor studies differentiate services by a color code that distinguishes service occupations: pink (feminized caretakers and servers such as waitress, teacher, nurse, secretary), gray (maintenance), and white collar (managerial, clerical), along with the blue collar working class. We further specify that these occupations are clearly polarized according to skill level from the most mentally labor-

Table 6.1
Different Categories of Services

I. Traditional Service Sector	- Examples of Service Industries: Transportation, Food, Financial Services & Banking, Insurance, Entertainment, Hotels & Tourism, Health care, Education, Advertising, Communications
II. Services in Terms of Labor Component	A. High-end Services: Mentally labor-intensive (White Collar) - Examples: Professionals
	B. Low-end Services: Manually labor-intensive (Pink & Gray Collar) - Examples: Personal services, Maintenance
III. High-End Service Activities in Core Niches	A. Non-Factor Services: Routinized support systems increasingly contracted out. - Examples: Accounting, Auditing, Legal, Insurance, Personnel, Data processing, Consulting, Engineering, Banking
	B. Factor Services: Vertically integrated knowledge intensive and high technology dependent.
	1. BDCs: Marketing and distribution dominate product conception and not production. - Examples: Marketing, Product conception
	2. PDCs: Technological innovation dominates product conception and production. - Examples: Research & Development, Technological innovation, Information packages

Notes: BDCs: Buyer-Driven Commodity Chains
       PDCs: Producer-Driven Commodity Chains

intensive to the most manually labor-intensive, as exemplified by professionals on the one hand and personal or maintenance workers on the other. This point has important implications for the study of core niches in that "internationally traded services are attractive because they are generally labor-intensive (for example, computer software, consultancy) and offer high value-added" (Price and Blair, 1989: 121).

The heterogeneity of service activities and commodities is so extensive that textbook definitions identified only one shared characteristic: intangibility. Intangibles, perishables, or nonstorables require instantaneous consumption and the immediate proximity of consumer and producer, as do personal services such as medical care. Our findings concerning the role of services in GCCs contradicts this premise. Services have expedited globalization exactly because they increasingly consist of information, which can be stored, codified, and transmitted over great distances. Since services such as product design, legal advice, chemical formulas, advertisements, brand names, and software programs can be used and reused, and sold and resold, they are in a sense nonperishables, at least until competitive pressures render them obsolete.

In this study we explicitly differentiate services according to their relationship to production. In order to do this we have synthesized some of the more successful efforts intended to classify "producer" services that are scattered in the literature. Producer or "intermediate" services are consumed by producers as opposed to private individuals and are not produced by public bodies or governments. They are also designated as "factor" or "disembodied" services because they include any service input in the process of production, whether in-house or sourced-out, which represents a factor of production just as capital and labor are factors of production.

Factor services are of particular importance to the upstream segment of PDCs. They are integral to production plans: (i.e., an engineering consultancy or architectural design) and interactive with the production process (i.e., building plans are continuously revised during construction). Because they are part of the production process, we identify product design and R&D as services even though such activities are conventionally identified as "support systems" within a larger industrial project and typically included in industrial statistics.[6]

In contrast, "nonfactor" services are "factor-embodied" or "product-embodied" services which represent a final product; that is, one buys the services of an accountant or a trip on an airline. Often, many nonfactor services combine into a single service such as a delivery system. We associate these services most closely with BDCs because they often involve support systems or auxiliary services such as insurance, communication, and information networks that are of particular importance to downstream market activities. They too can be vertically integrated into a larger production process or subcontracted out to autonomous economic units (firms).

SERVICES AND CORE NICHES OF GCCs

Core Niches in Services

Core activities and high-value-added activities are synonymous in GCC research. They represent one pole of the core-periphery dichotomy that "designates the unequal distribution of rewards among the various economic activities in the single overarching division of labor" in the world economy (Gereffi and Korzeniewicz, 1990: 47). "Core countries now accumulate wealth by concentrating on the service sector and on the most productive, high-value-added segments of manufacturing" (46) and, as a consequence, "core-country firms, rather than those in the semiperiphery . . . capture the lion's share of economic rents" (Gereffi and Korzeniewicz, 1990: 50).[7] Two important interrelated themes are revealed by Gereffi and Korzeniewicz (1990), but remain undeveloped: (1) the identification of high profit yields (such as those gleaned from services) with "core" activities, and (2) the implication that core capital is in a monopoly/monopsony position in GCCs because of its concentration in the service sector.

The dynamic of GCCs that keeps high value-added services in core countries and under the control of TNCs is currently self-perpetuating. This is because the impetus driving the constant structuring and restructuring of commodity chains currently is not to be found in manufacturing and industry (which are areas already populated by the semiperiphery), but in the high-end services where technology and information are now indivisible and indispensable.

The analysis of these core niches inhabited by high-end services is not only the logical compliment of the semiperiphery industrial export niches, but integral to any comprehensive analysis of GCCs. The role of services, which network and coordinate vast amounts of complex information across vast distances and over time, is crucial for GCCs to function, especially in a production environment characterized by the atomization of production and increased transactional intensity. In addition, high-end services are increasingly essential to a firm's efforts to raise productivity and therefore surplus value. This ability to coordinate production grants control over GCCs to the service activities characterizing core niches; and the greater the degree of atomization in production, the greater the control leverage of services.

Command over surplus value is anchored in command over the core niches of GCCs. For this reason, TNCs are concentrated and centralized in the upstream of PDCs and in the downstream of BDCs. Based in core niches, they are positioned to extend backward and forward linkages and to diversify. The Japanese general trading company (*sogo shosha*), for example, has integrated backward and horizontally into a wide range of nontrading activities in the BDCs in which it participates, in order to control manufacturers and primary producers (Dunning, 1989: 125). Similarly, the largest amounts of service activity investments expended by TNCs in PDCs has been in forward and horizontal linkages, meaning in the downstream core niches such as "sales subsidies, import and export merchants, general trading companies and large retail chains" (Dunning, 1989: 125).

This extension into the complementary core niches of PDCs and BDCs is facilitated by high-end service activities and driven by the intense competition that prevails in the core niches (upstream in PDC and downstream in BDC) of GCCs. The larger and more international an enterprise is, the more control it can exert directly and, more importantly, indirectly over other economic actors in the GCC. This control is strengthened by the atomization of production to the extent that smaller economic agents must conform to the economic demands emanating from core niches, which are expressed increasingly through the market rather than through hierarchy.

TNCs are beginning to master the information technology necessary to secure linkages throughout the entire GCC without necessitating ownership. The networks that GCCs span can be arranged "to create new capabilities and skills as well as favorable asymmetries in the marketplace" (Venkatraman, 1991: 140). The transactions between producers and input suppliers in PDCs and between buyers and contractors in BDCs can be electronically integrated or formatted for "obtaining differential benefits in the marketplace" (Venkatraman, 1991: 140).

Such integration is now imperative because of the compression of time and space afforded by information technology (see Schoenberger, chapter 3 in this volume). Black and Decker's time to market for new products was cut in half in 1985 and Ford's Taurus/Sable shortened its product development cycle by one year (Rockart and Short, 1991: 197). The doubling of "seasons" in the clothing industry is a clear example of the effect of compressed time on a BDC (see Gereffi, chapter 5 in this volume).

The integration of core services, such as R&D, telecommunication systems, product design, marketing, and sales, enables capital to coordinate and therefore directly and indirectly control geographically and economically dispersed segments of GCCs (Dumaine, 1992). These core services are also vital for maintaining market and technological advantages in the continuously transforming commodity chain.

The Role of Services in GCCs

Service activities interconnect the production process of GCCs in at least five interrelated ways: (1) what is produced; (2) how it is produced; (3) spatial coordination, such as transportation and telecommunications (which implies a time coefficient); (4) other "facilitating" services; and (5) distribution. Although these five service linkages permeate all GCCs, BDCs are primarily driven by a downstream or back-end service sector dynamic and PDCs are largely driven by a front-end or what we identify as an upstream service sector dynamic. An exposition of these five diverse nodes and categories of services will help differentiate these GCCs.

The important role services play in both buyer- and producer-driven chains can be conceptualized in terms of certain properties of GCC nodes or segments: the relations of production and the dominant organization of production.

(1) What is produced: Product conception and design as well as R&D is the pre-upstream segment of GCCs. These represent the very highest order of services in terms of prerequisite skill level and technology intensity. This segment is significantly linked to the GCC downstream flow of final distribution, particularly in BDCs, as buyers who ordered a product then become sellers of the product. Korzeniewicz provides an excellent analysis of this process and its social implications in his case study of Nike (see chapter 12 in this volume). This is an important part of both BDCs and PDCs, although its implication in each is quite different, as will be discussed further in the section on PDC and BDC competition.

(2) How it is produced: This reflects management decisions pertaining to the

organization of production and choice of technology. Such choices not only reflect economic goals such as enhanced efficiency, productivity, and profit maximization, but also the influence of other social forces such as class conflict and government policy. These high-end producer services are especially science-based and include R&D and technology innovation relevant chiefly to the up-stream segment of PDCs. They therefore have the effect of continuously trans-forming the production processes not only of core niches, but also of the rest of the commodity chain.

In addition, PDCs and BDCs are interlinked by three important categories of services:

(3) Transportation and telecommunications clearly dominate service industries and are critical to the national transborder flows essential for globalized pro-duction. They transmit information and courier products, components, and per-sonnel between commodity chain nodes. Transportation services have traditionally dominated the service sector and are typically a product-embodied service, although some firms have horizontally expanded to accommodate de-livery systems; for instance, large oil companies such as Shell and Exxon operate their own shipping lines. The revolution in container shipping, by profoundly transforming the transportation industry, has also transformed the territoriality of GCCs and the production processes of relevant industries such as fruit and vegetables. It should be noted that the East Asian NICs have made considerable advances in these service industries. Evergreen, a Taiwanese shipping line, is the largest in the world.[8]

Telecommunication services operate as both factors and nonfactors, but are of increasing importance as factor services. Firmware, for example, which embeds customized software inside firm-specific technology, is prominent in service industries (i.e., ATM [automated teller machine] banking facilities with read-only memory), while computer-aided design and manufacturing systems (CAD/CAM) are essential factors in today's textile industry. Because of the revolution in telecommunications, computer software, and information-process-ing services, whose "technological core" is the semiconductor (particularly the silicon chip), knowledge has become the most critical factor of them all (Hen-derson, 1989: 3). With the overview and quick response gained from knowledge over the means of production and over markets (including labor markets), key economic actors such as TNCs have the technological basis to coordinate and profoundly influence GCCs.

(4) Other service industries and sectors, such as financial, accounting, engi-neering, legal, insurance, consulting and support systems, are essential in fa-cilitating GCCs. Of these, core-nationality firms have cornered a significant market share (e.g., the "Big Eight" international accounting firms and several New York and London based advertising firms, Prudential in insurance, and Chase Manhattan in banking). Financial capital and banking is an enormous service sector in its own right and yet another layer of the GCC, but one requiring a separate analysis not possible here.

(5) Marketing services clearly dominate the downstream distribution segment of GCCs where a broad range of wholesale and retail networks, information technology (such as department stores' point-of-sale transactions), and the media are critical. These downstream service linkages are the most prominent feature of BDCs and, as mentioned, are closely related to upstream product design activities. Because global production networks require global markets, competitive downstream advantages in GCCs necessitate an international perspective.

PDCs AND BDCs

Buyer-Driven and Producer-Driven GCCs

The GCC framework has been considerably advanced by Gereffi's categorization of "two distinct governance structures" (see Gereffi, chapter 5 in this volume). Gereffi's model of "producer-driven" GCCs refers to "industries in which TNCs or other large integrated industrial enterprises play the central role in controlling the production system (including its backward and forward linkages) . . . [and are] most characteristic of capital- and technology-intensive industries like automobiles, computers, aircraft, and electrical machinery." In contrast, "buyer-driven" industries represent what the business literature once referred to as hollow firms (Riddle and Brown, 1988: 247). These are "merchandisers" (not "manufacturers") who "rely on complex tiered networks of subcontractors that perform almost all their specialized tasks" (see Gereffi, chapter 5 in this volume). These concepts delineate the critical "driving" or "coordinating" role played by services for GCCs.

Upstream research and development (R&D), product conception, and design activities impel the dynamic of PDCs because they are the focal point of capitalist innovation in the current restructuring of the world economy. Similarly, downstream high-end service activities of marketing and distribution continually shape and transform BDCs. Although all of these activities rely on knowledge inputs and innovative technology, the focus of the upstream segment of BDCs is product design rather than technology and is more immediately related to the downstream service activities of distribution, whereas upstream PDC service activities are characterized by capital-intensive technology and R&D.

Linkages between upstream and downstream core niches are highly developed in both PDCs and BDCs. The R&D, product conception, and design service activities of the upstream core niche drive PDCs. Marketing and distribution service activities associated with the downstream core niche provide the corollary for BDCs.

The barriers to entry represented by high-end service activities in core niches can be overcome only by the largest of economic actors. Although "big" is not enough, it is certainly necessary. High capital investment capabilities (to cover costly service overhead such as marketing and telecommunications networks) and other start-up costs are essential to enter or survive the competition. In

PDCs, access to the cutting edge of innovative technology and economies of scale are fundamental. Economies of scope are especially critical in BDCs. Skyrocketing service costs during the 1980s, due in part to the costs of new technology, and also in part to the comparatively high ratio of labor to productivity peculiar to services, have kept these barriers high (Nasa, 1992).

PDCs in Capitalist Competition

There are two different types of core niches in PDCs: the "systemic" and the "subsystemic" core niches (see Table 6.2). The systemic core niche represents a service or set of services that act as a module or paradigm for subsystems. The systemic core niches are highly capital- and technology-intensive, and thus are not open for broad competition. The products made by these niches are often defining of an industry, and myriad subsystemic niches are borne, adapting to the systemic niche. One notable example is the IBM personal computer (PC). IBM won against many other early competitors in the war for the PC market. Once IBM cornered the market with its brand of PCs, competitors were forced to predicate the development of related technology on the paradigm established by the IBM PC. Subsystemic producers were similarly relegated to producing subsystems, or parts, such as computer chips and floppy disks, that were adaptable to the IBM PC.

In PDCs, the highest barriers to entry exist in these systemic core niches where R&D, technological innovation, and telecommunication networks are concentrated on efforts to gain competitive advantages in production. Competitive advantage in systemic niches is primarily based on high-end service activities that expand productivity and capabilities via technology derived from R&D or innovations in the organization of production and information technology. Imposing barriers to entry keeps firm birth rates and also death rates low enough to enable TNCs to exert an oligopolistic force in these systemic niches. TNCs have a heightened concentration in high-growth, R&D-intensive, and profitable sectors within industries that congregate in systemic core niches. The pitched competition waged by TNCs in PDC systemic core niches conforms to what Schumpeterians and classical economists classified as "strong competition."[9]

Ironically, the high cost of this competition leads to defensive alliances in which TNCs join together to develop base technology using shared pools of capital and knowledge. For example, Toshiba and IBM have joined forces to develop flash memory computer chips, and both have joined Apple in endeavoring to produce the first multimedia computer. But markets and the high-value-added potential of key technology, which is the implementation of base technology, are never shared. This is the realm of strong competition.

Strong competition continually revolutionizes the capitalist mode of production. "Winner-take-all" advantages are captured by successful "first movers" because in the battle for control over systemic niches the winner establishes the paradigm for the entire industry. In the consumer electronics industry, Sony lost

Table 6.2
Core Service Niches in PDCs and BDCs

	PDCs	BDCs
I. Systemic Core Niches	1. Upstream-based and technologically-driven	1. Downstream-based and market-driven
	2. High degree of TNC interrelatedness (shared pool of knowledge, science & technology)	2. Low interrelatedness or parallel TNC activities
	3. Defensive alliances in the creation of base technology (in order to defray costs and speed technological development)	3. No alliances necessary
	4. Depends on paradigmic base technology (new industries may result from converging industries, such as media and computer technology)	4. Not dependent on paradigmic technology
	5. Product typically has high-technology component	5. Product typically does not have high-technology component (e.g., apparel)
	6. Means of production is capital-intensive	6. Means of production can be capital-intensive (e.g., food processing, or CAD/CAM in apparel)
	7. High value-added in key technologies and enhanced by economies of scale, and high entry barriers (e.g., information system packaging)	7. High value-added based on economies of scope (e.g., product conception in terms of a market strategy)
	8. Relative autonomy of Upstream and downstream high-end service activities	8. Simultaneity of downstream and upstream high-end service activities
	9. Strong competition	9. Weak competition
II. Sub-Systemic Core Niches	1. Routinized (non-factor) high-end services which provide support systems necessary to TNC, but not yielding high value-added. Same for PDCs and BDCs. - Examples: Accounting, Advertising, Legal services, Insurance, Data processing services	
	2. Smaller firms providing highly specialized, capital-intensive, high knowledge factors to PDCs as part of production process. These factors are typically contracted for by TNCs in systemic core niches.	2. Smaller firms providing intermediate or final product to BDCs downstream for final assembly & distribution. These products are typically contracted for by TNCs in systemic core niches.
	3. Smaller firms producing capital-intensive, high-knowledge products dependent on base technology generated by systemic core niches for sale downstream. They adapt and clone TNC products and drive prices down (e.g., home electronics)	3. Smaller firms producing final product for sale downstream in markets already established by TNCs. They adapt and clone TNC products and drive prices down (e.g., apparel)

Notes: BDCs: Buyer-Driven Commodity Chains
      PDCs: Producer-Driven Commodity Chains
      TNC: Transnational Corporation

one battle of the VCR wars when it failed to establish its Betamax system as the standard for the industry. When IBM won the first round of the microcomputer wars in the 1980s, its PC became the standard for a broad range of integrated products including terminals, disk drives, and software (such as Wordstar, which once dominated word processing). These niches are systemic because PDC industries are characterized by the production of interrelated and compatible technology. "The greater the number of other manufacturers with whom a manufacturer's equipment is compatible, the greater the market for their own equipment" (Rotemberg and Saliner, 1991: 99).

Information technology service industries provide the most striking examples of the consequences of such interconnectivity. The CIRRUS ATM (automated teller machine) network and the American Airlines Sabre CRS (computer reservation system) are two examples of information technology electronic networks. They each establish the dominance of the provider because of the participation in the system by rivals, whose value-added is enhanced by participation, although not as much as the provider (winner) who also gains proprietary rights that dictate the terms of participation. United's Apollo CRS system requires subscribers to book 95 percent of all flights with at least one United segment. CRS providers not only maintain first screen showing of its flights, but directly access the internal databases of other airlines, domestic and foreign, which is exploited by its marketing divisions (Rotemberg and Saliner, 1991: 107).

An important feature of the systemic core niche is that it is effectively integrated with the GCC's downstream core niche where marketing and distribution service activities reign. TNCs may outsource a myriad of intermediate production and service activities, but they typically vertically integrate these two core niches. Although marketing is not what drives the systemic core niche, it enables a firm to consolidate its position in and potentially dominate the market. For example, without the strengths of IBM's downstream marketing and distribution divisions, IBM's competitive advantages in becoming the paragon of the PC industry would have been diminished.

The subsystemic core niche is dependent on the systemic core niche. The subsystemic core niche is also capital- and technology-intensive, but to a lesser degree than the systemic core niche. This allows for greater competition, as more firms can afford to develop an improved microchip, floppy disk, keyboard, and so on. Although South Korean firms have been gaining market share in DRAM (dynamic random-access memory) chips (jumping from a 3 percent share in 1987 to 19 percent in 1991), they populate a subsystemic core niche because it still is dependent on Japanese patents and R&D for the chip-manufacturing equipment (Helm, 1992).

Once a paradigm is established, late arrivers must overcome the additional barrier to entry because of the reluctance of customers and related producer industries to absorb the costs of switching equipment that has already been installed and used for training. As a result, first-mover technology becomes standardized. The effect of standardization is twofold. It establishes a regime that "subsystemic" core niches must adapt to in developing new technology that depends on the systemic technology. It also pushes technology development along a trajectory shaped by market forces rather than by the intrinsic qualities of the winning product.

In both the systemic and subsystemic core niches of PDCs, competitive advantage is increasingly "a function of the rate of increase in knowledge rather than the absolute increment to the general stock of knowledge" (Mytelka, 1987: 50). This is because capitalist competition rapidly renders innovation or "key" knowledge into "base" knowledge that is accessible to all, but not the stuff of competition. As a result, by the time a patent is secured, it is already obsolete as a "key" innovation. This is particularly marked in telecommunications and data-processing industries where there is an inverse relationship between product life cycle and R&D cost.

This cycle is now at a frantic pace in both buyer- and supplier-driven commodity chains as innovation outpaces market growth (Hughes, 1990: 60). Each wave of innovation, in R&D or in marketing strategies, ratchets up competition which necessitates yet another wave of innovation (I) $[I{\rightarrow}C{\rightarrow}I'{\rightarrow}C'{\rightarrow}]$. Competitive pressures are not confined within industry boundaries, but emerge also from knowledge "spill-over and interaction" (Hughes, 1990: 61) among and between industries. These contribute to the multiplication of commodity markets. The birth of information technology as an industry was itself due to the convergence of electronics, telecommunications, and computers (Price and Blair, 1989: 117).

The increasing interdependence of technologies has also produced compulsive sequencing (i.e., miniaturized computers require equally miniature screens [Storper and Walker, 1989: 106]) and compulsive complementary systems (i.e., retail scantrons that read universal bar codes require automated cash registers, or Aetna Insurance Company's launch of the first private satellite in order to support its burgeoning information system). Services in particular require extensive support systems based on yet more services, which together make up packages of integrated services.

These steepen the already towering barriers to entry in the core niches of PDCs and BDCs and integrate upstream service activities in core niches more closely with downstream ones. The substantial capital investment required for a modern production facility is predicated on international sales and distribution networks. Costly telecommunications projects today can absorb the high cost of analog optic fiber, which is less costly to operate than digital systems, only by widening international markets.

Other advantages accrue to the linkage of downstream and upstream core niches. Otis Elevator Corporation's centrally coordinated electronic service system was among the first to provide senior management a bird's-eye view of its maintenance services (Rockart and Short, 1991: 208). It provides feedback essential for modifications and technology development in the upstream core niche, especially as firms grow more vigilant about customer preference in today's highly competitive economic environment. Otis's electronic service system also provides a valuable database for marketing, so that customized sales can be directed to the right block of consumers. This leveraged value-added provides enormous returns as new packages of products and services are "produced" without incurring additional costs.

BDCs in Capitalist Competition

In BDCs the highest barriers to entry exist in the downstream marketing and upstream product conception and design segments of the chain where telecommunications networks and innovation are directed at gaining competitive advantages in the marketplace. Competition waged in BDCs is as fierce as that waged in PDCs, but "weak" in the sense that it is centered in the realm of exchange where firms primarily vie for price, market, and wage advantage.

Core capital is concentrated in BDC core niches due to these barriers and is able to exert an oligopsonistic presence in BDCs because of their immense bargaining power, knowledge of markets, many retail outlets, and the ability to afford to take risks in an effort to sustain competitive advantage. Hollow firms such as Reebok and Nike tenaciously hold onto product conception, design, and marketing, the highest value-added activities, but farm out production, typically to the semiperiphery. As an additional bonus, their continued use of Southeast Asian manufactures frees them not only from the expense of manufacturing, but from the burden of primary input procurement (the upstream "extractive" segment of GCCs).

In BDCs the battle for market share takes full advantage of available technology but does not typically generate such technology. The coordinating advantages of BDCs are employed primarily to promote or sustain markets or to seek out and acquire cheaper or better quality inputs, including labor. The fight for market share is closely tied to upstream product-design service activities.

"While 'internationalization' refers simply to the geographic spread of economic activities across national borders, 'globalization' implies a degree of functional integration between these internationally dispersed activities" (see Gereffi, chapter 5 in this volume). This functional integration is accomplished via the coordinating advantages gathered in core niches. They enable distant production blocks and markets within and between GCC segments to be spatially coordinated in both PDCs and BDCs. Internationalization has led to globalization. As a result, the competitive advantages of economic actors in core niches are economies of scope, which depend on coordinating advantages (Dunning, 1989: 117). Coordinating advantages are possible only if the linkages interconnecting segments of a GCC and between different GCCs are of the highest efficiency and effectiveness.

Firms dominating BDCs in particular must maintain multiproduct lines in order to achieve economies of scope. In order to keep abreast of the market they must unceasingly modify, update, and ultimately replace each product line. This process is driven by innovations attending productive and design methods, such as CAD/CAM (computer-aided design and manufacture) in the garment and textile industries in the upstream segment of GCCs.[10] Once established, these innovations are easily imitated and exploited, not only by competitors of equal stature but by smaller producers. What cannot be readily imitated are the advantages gleaned by service activities in downstream core niches: market access, brand names, advertising, trademarks, retail outlets. In BDCs, upstream innovations in product design as well as production organization and GCC coordination are adapted to downstream requirements. One garment industry insider is cited by Bonacich and Waller: "It takes years to build that sort of sourcing and warehousing system. Liz [Claiborne] has the best people working for her throughout the world. And that creates a barrier to entry for other companies" (1992: 21).

In BDCs, innovations in the organization of production and distribution, which have been facilitated by information technology, have dramatically transformed the apparel industry. Apparel innovations exemplify the force the downstream core niche exerts on the rest of the GCCs. The retail industry became intensely competitive during the 1980s as mergers and acquisitions raised debt and operating expenses. Conventional department stores had relied on sustained markups for profits. Discount outlets and chains, which were boosted by the development of clothing manufacturers in the semiperiphery, can afford to pin profits on product turnover. Gross profit is not measured in terms of markup per product, but in terms of square feet of space! Walmart, for example, moves two times the amount of inventory through its stores as May Department Stores Company (Bonacich and Waller, 1992). These innovations in the organization of distribution took advantage of cheap production costs upstream, which facilitated the lowering of markups. It is important to understand, however, that it is the service activities downstream in the core niche of marketing and distribution, rather than innovations upstream, that coordinate and drive the rest of the BDC. For this reason, upstream and downstream core niches are more easily integrated in BDCs than PDCs.

The "media-zation" of capitalist consumption, which sells an ideology, set of values, and life style along with the product, adds to the pace and frenzy of capitalist competition in the downstream segment (i.e., advertisement and marketing) of GCCs. The packaging is actually *a part of* the product in BDCs. The Nike pump sneaker is less technology than hype; and although influential in the industry as a whole, it does not depend on interrelated technology as in the case of PDCs. For this reason, "state of the art" in BDCs remains subsystemic. An entirely new product does not necessarily prompt a qualitative technological shift built on the previous one.

In both BDCs and PDCs it is clear that the core niches necessitating high-end services are tremendously dynamic and competitive segments in GCCs. As any analysis of the GCC configuration makes abundantly clear, the technical, financial, marketing, and economic know-how that comprise high-end services have replaced embodied technology (the industrial means of production) as a firm's primary competitive advantage—an advantage often greater than those secured via traditional cost and efficiency allocations. But even this is not enough. "The key to longevity in dynamic, knowledge-intensive industries . . . is to be in a position to control the transformation of the market, rather than merely respond to changes in it" (Mytelka, 1987: 50). In PDCs the key is upstream; in BDCs it is downstream.

CONCLUSION

The atomization and globalization of production processes have had a profound impact on the growth of services. Not only did the number of service activities continue to proliferate to support the atomized production process, but services, in particular core niche services, have become essential to the viability of GCCs. They integrate and coordinate the myriad processes of production, without which the GCC will be incapable of functioning under the current conditions of intense competition.

The purpose of this chapter was to focus on services as a critical element of GCCs. Service activities that dominate the core niches of GCCs are "core" because they are among the few activities not farmed out by TNCs. TNCs have steadfastly retained command over core services, since these are not only high value-added, but allow TNCs to *control* the entire process of production and distribution. Core niche services are thus not simply auxiliary to the production and distribution processes, but are the essential driving forces.

The role of services is further elaborated in the context of two different types of GCCs: PDCs and BDCs. The more dynamic core niche in PDCs is upstream, where service activities generating product and technology innovation through R&D drive the commodity chain. In particular, the very high-end services, which we call systemic core niche services, control the trajectory of development characterizing the PDCs of particular industries. In BDCs, marketing and distribution represent the service activities that drive and coordinate the GCC.

A focus on services in GCCs is crucial for an analysis of the distinct processes of atomization and globalization that today characterize the restructuring of capitalism. Services provide linkages between commodity chain nodes, integrate and coordinate dispersed production activities, and provide the impetus for the continual transformation of GCCs.

NOTES

1. This concept was first introduced by Hopkins and Wallerstein, who defined a commodity chain as "a network of labor and production processes whose end result is a finished commodity." Gereffi and Korzeniewicz (1990) have extensively elaborated this model by analyzing production segments or nodes according to (1) commodity flows

to and from each node, (2) relations of production within each node, (3) organization of production, and (4) geographic loci of each node.

2. Services have facilitated this process. Services can raise labor productivity and efficiency, multiply products, circulate commodities, credit and money, offset risk, administer and manage production, and supply infrastructure for its expansion. They are, however, inextricably bound to commodity production and decidedly not postindustrial. Storper and Walker describe these activities as "office-based industries" (1989: 195–96).

3. Subcontracting is of utmost importance to GCC research. A fuller discussion, however, is not possible in this paper.

4. Neoclassical economists who depend on consumption as the penultimate measure of utility, the keystone of mainstream economics, argue that (1) goods and services both accomplish the same economic end—satisfaction—and (2) at the point of sale the two groups of activities are joined and therefore the division between the two, as products or factors, is largely artificial. Thus services are treated as another, albeit particular, good in most texts.

5. Other categorizations of services are based on material/immaterial characteristics such as "visible" (transport) versus "nonvisible" (fees or royalties), or distance-related features like "long-distance" versus "proximity-requiring," or information versus non-information services. An important distinction we do not address here is private versus public (government) services.

6. The importance of methodological problems associated with research on services is worth noting. One services expert, Dorothy Riddle, calculates that 40–60 percent of activities in extractive and manufacturing industries are in reality service activities, especially those related to high technology. She estimates that 80 percent of the cost of creating a new computer and 70 percent of the cost of a telecommunications switchboard are spent on services and software (1986: 240).

7. Gereffi and Korzeniewicz situate this dichotomy "in the single overarching division of labor that defines and bounds the world economy" (1990: 50). We instead limit this economic context to GCCs, which definitely do represent such an overarching division of labor. The GCC framework successfully untethers "the concept of core-periphery relations from any particular kinds of products, industries, countries, or regions" (Gereffi and Korzeniewicz, 1990: 48).

8. We thank Gary Gereffi for this example.

9. See Storper and Walker's discussion of weak and strong competition in connection with agglomeration (1989: 42–48).

10. Note that CAD/CAM technology is now base technology (Takahash, 1992).

REFERENCES

Bonacich, Edna, and Waller, David. 1992. "The Restructuring of the Pacific Rim Garment Industry." Paper presented at the Conference on the Globalization of the Apparel Industry, UCLA, 1992.

Dumaine, Brian. 1992. "Is Big Still Good?" *Fortune*, April 20, 1992, pp. 50–60.

Dunning, John H. 1989. "Trade and Foreign Owned Production in Services: Some

Conceptual and Theoretical Issues.'' In *Services in World Economic Growth*, edited by Herbert Giersch. Germany: Inst. für Weltwirtschaft an d. Univ. Kiel.

———. 1991. ''Governments—Markets—Firms: Towards a New Balance?'' *CTC Reporter*, No. 31.

Gereffi, Gary. 1989a. ''Development Strategies and the Global Factory.'' *Annals of the American Academy of Political and Social Science* 505:92–104.

———. 1989b. ''Rethinking Development Theory: Insights from East Asia and Latin America.'' *Sociological Forum* 4, 4:505–33.

———. 1990. ''New Realities of Industrial Development in East Asia and Latin America: Global, Regional, and National Trends.'' In *States and Development in the Asian Pacific Rim*, edited by Richard P. Appelbaum and Jeffrey Henderson. Newbury Park, CA: Sage Publications.

———. 1991. ''Memo to SSRC Mini-Conference on The New International Context on Development.'' May 31, 5 pp.

Gereffi, Gary, and Korzeniewicz, Miguel. 1990. ''Commodity Chains and Footwear Exports in the Semiperiphery.'' In *Semiperipheral States in the World-Economy*, edited by William G. Martin. Westport, CT: Greenwood Press.

Giersch, Herbert, ed. 1989. *Services in World Economic Growth*. Germany: Inst. für Weltwirtschaft an d. Univ. Kiel.

Gordon, David. 1988. ''Global Economy: New Edifice or Crumbling Foundation.'' *New Left Review*, London.

Gray, H. Peter. 1989. ''Services and Comparative Advantage Theory.'' In *Services in World Economic Growth*, edited by Herbert Giersch. Germany: Inst. für Weltwirtschaft an d. Univ. Kiel.

———. 1990. ''The Role of Services in Global Structural Change.'' In *Structural Change in the World Economy*, edited by Allan Webster and John Dunning. London: Routledge.

Grubel, Herbert G., and Walker, Michael A. 1989. ''Modern Service Sector Growth: Causes and Effects.'' In *Services in World Economic Growth*, edited by Herbert Giersch. Germany: Inst. für Weltwirtschaft an d. Univ. Kiel.

Helm, Leslie. 1992. ''A New Force in Chips.'' *Los Angeles Times*, August 17.

Henderson, Jeffrey. 1989. *The Globalisation of High Tech Production: Society, Space and Semiconductors in the Restructuring of the Modern World*. New York: Routledge.

Hughes, Kirsty S. 1990. ''Competition, Innovation, and Industrial Performance.'' In *Structural Change in the World Economy*, edited by John Dunning and Allan Webster. London: Routledge.

Mytelka, Lynn Krieger. 1987. ''Knowledge-Intensive Production and the Changing Internationalization Strategies of Multinational Firms.'' In *A Changing International Division of Labor*, edited by James A. Caporaso. Boulder, CO: Lynne Rienner Pub.

Nasa, Sylvia. 1992. ''Employment in Service Industry, Engine for Boom of 80's, Falters,'' *New York Times*, January 2.

Price, D. G., and Blair, A. M. 1989. *The Changing Geography of the Service Sector*, London: Belhaven Press.

Riddle, Dorothy. 1986. *Service-Led Growth: The Role of the Service Sector in World Development*, New York: Praeger.

Riddle, Dorothy, and Brown, Kristopher I. 1988. "From Complacency to Strategy: Retaining World Class Competitiveness in Services." In *Global Competitiveness: Getting the US Back on Track*, edited by Martin K. Starr. New York: W. W. Norton.

Rockart, John F., and Short, James E. 1991. "The Networked Organization and the Management of Interdependence." In *The Corporation of the 1990s: Information Technology and Organizational Transformation*, edited by Michael S. Scott Morton. New York: Oxford University Press.

Rotemberg, Julio J., and Saliner, Garth. 1991. "Interfirm Competition and Collaboration." In *The Corporation of the 1990s: Information Technology and Organizational Transformation*, edited by Michael S. Scott Morton. New York: Oxford University Press.

Sassen, Saskia. 1991. *The Global City*. Princeton, NJ: Princeton University Press.

Storper, Michael, and Walker, Richard. 1989. *The Capitalist Imperative: Territory, Technology and Industrial Growth*. New York: Basil Blackwell.

Takahash, Dean. 1992. "Big Money in Tiny Chips," *Los Angeles Times*, July 11.

United Nations Centre on Transnational Corporations. 1980–1990. *CTC Reporter*, New York: United Nations.

Venkatraman, N. 1991. "IT-induced Business Reconfiguration." In *The Corporation of the 1990s: Information Technology and Organizational Transformation*, edited by Michael S. Scott Morton. New York: Oxford University Press.

Woo, Myung. 1992. "New Dependence of the Korean Automobile Industry." PEWS XVI Conference.

Yotopoulos, Pan A. 1989. Discussant in Herbert Giersch, ed., *Services in World Economic Growth*. Inst. für Weltwirtschaft an d. Univ. Kiel.

7

Institutionalizing Flexibility: A Comparative Analysis of Fordist and Post-Fordist Models of Third World Agro-Export Production

Laura T. Raynolds

Over recent years, dramatic changes in financial circuits, productive technologies, and commodity markets have fundamentally altered the conditions of production. Throughout the world, states have been engaged in restructuring local economies to accommodate these changes and secure a place for local economic activity within shifting international circuits of accumulation. These transformations have reshaped capitalist production at the level of the firm, both in the internal organization and management of capital and labor, and in the nature of collaboration and competition between firms.

Given the historical primacy of export agriculture in many Third World countries, it is not surprising that changes in this sector have formed the locus of recent restructuring in many peripheral nations. Traditional agricultural exports—such as sugar, coffee, cocoa, and tobacco—which have long integrated Latin America and the Caribbean in the colonial-based international division of labor, have been undermined over the past decade by international marketing constraints, declining prices, and mounting global competition. As a consequence, nontraditional agricultural exports—including a wide array of specialty horticultural crops and off-season fruits and vegetables—have been greatly expanded to shore up falling export revenues and tap growing fresh food and luxury good markets in metropolitan centers.

Not only have the types of agricultural commodities being produced in Latin America and the Caribbean changed, but the organization of production has itself been fundamentally transformed. Firms have been reorganized in order to take advantage of new market opportunities while shielding themselves from new production risks. All firms, whether they be subsidiaries of very large transnational corporations or modest firms established by entrepreneurial capitalists of domestic or foreign origin, have had to cut costs and institutionalize flexible production systems in order to remain competitive under changing world economic conditions. Yet, given their differential endowments, the strategies employed by different firms and the likelihood of their success are quite varied. As this chapter will demonstrate, understanding the various ways in which firms in the nontraditional agricultural sector are constituted requires moving away from a restricted view of the sphere of agricultural production to an understanding of the differential role of firms in particular commodity systems—systems that integrate (1) raw material production; (2) processing, packing, and exporting activities; and (3) marketing and consumptive activities.

This article focuses specifically on the configuration of firms in the rapidly expanding nontraditional agricultural export sector of the Dominican Republic during the 1980s. Until recently the Dominican Republic exemplified the colonial legacy of the Third World in the international division of labor as a producer of low-value undifferentiated agricultural export commodities. Yet, over the course of the 1980s, traditional export revenues collapsed, fueling massive foreign exchange deficits. In the face of the growing economic crisis, the Dominican state and international financial organizations together identified the promotion of nontraditional agricultural exports as central to national economic revitalization and international solvency. Taking advantage of generous investor subsidies and rapidly expanding markets for new fresh fruits and vegetables, numerous firms were established in the nontraditional agricultural sector. This chapter explores the configuration of these firms to ascertain the potentially variable ways in which they institutionalize the production requirements of the changing world economy.

FORDIST AND POST-FORDIST MODELS OF AGRICULTURAL PRODUCTION

There has been a great deal of debate over the past decade as to whether the established model of capitalist production, commonly referred to as ''Fordist'' production, has given way to a more flexible ''post-Fordist'' production model. While this discussion has focused largely on changes taking place in manufacturing and service industries, its central propositions can equally be applied to transformations in agriculture. This chapter focuses on the implications of the post-Fordist argument for production organization.[1] In particular, I point to ways in which the dichotomization of production models has been overstated and suggest that a commodity-based research framework can help highlight some of the more nuanced changes in current production relations.

Fordism generally refers to the model of mass production for mass consumption that became the norm in the United States and Europe after World War II. At the level of the national economy, emphasis is placed on the social articulation of production and consumption (Aglietta, 1987; Lipietz, 1987). At the level of the productive unit, researchers note the growth of huge corporate manufacturing based on large, technologically rigid machinery and its association with the deskilling of labor (Piore and Sabel, 1984: 4). In agriculture, parallel production systems were established in the postwar period, perhaps most visibly in the giant Californian vegetable enterprises. Large corporations gained control over crops such as lettuce and instituted production systems often referred to as factories in the fields—with huge extensions of land, sophisticated technology, large-scale machinery, and numerous unskilled workers (Friedland, Barton, and Thomas, 1981; Thomas, 1985). Large-scale production was matched by lettuce's widespread consumption, aided by technological changes increasing its shelf life and transportability. The Fordist regime in capitalist countries was thus anchored in a "durable food" system, where mass production of standardized foods supplied large, undifferentiated consumer markets (Friedmann, 1987).

Similar patterns of mass production have been identified in Third World countries, particularly in export sectors. Agribusiness followed the large-scale U.S. model in establishing export-oriented plantations in Latin America (Burbach and Flynn, 1980). Production technologies, commodity specifications, and management practices all followed international standards (Sanderson, 1986). Importantly though, since mass production was not matched by mass national consumption of these commodities, this pattern reflects a more unstable pattern, which has been called "peripheral Fordism" (Lipietz, 1987).

According to a great many authors, the Fordist model of production has broken down since the 1970s and is increasingly being replaced by a more flexible, post-Fordist pattern of production. Piore and Sabel (1984) argue that the new production model is based on flexible specialization—batch production in small firms that are linked through dense networks and produce for niche markets. They suggest that post-Fordist production can out-compete the Fordist model because of flexibilities in work organization, product specification, and marketing strategies. Many studies have found that large manufacturing firms are undergoing a process of vertical disintegration whereby production is increasingly undertaken by small specialized firms linked through production contracts (Murray, 1987; Holmes, 1986). At the national level this shift in production organization is associated with the differentiation of consumer markets and the disarticulation of production and consumption (Aglietta, 1987; Lipietz, 1987).

Though less extensively documented, post-Fordist shifts in agricultural production essentially parallel those in other sectors. Analyzing the home of Fordist agriculture, California, recent studies of specialty crops note the vertical disintegration of production, where cultivation is being undertaken by dispersed contract growers and sharecroppers, under the direction of shippers and processing firms (FitzSimmons, 1986; Wells, 1984). Similar patterns of post-Fordist production are evident in Third World countries, where contract production of a range of commodities appears to be becoming increasingly common (Glover and Kusterer, 1990; Little and Watts, forthcoming).

Despite the resonance of the Fordist/post-Fordist categories in capturing important aspects of changing world economic conditions and shifting production patterns, this dichotomization appears to be more illustrative than real. As is common with dualistic models, what is noted as a sharp conceptual distinction between polar opposites, is not easily reconciled with reality. First, it is unclear to what degree the notion of the rise and crisis of Fordism captures actual historical changes in any, or all, capitalist national economies; second, it appears on investigation that most firms and markets fail to fit neatly into Fordist or post-Fordist categories (Williams et al., 1987; Sayer and Walker, 1992).

Rather than rejecting the post-Fordist thesis out of hand, I think this mixed empirical record presents a challenge for more exploratory research. The post-Fordist debates clearly point to some important social and economic changes. I take the central proposition regarding the organization of production to be that flexibility is becoming increasingly important for firms and sectors. One question that remains open is how firms institutionalize this flexibility, (1) in the volume and differentiation of their products, (2) in their management and internal factor mix, and (3) in their relations with other firms as either suppliers or buyers.

A commodity-based approach is well suited for addressing this issue because it focuses on the configuration of firms within a network of related enterprises, from the point of raw material production through processing/packaging/shipping stages and on through the marketing and consumption of commodities. Commodity-based research has proved very insightful in analyzing Latin American and Caribbean agricultural export systems, specifying the organization of production, the configuration of exporting, the organization of markets, and the creation of consumer demand (Mintz, 1986; Tomich, 1990; Trouillot, 1988). There are two complementary conceptualizations of this approach. Friedland (1984) proposes a "commodity systems analysis" for the study of agriculture that focuses on the organization of production (including production scale, labor organization, and the role of science and technology) and its integration into marketing and distribution systems. Hopkins and Wallerstein (1986) outline a similar approach, which emphasizes the interlocking "nodes" of production that go into creating a finished commodity. This latter formulation is more sensitive than the former to the links between component production processes, the geographical location (and potential dispersion) of production, and the variability of "commodity chains" over time. Yet Friedland's approach more carefully avoids the reification of commodity systems and places greater emphasis on microproduction relations.

THE EXPANSION OF NONTRADITIONAL FRESH FRUIT AND VEGETABLE EXPORTS

The recent collapse in the Dominican Republic's colonial-based agricultural export economy generated a rapid rise in nontraditional agricultural exports during the 1980s. Revenues from the country's major traditional export earner, sugar, plummeted as a result of declining world prices, rising use of chemical sweeteners, and diminished access to preferential marketing agreements. In order to compensate for declining export earnings and shore up the national economy, which was weakened by escalating foreign debt, new export commodities were widely promoted. This process of export substitution was politically configured and supported by the Dominican state in conjunction with its major trading partner, the United States, and international financial institutions.

Shifting U.S. policies toward the Caribbean played a central role in propelling the growth of Dominican nontraditional commodities, in large part by undermining established export markets and necessitating the search for alternative exports. The United States reduced the Dominican Republic's sugar quota by 64 percent between 1983 and 1988, causing a loss in foreign exchange earnings of well over US$ 200 million (C/CAA, 1988:9; USDA/ERS, 1990: 57–58). While the U.S. Caribbean Basin Initiative was championed for strengthening regional trade, particularly in nontraditional commodities, its impact has been relatively modest. Pressures from international financial organizations have, in contrast, been quite important in stimulating nontraditional exports. In the face of the country's substantial foreign debt, the Dominican state has been obliged to submit to structural adjustments and recast national policies according to the neoliberal model of the International Monetary Fund (IMF) and the World Bank (Ceara Hatton, 1984). This approach focuses on stimulating private sector investments, particularly in exports, as a way of increasing economic growth and foreign debt repayment.

Nontraditional exports, defined as all those *except* coffee, cocoa, tobacco, and sugar and its derivatives, received the greatest subsidies.[2] Firms in this sector were granted income tax and import duty exonerations from 30 to 100 percent (Law #409), as well as tax credits valued at 15–25 percent of exports (Law #69) (Investment Promotion Council, 1987). In addition, nontraditional agricultural exporters were given state-subsidized loans and inexpensive access to state lands being retired from sugarcane production.

These incentives stimulated a boom in nontraditional exports in the 1980s. Export revenues from nontraditional agricultural and agroindustrial commodities almost doubled over the course of the decade, rising from US$ 58 million in 1979 to US$ 110 million in 1989 (CEDOPEX, 1979–1989). As with traditional exports, the vast majority of these new exports were destined for U.S. markets. Over 120 new firms or firm expansions participated in this boom, representing a growth in combined foreign and domestic investments of well over US$ 100 million.[3] The most dramatic increase in export revenues in the mid-1980s came from the following four fruit and vegetable categories: (1) melons, with earnings rising from US$ 0.1 to US$ 3.1 million between 1979 and 1986; (2) pineapples, with earnings rising from US$ 0.03 to US$ 1.9 million between 1979 and 1986; (3) winter vegetables (most importantly tomatoes and green peppers), with earnings rising from US$ 1.7 to US$ 8.5 million between 1979 and 1986; and (4) oriental vegetables (most importantly Chinese eggplants, fuzzy squash, and hot peppers), with earnings rising from US$ 1.5 to US$ 5.0 million between 1979 and 1986 (CEDOPEX, 1979–1989).

Nontraditional agricultural export firms based in the Dominican Republic vary greatly in terms of their size and asset levels. While the average investment of fresh fruit and vegetable firms is roughly US$ 1.5 million, investment patterns differ markedly by commodity area.[4] Pineapple firms represent by far the largest enterprises in this sector, with assets averaging US$ 8.6 million. Vegetable firms are relatively modest, with the vast majority of oriental and winter vegetable enterprises recording investments of under US$.8 million. The firms involved in melon exporting range from quite modest to very large ventures.

Ownership patterns in fresh fruit and vegetable exporting are similarly quite varied. Forty-four percent of nontraditional agricultural firms are foreign controlled, while 47 percent are Dominican owned. Most of the foreign investment in this sector is from the United States, in keeping with the general predominance of U.S. investment in the Dominican economy (U.S. Embassy, 1991: 2). The major pineapple exporters are all foreign controlled transnational corporate subsidiaries. Sixty-four percent of melon firms are similarly dominated by foreign capital, but this includes both large corporate investments and entrepreneurial capital. Ownership of winter vegetable enterprises is evenly divided between local and non-Dominican interests, with entrepreneurial capital predominating in both cases. While 67 percent of oriental vegetable export firms are owned by Dominican residents, almost all of these entrepreneurial investors are first-generation Japanese, Taiwanese, or Chinese migrants.

THE ORGANIZATION OF THE FRESH FRUIT AND VEGETABLE COMMODITY CHAIN

The diverse nontraditional agricultural export firms located in the Dominican Republic operate within a relatively new global fresh fruit and vegetable commodity system. International fresh produce trade has increased significantly in the past two decades because of technological changes, which have improved refrigerated shipping infrastructure and increased the transportability of fresh commodities, and changing consumption patterns, which have vastly increased the demand for fresh "healthy" fruits and vegetables (Islam, 1990; Mackintosh, 1977). These developments have in turn led to (1) a seasonal extension of production, through a geographic dispersion of production locations and biochemical alterations in plant requirements and storage capacities, and (2) a proliferation of products, including a vast array of "exotic" fruits and vegetables which have captured an increasing share of the fresh produce market (Friedland, 1991).

The global fresh produce commodity chain consists of three interlocking processes: (1) raw material production; (2) combined processing, packaging, and exporting activities; and (3) marketing and consumptive activities. As depicted in Figure 7.1, how these activities are carried out varies and may be undertaken within the produce-exporting firm itself, or by other associated firms.

Analysis of the different ways in which fresh fruit and vegetable firms individually and collectively coordinate the movement of commodities from the point of production in the Dominican Republic, to the point of consumption in the United States, provides critical insights into the nature of nontraditional agricultural export firms as well as the configuration of the overall commodity chain. In particular, this approach highlights the potentially varied ways in which firms may cut costs and institutionalize flexibilities throughout the entire productive process. While I contrast firm production strategies by commodity area, I do not mean to suggest that the technical characteristics of particular commodities determine these strategies, or that they are fixed over time and space, but rather that these contrasts may illuminate important variations in the technical, economic, and political conditions of firms.[5]

Raw Material Production

Fresh fruit and vegetable exporters can organize their produce supply systems in three major ways. First, following an open market system, firms can purchase commodities on the local market, either directly from producers or from merchants, at the going price and when needed. Exporters are thus not engaged in the agricultural production process at all. Second, following an internal production system, firms can engage directly in farming activities in plantation enterprises using hired labor. These firms thus combine, under centralized management control, agricultural production with processing, packaging, and exporting activities.

There is an important third method of procuring produce—via a contract production system—which essentially falls between the two systems outlined above. Here firms enter formal agreements with producers which specify, in advance, that they will purchase a particular quantity of produce, of a particular quality, according to a particular time schedule. The pricing system is agreed upon in advance, though actual prices may be fixed or pegged to the market rate at the time of shipment. As part of the contract, purchasing firms agree to supply specified production inputs, typically including credit as well as technical products and services, and producers agree to follow the production guidelines established by the purchasing firm. Exporters involved in this system thus gain some control over product quality, quantity, and timing in exchange for assuming some of the costs and risks of agricultural production.

Fresh fruit and vegetable firm managers in the Dominican Republic assert that the major reason for choosing among these raw material production systems is to assure the consistent quality of produce. Fresh agricultural commodities are by definition highly perishable, suffering greatly from excess handling and storage, and have highly variable physical characteristics. Yet their final retail price hinges primarily on high quality and the meeting of detailed physical standards.

Figure 7.1
Fresh Fruit and Vegetable Commodity Chain

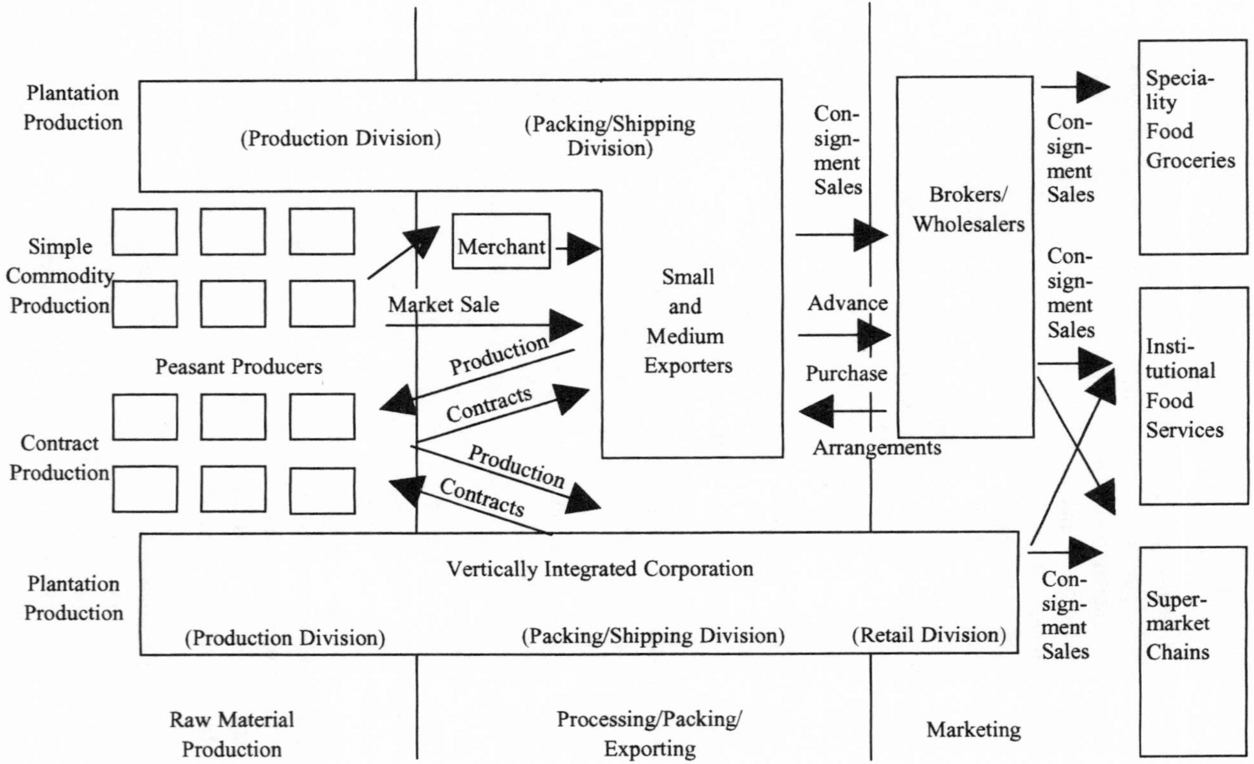

Table 7.1
Forms of Raw Material Production

Production Systems	Percentage of Production				
	All Ag. N=21	Pineapple N=2	Melon N=4	Oriental Veg. N=7	Winter Veg. N=4
Open Market[1]	12	-	-	14	50
Contract[2]	22	4	30	35	-
Internal[3]	66	96	70	51	50
Total	100	100	100	100	100

Source: Personal interviews with firm managers, 1990-1991.
Notes: [1]A market system is where raw materials are purchased on the open market with no prior contracts. [2]A contract system entails production by out-growers under firm contracts. [3]An internal production system is where land and capital are under direct firm control.

The combination of these natural and market factors mitigates against open market purchases of fresh produce exports and supports more tightly controlled production systems. Firm managers report that limiting costs and assuring a timely and sufficient supply of produce are the other major reasons for engaging in particular agricultural production systems.

Fresh fruit and vegetable export firms in the Dominican Republic rely primarily on internal plantation production for 66 percent of their produce, and secondarily on contract production for an additional 22 percent of their raw material. Yet, as demonstrated in Table 7.1, firms in different commodity areas tend toward different patterns of raw material production. While direct agricultural production is important for all commodities, this plantation form is used almost exclusively in pineapple production. Pineapple cultivation demands heavy capital investments, since these plants require over a year to mature. These investments do not pose a major problem for the wealthy transnational corporations that dominate the export sector, but they make this commodity ill-suited for Dominican peasant production. Pineapple firms argue that plantation production allows them to guarantee their supply of high-quality produce and to cut costs via administrative efficiency.

Contract production is most important in oriental vegetables and melons. Though these labor intensive, short-cycle crops might be purchased on the open market, exporting firms are very concerned with assuring timely and sufficient produce supplies. Melon firms need to guarantee high-quality stocks in time to hit a very tight market window, which is defined by U.S. melon harvests. While oriental vegetable exporters ship year-round, they need to assure the availability of crops previously unknown in the Dominican Republic. Though oriental vegetable and melon exporters cultivate some of their own produce, the smaller firms in this sector cannot afford the fixed investments required in full plantation production. By contracting out production, exporting firms are able to pass many of the substantial production risks and costs, particularly for land and labor, onto peasant contract growers. In addition, since contracts last only for a short production cycle, firms maintain a great deal of flexibility in the amounts and types of commodities supplied.

Only in winter vegetables is there a significant reliance on open market purchases of export commodities, since these short-cycle crops are readily available in the Dominican market. Exporting firms involved in this sector can avoid direct production costs and maximize their product flexibility through open market purchases. These cost savings are particularly important for winter vegetable exporters who, as previously noted, have relatively modest assets. Yet, despite their interest in cutting costs, winter vegetable firms produce half of their own produce in order to assure timely access to high-quality commodities.

Processing, Packaging, and Exporting

Contrary to the common perception that fruits and vegetables are sold fresh from the field, the intermediary handling of these commodities is quite complex. To avoid spoilage, intermediary operations must proceed smoothly and quickly. Fresh produce must be washed, sorted, packed, cooled, transported nationally, and shipped internationally—all according to an elaborate set of internationally approved standards. Even under the best conditions, these commodities must reach their market destination within a week or two or they will spoil. The organization of an effective system for undertaking these operations is crucial for the success of fresh fruit and vegetable exports and requires the knowledge and satisfaction of strict biological, marketing, and import requirements (Islam, 1990: 11).

To enter the United States, fresh produce must satisfy strict health and safety guidelines. Import regulations designed to protect the U.S. population from unsanitary food and prevent the spread of plant diseases act as critical nontariff barriers to trade that are not fully understood or easily met by exporters without U.S. affiliates (Islam, 1990: 52). In the Dominican fresh fruit and vegetable sector, large pineapple corporations have their containers inspected by a U.S. Department of Agriculture representative before they are sealed so that they may pass unhampered through U.S. customs. This advance monitoring is prohibitively expensive for smaller firms, which consequently suffer severe delays at the port of entry and have lost numerous shipments of produce because of findings of pests and pesticide residues.

The perishability of fresh produce demands that transportation systems, particularly overseas shipping, be timely and efficient. Despite their proximity to the United States, exporters of Dominican produce are hampered by insufficient and expensive freight services. Most boats travel via Puerto Rico, adding five days onto the three-and-a-half-day trip from the Dominican Republic to Miami

Table 7.2
Marketing Links of Agricultural Export Firms

Marketing Links	Percentage of Firms				
	All Ag. N=22	Pineapple N=2	Melon N=5	Oriental Veg. N=6	Winter Veg. N=3
Parent Company	4	100	40	-	33
Related Company[1]	62	-	60	17	33
Broker/Wholesaler	34	-	-	83	33
Total[2]	100	100	100	100	99

Source: Personal interviews with firm managers, 1990-1991.
Notes: [1]Related companies include branch offices of Dominican-based firms and corporate investors. [2]Totals may not sum to 100 due to rounding error.

(World Bank, 1985: 91). Since fruits and vegetables degenerate within a week, this indirect routing can cause entire shipments to spoil. Refrigerated sea freight costs from the Dominican Republic to the United States may easily match the value of the produce; at twice that price, few exporters can afford to air-freight their products (World Bank, 1985:91). The most important distinction between the shipping options of Dominican-based fresh produce exporters is between those few companies that own their own vessels (including Dole Foods, Chiquita Brands, and a subsidiary of Sea Board Corporation) and those that must rely on commercial services.

As demonstrated in Table 7.2, there is greater variation in the relations under which fresh fruits and vegetables are exported. Pineapple corporations ship goods to parent company offices in the United States, thereby tightly integrating their production, packing and shipping, and retail divisions. This vertically integrated system assures the rapid and controlled movement of fresh produce from Caribbean packing sheds to U.S. company distributors, and permits the similarly rapid return of information regarding any problems encountered en route.

The exporting relations of oriental vegetable firms are strikingly different—their produce is predominantly sold on consignment to independent brokers/wholesalers in the United States. Under this arrangement, importers take a 13–15 percent commission on the selling price, with the balance going to the exporter (World Bank, 1985: 92). Exporting firms thus absorb the costs of transportation as well as losses from damage in transit. Since exporters have no way of verifying the condition of the produce on arrival or the price at which it was sold, this relation is typically fraught with tension. Oriental vegetable exporters attempt to overcome these uncertainties by building up long-term personal relations with importers, from their own ethnic group if possible.[6]

The majority of melon exporters, those that do not have U.S. parent firms, have advance purchase agreements with either U.S. corporate investors or U.S.

branch offices. Dominican-based exporters are thus able to share transportation costs and risks, guarantee product prices, and even sometimes access productive capital. These contractual relations limit exporting uncertainties and help ensure that produce-marketing criteria and import standards are met before shipments leave the Dominican Republic. As noted in Table 7.2, only winter vegetable firms are involved in all three exporting relations.

Marketing

Since there is very limited demand for fresh fruits and vegetables in the Dominican Republic, firms in this sector are at the mercy of the U.S. market, the primary destination of all major exports in this sector. For exporting firms to be successful, they must be linked to distribution systems which effectively supply the major U.S. outlets for fresh produce: supermarket chains; specialty food groceries; and institutional food services. Close links with these distribution systems are critical because of (1) the high degree of concentration found in fresh produce trade, and (2) the importance of obtaining accurate marketing information and undertaking promotional activities for specific commodities (Islam, 1990: 65). Very large firms with important market shares can attempt, with some success, to shape their export markets, but minor exporters must respond as best they can to changing market conditions. Fresh fruit and vegetable exports from the Dominican Republic appear to enter three distinct agrofood marketing networks.

Oriental vegetables enter growing specialty food networks since they are not widely produced or consumed in the United States. This produce is sold either to ethnic restaurants or to specialty grocery stores catering to Asian migrant communities and gourmet cooks. While U.S. oriental vegetable consumption has increased in response to the rising popularity of ethnic cuisine and the growing size and purchasing power of migrant populations, neither exporters nor broker/ wholesalers have had much influence over these trends. The relatively modest enterprises involved in this sector cannot afford the expensive advertising necessary to introduce these "exotic" foods to the mass U.S. consumer market, and only a few oriental vegetables, such as snow peas and Chinese eggplants, make it into large supermarkets. While ethnic ties may help news travel through this marketing network, broker/wholesalers have not relayed information on import restrictions and Dominican-based oriental vegetable exporters have had trouble satisfying U.S. customs requirements.

Melons and winter vegetables enter off-season produce circuits, reaching the U.S. market during the winter months and taking advantage of the growing demand for year-round fresh produce. These products are sold to supermarkets, greengrocers, and institutional food services. Since melons, tomatoes, green peppers, and other such foods are already part of the average summer food basket, the marketing challenge has been to extend the period in which these items are purchased. The recent rise in health-conscious eating has increased the year-round demand for fresh fruits and vegetables. This demand has been stimulated in part by extensive advertising by the off-season produce industry, often through lobbying groups involving both producers and distributors. Given their tighter marketing networks, winter produce exporters located in the Dominican Republic have greater access to market intelligence and importing information than oriental vegetable exporters. While sales of Dominican produce benefit from rising demand, they are greatly influenced by U.S. production patterns as well as those in competing Latin American countries. A few melon and winter vegetable exporters based in the Dominican Republic benefit from coordinated planting with parent firms or related companies located in the United States.

Pineapples from the Dominican Republic enter global sourcing networks governed by Dole Foods and Chiquita Brands, two of the largest distributors of fresh produce in the world. These companies sell to major supermarket chains and institutional food services. Through expensive advertising and promotional efforts, these companies have strengthened the brand loyalty of both retail enterprises and consumers. They have increased pineapple consumption through extensive advertising as well as through product differentiation schemes which, for example, provide in-store preparation of pineapple products. Dole and Chiquita retail divisions effectively shape their markets and convey projections through the company network to be used in planning pineapple planting and harvesting. Since these two corporations dominate the world pineapple market, the competitiveness of Dominican pineapples depends largely on relative production costs in their alternative production sites.

FLEXIBLE RESPONSES TO CRISIS

As previously suggested, all firms must accommodate the changing conditions of doing business in a post-Fordist world, but the ways in which they do so may vary. Having laid out the basic configuration of agricultural export firms operating in the Dominican Republic and their differential insertion into the fresh fruit and vegetable commodity chain, it is possible to identify more clearly the ways in which these firms cut costs and institutionalize flexibilities. I focus this discussion on recent experiences in oriental vegetables and pineapples, two of the areas of greatest transformation in the Dominican nontraditional agricultural export sector.

Oriental vegetable exporting from the Dominican Republic during the 1980s in many ways epitomized the post-Fordist model of production—production was organized by small enterprises linked through a network of contracts producing specialty foods for niche markets. Most cultivation was undertaken by two to three thousand peasant producers working on short-term contracts with a dozen small entrepreneurial firms (Listin Diario, 1989). These firms in turn were tightly linked through personal as well as market ties to ethnic marketing chains that served a growing U.S. niche market for exotic vegetables. Yet, despite their post-Fordist character, the flexibility of oriental vegetable firms was restricted to their raw material production systems, and exporters have suffered greatly in recent years from their limited marketing agility.

At its height in the mid-1980s, oriental vegetables accounted for roughly 11 percent of total Dominican nontraditional agricultural export earnings (CEDO-PEX, 1988). Earnings from this produce have declined significantly in recent years because of a persistent failure by exporters to meet strict U.S. import requirements. Between 1987 and 1988, the U.S. Food and Drug Administration placed Dominican shipments of major oriental vegetables under ''automatic detention'' because of findings of excess pesticide residues (Murray and Hoppin, 1992). In 1989, several more oriental varieties were restricted entry to the United States, this time because of pest infestations (Listin Diario, 1989).

Oriental vegetable exporting firms tried first to circumvent these restrictions by manipulating their marketing activities. When exports of particular firms were initially restricted, many enterprises simply started shipping under other names. Since these were not name-brand commodities, this strategy worked until all oriental vegetables from the Dominican Republic were restricted. Exporters then tried to diversify into unregulated markets. While many exporters increased shipments to Canada, this strategy depended largely on the improper relabeling of goods for reexport to the United States, since Canadian demand for this produce is limited.

Oriental vegetable firms were then forced to make more drastic changes in their production systems. Between 1988 and 1989, major exporters reported a 57 percent decline in cultivated area (JACC, 1989: 27-28). By 1990, virtually all contracts for oriental vegetables had been discontinued. Since many firms had limited fixed investments, they were able to close down their operations virtually overnight as markets contracted. Enterprises run by first-generation Asian migrants with few local ties left the Dominican Republic within a year to start again in Central American countries from which oriental vegetables were not restricted. Firms with greater local ties focused on diversifying into new commodity areas.

In contrast to oriental vegetables, pineapples exported from the Dominican Republic in the 1980s were produced following what is often characterized as a Fordist model, based on large-scale production by vertically integrated corporations oriented toward mass consumer markets. Pineapple cultivation occurred almost exclusively on large-scale plantations managed directly by subsidiaries of Dole Foods and Chiquita Brands. The movement of these fruits from the point of production, through intermediary processing, packing, and shipping, and on to the U.S. market were all managed by interlocking corporate divisions. While these firms have relatively rigid raw material production systems (in keeping with their Fordist characterization), their recent success can largely be attributed to their highly flexible marketing capacity.

Pineapples have displayed the most rapid and consistent growth of any commodity in the Dominican fresh fruit and vegetable export sector. In 1980, pineapples contributed only 1 percent of nontraditional agricultural export earnings;

by 1989 they made the largest contribution to fresh produce exports, with 14 percent of the total value (CEDOPEX, 1979–1989). This growth was fueled by Dole and Chiquita in large part to compensate for production losses in Central American subsidiaries plagued by labor unrest and other problems. One of the major reasons for locating in the Dominican Republic was the availability of cheap state land that was being taken out of sugarcane production. Chiquita and Dole have been able to dramatically reduce their fixed plantation investments by producing on state land that they rent at concessionary prices. The Dominican Republic's low wages, which are among the lowest in the region (Bobbin Consulting Group, 1988), also helped attract these new investments. Despite the strength of their global sourcing systems in compensating for natural harvest fluctuations and in increasing their negotiating power over individual states, Chiquita and Dole have had trouble ensuring the profitability of their Dominican plantations. Though they have seriously contemplated pulling out, they cannot easily walk away from the roughly US$ 8.6 million they have invested in the Dominican Republic.

These transnational corporations have much greater flexibility in their marketing activities. Chiquita Brands and Dole Foods benefit from tremendous economies of scope, as well as economies of scale, which enable them to introduce new fresh fruits and vegetables to mass consumer markets under their well-known labels. Thus, while the oriental vegetable industry has largely been limited to niche markets for their exotic produce, Chiquita has successfully introduced exotics such as kiwi fruit and mangos to supermarket shoppers via huge advertising campaigns (Olsen, 1991). Dole has been similarly successful in its product differentiation schemes as well as in developing major markets in Europe and the Pacific (Castle and Cooke, 1988). This market power gives these corporations a type of flexibility and competitive edge unknown to smaller firms that may be more flexible in their production organization.

CONCLUSIONS

This study lends empirical support to my contention that the post-Fordist literature overstates the dichotomy between firms organized around Fordist and flexible specialization models. There is in fact a substantial range in the ways in which firms are organized, even in new and rapidly expanding sectors such as the nontraditional agricultural export sector in the Dominican Republic. It is not necessarily clear that one organizational pattern predominates or provides greater resiliency in the face of mounting world economic competition and volatility. While all firms must clearly institutionalize points of flexibility and cost-saving mechanisms, the ways in which this is done can, and do, vary. This evidence of organizational diversity should not be surprising. What is perhaps surprising is that scholars have expended so much energy trying to demonstrate that successful economic organization must, in some deterministic way, fit into a single post-Fordist mold (Sayer and Walker, 1992).

Post-Fordist interpretations tend to overstate the economic opportunities afforded small firms by their flexible production systems and understate the limitations that may be placed on these enterprises by restricted assets and/or limited market niches. As suggested in the experience of Dominican-based oriental vegetable enterprises, this flexibility may provide firms with the capacity to respond rapidly to crisis and even, if necessary, relocate from one country to another, but it does not necessarily give firms the power to resolve the crisis itself. In this case, entrepreneurial capitalists lost some US$ 16 million in a single year, bankrupting many small firms (JACC, 1989: 27-28). For the peasant producers involved in the contract production of oriental vegetables, this system did not engender a return to idyllic craft production. And yet, when contracts were canceled, producers were left worse off, often with degraded agricultural resources, no profits, and no viable markets for their produce.

Analysis of Fordist production patterns often overstates the rigidities of large-scale vertically integrated production systems and understates the flexibilities available to corporations able to efficiently bring to market new and diverse commodities. As suggested in the experience of pineapple transnationals in the Dominican Republic, what these firms may lack in the ability to rapidly alter their production patterns, they more than make up for through their impressive capacity for innovation and market penetration, which allows them not only to respond to market changes, but indeed to shape them. The enormous economic and political power of these firms has made pineapples the most rapidly growing segment of Dominican nontraditional exports. In ascertaining the benefits of this growth it is critical to recall that the expansion of Dominican fresh produce exports has been built on a series of state concessions that limit local returns from this export boom. Since firms pay few taxes, subsidized land rents, and rock-bottom wages, the net benefits to the national economy and the Dominican population are open to question.

NOTES

I would like to thank Philip McMichael and the editors for their helpful comments on an earlier version of this paper, and acknowledge the support of the Inter-American Foundation Graduate Fellowship Program and the Equipo de Investigación Social, Instituto Technológico de Santo Domingo, which made my field work possible. The views presented here are those of the author and not necessarily those of these individuals or institutions.

1. See Raynolds (forthcoming) for a fuller treatment of the national political economic shifts that are often noted in this debate.

2. Nontraditional exports are politically defined as those commodities on which a country is considered to not be overly dependent, and thus varies over time and across states. The Dominican concept is best defined in incentive legislation, Law #409 (Banco del Comercio, 1982).

3. These figures are calculated from the Departamento Técnico Agroindustrial registry of Law #409 beneficiaries.

4. The following data are from personal interviews with managers of forty-four non-traditional firms representing major commodity areas in 1990–1991, as well as the U.S. Department of Commerce, Caribbean Basin Investment Survey databank, and the Dominican Departamento Técnico Agroindustrial registry of beneficiaries under Law #409, 1983–1989.

5. For example, in my interviews, 37 percent of firm managers reported that they had altered their supply systems within the previous five years.

6. For example, exporters of Japanese origin complain that they are penalized by the fact that the major U.S. brokers/wholesalers for their products are of Chinese descent.

REFERENCES

Aglietta, Michel. 1987. *A Theory of Capitalist Regulation: The U.S. Experience*. Translated by David Fernbach. London: Verso Books.

Banco del Comercio Dominicano. 1982. "Ley 409 Sobre Incentivo y Protección Agroindustrial." Santo Domingo: Dr. Milton Messina y Asociados.

Bobbin Consulting Group. 1988. "Sourcing: Caribbean Option." Columbia, SC: Bobbin Consulting Group.

Burbach, Roger, and Flynn, Patricia. 1980. *Agribusiness in the Americas*. New York: Monthly Review Press.

Castle and Cooke, Inc. 1988. *1988 Annual Report*. Castle and Cooke, Inc.

C/CAA (Caribbean/Central American Action). 1988. "In Caribbean Basin, Sugar is a Tough Habit to Break." *Caribbean Action* 1: 9.

Ceara Hatton, Miguel. 1984. *Tendencia Estructurales y Coyuntura de la Economía Dominicana 1968–83*. Santo Domingo: Nuevas Rutas.

CEDOPEX (Centro Dominicano de Promoción de Exportaciones). 1979–1989. *Boletin Estadístico (Various Editions)*. Santo Domingo: CEDOPEX.

FitzSimmons, Margaret. 1986. "The New Industrial Agriculture: The Regional Integration of Specialty Crop Production." *Economic Geography* 62(4): 334–53.

Friedland, William. 1984. "Commodity Systems Analysis: An Approach to the Sociology of Agriculture." In *Research in Rural Sociology and Development*, edited by Harry K. Schwarzweller, pp. 221–35. Greenwich, CT: JAI Press.

———. 1991. "The New Globalization: The Case of Fresh Produce." Paper presented at the Workshop on the Globalization of Fresh Fruit and Vegetable System, University of California, Santa Cruz (Dec. 1991).

Friedland, William H.; Barton, Amy E.; and Thomas, Robert J. 1981. *Manufacturing Green Gold: Capital, Labor, and Technology in the Lettuce Industry*. Cambridge: Cambridge University Press.

Friedmann, Harriet. 1987. "The Family Farm and the International Food Regimes." In *Peasants and Peasant Societies*, edited by Teodor Shanin, pp. 247–58. New York: Basil Blackwell.

Glover, David, and Kusterer, Ken. 1990. *Small Farmers, Big Business: Contract Farming and Rural Development*. New York: St. Martin's Press.

Holmes, John. 1986. "The Organization and Locational Structure of Production Subcontracting." in *Production, Work, Territory*, edited by Alison Scott and Michael Storper, pp. 80–106. Boston: Allen and Unwin.

Hopkins, Terence, and Wallerstein, Immanuel. 1986. "Commodity Chains in the World-Economy Prior to 1800." *Review* 10, 1:157–70.

Investment Promotion Council of the Dominican Republic. 1987. "Investing in the Dominican Republic." Santo Domingo: Investment Promotion Council.

Islam, Nurul. 1990. "Horticultural Exports of Developing Countries: Past Performances, Future Prospects, and Policy Issues." Washington D.C.: International Food Policy Research Institute, Research Report #80.

JACC (La Junta Agroempresarial de Consultoría y Coinversión, Inc.). 1989. "La Producción y Exportación de Vegetales Chinos." *Agroempresa*, November-December, pp. 26–27.

Lipietz, Alain. 1987. *Miracles and Mirages: The Crisis of Global Fordism.* Translated by David Macey. London: Verso Books.

Listin Diario. 1989. "Ve Podrían Levantar Sanciones en Breve." *Listin Diario (Santo Domingo)*, August 14, p. D-1.

Little, Peter D., and Watts, Michael. Forthcoming. *Living Under Contract: Contract Farming and Agrarian Transformation in Sub-Saharan Africa.* Madison: University of Wisconsin Press.

Mackintosh, Maureen. 1977. "Fruit and Vegetables as an International Commodity: The Relocation of Horticulture Production and its Implications for the Producers." *Food Policy* 2:277–92.

Mintz, Sidney W. 1986. *Sweetness and Power: The Place of Sugar in Modern History.* Harmondsworth, England: Penguin Books.

Murray, R. 1987. "Ownership, Control and the Market." *New Left Review* 164: 87–112.

Murray, Douglas, and Hoppin, Polly. 1992. "Recurring Contradictions in Agrarian Development: Pesticide Problems in Caribbean Basin Nontraditional Agriculture." *World Development* 20 (4):597–608.

Olsen, Thomas. 1991. "Chiquita Pits Fresh Marketing Against Mystery of Mangos." *Cincinnati Business Courier*, June 3, pp. 1–12.

Piore, Michael J., and Sabel, Charles F. 1984. *The Second Industrial Divide: Possibilities for Prosperity.* New York: Basic Books.

Raynolds, Laura T. Forthcoming. "The Restructuring of Export Agriculture in the Dominican Republic: Changing Agrarian Production Relations and the State." In *Agro-Food System Restructuring on a World Scale: Toward the Twenty-First Century*, edited by Philip McMichael. Ithaca, NY: Cornell University Press.

Sanderson, Steven. 1986. *The Transformation of Mexican Agriculture: International Structure and the Politics of Rural Change.* Princeton, NJ: Princeton University Press.

Sayer, Andrew, and Walker, Richard. 1992. *The New Social Economy.* Cambridge, MA: Basil Blackwell.

Thomas, Robert J. 1985. *Citizenship, Gender, and Work: Social Organization of Industrial Agriculture.* Berkeley: University of California Press.

Tomich, Dale. 1990. *Slavery and the Circuit of Sugar: Martinique and the World Economy, 1830–1848.* Baltimore: Johns Hopkins University Press.

Trouillot, Michel-Rolph, 1988. *Peasants and Capital: Dominica in the World Economy.* Baltimore: Johns Hopkins University Press.

USDA/ERS (U.S. Department of Agriculture, Economic Research Service). 1990. "U.S. Sugar Imports Under Quotas, by Country, 1984/85-1989/90." *Sugar and Sweetener*, March.

U.S. Embassy, Santo Domingo, Economic Section. 1991. "Foreign Economic Trends for the Dominican Republic." Santo Domingo: U.S. Embassy.

Wells, Miriam. 1984. "The Resurgence of Sharecropping: Historical Anomaly or Political Strategy?" *American Journal of Sociology* 90: 1–29.

Williams, Karel; Cutler, Tony; Williams, John; and Haslam, Colin. 1987. "The End of Mass Production?" *Economy and Society* 16(3): 405–39.

World Bank. 1985. *Dominican Republic: Economic Prospects and Policies to Renew Growth*. Washington D.C.: World Bank.

PART III

The Geography of Commodity Chains

8

The New Spatial Division of Labor and Commodity Chains in the Greater South China Economic Region

Xiangming Chen

The international division of labor has always been a key focus for studying the different roles and relative positions of countries at varied development levels in the economic hierarchy of the world-system. Two major shifts have occurred in the international division of labor. Amid the continued geographical fragmentation and dispersion of manufacturing processes at the global level, there is increasing concentration and integration of industrial and commercial activities of various regional scales.

These two parallel processes have begun to reshape the international division of labor into more complex and tightly connected networks of sourcing, manufacturing, and marketing that cut across the geographical and political boundaries of nation-states. The key questions are: (1) What are the characteristics of the division of labor in these regional networks? (2) What factors shape these regional divisions of labor? (3) What are the consequences of regional economic integration for the countries involved? In this chapter I attempt to answer the above questions by focusing on the division of labor in an emerging regional economic network—the Greater South China Economic Region (hereafter GSCER).

THE EMERGENCE OF THE GREATER SOUTH CHINA ECONOMIC REGION (GSCER)

The origin of the GSCER may be traced to some ideas floated in the second half of the 1980s about economic cooperation among China, Hong Kong, and

Taiwan, based on their comparative advantages: China's cheap land, raw materials, and labor; Hong Kong's links to world markets, international financial services, and transport hub; and Taiwan's capital, manufacturing technology, and management expertise. Scholars and business analysts in China, Hong Kong, and Taiwan have proposed such concepts as "the Greater China Common Market," "the Greater Chinese Economic Community" (see Lu and Zheng, 1990), "the Chinese Productivity Triangle" (Kraar, 1992), and "the Triangular Chinese Economy" (Lampton et al., 1992). Lee (1991) identifies Greater China (China's Fujian and Guangdong provinces, Hong Kong, and Taiwan) as a new growth zone. As Greater China has a broader spatial connotation, I use the GSCER to characterize the special economic relations and new spatial division of labor among China's Fujian and Guangdong provinces, Hong Kong, and Taiwan, while reserving the term "Southern China" for Fujian and Guangdong. Map 8.1 lays out the spatial boundaries of economic integration in the GSCER.

The initial stimulus to economic cooperation among Southern China, Hong Kong, and Taiwan emerged in the late 1970s, when China began to implement domestic economic reform and an open development policy. The primary objectives of this policy were to introduce direct foreign investment (DFI), to adopt advanced foreign technology, and to speed up China's exports. In 1978 the Chinese government designated Fujian and Guangdong as the first two provinces for experimenting with economic reform and open policy. In 1979–1980 China set up four Special Economic Zones (SEZs): three (Shenzhen, Zhuhai, Shantou) are along Guangdong's coast and one (Xiamen) is a port city in Fujian. In 1984 China designated Fourteen "open" coastal cities, two of which (Guangzhou, Zhanjiang) are in Guangdong and another (Fuzhou) is in Fujian. In 1985 China opened three river deltas in its coastal region to DFI. While the Pearl River Delta includes several of Guangdong's cities and counties, the southern Fujian delta forms a triangle among the cities of Xiamen, Zhangzhou and Quanzhou. In 1988 China upgraded the Hainan SEZ to a province (see Map 8.1 and Chen, 1991).

Although China's open coastal development strategy is no longer confined to Guangdong and Fujian, the two provinces ranked first and third (among China's twenty-nine provinces, central government municipalities, and autonomous regions) in the growth of gross industrial output during 1980–1990 (SSB, 1981: 19; 1991c: 11). During 1985–1991 Guangdong averaged 43.7 percent of the total DFI in China, accounting by far for the largest provincial share, whereas Fujian's share was 7.5 percent, ranking fourth behind Guangdong, Beijing, and Shanghai (Chen, 1993: Table 2). Did rapid growth and large DFI qualify Fujian and Guangdong as partners in a "triple alliance" with Hong Kong and Taiwan?

Table 8.1 shows the basic indicators on Fujian, Guangdong, Hong Kong, and Taiwan. Although Fujian and Guangdong have much larger populations and areas, they trail Hong Kong and Taiwan in gross domestic product (GDP) and have a much larger gap with Taiwan. While Fujian and Guangdong have rela-

Map 8.1
The Extent of the Greater South China Economic Region (GSCER)

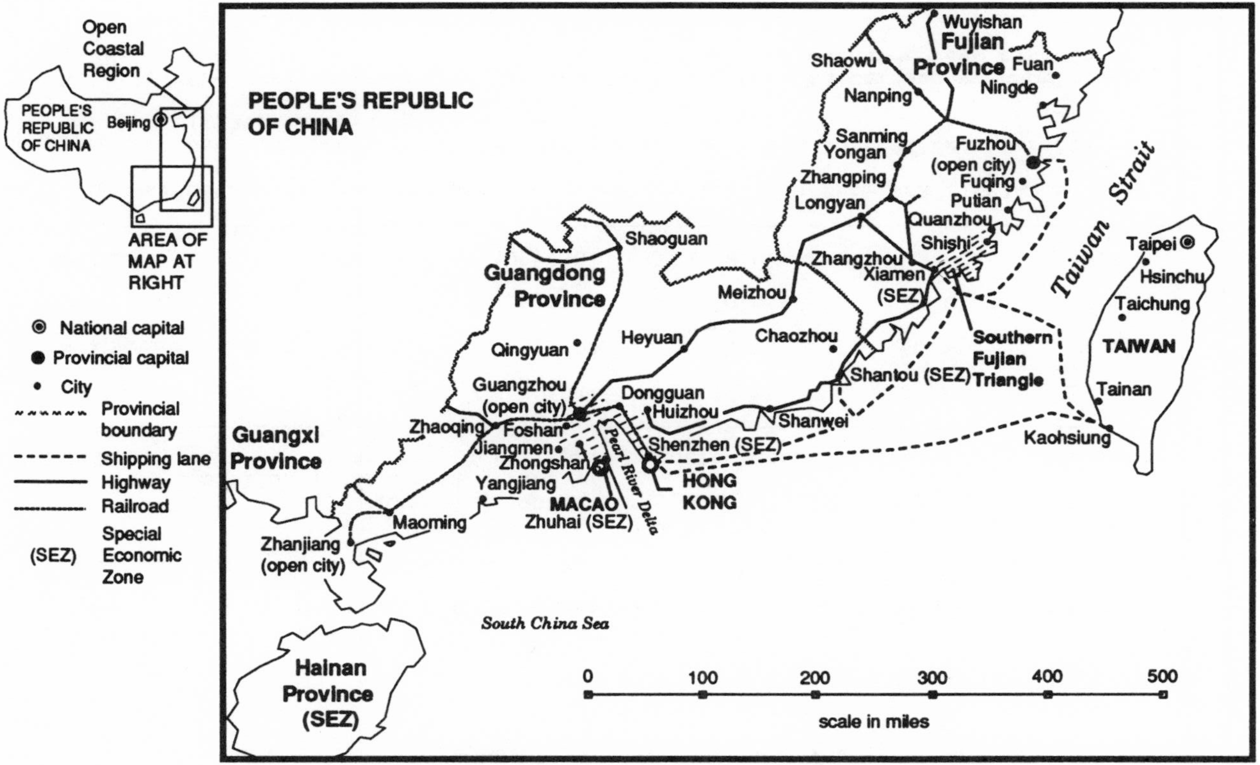

Table 8.1
Basic Indicators on China's Fujian and Guangdong Provinces, Compared with Hong Kong and Taiwan

Unit	Population (millions)	Area (thousand sq. km.)	GDP (US\$ millions)	Distribution of Gross Domestic Product (%)		
				Agriculture	Industry	Services
Fujian	27.5	121	6,104[a]	33.7	39.6	26.7
Guangdong	63.5	212	19,510[a]	31.8	40.7	27.5
Hong Kong	5.6	1	36,530	0.0	29.0	70.0
Taiwan	19.7	36	105,750	6.0	48.0	46.0

Sources: Data on Fujian and Guangdong are for 1986 and from SSB (1987a, 5-7, 24; 1987b, 34, 42). Data on Hong Kong and Taiwan are for 1987 and adapted from Gereffi (1990, table 1.1).

Note: a. The GDP figures on Fujian and Guangdong were in Chinese yuan originally and converted to U.S. dollars using the 1986 exchange rate of 3.45 yuan = US\$1.

tively big agricultural sectors, the weight of their industrial sectors in overall GDP is similar to that of Hong Kong and Taiwan.

Fujian and Guangdong's GDP sustained annual growth rates of 11 percent and 13 percent during 1978–1989 (Wu, 1991: 24), exceeding the rate of GDP growth in Hong Kong and Taiwan during the same period of time and even during their most dynamic growth from the mid-1960s through the early 1980s. Guangdong's agricultural labor as a share of total labor declined from 74 percent in 1978 to 54 percent in 1989, while its industrial labor force rose from 14 percent to 25 percent. The Guangdong economy also became more oriented to light and processing industries. Its ratio of heavy to light industries changed from 42:58 in 1978 to 31:69 in 1989 (Maruya, 1992: 5). The rapid growth of Guangdong's light industries was driven by a strong export surge. With only 6 percent of China's population, Guangdong accounts for 21 percent of the country's total exports (Kraar, 1992: 125). Thus Guangdong's dynamic economic growth in the 1980s was based on highly labor-intensive and export-oriented industrialization, similar to what Hong Kong and Taiwan experienced in the 1960s.

The foregoing is not intended to be a close comparison of highly comparable cases. The rapid economic growth of Fujian and Guangdong is partially a function of their very small initial bases and the pent-up demand for goods and services in China's old central planning regime. Nevertheless, the pace and pattern of Fujian and Guangdong's industrialization in the 1980s, coupled with their large populations and land, render the two Chinese coastal provinces complementary partners, with Fujian being the "junior" one of the two, in a new division of labor with Hong Kong and Taiwan in the GSCER.

ECONOMIC LINKS IN THE GSCER

Southern China's economic links with Hong Kong and Taiwan were shaped by different historical antecedents. Guangdong has had a longer, stronger, and closer economic connection with Hong Kong than with Taiwan. Between 1842, when Hong Kong became a British colony, and the founding of the People's Republic in 1949, Hong Kong functioned as an entrepôt for goods entering and leaving China. Guangdong has remained Hong Kong's primary hinterland. In comparison, Fujian has stronger ties with Taiwan than with Hong Kong. In the seventeenth century, many Fujianese emigrated to Taiwan to avoid imperial meddling and poverty (McGregor, 1992). These historical conditions have a direct bearing on how the recent economic links in the GSCER are formed.

The opening of Guangdong and Fujian in the late 1970s led to rapidly growing trade among China, Hong Kong, and Taiwan. Total China–Hong Kong trade increased from US$5.6 billion in 1980 to US$26.3 billion in 1987, a rise of 5.3 times. More remarkable is that entrepôt trade (passing through Hong Kong to and from China) soared from US$1.8 billion to US$18.4 billion, five times faster

Figure 8.1
China's Trade with Taiwan via Hong Kong, 1977–1993

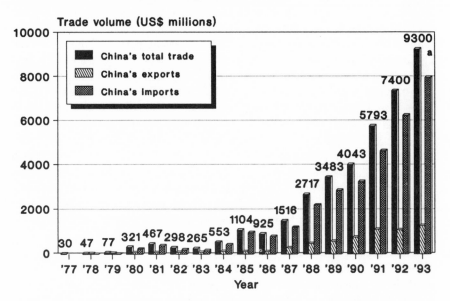

Source: The Economist (1992: 31); Jia (1992: 280); Kraar (1992: 125); Lardy (1987: 7); *People's Daily* (February 24, 1993: 5); SSB (1991c: 97).

[a]Projected.

than direct trade, which grew from US$3.8 billion to US$7.9 billion during 1980–1987 (Vogel, 1989: 67).

This renewed and enhanced entrepôt role of Hong Kong reflects the entrance of Taiwan into the China–Hong Kong trading diad as a third party. The volume of indirect trade between China and Taiwan rose from an estimated US$30 million in 1977 to US$7,400 million in 1992, an annual growth rate of about 45 percent (Figure 8.1). At this rate, China could replace the United States as Taiwan's biggest trading partner by the year 2000 (Kraar, 1992). The breakdown of exports and imports shows a huge trade balance in Taiwan's favor, resulting from the very different contents of trade flows between the Taiwan Strait. While China's exports to Taiwan are mainly agricultural and industrial raw materials and some semiprocessed goods, Taiwan exports to China primarily textile and consumer electronics products and machinery, which are much higher value-added. Figure 8.2 shows that the indirect trade between China and Taiwan as a share of their total trade also increased rapidly. Of China's US$4.5 billion in imports from Hong Kong in the first half of 1988, US$890 million (20 percent) came from Taiwan, second only to Japan (US$1.6 billion) and ahead of the United States (US$540 million) and South Korea (US$470 million) (Taira, 1988: 1). Measured by the volume of trade, the economic relations between China and Hong Kong

Figure 8.2
Indirect China-Taiwan Trade as Percentages of Their Total Trade, 1977–1992

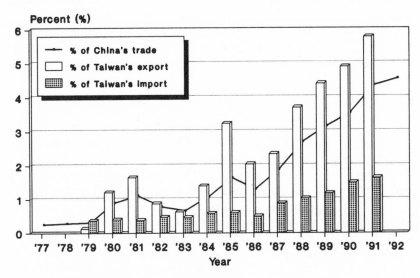

Source: The Economist (1992: 31); Jia (1992: 280); Kraar (1992: 125); Lardy (1987: 7); *People's Daily* (February 24, 1993: 5); SSB (1991c: 97).

began to tighten from the early 1980s, while a triangular trading network involving Taiwan emerged in the mid-1980s and became consolidated toward the end of the decade. In the first 10 months of 1991, three-way trade (among China, Hong Kong, and Taiwan) reached US$68 billion (Lampton et al., 1992: 1).

Investment also functions as a strong mechanism for integrating Southern China, Hong Kong, and Taiwan. Hong Kong and Macao[1] accounted for an average of 61 percent of total DFI in China during 1985–1989 (SSB, 1986: 582; 1990a: 654). It was reported that Hong Kong and Macao invested US$4 billion in China in 1991 alone, whereas China may have US$13–$15 billion invested in Hong Kong (Lampton et al., 1992: 1). Direct investment from Hong Kong and Taiwan in China has overwhelmingly been concentrated in Fujian and Guangdong provinces. In Guangdong province, approximately 90 percent of the DFI cases and 70 percent of the DFI capital have come from Hong Kong and Macao (SSB, 1987b: 341). In Fujian, about 60 percent of the DFI are from Hong Kong (SSB, 1991a: 320).

In spite of the continued ban on direct investment, Taiwan's Ministry of Economic Affairs (MOEA) allowed small businesses to make indirect investment (via a third party) on the mainland. Prior to 1987 the amount of Taiwan investment in China was relatively small and difficult to estimate. For 1988 and 1989 the figure was reported to be around US$600 million (Moore, 1990: 84), for a cumulative total of US$1.3 billion since 1987 (Baum, 1990: 29). Recent sources (Cheng, 1992; Kraar, 1992; Lampton et al., 1992; Lee, 1991) report that between 2,500 and 4,000 Taiwan companies invested around US$3 billion in China during 1986–1991 through third-party channels, with US$1.2 billion in 1991 alone. The heavy concentration of Hong Kong and Taiwan investments in Guangdong and Fujian reflects the growing spatial and economic integration within the GSCER, especially in the second half of the 1980s.

THE NODES OF INVESTMENT FLOWS IN THE GSCER

The growing economic integration of Southern China, Hong Kong, and Taiwan is anchored on several key nodes, which are defined as centers that send or absorb investment flows and serve as major production sites and service links in the GSCER. These nodes are arrayed at three levels. The dominating node in the GSCER, Hong Kong transmits a huge volume of goods to and from China and sends heavy capital flows into Guangdong and Fujian.

Shenzhen, which borders Hong Kong (see Map 8.1), is a single second-tier node in the GSCER. During 1979–1985 Hong Kong and Macao, predominantly the former, accounted for 98 percent of the DFI cases and 88 percent of the contracted capital in Shenzhen (see Table 8.2). Period data for 1979–1990 show that the figures dropped to 93 percent and 76 percent, respectively (SZYBEC, 1991: 141). In 1989, when annual official reporting of Taiwan investment in Shenzhen began, Taiwan emerged as the second largest investor behind Hong Kong in DFI cases, even though its average case was less capitalized than Hong Kong, Japan, and the United States. In 1990 Taiwan was ahead of Japan and the United States in cases of investment, amount of capital contracted, and average capital intensity (which also surpassed Hong Kong and Macao). During 1979–1990 Taiwan contributed 78 investment cases and US$72.3 million in capital to Shenzhen (SZYBEC, 1991: 141). Thus 90 percent of Taiwan's cumulative investment cases and 81 percent of its total capital in Shenzhen in the 1980s were committed in 1989 and 1990.

There are three third-tier nodes: Guangzhou, Xiamen, and Fuzhou. Guangzhou, Guangdong's capital and one of the fourteen open cities named in 1984, has been the largest southern Chinese city in population, industrial output, and overseas trade. Xiamen, one of the four SEZs created in 1979–1980, has long been an important port city across the water from Taiwan. Fuzhou, Fujian's capital and one of the fourteen open cities, is Fujian's largest industrial center and a major seaport for foreign trade (see Map 8-1 for the locations of the three cities).

Table 8.3 cross-classifies the selected locations and industries for Taiwan investment in China for 1991. (Earlier data are not available.) The four key nodes on mainland China together accounted for 45.3 percent of the investment cases and 43.6 percent of the contracted capital. Guangdong and Fujian combined received 67.1 and 58.2 percent of the investment cases and capital. Although

Table 8.2
Direct Foreign Investment (DFI) in Shenzhen by Nationality, 1979–1985, 1989, and 1990

Country	1979–85			1989			1990		
	(1) DFI Case	(2) DFI[a] Volume	(3) (2)÷(1)	(1) DFI Case	(2) DFI Volume	(3) (2)÷(1)	(1) DFI Case	(2) DFI Volume	(3) (2)÷(1)
Hong Kong, Macao	3,435	2,075.8	0.6	630	402.1	0.6	699	547.3	0.8
Taiwan	--	--	--	25	9.9	0.4	45	48.4	1.1
Japan	24	40.8	1.7	16	11.3	0.7	12	10.6	0.9
United States	18	74.6	4.1	16	22.9	1.4	16	12.5	0.8
United Kingdom	3	15.2	5.1	--	--	--	2	7.8	3.9
France	--	--	--	9	2.5	0.3	1	0.1	0.1
Australia	5	25.5	5.1	2	0.5	0.2	2	5.5	2.8
Singapore	13	64.6	5.0	2	3.3	1.6	5	31.3	6.3
Malaysia	--	--	--	--	--	--	1	0.2	0.2
Thailand	2	22.3	11.2	1	25.9	25.9	2	10.9	5.5
Philippines	1	0.5	0.5	2	1.2	0.6	1	0.1	0.1
Indonesia	1	0.4	0.4	--	--	--	1	0.2	0.2

Sources: SSB (1991d 284-94), SZYBEC (1986, 53).

Note: a. In US$ millions.

Table 8.3
Taiwan's Capital Investment in China via Third Parties, by Selected Location and Industry, 1991

Industry	Shenzhen (1[a]) (2[b])		Guangzhou (1) (2)		Xiamen (1) (2)		Fuzhou (1) (2)		Guangdong[c] (1) (2)		Fujian[c] (1) (2)		Shanghai (1) (2)		Beijing (1) (2)		Others[d] (1) (2)	
Electronic and electric appliances	11	13.3	3	3.2	8	4.3	1	0.1	4	0.7	3	0.8	4	6.6	--	--	8	2.6
Textiles	--	--	--	--	1	5.0	--	--	1	0.3	--	--	1	5.3	--	--	1	2.7
Garments and footwear	1	0.1	1	0.8	2	0.6	7	5.9	2	0.4	4	2.5	2	1.4	--	--	7	1.6
Leather and fur products	--	--	1	0.2	--	--	--	--	2	1.5	--	--	--	--	--	--	3	0.5
Food and beverage processing	1	0.2	--	--	1	0.2	1	1.8	2	1.8	3	1.8	1	2.7	3	6.0	7	4.9
Plastic and rubber products	15	12.9	7	2.5	4	3.9	3	1.7	12	7.4	3	1.4	4	2.8	--	--	10	21.9
Pulp paper and products	1	1.0	--	--	--	--	--	--	2	0.6	--	--	--	--	--	--	2	0.8
Timber and bamboo products	2	0.6	--	--	1	2.1	1	0.1	1	0.8	3	0.2	2	1.3	--	--	5	1.1
Non-metallic minerals	1	1.4	1	0.5	1	0.2	--	--	3	2.2	1	0.06	2	0.6	--	--	3	0.7
Basic metals and metal products	6	6.8	1	0.1	1	0.02	--	--	2	0.7	--	--	1	0.03	--	--	3	2.0
Chemicals	1	0.3	--	--	1	0.07	1	0.5	1	0.2	--	--	1	0.7	--	--	4	1.3
Total	39	36.6	29	7.3	20	16.4	14	10.1	32	16.6	17	6.8	18	21.4	3	6.0	53	40.1
(2) ÷ (1)	0.9		0.3		0.8		0.7		0.5		0.4		1.2		2.0		0.8	

Source: MOEA (1991, 65–66).

Notes: a. DFI cases.
b. DFI volume in US$ millions.
c. Locations in Guangdong and Fujian other than Shenzhen, Guangzhou, Xiamen, and Fuzhou.
d. Areas other than those identified.

Shenzhen and Guangzhou had more investment cases than Xiamen and Fuzhou in 1991, the two Fujian cities have emerged as favored sites for Taiwan investment. Before 1988 Xiamen's largest overseas investor was Hong Kong. In 1988 Taiwan provided 53 percent of the DFI in Xiamen, outinvesting Hong Kong in that year. As of October 1991, Taiwan investment accounted for 42.4 percent of Xiamen's DFI cases and 42.1 percent of its contracted capital (*Tegu yu Kaifang Chengshi Jingji*, 1992). The evidence suggests that Taiwan is surpassing Hong Kong as the largest overseas investor in Xiamen. By May 1990 Fuzhou set up over 100 projects involving Taiwan capital, trailing behind only Xiamen and Shenzhen (Silk, 1990).

Table 8.3 also shows that Taiwan investment in Guangdong and Fujian is oriented toward labor-intensive industries. Plastic and rubber products, electronic and electric appliances, and garments and footwear ranked one, two, and three in investment cases and contracted capital. Taiwan investment in plastic and rubber products is heavily concentrated in Guangdong, especially Shenzhen and Guangzhou, while the garments and footwear industries in Fujian, especially Fuzhou, absorbed more Taiwan investment than their counterparts in Guangdong. The labor-intensive feature of Taiwan investment in Southern China is further revealed by the greater capital intensity of Taiwan's investment projects in Shanghai, Beijing, and other locations outside Guangdong and Fujian. The labor-intensive investments of Hong Kong and Taiwan in Guangdong and Fujian reflect a new spatial division of labor and the formation of commodity chains, which link together the economies within the GSCER and between the region and the global economy.

THE DIVISION OF LABOR AND COMMODITY CHAINS

Each commodity chain consists of flows between the nodes, the relations of production, the dominant organization of production, and the geographical loci of the operation in question (Hopkins and Wallerstein, 1986: 162). Gereffi and Korzeniewicz (1990: 50–51) emphasize the importance of including both forward and backward links from the production stage in defining a commodity chain. Their empirical study of the global footwear industry focused on four major segments: raw material supply, production, exporting, and marketing and retailing. Within this framework, I conduct a limited commodity chain analysis of the links between the raw material supply, production, and marketing of athletic shoes in the GSCER.

Fujian is known for its long history and good skills in making shoes. In 1986 the shoe industry accounted for 2.9 percent of Fujian's total industrial output and 10.8 percent of its exports. In recent years the city of Putian, located between Xiamen and Fuzhou (see Map 8.1), has become China's major production site for athletic shoes. It has more than forty factories that employ over 60,000 workers. Fujian is capable of making 7 million pairs of athletic shoes annually, over one-third of which are exported, earning US$10 million in foreign exchange

Figure 8.3
The Formation of an Athletic Shoe Commodity Chain in the GSCER and Beyond

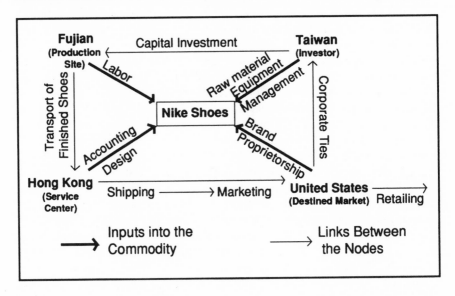

(Zhang, 1988). Although shoemaking has been one of Taiwan's major export industries, it has recently been squeezed, together with other labor-intensive industries, by rising labor costs, domestic industrial upgrading, and external competition. To find a way out, an estimated 80 percent of the shoemakers in Taiwan have moved all or some of their production facilities to nearby mainland locations (Baum, 1991), especially to Fujian (see Table 8.3).

Recently, three China-Taiwan athletic shoe joint ventures, through which Nike Inc. places a lot of orders, moved from their original locations in Beijing and Shanghai to Putian in Fujian. Most of the raw materials come from Taiwan through Hong Kong to Fujian. Nike keeps at each shoe factory several Taiwanese resident managers who have been in the shoe business for years and speak the same local dialect. Nike's Hong Kong staff handles accounting and designs, makes sure the sample and raw materials reach the factories on time, and ships the finished Nike shoes out of China through Hong Kong toward their destined markets, mainly the United States (Chang, 1990; also see M. E. Korzeniewicz, chapter 12 in this volume). Figure 8.3 shows the various inputs from four geographical loci into Nike shoes and the links between the four nodes in the chain. This commodity chain not only spans Taiwan, China (Fujian), and Hong Kong, but stretches out across the Pacific Ocean to the United States.

Similar commodity chains also have taken shape in other labor-intensive industries that link the GSCER to the world and U.S. markets. Toys, for instance, are designed in Hong Kong, assembled in Southern China (often with a Taiwan-made chip for talking dolls), and finally packaged and shipped from Hong Kong to various countries. A Hong Kong trading firm, which used to source entire jogging suits from Taiwan for such U.S. retailers as Woolworth, now has them sewn in Guangdong with velour from Taiwan (Kraar, 1992: 125).

This new division of labor in the GSCER may no longer be confined to typical labor-intensive industries. General Motors, the U.S. automaker, has recently unveiled a long-range plan for including both Taiwan and China in the mutual supply and exchange of components and parts in the Asia-Pacific region. GM's primary objective is to use its cooperative ties with Taiwan to penetrate the mainland market. In the eventual division of labor, Taiwan and China will be engaged in the mutual supply and exchange of components and parts for GM cars and even joint production of whole cars for the United States, Taiwan, China, and other markets. To achieve that long-term goal, GM and its Taiwan partner, Chinese Automobile Co. Ltd., have already established a joint venture in Hong Kong, which has been authorized to sell GM cars to China (IDIC, 1992: 4).

The differential roles of China, Taiwan, and Hong Kong raise the crucial question about the distribution of economic surplus among participants in the commodity chain of a given industry stretching across political and geographical boundaries. Gereffi and Korzeniewicz (1990: 50) contend that core-country firms, with their diverse retail outlets at the service end of the chain, reap the lion's share of economic surplus, while the NIC footwear manufacturers benefit much less by using their comparative advantage of lower labor cost at the production stage. Extending this logic to the division of labor in the GSCER, I argue that Taiwan and Hong Kong as semiperipheral economies secure greater surplus than China as a peripheral manufacturer of labor-intensive goods.

This unequal distribution of surplus is partly a result of the dominant type of Taiwan's production organizations in Fujian. Before 1987, of the nineteen Taiwan-invested firms in Xiamen, joint ventures accounted for 57.9 percent, wholly owned ventures 26.3 percent, and cooperative ventures 15.8 percent. Of the 118 Taiwan-invested firms approved by mid-1989, Taiwan's wholly owned ventures as a share of the total had increased to 73.7 percent (Luo and Chen, 1989: 32). Taiwan investors have preferred wholly owned ventures because the majority of them bring their own raw materials, capital, technology, equipment and finally export the products; the only factor of production they need is cheap mainland labor for assembly and finishing.

Using their established sourcing networks, the Taiwan companies with manufacturing operations in Southern China are able to procure better, albeit somewhat more expensive, raw materials from Taiwan itself or from places like Japan and South Korea, than Chinese companies can.[2] To the extent it is possible and profitable to use cheaper raw materials in China, the Taiwan companies can lower costs further and reap bigger profits at the marketing end of the chain. Relying on well-established and far-reaching export networks, extensive experience with core markets, and "brand loyalty" via huge marketing budgets, Taiwan and Hong Kong companies with products manufactured in China could maximize the markup in selling them through Hong Kong to the overseas buying offices of large chain discount stores (e.g., Kmart) or to wholesalers in the United States (see Gereffi chapter 5 in this volume).

EXPLAINING THE DIVISION OF LABOR IN THE GSCER

World System Dynamics and Comparative Economic Advantages

From a world system perspective, the growing economic integration of Southern China, Hong Kong, and Taiwan is a regional reflection of and response to the global economic transformation. The international division of labor is constantly restructured by the realigned niches of countries as they experience mobility in the global and regional economic systems. The upward movement depends on countries' capacities to initiate and/or react to changing comparative advantages. The industrial flexibility of Japan, South Korea, and Taiwan, coupled with their relative state autonomy (central coordination, bureaucratic planning), propelled the three countries to climb the economic hierarchy in a global and East Asian context (Cumings, 1984).

As Japan moved into the core, and the East Asian NICs into the semiperiphery, they began to shift labor-intensive industries down to such labor-surplus, low-wage countries as China, Indonesia, Thailand, and Malaysia. For Taiwan specifically, the end of the 1980s brought about worsening labor shortages and rising labor costs. Taiwan's labor force shrank slightly in 1990 for the first time, while the labor force participation rate dropped to 58.2 percent, the lowest in five years. Meanwhile, pay raises averaged 12.2 percent annually during 1987–1990, faster than productivity gains of 8.3 percent a year (Baum, 1991).

To respond to these problems, Taiwan reoriented its overseas investment. In 1986 only 13.5 percent of Taiwan's overseas investment went to the ASEAN countries (minus Singapore), while the figure for 1991 soared to 41.7 percent. The estimated US$3 billion Taiwan investment in China during 1986–1991 amounted to about one-third of Taiwan's total overseas investment in that period (MOEA, 1991). High labor costs in Hong Kong, which are at least five times as much as labor costs in Shenzhen (already the highest in Guangdong) and nine times the average wage rate in the rest of the province, coupled with a service-oriented economy (see Table 8.1), have been pushing Hong Kong's labor-intensive manufacturing industries into Southern China. It is estimated that Hong Kong companies now control at least two-thirds of the approximately 25,000 factories with overseas capital that have been created in Guangdong since 1978, employing more than 2 million workers; the figure doubles to 3 or 4 million if jobs generated indirectly by Hong Kong investment are included. In the meantime, manufacturing employment in Hong Kong dropped from a peak of 990,000 in 1981 to 849,000 in 1985, and declined further to 654,662 in September of 1991. Ten years ago, Hong Kong had 3,200 toy factories; today 97 percent of such manufacturing takes place across the border (ADB, 1985: 147; *The Economist*, 1991: 21; Kraar, 1992: 125; Lu and Zheng, 1990: 48; Shapiro, 1992: 79–80).

Although the world-system and comparative-advantage explanations are powerful, they fail to account for why Hong Kong and Taiwan did not make labor-intensive manufacturing investment in China throughout the 1970s, when Hong Kong was already moving toward a service-oriented economy and Taiwan was beginning to upgrade its industrial structure to greater capital intensity and technological complexity. The timing of economic integration among Southern China, Hong Kong, and Taiwan warrants a state-centered political explanation.

Political Shift and State Policy

It is no coincidence that Hong Kong's trade with and investment in China picked up considerably from the late 1970s, when China opened up its southern border. Since the late 1970s, China's political stance toward Hong Kong, through the negotiation and signing of the Sino-British accord, has continued to influence Hong Kong's confidence and behavior in economic cooperation with China.

From 1986 on, a series of policy moves helped ease and warm up China-Taiwan relations. The formation of the Democratic Progressive Party (DPP) in September 1986 marked the beginning of accelerating democratization in Taiwan. In November 1987 the Red Cross Society in Taiwan began processing applications for mainland visits. In July 1988 the State Council of China promulgated provisions to promote economic and technological exchange with Taiwan. In May 1989 Taiwan's vice-premier recommended that Taiwan companies be allowed to set up branches in Hong Kong to trade with China, legitimizing what was already happening (Seymour, 1989). In January 1991 the Strait Exchange Foundation (SEF) in Taiwan—a formally private but semiofficial institution—began operation. It is no surprise that these reciprocal policy measures played an important role in facilitating indirect trade between China and Taiwan and the latter's investment in the former (also see Jia, 1992).

To explain the spatial concentration of Hong Kong and Taiwan investment in specific cities in Fujian and Guangdong, we need to go beyond the broad political and ideological shifts to identify the effect of location-specific policies. In the late 1970s both Guangdong and Fujian provinces were granted the status of reform experimental regions, and with it, considerable local autonomy in economic development and foreign trade. In 1988 Shenzhen and Xiamen were given provincial authority in economic planning. In August 1988 Xiamen issued preferential policies for Taiwan investors, including the exemption of corporate tax for the first four years and half the normal rate for the next five years (if industrial and agricultural projects have a contract life exceeding 10 years). In January 1989 Fuzhou announced special preferences for Taiwan in investment. In 1990 Guangzhou, Shantou, and Zhuhai (see Map 8.1) followed suit by offering competing favorable treatments to Taiwan investors (Silk, 1990: 36–37). These location-specific policies contributed to the sharp rise in Taiwan investment in Shenzhen, Xiamen, and other major cities of Guangdong and Fujian during 1988–1991.

While China's open policy created a favorable macro atmosphere for Hong Kong and Taiwan investments, it is not sufficient to narrow the fundamental difference between Hong Kong and Taiwan's capitalist and China's state socialist economies. The location-specific financial incentives helped improve the local investment environments in China, but they cannot fully account for the fact that Hong Kong and Taiwan investments have diffused beyond the several major locations (favored by differential policies) to other cities in Guangdong and Fujian.[3]

Sociocultural Similarity, Kinship Ties, and Regional Identity

Guangdong province has had a very close historical and sociocultural connection with Hong Kong through shared kinship ties, regional identity, and local dialects. While some Shanghai industrialists emigrated to Hong Kong in the late 1940s, the total number of Shanghainese in Hong Kong was estimated to be only 4 percent. The majority of Hong Kong Chinese trace their origins to various parts of Guangdong province. A large minority (11 percent) of the Hong Kong population have ancestral roots in the Chaozhou and Shantou region (Wong, 1988: 6, 179), while a smaller percentage emigrated from Meixian (Meizhou now) in northeastern Guangdong (see Map 8.1). Despite their regional variations, Hong Kong remains predominantly and essentially Cantonese (Vogel, 1989).

Taiwan's sociocultural, kinship, and regional ties with Guangdong and Fujian, especially the latter, are longstanding, extensive, and deep-rooted. Historically, ambitious Taiwanese families that had emigrated to the island from Fujian sent members back across the Strait to such cities as Xiamen and Fuzhou to study or facilitate family business (Greenhalgh, 1984). China estimated that 70 percent of the population in Taiwan have ancestral and kinship ties with southern Fujian (Song and Gao, 1990: 28), where the open triangle is situated (see Map 8.1). About 800,000 people in Hong Kong and Macao also have kinship ties to Fujian (Wang, 1990: 47).

The role of kinship ties in facilitating Hong Kong and Taiwan investments in South China lends supporting evidence to Granovetter's embeddedness argument, which stresses the role of concrete personal relations or networks of such relations in generating trust in economic transactions (1985: 490). Smart and Smart (1991: 226) suggest that an investment from a Hong Kong entrepreneur can be made to reactivate his or her social connections in China. The kinship and friendship relations of a Hong Kong investor are social connections and resources that he or she can use to participate in a relationship of gift exchange, thus gaining introductions to local officials and circumventing bureaucratic red tape. The effect of kinship ties is reinforced by regional or local affiliation. Overseas Chinese businessmen in Hong Kong, Taiwan, and the Southeast Asian countries tend to invest in their place of ancestry or birth (see McGregor, 1992). One survey found that up to 70 percent of foreign-owned enterprises in the Pearl River Delta region (see Map 8.1) were either directly set up by overseas Chinese or with their help (Xu and Li, 1990: 61). In Guangdong and Fujian provinces, the Cantonese, Chaozhou, and *Minnan* (southern Fujian) subcultures further strengthen the role of kinship ties and same-place identity in inducing Hong Kong and Taiwan investments.

While a sociocultural perspective offers great insight into the process and concentration of Hong Kong and Taiwan investments in Guangdong and Fujian, the sociocultural and kinship ties, which had been a historical constant, began to exert their overdue effect only in the context of China's economic and political openness in the 1980s. The interaction between the political and sociocultural factors becomes more apparent in conjunction with the complementary explanation of geographical proximity.

Geographical Proximity and Locational Advantages

Hong Kong sits on Guangdong's border, while Fujian is the closest mainland province to Taiwan. The short physical distance is "shortened" further by the closely integrated and increasingly open border between Hong Kong and Shenzhen, which approximates what Herzog calls the transfrontier metropolis. This phenomenon of an international spatial division of labor, exemplified by the *maquiladora* industrialization program along the U.S.–Mexico border region, owes its formation to the frequent movement of population, industry, and capital across the previously guarded yet increasingly permeable territorial boundaries of nation-states (Herzog, 1991: 519–22). Hong Kong businessmen now commute freely across the border to supervise production in Shenzhen and the other Guangdong cities in the Pearl River Delta daily or weekly (Lee, 1991). A new superhighway between Hong Kong and Guangzhou, scheduled to be completed in 1993, will cut road travel time from four hours to slightly more than one. This will further speed up and cement the economic and spatial integration between Hong Kong and the Pearl River Delta.

Fujian has a less favorable geographical position. It is not only farther away from the main entry point of Hong Kong, but cannot use its ports for direct shipping across the 100-mile-wide Taiwan Strait. Fujian's less developed rail and road networks also make it difficult for Hong Kong and Taiwan investors to access its mountainous locations away from the coast. Nevertheless, Taiwan investors have begun to pursue large-scale land development for manufacturing and commercial purposes between the key coastal nodes of Fuzhou and Xiamen. Until the transportation system is improved further and direct shipping between Taiwan and Fujian occurs, Hong Kong and Taiwan investors will continue to favor the coastal cities, especially those close to Hong Kong. Highlighting the effects of distance and transportation is not intended to minimize other complementary explanations. They coalesce in a temporal conjuncture in explaining the emergence of a new division of labor in the GSCER with strong implications for the region and beyond.

IMPLICATIONS OF SPATIAL AND ECONOMIC INTEGRATION IN THE GSCER

The major implications of economic integration in the GSCER stem from the basic fact that two coastal provinces of socialist China are intimately tied with Hong Kong and Taiwan into the global system of contemporary capitalism through a new spatial division of labor. These implications are identified and examined briefly at different levels.

At the global level, although the GSCER remains an informal and uncoordinated economic bloc, its collective external impact and evolving internal ties strongly affect the world economy and some core countries. China's trade surplus with the United States, for example, grew rapidly from US$3 billion in 1988 to US$13 billion in 1991. Much of this increase was accounted for by China's exports of shoes and toys to the United States made by Taiwan and Hong Kong–invested factories on the mainland (Lampton et al., 1992: 6). Taiwan's shoe exports to the United States in 1990, for example, dropped 23.2 percent, while China's shoe exports to the United States rose 105.0 percent (Cheng, 1992). Given the increasing economic interdependence of the GSCER, the United States will find it impossible to apply economic or political sanctions against China (e.g., withdrawal of most-favored-nation status) without affecting the economic interests of Hong Kong and Taiwan (Lampton et al., 1992).

At the regional level, the spatial integration between Hong Kong and Guangdong, especially Shenzhen and its surrounding region, may lead to the eventual annexation of Shenzhen by what will be the Hong Kong Special Administrative Region in 1997. Ironically, this will mean that Hong Kong must shift resources to support the vast, less developed hinterland, thus becoming a "captive city" even before 1997 (MacPherson, 1991). The establishment of direct trade and investment between Taiwan and China, which may only be a matter of time, may diminish Hong Kong's role as a crucial and profitable nexus for shipping, tourism, and even banking (see Broadfoot, 1990). Given Hong Kong's strengths in international banking (chief financier and guarantor for many DFI projects in China), location (contiguous with Guangdong), and prospective political status (the 1997 return to China), however, it is unlikely that Taiwan will displace Hong Kong as the main commercial-industrial link to China. Assuming that direct trade and investment may create new areas and forms of cooperation, we may even see more complementary roles for Taiwan and Hong Kong in the development of the GSCER.

Although Taiwan will benefit from a more direct economic relationship with China, it faces several challenges and dilemmas in dealing with China. Dependence on trade with China and its cheap raw materials could subject Taiwan to the political will of the mainland government trying to push the "one country, two systems" plan for reunification. Continued heavy flows of industrial capital from Taiwan to China may lead to deindustrialization in some of the island's manufacturing sectors. Taiwan's massive manufacturing investment in China is making the mainland a new competitor for the island's traditional exports.

Within China, the most favorable economic policies granted to Guangdong and Fujian provinces, especially to their SEZs, through the 1980s and their effect on rapid growth in Southern China have created some economic gaps and policy conflicts with the northern portions of the coastal region. A recent study (Lampton et al., 1992) found that people outside of Guangdong and Fujian want to extend the "exclusive" relationship between Hong Kong and Guangdong on the one hand, and between Taiwan and Fujian on the other, to a much larger portion of China. The central government has intervened to redress the regional and local imbalances. In 1990 the central government unveiled a grand plan for developing Pudong near Shanghai. This plan was intended to shift the policy focus away from the favored south to the central and northern parts of China. Deng Xiaoping's visit to Guangdong in early 1992 suggested that the central government not only would continue its favorable policy toward Southern China, but may promote the region as a model for the rest of the nation. The interventions from the center may reshape the already differentiated regional interests in ways that will generate more regional competition and conflict and weaken the central government. The multiple effects of Southern China's economic integration with Hong Kong and Taiwan on China's internal political and economic development constitute a significant research agenda beyond the scope of this chapter.

This study concludes that although systematic political and economic differences prevent the GSCER from becoming an organized trading bloc, it has developed a "natural" division of labor among its three separate economies in the global production system. Generalizing from this case to its implications for commodity chains research, I advance two broad propositions. First, the formation of commodity chains in a regional division of labor requires that different parts of the region contribute complementary elements of the chain, that is, raw materials, readily available capital, abundant and low-cost labor, nodes with good transport facilities, and marketing networks. Social resources (shared culture or subculture, kinship ties, common language, same-place identity) also play a crucial role in shaping regional economic networks and commodity chains. The emergent "triangle" of Singapore, Malaysia, and Indonesia (see Parsonage, 1992) and the new triangular economic ties among the United States, Canada, and Mexico through NAFTA are cases for future comparative study. Second, commodity chains are no longer formed only across the geographical boundaries of capitalist and market-oriented economies. The deeper insertion of China and the former socialist states in Eastern Europe means that commodity chains will increasingly stretch over and through ideological barriers and political boundaries. Future research should address broader and more varied propositions about how the complex interaction among economic, political, sociocultural, and spatial factors is shaping the size, type, and geographical location of commodity chains in global and regional economic networks.

NOTES

This research was supported in part by a grant from the Campus Research Board of the University of Illinois at Chicago. I am grateful to Gary Gereffi, Xiaoyan Hua, Miguel Korzeniewicz, James Norr, William Parish, David Rubinstein, Mildred Shwartz, and Ezra Vogel for their comments and suggestions on an earlier draft. Many thanks are due to Raymond Brod for his skilled production of the maps and to Mr. Ming Chang in the Commercial Division of the Chicago Office of the Coordinating Council for North American Affairs of Taiwan (Republic of China) for supplying some of the most recent data.

1. Investment flows from Hong Kong and Macao have been lumped together in China's official statistics. But Macao accounts for an extremely insignificant share of the sum of the two, less than 4 percent in 1992.

2. Interview with a Chinese national who is involved in buying toys and other products made by Taiwan– or South Korea–China joint-venture factories in China to sell them to the U.S. wholesalers, April 1992.

3. As an indicator of this spatial diffusion, the share of DFI in Guangdong and Fujian accounted for by the four key nodes (Table 8.3) declined from 64 percent in 1987 to 51 percent in 1990 (SSB, 1988: 440, 443; 1991b: 509, 512).

REFERENCES

ADB (Asian Development Bank). 1985. *Key Indicators of Developing Member Countries of ADB*. London: Macmillan Reference Books.

Baum, Julian. 1990. "The Mainland Dilemma." *Far Eastern Economic Review* (Oct. 18):29–36.

———. 1991. "Taiwan's Building Block." *Far Eastern Economic Review* (May 2):36–37.

Broadfoot, Robert. 1990. "The Impact of PRC-Taiwan Ties on Hong Kong." *The China Business Review* (Sept.-Oct.):38.

Chang, David. 1990. "Speaking the Same Language." *The China Business Review* (Sept.-Oct.):39.

Chen, Xiangming. 1991. "China's City Hierarchy, Urban Policy and Spatial Development in the 1980s." *Urban Studies* 28 (June):341–67.

———. 1993. "China's Growing Integration with the Asia-Pacific Economy: Subregional and Local Dimensions, Determinants, and Consequences." In *What Is in a Rim? Critical Perspectives on the Pacific Region Idea*, edited by Arif Dirlik, chapter 6. Boulder, CO: Westview Press.

Cheng, Chu-yuan. 1992. "Liangan Jingmao Guanxi de Jingji Xiaoguo" (The Economic Effects of Trade Across the Strait). *Jingji Ribao* (Economics Daily), June 13.

Cumings, Bruce. 1984. "The Origins and Development of the Northeast Asian Political Economy: Industrial Sectors, Product Cycles, and Political Consequences." *International Organization* 38 (1):1–40.

The Economist. 1991. "Asia: As Close As Teeth and Lips." August 10, pp. 21–22.

————. 1992. "Taiwan: China's Snare." (January 4):30–31.

Gereffi, Gary. 1990. "Path of Industrialization: An Overview." In *Manufacturing Miracles: Path of Industrialization in Latin America and East Asia*; edited by Gary Gereffi and Donald L. Wyman, pp. 1–31. Princeton, NJ: Princeton University Press.

Gereffi, Gary and Korzeniewicz, Miguel. 1990. "Commodity Chains and Footwear Exports in the Semiperiphery." In *Semiperipheral States in the World Economy*, edited by William G. Martin, pp. 45–68. Westport, CT: Greenwood Press.

Granovetter, Mark. 1985. "Economic Action and Social Structure: The Problem of Embeddedness." *American Journal of Sociology* 91 (Nov.):481–510.

Greenhalgh, Susan. 1984. "Networks and Their Nodes: Urban Society on Taiwan." *The China Quarterly* 99 (Sept.):529–52.

Herzog, Lawrence A. 1991. "Cross-national Urban Structure in the Era of Global Cities: The US-Mexico Transfrontier Metropolis." *Urban Studies* 28 (Aug.):519–33.

Hopkins, Terence K., and Wallerstein, Immanuel. 1986. "Commodity Chains in the World Economy Prior to 1800." *Review* 10 (Summer):157–70.

IDIC (Industrial Development & Investment Center). 1992. *Taiwan Industrial Panorama* 20, no. 5 (May), Taipei, Taiwan.

Jia, Qingguo. 1992. "Changing Relations Across the Taiwan Strait." *Asian Survey* 32 (March): 277–89.

Kraar, Louis. 1992. "A New China without Borders." *Fortune*, October 5, pp. 124–28.

Lampton, David M., et al. 1992. *The Emergence of "Greater China."* A report on a project of the National Committee on U.S.-China Relations, Inc. New York.

Lardy, Nicholas R. 1987. *China's Entry into the World Economy*. Lanham, MD: University Press of America.

Lee, Dinah. 1991. "Asia: The Next Era of Growth." *Business Week*, November 11, pp. 56–59.

Lu, Chaoming and Zheng, Tianxiang. 1990. "Yianhai Fazhan Zhanlue Xingjianyi" (New Proposals for the Coastal Development Strategy). *Tequ yu Kaifang Chengshi Jingji* (Special Zone and Open City Economy) 5:45–48.

Luo, Hui, and Chen, Ming. 1989. "Qiantan Xiamen Tequ Yinjin Taizi de Tezheng yu Qianjing" (A Preliminary Analysis of the Characteristics and Prospect of Taiwan's Capital Investment in Xiamen). *Tequ yu Kaifang Chengshi Jingji* (Special Zone and Open City Economy) 10:31–34.

MacPherson, Kerrie L. 1991. "Hong Kong: A Captive City?" *Asian Outlook* 26 (May-June):13–17.

Maruya, Toyojiro. 1992. "The Development of the Guangdong Economy and Its Ties with Beijing." *China Newsletter* (JETRO) 96 (Jan.-Feb.): 2–14.

McGregor, James. 1992. "Overseas Chinese Quietly Invest at Home." *The Wall Street Journal*, June 16, p. A6.

MOEA (Ministry of Economic Affairs). 1991. *Statistics on Outward Investment*, December, Taipei, Taiwan.

Moore, Jonathan. 1990. "The Upstart Taipans." *Far Eastern Economic Review*, April 19, pp. 84–86.

Parsonage, James. 1992. "Southeast Asia's 'Growth Triangle': A Subregional Response to Global Transformation." *International Journal of Urban and Regional Research* 16 (June): 307–17.

Seymour, James D. 1989. "Taiwan in 1988: No More Bandits." *Asian Survey* 29 (Jan.): 54–63.

Shapiro, Fred C. 1992. "Letter from Hong Kong." *The New Yorker* 68 (June 29): 74–82.

Silk, Mitchell A. 1990. "Silent Partners." *The China Business Review*, September-October, pp. 32–40.

Smart, Josephine, and Smart, Alan. 1991. "Personal Relations and Divergent Economies: A Case Study of Hong Kong Investment in South China." *International Journal of Urban and Regional Research* 15 (June): 216–33.

Song, Yu, and Gao, Shengyu. 1990. "Renshi Xiamen Tequ" (Understanding the Xiamen SEZ). *Tequ yu Kaifang Chengshi Jingji* (Special Zone and Open City Economy) 8:27–28.

SSB (State Statistical Bureau). 1981, 1986, 1990a. *Zhongguo Tongji Nianjian* (China Statistical Yearbook). Beijing: China Statistical Press.

———. 1987a, 1991a. *Fujian Tongji Nianjian* (Fujian Statistical Yearbook) Beijing: China Statistical Press.

———. 1987b. *Guangdong Tongji Nianjian* (Guangdong Statistical Yearbook). Beijing: China Statistical Press.

———. 1988, 1991b. *Zhongguo Chengshi Tongji Nianjian* (China Urban Statistical Yearbook). Beijing: China Statistical Press.

———. 1991c. *Zhongguo Tongji Zhaiyao* (China Statistical Abstract). Beijing: China Statistical Press.

———. 1991d. *Shenzhen Tongji Nianjian* (Shenzhen Statistical Yearbook). Beijing: China Statistical Press.

SZYBEC (Shenzhen Yearbook Editorial Committee). 1986, 1991. *Shenzhen Jingji Tequ Nianjian* (Shenzhen Special Economic Zone Yearbook). Hong Kong: Hong Kong Economic Herald Press.

Taira, Kimiaki. 1988. "Hong Kong—Ever Entrepôt." *China Newsletter*, Japan Export Trading Corporation (JETRO) 77 (Nov.-Dec.):1.

Tequ yu Kaifang Chengshi Jingji. 1992. "Taishang Chengwei Xiamen Jingji Tequ Fazhan de Zhongyao Liliang" (Taiwan Businesses Have Become an Important Force in Xiamen's Economic Development) 2:41.

Vogel, Ezra F. 1989. *One Step Ahead in China: Guangdong Under Reform.* Cambridge, MA: Harvard University Press.

Wang, Zhaoguo. 1990. "Fahui Huaqiao Youshi Fanrong Fujian Jingji" (Making the Fujian Economy Prosperous with the Overseas Chinese Advantage). *Tequ yu Kaifang Chengshi Jingji* (Special Zone and Open City Economy) 10:47–48.

Wong, Siu-lun. 1988. *Emigrant Entrepreneurs: Shanghai Industrialists in Hong Kong.* Hong Kong: Oxford University Press.

Wu, Si. 1991. "Yianhai Zhongguo de Jingji Qifei" (The Economic Take-off of the "Coastal China"). *Tequ yu Kaifang Chengshi Jingji* (Special Zone and Open City Economy) 8:24–29.

Xu, Xue-qiang, and Li, Si-ming. 1990. "China's Open Door Policy and Urbanization in the Pearl River Delta Region." *International Journal of Urban and Regional Research* 4 (March): 49–69.

Zhang, Li. 1988. "Jiaqiang Min-Tai Jingji Hezuo Cujin Xiangzhen Gongyie Fazhan" (Strengthening Fujian-Taiwan Economic Cooperation and Facilitating the Development of Township Industries). *Tequ yu Kaifang Chengshi Jingji* (Special Zone and Open City Economy) 3:58–62.

9

Commodity Chains and Industrial Restructuring in the Pacific Rim: Garment Trade and Manufacturing

Richard P. Appelbaum, David Smith, and Brad Christerson

INTRODUCTION: COMMODITY CHAINS AND EXPORT NETWORKS IN THE GLOBAL ECONOMY

In today's manufacturing system, production is dispersed across the globe. Particularly noteworthy is the rapid expansion of industrial exports from Third World countries, especially the NICs of East Asia and Latin America. These changes call for a reformulation of development theory. Contrary to the arguments of the early neo-Marxist dependency theorists, it is clearly no longer true that all developing countries export low-priced primary goods to core countries in an "unequal exchange" for more costly manufactured goods. But while industrialization has become prevalent throughout the Third World, it has had differential impacts on development—leading to "economic miracles" in some countries and low-wage labor exploitation and continued poverty in others. Simplistic notions from neoclassical economics and modernization theory depicting the rise of manufacturing as an unproblematic stage of economic "takeoff" must also be rejected.

Instead, we must look at both the nature of manufacturing activities and the specific linkages that connect industries to global markets and transnational corporations. While some peripheral countries are primarily "export platforms" for simple, low-technology, labor-intensive goods made by low-wage unskilled workers, industrial upgrading in many of the NICs has led to a shift from commodities like textiles, apparel, and footwear to "higher-value-added items that employ sophisticated technology and require a more extensively developed, tightly integrated local industrial base'' (Gereffi, 1992: 92) such as computers, semiconductors, numerically controlled machine tools, VCRs, televisions, and sporting goods. Gereffi notes that this pattern does not simply reflect new products, but involves the continuous upgrading of new production processes for old ones.

This understanding of an increasingly integrated global economy where countries come to occupy distinct export niches and where industrial upgrading is a key strategy, leads Gereffi to argue that global ''commodity chains'' should be the central object of analysis. This idea, which in many ways parallels the ''value chain'' of economist Michael Porter (1990a and 1990b) or the ''production chain'' of geographer Peter Dicken (1992), draws on Hopkins and Wallerstein's (1986: 159) definition of the commodity chain as ''a network of labor and production processes whose end result is a finished commodity.'' Gereffi and Korzeniewicz (1990) conceptualize these chains as consisting of a number of ''nodes'' that comprise the pivotal points in the production process: extraction and supply of raw materials, the stage(s) of industrial production, export, and marketing. Each node is itself a network connected to other nodes concerned with related activities; local, regional, national, and world economies are seen as ever more intricate web-like structures of these chains.

One key insight of Gereffi's framework is the possibility that these nodes, rather than national economies, are the locus where surplus or profits accrue; another is the emphasis on marketing as a critical link. In fact, in low-cost production (as in the footwear or garment industries), the principal profits are not realized in manufacturing, but rather in marketing, retailing, and design— activities that typically remain in core countries. Essentially, core-controlled firms are extracting ''monopoly rent'' based on their ownership of brand names and trademarks and their expertise in both design and manipulation of consumer tastes through advertising (see M. Korzeniewicz on athletic footwear, chapter 12 in this volume).

Ultimately, global inequality and Third World development and underdevelopment are defined by the positions societies occupy in these multiplex networks of worldwide economic production and exchange. All commodities undergo a sequence of transformation from raw materials to finished products to packaged and marketed goods: their geographic linkages and connections create a spatially bounded structure for the world-economy. Differential profit and surplus are generated at various nodes along these commodity chains. These patterns are not entirely uniform, and the highest profits and the most surplus extraction are not always located at the beginning, middle, or end of the commodity chain, but vary according to particular circumstances and commodities.

According to Porter's (1990b) reasoning, firms that produce for high-value export niches create barriers to entry for competing firms by developing innovative process technologies, offering products of superior quality, and by establishing brand reputations based on cumulative marketing efforts. Their advantages are often location-specific, entailing geographical proximity to research centers, world-class component suppliers, competing firms, and the most sophisticated consumers of their products (which promotes global competitiveness). Conversely, low value or "peripheral" nodes on any commodity chain are comprised of large numbers of competing firms (Wallerstein et al., chapter 2 in this volume). Firms that produce for low-value export niches rely on cost advantages such as cheap labor, raw materials, and economies of scale made possible by machinery and equipment available worldwide. These advantages can be easily replicated by other firms around the globe (Porter, 1990b). The reduction of communication and transportation costs allows firms in these niches to scour the globe for the cheapest mix of labor and materials. Thus low-value "peripheral" nodes tend to be geographically dispersed (Wallerstein et al., chapter 2 in this volume).

In this extension of the Hopkins-Wallerstein-Gereffi-Korzeniewicz argument, "core" activities in the commodity chain are those where the principal profits are realized; core nations (or, more likely, regions within nations) are those where core activities are spatially concentrated in industrial districts (Porter, 1990a, 1990b; Scott, 1988; Piore and Sable, 1984; Storper and Christopherson, 1987). The entire debate about development strategies shifts to encompass regional- (and even firm-) specific efforts at industrial upgrading, thereby allowing these actors to control global marketing channels.

GLOBALIZATION AND THE APPAREL INDUSTRY IN THE POSTWAR PERIOD

The period we have chosen to examine (1978–1987) might be best characterized as a "settling out" of the globalization of the garment industry. The most rapid period of globalization occurred during the 1960s. Between 1963 and 1973, for example, world exports of textiles more than tripled in current dollars, while world exports of apparel grew nearly sixfold. This pattern of growth has continued until the present time, although at a considerably diminished rate. Global textile exports (in current dollars) grew 114 percent between 1973 and 1979, and 60 percent between 1979 and 1987. Similarly, global apparel exports grew 181 percent between 1973 and 1979, and 132 percent between 1979 and 1987 (all figures are from Dickerson, 1991: ch. 6).

During the postwar period, East Asia became a dominant force in the global garment industry (Salaff, 1992; Cheng and Hsiung, 1992; Deyo, 1992). Japan pioneered the shift from Europe to Asia immediately after the war, offering low wages along with high-quality production in the manufacture of textiles, prints, and apparel. By 1963 the roster of the top five global exporters comprised both European and Asian producers, including Italy (15.5 percent), Hong Kong (11.0 percent),[1] Japan (9.6 percent), France (9.1 percent), and West Germany (6.8 percent). Fourteen years later, the Asian shift had become even more pronounced. Although Japan was no longer among the top fifteen exporting nations (having long since completed its shift away from low-wage, low-value-added manufacturing), Hong Kong had become the world's leading apparel exporter (13.1 percent of the world's total), followed by Italy (11.1 percent), South Korea (9.2 percent), West Germany (6.2 percent), and Taiwan (6.1 percent) (Dickerson, 1991: 153).

By 1980 China, Hong Kong, South Korea, Japan, and Taiwan together accounted for nearly a quarter (24 percent) of global textile exports, and 11 percent of imports—the latter in large part to feed their growing apparel export industries (which had reached 29 percent of world apparel exports by 1980). During the next seven years, these five countries strengthened their share in world textile exports (to 31 percent), textile imports (to 17 percent), and apparel exports (to 33 percent). Hong Kong and China together accounted for 14 percent of world textile exports in 1987; Hong Kong had emerged as the world's leading exporter of apparel by the early 1970s, a position it still retains (by 1987 Hong Kong accounted for 13 percent of world apparel exports). During the same period (1980–1987), the United States had emerged as a major market for global apparel exports; the North American share of the world market grew by more than half, from 18 percent in 1980 to 28 percent in 1987 (all figures are from Dickerson, 1991: ch. 6).[2]

In the most recent years there are signs of further change in the international geography of textile and apparel production. While the established industries in the East Asian NICs continued high-volume garment production and experienced absolute export growth in the 1980s, in some other Pacific Rim countries newly created apparel industries increased capacity at a much more rapid rate. China, Thailand, Indonesia, and Malaysia all registered very large growth rates that pushed each nation's clothing export totals far above the half-billion-dollar mark, while some Central American and Caribbean countries went from nominal apparel exports to production for the world market that topped the $100 million mark (Costa Rica, Dominican Republic, Haiti, and Jamaica) (Bonacich and Waller, n.d.: Table 2). By the early 1990s manufacturers in the garment business in the United States, Hong Kong, and South Korea made it clear that such far-flung sites as Vietnam, Guatemala, Burma, North Korea, and Mongolia were either targets of planned investment in export-oriented garment factories or had already gone on-line.

What are the driving forces determining industrial location in the Pacific Rim garment industry—that is, the points at which the garment commodity chain "touches down"? There are several interrelated factors that must be considered.

- Labor costs have remained much lower in East Asia (including the semiperipheral NICs of Hong Kong, Taiwan, Singapore, and South Korea) than in North America or Japan throughout the 1980s, while quality has been high. And the labor costs in China, Southeast Asia, and the Caribbean are but a fraction of wages even in nations like Hong Kong or South Korea, which helps to explain why these areas were the fastest growing.

- Protectionism in core countries, such as the comprehensive international Multifiber

Arrangement (MFA) in 1974 (Moon, 1987: 116–19; for more details see Aggarwal, 1985), has led to the development of a negotiated "quota" system with the major Asian producers, limiting the number of units of particular types of garments that can be imported to the United States each year. While there are some ingenious ways to "get around" these restrictions, they clearly impact exports from the affected countries, and lead to the development of new sources (or new products) elsewhere.

• Industrial flexibility—the ability to quickly produce what buyers demand—has grown rapidly in the postwar period, thanks to technological developments such as "quick response" (just-in-time) delivery systems. Although the highly labor-intensive apparel industry has been resistant to full mechanization (Bonacich and Waller, n.d.: 24), precision equipment and computer-assisted design can help countries with maturing industries retain their competitive edge, particularly in the specialized (and limited-size) market niches for expensive fashion articles. This may account for some of the continued export growth (or, at least, slower decline) of the garment industry in places like South Korea and Taiwan, where wage pressures greatly diminished competitive advantage over the last decade.

DATA AND METHODS

In this chapter we explore the spatial structure of two garment commodity chains, one of high value (wool men's suits) and one of low value (women's synthetic blouses), to explore the determinants of where particular nodes "touch down." We expect that high-value nodes (wool men's suits) on the commodity chain will be spatially concentrated, while low-value nodes (blouses of synthetic fiber) will be spatially dispersed. We further anticipate that producers of high-value finished garments (men's wool suits) will tend to be located in the same countries as globally competitive suppliers (high-quality wool fabric suppliers), while producers of low-value garments—which rely more heavily on cheap labor strategies—will be less likely to locate near fabric suppliers.

We chose men's wool suits and women's synthetic[3] blouses because they represent relatively distant segments of the apparel industry, both in terms of value-added and their degree of responsiveness to changes in fashion. Following Gereffi (1992), we operationalize value-added as the per-unit export value of the final product. Other things being equal, we reason, a more expensive commodity reflects higher-skilled production (as well as greater opportunity for profit-taking) than a less expensive one. By this standard, men's wool suits represent a fairly high degree of value-added production in the global garment industry. In 1987, for example, the average export value of men's wool suits was $145.20. In contrast, women's synthetic blouses averaged only $7.96.[4] Men's wool suits comprise a small but consistently high and growing value-added segment of the apparel market, while women's synthetic blouses typify a rapidly growing segment centered on the production of inexpensive women's wear. The percentage of total world exports of men's wool suits and women's synthetic blouses in 1987, for the leading exporting nations, are presented in Tables 9.1 and 9.2.

We use world trade data obtained from the United Nations to analyze these

Table 9.1
Men's Wool Suits Commodity Chain: Top Exporters, 1987 (Percentage of Total World Exports)

Country	Wool	Fabric	Suits
Australia	58	0	0
New Zealand	18	0	0
Italy	0	41	27
West Germany	0	11	17
United Kingdom	3	14	2
France	3	5	3
South Korea	0	2	7
Yugoslavia	0	0	5

Table 9.2
Women's Synthetic Blouse Commodity Chain: Top Exporters, 1987 (Percentage of Total World Exports)

Country	Fiber	Fabric	Blouses
West Germany	19	11	7
United States	12	3	0
Italy	9	10	3
Japan	8	16	0
South Korea	5	12	10
France	3	5	3
China	0	6	8
Hong Kong	0	3	15
Taiwan[a]	0	3	8

Source: United Nations Statistical Office.

[a]Taiwan values are rough estimates based on cross-references of Taiwanese trade data and U.S. Department of Commerce data.

two commodity chains. The years 1978 and 1987 offered the highest number of reporting countries using the same commodity coding scheme.[5] U.N. trade data provide both value and volume measures of trade flow. Volume, ideally, would be the more consistent measure because it eliminates the inconsistency of value due to fluctuating exchange rates (U.N. data convert the value of the trade flow into U.S. dollars using current exchange rates). However, there is an even greater problem with using volume as the unit of measurement because different countries use different volume measures: some use the actual unit number of garments exported and others use total weight of garments exported. Because these two measures are not compatible, we used value instead of volume for our unit of measurement.

The rapid expansion of world trade between the 1970s and the 1980s renders it impossible to standardize levels of flow for comparison across time, even if the values are transformed into constant dollars by using a price index. We therefore used percentage of total world export value as our unit of measurement. Data on exports from and imports to Taiwan are not available through U.N. sources because the United Nations does not officially recognize Taiwan. Since Taiwan is a principal exporter of garments, this represents a serious difficulty for our analysis. In order to incorporate exports to and from Taiwan, we used Taiwanese sources and U.S. Department of Commerce data. Since export categories did not match the U.N. trade data perfectly, the values of trade to and from Taiwan are estimates.

We use geographic information systems (GIS) to provide visual map representations of bilateral commodity flows. These maps can expose regional trading blocks, spatial concentration and dispersal, and niche specialization. GIS maps have an enormous heuristic value because they visually depict information that can be used to identify trends and generate hypotheses. U.N. trade data used in conjunction with GIS systems can provide a good first-cut approximation of the spatial structure of commodity chains. A network in a GIS is simply a group of lines that connect origins to destinations. In order for trade flows to be represented visually, a network of lines must be created connecting each country with every other country. To simplify this task, we ignored every flow that did not exceed 1 percent of total world exports in each commodity we examined. This limited the number of lines we had to draw to approximately 300. The flows exceeding 1 percent of total world exports, when added together, typically accounted for between 50 percent and 80 percent of total world exports. Different magnitudes of flow can be visually represented by different thicknesses in the lines. Our maps display four different levels of bi-national trade flows for each year: 1.0–2.5 percent of total world exports (in U.S. dollars); 2.5–5.0 percent; 5.0–10.0 percent; and more than 10.0 percent. Arrows were placed along the lines to indicate direction.

MEN'S WOOL SUITS AND WOMEN'S SYNTHETIC BLOUSES

The Men's Wool Suit Commodity Chain

Sheep's Wool Exports

In examining the global trade data for exports of sheep's wool, a number of features stand out. First, Australia—and secondarily New Zealand—account for nearly two-thirds of all exports in this commodity. In 1978 Australia exported 44.1 percent of the world's wool, New Zealand 19.0 percent. By 1987, Australia's global dominance had increased to 58 percent of all wool exports, with New Zealand slipping to 18 percent. Second, Japan strongly dominated Australia's export market. In 1978, 19.4 percent of all global wool exports were from Australia to Japan, a figure that dropped to 15.3 percent by 1987. Since Japan is a major exporter neither of wool textiles nor of men's wool suits, we may conclude that a substantial portion of these imports are either destined for domestic consumption or for use in other woolen export garments. Third, between 1978 and 1987 the Asia trade has expanded to include China, which is the principal new Asian importer of Australian and New Zealand wool. This reflects China's growing role as a low-wage manufacturer of apparel, largely for U.S., Hong Kong, and Taiwanese capital. Fourth, there seems to be a slight trend toward greater diversity of significant bilateral export flows. The roster of major importing countries has expanded to include China (previously noted), Poland, Turkey, and Australia itself (although Greece is no longer included). Finally, Australia and New Zealand clearly export to two major trading blocks, Asia and Europe. In 1987 the former included India, China, South Korea, and Japan; the latter, Italy, France, West Germany, England, Belgium, and Poland. European wool imports reflect an importance of wool textiles and apparel that dates to the (European) industrial revolution; Asian wool imports are of much more recent vintage and indicate the shifting geographical fortunes of this industry.

Wool Fabric

Wool fabric is the intermediate link between woolen fibers and garments. Compared to raw wool exports, trade in wool fabrics is more diversified and more centered on Europe. Apart from a small amount of exports from Japan to the United States (1.1 percent of world total exports in 1978, 1.4 percent in 1987) and from China to Hong Kong (1.7 percent in 1987), virtually all significant wool textile importing and exporting occurred within Europe in both years. Italy is the leading exporter, accounting for roughly 40 percent of the world total in both years. Nearly all wool textile producers in Italy are located in the northern cities of Prato and Biella. Industry associations, joint reasearch facilities, local investments in infrastructure, and proximity to the world's most sophisticated consumers of fashion clothing provide advantages to these producers that cannot be replicated anywhere else on the globe (Porter, 1990b). Britain, which followed Italy at 20.6 percent in 1978, saw its share drop significantly (to 14.1 percent) in 1987. The leading European wool textile importers in 1987 included West Germany, France, Britain, the Netherlands, Austria, Greece, Belgium, and Switzerland; other major wool textile importers included Japan (from Italy), the United States (from Britain, Italy, and Japan), Canada (from Italy), and Hong Kong (from China). European (and Italian) dominance in the production of wool fabrics thus remains uncontested in the global export economy, and there has been no move toward sourcing production in Asia.

Men's Wool Suits

As with woolen textiles, men's wool suit exports center on Europe, with a much smaller secondary source in Asia. In 1978 Asian exports of men's wool suits accounted for only 11.3 percent of the world total, a figure that remained roughly the same (at 11.7 percent) in 1987. At the same time, exports within Europe as well as from Europe to the United States accounted for a large part of global trade in this commodity (see Map 9.1). The United States remained the largest single market over the period under study, growing from 25.6 percent of the world total in 1978 to 32.2 percent in 1987. During the same period, Italy became the predominant European exporter, with the United States its principal trading partner. West Germany dominated world exports of men's wool suits in 1978, accounting for 25.0 percent of the world total, with Italy following at 18.3 percent. By 1987 (see Map 9.2), Italian exports reached 27.4 percent of the world total, largely because of the U.S. market, and Italy displaced France as the United States' chief supplier (Italian exports to the United States accounting for 14.3 percent of the world total). Italian wool suit producers are spatially concentrated around wool fabric producers of the north. Geographic proximity to suppliers of the world's finest wool textiles, the demands of sophisticated Italian consumers, and the image of Italian fashion sense created by the brand reputations of Giorgio Armani, Gianni Versace, Valentino, and others, allow Italian producers to dominate this high-value niche. Thus, by 1987—with the exception of Korea—men's wool suit exports were dominated by Europe, with Italy the prime exporter and the United States its chief market.

Commodity Chain Analysis

World export patterns have changed very little over the nine-year period. While wool exports continue to originate primarily in Australia and New Zealand, textile exports remain centered in Europe, as do exports of the final product (mainly in Italy and Germany). This specialization increased between 1978 and 1987, as Italy increased its dominance in fabric and suit production and Australia captured a still larger share of wool exports. Suit exports have become stronger in Europe over the period, with only Korea playing an Asian role; Italy has increased its dominance, but some new low-wage countries have made an appearance as well. While a few low-wage countries export to Europe and the United States (in 1987, notably Poland, Morocco, and the Dominican Republic), this remains an essentially high-value-added "core" node spatially concentrated in relatively high-wage economies that traditionally specialized in the production of woolen textiles and apparel. These tendencies give support to our expectation that production in high-value niches tends to be spatially concentrated.

Women's Synthetic Blouses

Synthetic Fibers

Japan was the only significant Asian exporter in both 1978 and 1987, accounting for 6.8 percent of world trade in 1978 and 8.0 percent in 1987. The remaining principal export flows centered first in Europe, and secondarily in the United States. In 1978 U.S. exports of synthetic fibers to Canada and Hong

Map 9.1
Men's Wool Suits, 1978, Atlantic Region

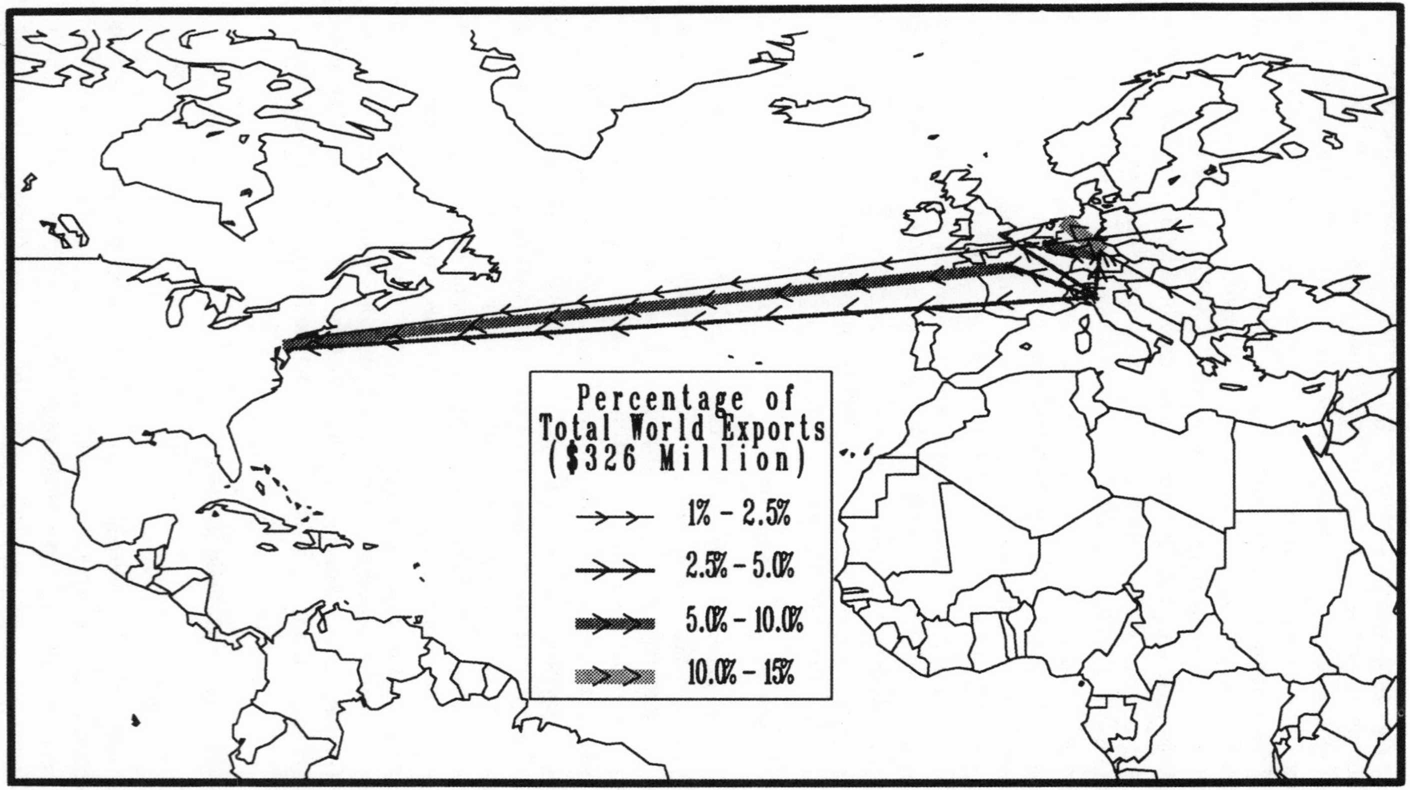

Percentage of
Total World Exports
($326 Million)

1% – 2.5%

2.5% – 5.0%

5.0% – 10.0%

10.0% – 15%

Map 9.2
Men's Wool Suits, 1987, Atlantic Region

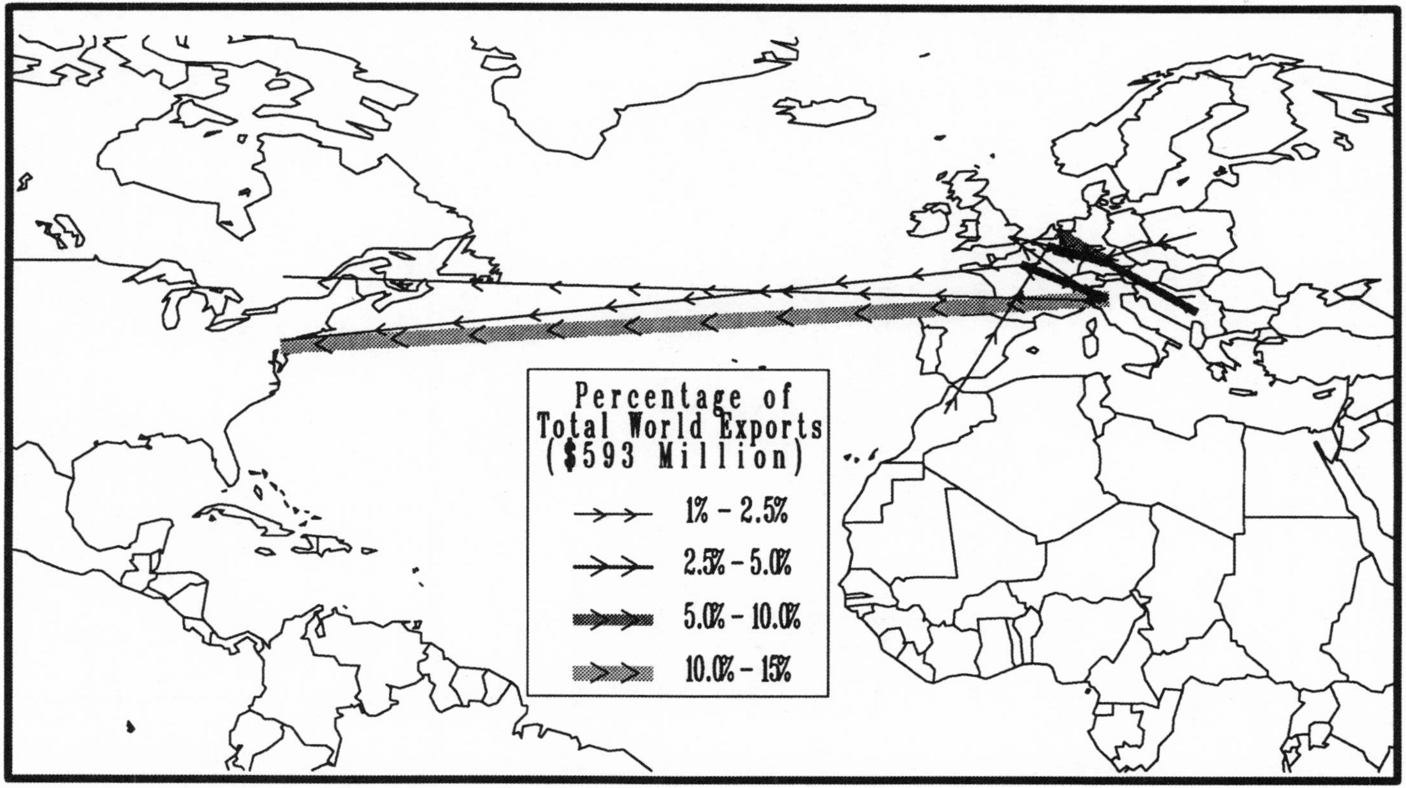

Percentage of
Total World Exports
($593 Million)

1% – 2.5%

2.5% – 5.0%

5.0% – 10.0%

10.0% – 15%

Kong accounted for 3.7 percent and 1.8 percent, respectively; by 1987 the only principal U.S. market was Canada (1.1 percent). West Germany dominated European exports of synthetics in both years, reaching 13.7 percent in 1978 (chiefly with Britain and Italy, and secondarily with Belgium, France, and the Netherlands), but dropping to only 7.9 percent in 1987 (with Italy, Britain, Belgium, and France). The production of synthetic fibers is thus concentrated in northern Europe, with some secondary production for export in the two most industrialized countries of East Asia (Japan and Korea).

Synthetic Fabric

In 1987 these textiles were exported mainly from Japan, Korea, China, Italy, and Germany. Hong Kong was the largest single market for exports (accounting for 29.5 percent of total world imports), but the United States, Singapore, Saudi Arabia, China, France, the Netherlands, and England also imported significant amounts. In part because of growing Hong Kong imports, East Asian exports of synthetic fabrics grew by nearly one-third during the period, from 34.2 percent of total world trade in 1978 to 41.2 percent in 1987. Conversely, intra-European trade declined by half, from 29.8 percent to 14.6 percent of the world total.[6] Japan was the principal Asian exporter in both years, although Japanese exports dropped from 19.4 percent of the world total in 1978 to 15.9 percent in 1987, as South Korea emerged as a principal exporter (South Korean exports grew from 5.3 percent to 11.7 percent during the period). In 1978 Korea was the only other Asian nation with significant exports of synthetic fabric; by 1987 Korea had been joined by Hong Kong and China. United States imports in both years came primarily from Japan, and secondarily from Italy.

Women's Synthetic Blouses

Asian exports accounted for roughly half of the world's total in both years; European exports (including Poland, Yugoslavia, Hungary, and Greece) declined from only 15.5 percent to 8.7 percent. Maps 9.3 and 9.4 clearly show a growing dispersion of exports to low-wage areas. While Hong Kong alone accounted for 26.3 percent of world exports in 1978, that figure had dropped to 15.5 percent by 1987, as China, Indonesia, Sri Lanka, and Malaysia all emerged as significant exporters. The United States provided the principal and rapidly growing market for Asian exports during the period, accounting for 24.3 percent of world imports in 1978 and 32.1 percent in 1987 (there is no significant trade between the United States and Europe in this commodity in either year). Europe is primarily a regional market, with even intraregional trade declining over the period.

Commodity Chain Analysis

Production along the synthetic women's blouse commodity chain is considerably more globally dispersed than that of men's wool suits. The U.S., Japan, and the industrialized nations of Europe provide the fiber and fabric, while an ever increasing number of low-wage Asian countries account for most of the

Map 9.3
Women's Synthetic Blouses, 1978, Pacific Region

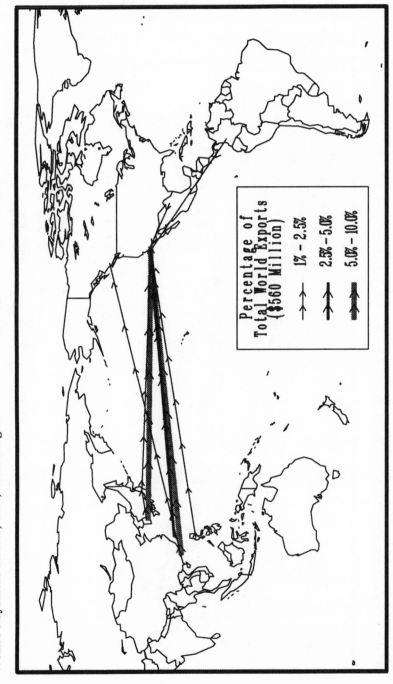

Percentage of
Total World Exports
($560 Million)

1% – 2.5%

2.5% – 5.0%

5.0% – 10.0%

Map 9.4
Women's Synthetic Blouses, 1987, Pacific Region

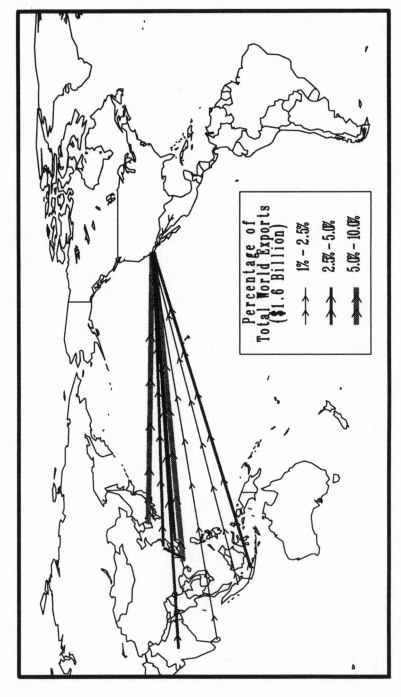

Percentage of
Total World Exports
($1.6 Billion)

1% – 2.5%

2.5% – 5.0%

5.0% – 10.0%

world's blouse exports. This chain became more dispersed and more centered on Asia between 1978 and 1987. These tendencies give support to our expectation that production in low-value niches tends to be spatially dispersed.

The Concentration of Suppliers and Producers

As we noted earlier, Porter (1990b: 80) argues that in a globalized, highly competitive world economy, "the presence in [a] nation of related and supporting industries that are internationally competitive" is a major determinant of whether firms within that nation are globally competitive. This tendency to cluster geographically is most evident in high-value niches, which rely on these advantages more heavily than cheap labor and materials, which form the basis of low-value niches. Translating this into the language of commodity chains, certain nodes on particular commodity chains, especially in high-value niches, will tend to cluster together in the same nations.

As a way to test Porter's assertion, we conducted a Pearson's R correlation analysis to examine whether globally competitive garment producers and globally competitive fabric producers tend to be clustered together in the same nations. We assume that the value of exports coming from a nation is a good measure of that nation's competitiveness in the industry. We correlated the export values of fabric and garments for both men's wool suits and women's synthetic blouses for 1978 and 1987.

The correlation between exports of synthetic fiber and synthetic fabric was relatively high and did not change over the time period (for 1978, $r = 0.76$; for 1987, $r = 0.77$). On the other hand, the correlation between exports of synthetic fabric and synthetic blouses was relatively low, although statistically significant in both years; it did increase significantly between 1978 and 1987 (from $r = 0.34$ to $r = 0.58$). Conversely, in both 1978 and 1987 there was no correlation between exports of wool fiber and wool fabric ($r = 0.01$ in both years), while the correlation between exports of wool fabric and wool suits was relatively high and statistically significant in both years. The tendency of these two nodes to locate in the same nation strengthened significantly over the ten-year period ($r = 0.66$ and $r = 0.88$ respectively).[7]

The results of this analysis suggest the following two tendencies: (1) Globally competitive wool fabric producers and globally competitive wool suit producers tend to be located in the same country. The correlation between these two export products increased between 1978 and 1987, indicating that these two segments of the commodity chain have become more spatially concentrated over the period. (2) Geographic clustering of globally competitive synthetic fabric producers and globally competitive synthetic blouse producers is much less pronounced than for wool fabric and wool suit producers. However, the correlation between these two export products increased substantially between 1978 and 1987, indicating that these two nodes of the commodity chain have become more spatially clustered over time because of the development of synthetic fabric industries in East

Asia. These tendencies support our belief that producers in high-value niches rely more heavily on geographic proximity to suppliers than producers in low-value niches.

CONCLUSIONS

Evidence from men's wool suit production, which is highly concentrated and centered on Europe (particularly Italy), and women's blouses of synthetic fiber production, which is dispersed among an ever increasing number of low-wage Asian nations, supports our belief that high-value "core" nodes in a commodity chain tend to be spatially concentrated, while low-value "peripheral" nodes remain spatially dispersed. Firms in high-value nodes rely on *location specific* sources of competitive advantage such as proximity to research centers, to world-class input suppliers, and to sophisticated consumer markets in order to create barriers of entry into their node. Firms in low-value nodes rely on sources of competitive advantage that are not location-specific (i.e., cheap labor and materials); thus capital searches the globe for ever cheaper mixes of labor and materials.

An examination of the correlations among fiber, fabric, and garment exports support our expectation that producers of high-value garments will tend to be located in the same countries as globally competitive fabric suppliers, while producers of low-value garments will be less likely to locate in the same country as globally competitive fabric suppliers. Firms in "core" nodes derive competitive advantage from geographic proximity to world-class suppliers, while firms in "peripheral" nodes less often do, as they primarily rely on finding sources of cheap labor and materials. However, our data show that as East Asian countries develop synthetic fabric production capabilities, synthetic fiber and synthetic blouse producers are increasingly located in the same nation.

Our case studies of South Korea and Hong Kong (reported elsewhere; see Appelbaum and Smith, 1992; Appelbaum and Gereffi, 1992) suggest that there are multiple locational determinants for garment production, including availability of quota, production quality, labor costs, fabric availability, and timeliness of delivery. Among nations that possess sufficient quota, garments that require high levels of quality, quickness of delivery, and flexibility in the alteration of style, tend to be manufactured in higher-wage areas that have tightly integrated local "industrial districts" such as Hong Kong and Seoul. Thus production of high-value garments, again, tends to be spatially concentrated. Garments that allow for high-volume standardized production and that do not require quick delivery or high quality, tend to be produced in low-wage areas. Production of low-value garments, therefore are spatially dispersed among low-wage countries.

NOTES

1. Hong Kong figures include re-exports of garments manufactured in whole or in part elsewhere (primarily China), and exported under Hong Kong quota; re-exports grew from

2.1 percent of Hong's total in 1973 to 21.9 percent in 1987 (Dickerson, 1991: 153), reflecting Hong Kong's changing role from local low-wage garment production to a control center for global manufacturing processes.

2. During the same period (1980–1987), European apparel imports declined from 58 percent to 52 percent of the world total, while Third World imports declined from 12 percent to 8 percent (Dickerson, 1991: 150).

3. Synthetic fibers include primarily polyesters and polymides (such as nylon), which are made from petrochemical products.

4. Nine countries reported the number of units exported, as well as the dollar value of exports. (These countries were China, Hong Kong, Cyprus, Norway, Malyasia, New Zealand, Singapore, Sri Lanka, and Jamaica.) The price-per-unit figures were computed by dividing the dollar value of exports by the number of units exported for these ten countries, for each commodity.

5. Men's wool suits are classified under SITC 842.21; women's synthetic blouses under SITC 843.52. The latter category consists of "man-made fibers other than knitted or crocheted" and includes blends as well as purely synthetic fabrics.

6. Intraregional trade is a significant portion of these totals: in 1987, for example, intra-Asian trade accounted for 18.8 percent of the world total (or 67.4 percent of all exports originating in an Asian country), while intra-European trade accounted for 14.6 percent (or 52.3 percent of all exports originating in a European country).

7. The r values were converted to z values to test the significance of the difference between the two r's using the formula $z = (\frac{1}{2}) [\ln (1 + r) - \ln [1 - r]$ (Snedecor and Cochran, 1989: 188). Normally this test is limited to comparisons of two independent samples. Since we are using every country that reported exports for these two years, ours is neither a sample (it is the population), nor is it independent. Therefore, this is not a test of statistical significance, but rather a conservative criterion of whether or not the differences in r were substantial.

REFERENCES

Aggarwal, Vinod. 1985. *Liberal Protectionism: The International Politics of Organized Textile Trade*. Berkeley: University of California Press.

Appelbaum, Richard, and Arnold, Christopher. 1993. "Space and the Global Economy: How Forces of Dispersal and Concentration are Reshaping the Contemporary Los Angeles Garment Industry." To appear in *Geographic Information Systems: A Handbook for the Social Sciences*, edited by Carville Earle, Leonard Hochberg, and David Miller. New York: Basil Blackwell.

Appelbaum, Richard, and Gereffi, Gary. 1992. "Points of Profit in the Garment Commodity Chain." Paper presented at the UCLA Center for Pacific Rim Studies conference, "The Globalization of the Apparel Industry in the Pacific Rim" (May 15–18).

Appelbaum, Richard, and Smith, David. 1992. "Locational Determinants of Garment Production in the Global Economy: the Cases of Hong Kong and South Korea." Center for Global Studies, University of California at Santa Barbara, October.

Bonacich, Edna, and Waller, David. n.d. "The Restructuring of the Pacific Rim Garment Industry: A Perspective from the United States." University of California-Riverside: Department of Sociology.

Cheng, Lucie, and Hsiung, Ping-Chun. 1992. "Women, Export-Oriented Growth, and the State: the Case of Taiwan.'' In *States and Development in the Asian Pacific Rim*, edited by Richard P. Appelbaum and Jeffrey Henderson. Newbury Park, NY: Sage Publications.

Deyo, Fred. 1992. "The Political Economy of Social Policy Formation: East Asia's Newly Industrialized Countries." In *States and Development in the Asian Pacific Rim*, edited by Richard P. Appelbaum and Jeffrey Henderson. Newbury Park, CA: Sage Publications.

Dicken, Peter. 1992. *Global Shift: The Internationalization of Economic Activity* 2d ed. New York: The Guilford Press.

Dickerson, Kitty G. 1991. *Textiles and Apparel in the International Economy*. New York: Macmillan.

Frobel, Folker; Heinrichs, Jurgen; and Kreye, Otto. 1982. "The Current Development of the World Economy: Reproduction of Labour and Accumulation of Capital on a World Scale." *Review* 5(4):507–55.

Gereffi, Gary. 1990. "Changing Roles of the NICs in the World Economy: Challenges to Development Theory." Paper presented at the 12th World Congress of Sociology (July 9–13), Madrid, Spain.

———. 1992. "New Realities of Industrial Development in East Asia and Latin America: Global, Regional, and National Trends." In *States and Development in the Asian Pacific Rim*, edited by Richard P. Appelbaum and Jeffrey Henderson. Newbury Park, CA: Sage Publications.

Gereffi, Gary, and Korzeniewicz, Miguel. 1990. "Commodity Chains and Footwear Exports in the Semiperiphery." In *Semiperipheral States in the World-Economy*, edited by William G. Martin. Westport, CT: Greenwood Press.

Hopkins, Terence K., and Wallerstein, Immanuel. 1986. "Commodity Chains in the World-Economy Prior to 1800." *Review* 10, 1: 157–70

Moon, Chung-in. 1987. "Trade Frictions and Industrial Adjustment: The Textiles and Apparel Industry in the Pacific Basin." *Pacific Focus* 2(1) 105–33.

Piore, M. J., and Sabel, C. F. 1984. *The Second Industrial Divide: Possibilities for Prosperity*. New York: Basic Books.

Porter, Michael E. 1990a. "The Competitive Advantage of Nations." *Harvard Business Review*, March-April, pp. 73–93.

———. 1990b. *The Competitive Advantage of Nations*. New York: The Free Press.

Rothstein, Richard. 1989. *Keeping Jobs in Fashion: Alternatives to the Euthanasia of the U.S. Apparel Industry*. Washington, D.C.: Economic Policy Institute.

Salaff, Janet W. 1992. "Women, the Family, and the State in Hong Kong, Taiwan, and Singapore." In *States and Development in the Asian Pacific Rim*, edited by Richard P. Appelbaum and Jeffrey Henderson. Newbury Park, CA: Sage Publications.

Scott, A. J. 1988. "Flexible Production Systems and Regional Development." *International Journal of Urban and Regional Research* 12: 171–86.

Scott, A. J., and Kwok, E. C. 1989. "Inter-firm Subcontracting and Locational Agglomeration: A Case Study of the Printed Circuits Industry in Southern California." *Economic Geography* 65: 48–71.

Snedecor, George W., and Cochran, William G. 1989. *Statistical Methods*. Ames: Iowa State University Press.

Storper, M., and Christopherson, S. 1987. "Flexible Specialization and Regional Industrial Agglomeration: The Case of the U.S. Motion Picture Industry." *Annals of the Association of American Geographers* 77: 104–117.

10

Strategic Reorientations of U.S. Apparel Firms

Ian M. Taplin

INTRODUCTION

The enhanced integration of production across geopolitical boundaries since the 1970s highlights the restructuring endemic to many industries in high-wage economies of the West. Relatedly, many firms have developed flexible production systems that provide speedier product delivery and permit economies of scope to be realized for small-batch product lines. Such specialized commodity production has sometimes resulted in the reconfiguration of firms within networks of related firms that are integrated as stages of a commodity chain. This chapter examines such a restructuring now taking place in the global apparel industry, paying particular attention to the strategic reorientation of U.S. apparel manufacturers.

Because apparel manufacture has become an important part of the export-led growth strategies of newly industrializing countries (NICs), U.S. firms, faced with low-wage competition for globalized production, have responded in several ways. Some have moved production overseas, others have developed domestic contracting, while still others have further rationalized the manufacturing system, innovating technologically and restructuring work to attain significant productivity increases. In each case, I will show how strategic choice is shaped by a desire among firms to remain high-value-added extractors in the apparel commodity chain.

INTEGRATED GLOBALIZED PRODUCTION

Macroeconomic changes associated with a succession of crises in the early and mid-1970s have provoked systematic restructuring of many firms and industries in Western economies during the 1980s (Kolko, 1988). In particular, high production costs (often a function of inflexible labor practices and rising social wage costs) and market saturation in some consumer durables have resulted in eroded profit margins for firms. Much of the restructuring has also been linked with significant increases in the globalization of trade and production, especially since NICs are proving attractive sites for U.S. firms seeking to relocate parts or all of the manufacturing process in a low-wage region (Ross and Trachte, 1990).

Because many of the NICs predicated their development on export-led growth strategies in which key manufacturing industries figured prominently, they were able to capitalize upon their comparative advantage in low labor costs at a time when consumer spending remained buoyant in high-wage economies (Deyo, 1987). While these strategies do not necessarily guarantee an explosive growth in GNP (see for example Latin American countries during the 1980s [Evans, 1987]), they can have the potential to force changes upon production forces in manufacturing industries in the West.

This is particularly the case with fragmented commodity production, a component of the new international division of labor that underlies globalized manufacturing. In such instances, industries, as Gereffi and Korzeniewicz (1990: 65) note, become stratified according to the economic value-added created by different sets of producers. By disaggregating the various stages of commodity production and identifying pivotal points in such a process, commodity chains provide a means of determining not just geographic specialization but the relative "value" of such tasks that accrue to firms in the form of profit.

Clothing Commodity Chains

In apparel, the commodity chain includes raw material suppliers, design and garment preparation specialists, manufacturers who assemble the product, and firms specializing in the distribution and retail of the finished product. Forward and backward linkages, from retailers who sell the product to textile companies that supply the fabric, locate apparel manufacturers between two sectors that increasingly have become concentrated in recent decades. Furthermore, apparel manufacturers in different regions of the country, operating in different sectors of the industry, face distinct organizational imperatives. In the New York area, traditionally the center of the industry, more specialized, high-fashion garments and sportswear now predominate. Southern California has similarly become associated with sportswear. Centered in Los Angeles around a system of small, agglomerated firms in a vertically disintegrated production system, the production of highly differentiated garments characteristic of sportswear flourishes. In both

Figure 10.1
Apparel Commodity Chains

a. **Standardized, Mass-Production Chain**

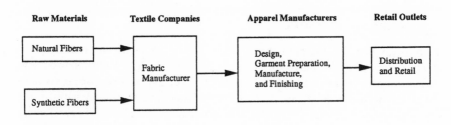

b. **Fashion-Oriented Chain**

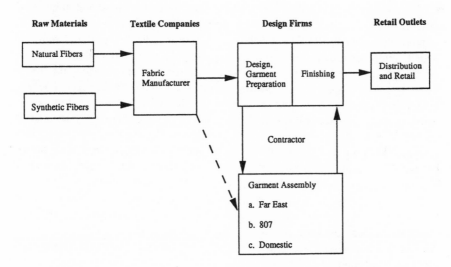

areas fashion-oriented production, requiring small-batch, differentiated commodity manufacture with a high rate of product turnover, has become prevalent. This contrasts with the less fashion-sensitive, large-volume, standardized production systems associated with many products in the Men's and Boys' wear markets, which in recent decades are more likely to be found in the southeastern region of the United States.

As I will discuss later, this indicates that two commodity chains exist in apparel production, with two regional poles in the fashion-oriented segment. Figure 10.1 presents a schematic breakdown of these chains. Because different production links in the commodity chain occur *within* the United States, a core country, it suggests that countries are not the most appropriate unit of analysis in talking about globalized production in apparel. Furthermore, industry sectoral differences demonstrate the saliency of local rather than national production systems as parallel commodity chains are integrated into global production networks.

THE CASE OF APPAREL

In many respects apparel appears to be an industry in which product manufacture is destined to move to labor-abundant NICs. It is labor-intensive and low-skilled, production is difficult to mechanize, and in many sectors small-batch requirements are the norm. It is a highly competitive industry with 15,926 establishments employing 1,0835,200 workers in 1987. In terms of employment trends, overall employment in 1987 declined to 88 percent of the 1954 level, with a steady decline in all sectors since 1973. The two largest segments of the industry, Men's and Boys' and Women's and Misses' wear, are the focus of this study.

As one can see from Table 10.1, the decline in employment and number of establishments has not been universal. In fact, the rise in the number of small establishments in Women's and Misses' clothing is indicative of the viability of small, agglomerated firms that have found niches in specialized production, either as design and garment preparation specialists or as "cut, make, and trim" subcontractors to such firms. Likewise, the increase in the average size of Men's and Boys' clothing firms and the greater decline of small and medium-sized firms in this sector suggest that manufacturing efficiencies here are more readily available in larger organizations.

It is interesting to note that Women's and Misses' clothing firms, with lower levels of apparent capitalization than Men's and Boys' clothing and a manufacturing norm that appears to be shifting toward the smaller firms, nevertheless maintain similar levels of value-added per production worker-hour than in Men's and Boys' wear. Despite new capital expenditures per employee in 1987 that were 83 percent of those in Men's and Boys' wear ($546.30 as opposed to $654.40), value-added was practically the same (a mere 4 percent differential, or $17.60 as opposed to $18.33).

Although raw materials constitute 50–60 percent of production costs, at 25–40 percent labor remains an important cost ingredient. Consequently, wage rates have been and continue to be a crucial factor in managerial decisions regarding the location of production (de la Torre, 1986). Wage-depressing tactics remain omnipresent in the industry, made possible in part by a reliance on female and in some areas (California and New York) immigrant labor.

Women represent 81 percent of the labor force and minorities 27 percent. Relative to average manufacturing wages, apparel wages have declined from 77 percent in 1950 to 54 percent in 1987 (OTA, 1987: 7). Slow productivity growth, attributable to the difficulty of mechanizing production, and the low-skill com-

Table 10.1
Clothing Establishments by Employment Size

Women's & Misses Outerwear

Establishments with	1977	1982	1987
1-19 Employees	5463	5765	6040
20-99	4495	4149	3045
100-249	848	747	601
250 or more	207	209	171
TOTAL	11,013	10,840	10,252
Total # of Employees	441,70	419,300	348,600
Average Establishment Size	40	39	34

Mens & Boys' Outerwear

Establishments with	1977	1982	1987
1-19 Employees	1153	913	645
20-99	1190	1008	832
100-249	848	711	626
250 or more	559	440	410
TOTAL	3750	3072	2513
Total # of Employees	463,200	373,900	337,000
Average Establishment Size	124	122	134

Source: U.S. Department of Commerce, Census of Manufacturers
Selective Years.

position of the labor force are reasons employers frequently give for such differentials (Cline, 1987: 91). Such wage erosion, however, has enabled the industry to avoid massive employment losses in the face of sustained NIC imports. Lagging textile costs have accompanied apparel wage depression, especially since the 1980s when textile price increases were lower than inflation. Consequently, profits have remained healthy for many firms in apparel (U.S. Department of Commerce, 1990).

Growth of Apparel Imports

Much of the restructuring that has occurred in the industry since the early 1970s has been in response to, or taking advantage of, low-cost production overseas. Although apparel, like textiles, has been among the most highly protected sectors since the turn of the century, it has witnessed significant import penetration in the last two decades. Because domestic apparel consumption has risen at a much slower rate than import growth (2.7 percent annually over the same period [Cline, 1987: 3]), such increased import penetration has resulted in a secular decline of domestic production. Ninety percent of imports come from low-wage countries, with the East Asian Big Four (Hong Kong, Taiwan, South Korea, and China) accounting for 60 percent of total U.S. apparel imports in 1987. While low-wage NICs have capitalized on their comparative advantage in labor costs, an overvalued dollar and rising U.S. incomes have further stimulated this secular supply shift.

As a system of managed trade, the Multi-Fiber Agreements (MFA) have never kept up with rapid shifts in trade flows and product cycles, nor with the rapid expansion of product demand in new areas (Nehmer and Love, 1985). However, they have provided a measure of protection for some domestic producers, stimulating adjustment strategies and the deployment of sophisticated technology and reorganized production systems. But in other instances, trade restrictions have protected firms without encouraging restructuring and rationalization. Or, as in the case of production in Mexico, they have enabled firms to seek cost-lowering subcontracting strategies while keeping production close to domestic markets.

DOMESTIC FIRM RESPONSES TO IMPORT PENETRATION

The strategic response of U.S. firms to the growing import penetration of domestic markets has been several-fold. Some firms have concentrated on revitalizing production through capital investments, technological change, and the use of new manufacturing systems (AAMA, 1988; OTA, 1987). Others have downsized, retaining the design and pre- and postassembly stages, but subcontracting the sewing or garment assembly stages. The latter can entail (1) the increase of domestic subcontracting, especially in or to regions where immigrant labor facilitates low wage rates, or (2) use of U.S. tariff provisions limiting duties on garments assembled offshore. In both instances, high-skilled garment preparation tasks remain in the core firm while the lower-skilled, labor-intensive (low-value-added) garment assembly work is subcontracted out. Guess? is a Los Angeles–based private label sportswear firm that has successfully utilized domestic contracting, mainly in southern California where its 100 contractors employ approximately 7000 workers (*Los Angeles Times*, August 5, 1992). Meanwhile, Gitano, a private label casual clothes company based in New York, relies upon a mix of 807 and Asian contract manufacturing to keep its costs low enough to sell in mass merchandisers (*Forbes*, February 23, 1987).

A third variation occurs when (3) the entire cut, make and trim operation is done overseas. Here, a U.S.-based design firm or retailer procures raw materials from overseas, then contracts out or licenses the entire manufacturing of the product to a NIC firm. Working to strict specifications, the overseas firms effectively manufacture to order. This type of arrangement is found among many of the private label firms (for example The Gap, The Limited, Liz Claiborne and Esprit) whose successes during the 1980s have been through their judicious use of multiple sources of low-cost international manufacturing.

Given the above, what determines the different strategic reorientation of firms as they attempt to cope with import penetration? Also, what do the various alternative strategies at the firm and sector levels tell us about globalized production and the reconfiguration of commodity chains?

If firms are to extract maximum economic value-added, they must push cost lowering onto the preceding unit in the commodity chain, insofar as possible up to textile companies who impose their own producer-driven costing. However, cost is a necessary but not always sufficient factor in determining competitiveness. In the fashion-oriented chain, for example, the imperative is often speed of product delivery. Flexible production systems and proximity to market, therefore, can be as important as wage factors in shaping decisions regarding the organization and location of production.

STRATEGIC REORIENTATIONS

Aside from costs, decisions regarding the location of manufacture are shaped by various factors that include the nature of the product, institutional regulation of labor markets (both at home and overseas in NICs), changes in the regulation and management of international trade, secular shifts in consumer demand, and supplier-vendor pressures. While labor costs remain important their salience is mediated by these other constraining factors.

Traditionally, apparel has been difficult to mechanize because the limpness of cloth prevents mechanical handling and fashion volatility limits standardized volume production. Not surprisingly, low levels of capital intensity persist in many sectors of the industry, although in the less fashion sensitive Men's and Boys' wear sector, capitalization rates are higher (OTA, 1987). Even here, however, complete automation of production has not been possible with efforts instead focusing mainly upon non-sewing operations in the pre-assembly stage.

Since the late 1970s the institutional regulation of labor markets has been subordinated to meeting the needs of employers, in particular giving them a freer hand in their utilization of labor. Poorly regulated labor markets, particularly weak government enforcement of workplace health and safety and few sanctions on employers for illegal employment practices have resulted, since the 1980s, in a rebirth of sweatshops in regions where immigrant labor is available. In regions such as southern California, Miami and New York/New Jersey many contractors have been able to use a Third World labor force in what amounts to de facto Third World labor market conditions (Blumenberg and Ong, 1992). Meanwhile, the southeastern states continue to provide an institutional environment hostile to unions, with minimal government interference, low taxes and the availability of a surplus black labor force (Falk and Lyson, 1988). In each case, low wages, relative to other manufacturing sectors, can be maintained.

The structure of international trade, its management, and variations in the enforcement of quotas clearly shape production decisions (Appelbaum et al., chapter 9 in this volume). Whether firms use overseas production, and if so where it is located, also depends upon labor and shipping costs, product quality criteria, and speed of delivery—all of which are assessed in light of market forces and organizational imperatives that influence domestic demand for the product. Despite the push of clothing exports from the NICs, it is important to remember that globalized production has also been driven by developed country firms' search for low-cost production. As Dicken (1992: 257) notes, this is a somewhat paradoxical situation given that the clothing imports that cause such concern in the United States are in fact often organized by U.S. firms locating production overseas.

Since the late 1960s new marketing strategies have been developed by manufacturing and design firms in conjunction with new apparel products for different life styles. Instead of marketing products that factories could best produce, they now place more attention on producing what the market demands. The growth of female labor force participation brought new clothing demands from women, and the trend towards more casual dressing by men decreased the demand for suits and increased the diversity of men's sportswear (*Wall Street Journal*, July 2, 1991 and March 23, 1992). Consumer spending on apparel increased during the 1980s, reflecting changes in the level and distribution of income. Not surprisingly, many of these changes are intricately linked with the structure of retailing. As Gereffi points out in chapter 5 of this volume, the buyer-driven pressures imposed by retailers decisively shape many manufacturing strategies by imposing cost, quality and increasingly flexibility imperatives.

Despite a large number of apparel retailers in *absolute* terms, a small number of very large retail chains have increased their market power over recent decades. Department stores, mass merchandisers and off-price retailers have created large niches in which they are able to exercise oligopsony power. Oversupply of retail space since the mid-1980s, at a time when consumer spending growth slowed and operating costs continued to rise, heightened the pressure upon retailers (Stern, 1986). Together with high interest payments, occasioned by leveraged buy-outs during the 1980s, these factors have forced the remaining large retailers to increase their margins (markups). In the case of mass merchandisers and off-price retailers, volume buying is used to extract further price concessions from suppliers (Scott and Lee, 1991: 7).

Technological innovations have indirectly aided retailers to further squeeze manufacturers. Accompanying a move to six or eight fashion seasons annually, many retailers now use Electronic Data Interchange (EDI) systems to revolutionize their relationships with suppliers. Such systems (basically an electronic cash register) track sales and enable orders to be placed for restocking on a daily or weekly basis (Sprinkle et al., 1992). Doing this gives stores a productivity edge as they pass inventory costs onto the supplier (Friedman, 1988: 19).

The concentration that has occurred in the textile industry since the 1970s, associated with high capital intensity and technological innovation, has increased the efficiency of that sector (OTA, 1987) and created oligopoly power. Open-ended spinning dramatically increased spinning speed; the shuttleless loom achieved similar results for the weaving process (Dicken, 1992: 249). Because textile companies maximize efficiency through economies of scale, their move towards standardized volume production runs counter to the needs of most small apparel companies. While many large apparel manufacturers have benefitted from lower fabric costs following these changes, small firms requiring limited quantities of varied items have not. The unwillingness of U.S. textile companies to supply the latter's needs on a regular basis has caused many small apparel companies to purchase fabric overseas. Not surprisingly, this can lead to overseas manufacture where the "cut, make and trim" parts of the operation are performed in the same geographic area where the fabric has been purchased.[1]

Determining a production strategy in an environment of unprecedented economic uncertainty is a difficult task facing apparel firms. Their response has been varied, depending largely on the sectoral-specific constraints imposed upon them. In the remainder of the chapter I discuss first the various forms of decentralized production and the rationale behind choices between domestic, 807 tariff arrangements, or Far East outsourcing. Then I examine revitalization efforts, both in terms of upgrading product quality and niche marketing, as well as new manufacturing systems developed by some of the large, mass market firms.

OVERSEAS SOURCING: THE FAR EAST

The factors uppermost in strategic decisions about sourcing are cost, quality, control, risk, investment and response time (AAMA, 1986). The benefits of manufacturing in the Far East are primarily cost related although high quality is also very significant. Containerized shipping has lowered freight costs and telecommunications innovations have improved coordination of production between U.S. firms and overseas contractors. In the Asian Big Four (Hong Kong, South Korea, Taiwan, and China), well developed infrastructures that facilitate the production and shipment of goods are in place. Investments are relatively secure, and control over facets of the production process are unproblematic for the firm responsible for the sourcing.

In general, unit labor costs in the Far East are one quarter those of the southern United States, but within this geographic area differences in wage rates abound. In 1991, for example, hourly compensation costs were as low as $0.24 in China and $0.25 in India compared with $3.74 in Taiwan and $3.74 in Hong Kong. Taiwan and Hong Kong, the highest labor cost Asian suppliers, have seen labor costs rise about 10 percent annually over the past decade whereas the lower-cost suppliers', such as India and China, rates have remained stable. Not surprisingly, some of the greatest growth in apparel exports has come from the "new" low wage nations of this area as the East Asian NICs have lost much of their cost competitiveness.[2]

Although fabric prices can be as low as 60–80 percent of U.S. textile costs and power costs are the same, factory supply costs in the Far East are 125 percent of that of southern U.S. manufacturers and productivity is 65 percent of U.S. levels (AAMA, 1986: 30). After duty and freight differentials are factored in, the advantage of overseas production is reduced. If one then introduces a product turnaround time of four months, quality control problems with new manufacturers and the difficulty of resupplying fast-selling items, Far Eastern sourcing loses some of its attractiveness.

OVERSEAS SOURCING: 807 PROGRAMS

Using the same set of criteria for evaluation purposes, cost, geographic proximity to the United States, and political stability are among the most important issues in selecting 807 programs. Established in 1965, item 807 levies duty only on the value-added of U.S. products assembled overseas. A new program (807A) was added in 1987 that further liberalized the re-import of goods. By 1989, 10 percent of total U.S. apparel imports entered under these program terms (U.S. Department of Commerce, 1990).

In the Caribbean region and Mexico, labor costs have remained proportionally lower over the last decade than those found even in the southern United States. Labor is abundant in these areas, especially young, single females who comprise the majority of workers. The Dominican Republic and Mexico, countries where capital investment by subsidiaries of U.S. firms are located, are both considered politically "sound." The closeness of these areas to the United States means freight costs are substantially lower than from Asian countries. More importantly, product turnaround time is dramatically shorter: three to five weeks from receipt of order, including production, transportation, and distribution to U.S. retailers (AAMA, 1986). In many of the more volatile fashion markets or with product lines that unexpectedly need restocking, such time factors are important.

Despite the saving in production costs, 807 arrangements nevertheless have problems. With the exception of Mexico, other nations lack developed infrastructures that are necessary for smooth production. Also, many firms with 807 dealings have had problems with corrupt customs officers and find it difficult to factor in a reliable and predictable cost structure for such problems.[3] Quality of workmanship can be a problem, but firms using 807 endeavor to establish long-term relationships with contractors who can eventually meet the stipulations placed upon them. While their comparative advantage in cost and abundant labor make these nations attractive to U.S. firms, the infrastructural limitations and quality problems hamper their ability to predicate sustained economic growth on the export of manufactured goods.

DOMESTIC SOURCING

U.S. apparel manufacturers, especially those in the volatile fashion-oriented sector, traditionally have relied on vertical production systems involving local contracting out of parts of the manufacturing process. Fast response time, particularly the ability to quickly fill diverse orders, can complement low costs as a key manufacturing variable. The proliferation of small Women's and Misses' outerwear firms, a sector where the rate of product turnover is high, suggests the persistence of such a pattern in the fashion-oriented commodity chain. Earlier analyses of aggregate employment changes captured this trend (ILGWU, 1985); more recent case studies substantiate its continued existence (Bonacich, 1990; Lin, 1989).

Options to utilize domestic sourcing are determined by the following major advantages. First, it offers immediate access to additional output without adding to fixed labor costs. This type of flexibility is found in the Los Angeles area garment industry where Women's and Misses' sportswear can be turned around in as little as ten days.

Second, immigrant labor markets in key regions of garment production provide abundant low-wage labor for contractors, many of whom are immigrants themselves. Because immigrant entrepreneurs traditionally have played an important role in the development of the garment industry (associated with the ease of entry, low capital overheads, and lower than average profit levels in the industry), apparel manufacturing has tended to proliferate in areas of large immigrant populations (Waldinger, 1986; Light and Bonacich, 1987). Currently, contracting in the Los Angeles garment industry is a haven for Korean and more recently Vietnamese entrepreneurs. Relying upon a pool of immigrants (legal and illegal), mainly Hispanic women and children, such entrepreneurs have been able to keep their operating costs low by paying below minimum wages, requiring unpaid overtime work, and ignoring many of the standard workplace practices mandated by the federal and state government.[4]

Relatedly, the 1989 changes in homeworking laws by the U.S. Labor Department permit certain companies to hire employees to work at home, thus providing contractors with yet another potential low-overhead labor supply. Even though registration and record keeping procedures are mandated, estimates (from between 8,000 and 125,000 people or 1 and 14 percent of the total apparel labor force) vary widely as to those who actually do contract apparel work at home (*Wall Street Journal*, 19 September 1988). Although most firms that use homeworkers do so as part-timers to supplement core operations, one presumes that their use will continue at current levels and possibly rise.

Fourth, contracting can enable firms to circumvent union contracts, either as a temporary "cost-saving" measure or as part of a longer term de-unionization strategy. Poorly regulated labor markets, large female immigrant populations, and the proliferation of small work sites, characteristic for contract shops, make union organizing difficult. Not surprisingly, unions such as the ILGWU have seen their strength erode over the past decades in areas such as southern California (Laslett and Tyler, 1989).

Obviously infrastructure, control and risk are not problematic when dealing with domestic sourcing. Quality can vary, but again competition among contractors has a quality control effect that can only benefit the firm placing the order. Finally, many private label firms have been able to exert a downward pressure on contractors' unit charges by threatening to move offshore with production contracts. Except in the southeastern United States where labor shortages have been reported since the late 1980s and some firms have been forced to use 807 sourcing, tight labor markets have not been a problem.

Domestic sourcing can provide design firms with low-cost production that is both flexible and speedy. That, together with high levels of reliability and quality, enable many of them to retain their competitive edge. This is especially evident in the Women's and Misses' sector where high rates of product turnover and speedy product delivery practically necessitate proximity of design firms to their contractors. Pressured by retailers to meet both cost and time criteria, design firms can remain competitive by keeping the prices to contractors low. The latter, in turn, rely upon wage-depressing tactics to retain a profit margin in their low-value-added place in the commodity chain.

DOMESTIC PRODUCTION CHANGES

Traditionally, very few production economies of scale existed in apparel. However, the advent of microprocessor technology has, since the late 1970s, facilitated automation of some production tasks. Its major impact though, has come in the garment preparation and garment handling stages, yielding greater production flexibility. This, and related organizational changes that restructure the production process, are the principal areas that domestic manufacturers developed to remain competitive.

The introduction of computer-aided design (CAD) systems had, by the mid-1980s, reduced the time spent producing patterns by up to one-third (Hoffman and Rush, 1988). Together with computer-controlled cutters (CCC) and automatic spreading machines, such systems improved the speed with which materials for sewing were prepared, cutting labor needs by one-half and reducing material wastage by as much as 25 percent for patterned garments (OTA, 1987). Given the high-skill, higher-wage of graders, markers and cutters, labor force reductions here have led to significant cost savings.

Because as much as three-quarters of the time spent by sewing machine operators is positioning garment pieces rather than in actual sewing, the focus of many improvements has been in the area of materials handling (Sieling and Curtin, 1988: 28). Technological innovation in peripheral sewing operations and improved sewing machine flexibility have partially automated production, especially in the standardized product market (Shepherd, 1987). Such changes have led to productivity increases which, since the early 1980s in Men's and Boys' suits, for example, have averaged 6 percent per annum (Sieling and Curtin, 1988: 25). However, difficulties in completely automating production have forced many firms to experiment with alternative production systems.

In the traditional bundle system, pieces of up to 25 garments are cut and tied in bundles to be assembled by sewing machine operators. Under such a system, inventory costs are high and production cycle time is slow as garment assembly can take up to 10 days. Many large Men's and Boys' wear firms have introduced modular manufacturing to overcome these problems (AAMA, 1988). Relying on quota-driven teams of workers in which each worker performs a standardized sewing task, such a system can reduce turnaround time to several hours. By dramatically cutting the production cycle times as well as significantly lowering inventory costs, such a system can provide manufacturers with productivity increases, quality-based production controls plus flexibility. This enables them to be more responsive to the buyer-driven pressure from retailers. When made part of EDI systems, which more and more retailers are introducing, it also enables manufacturers to monitor production and ensure they meet the fluctuations in retail needs (*New York Times*, October 1, 1988; U.S. Department of Commerce, 1990). Finally, because management transfers much of the supervision of the work force to the team, where group-based productivity norms effectively ''pace'' workers, any resulting work intensification is diffused through work-based subcultures of self-exploitation.

The core of the above revitalization efforts have focused upon cost lowering through improved product flow and reductions in fabric wastage, while simultaneously providing management with greater control over the production process. Lowered inventory costs and a more efficient use of workers have proved beneficial, especially for large firms in standardized markets and where increased market share has been the strategic goal. In casual wear (e.g., sweatshirts where sewing tasks are standardized and simple yet the product is bulky, high productivity and high weight to labor ratios provide U.S. firms with a competitive edge over their overseas competitors. Table 10.2 illustrates this with a comparison of T-shirt production in the United States and through 807 arrangements.

RECONFIGURED COMMODITY CHAINS

The logic of the new international division of labor for a product such as clothing is impeccable. But the politics of quotas and buyer-driven pressure from retailers, the latter conflating cost lowering with simultaneous demands for flexibility in production, have added complexity to what otherwise might be a simple and predictable outcome.

Table 10.2
Cost Comparison: T-shirts ($/Dozen)

	U.S.	807 Product
Fabric, Trim & Cutting	$11.15	$11.15
Assembly Labor	$4.65	$1.76
Freight, Duty & Documentation	---	$4.13
TOTAL	$15.80	$17.04

Source: American Apparel Manufacturers Association, 1986.

Retailers

At the end of apparel commodity chains, retailers continue to exercise oligopsony power, reaping high profits following a move towards improved wholesale distribution efficiencies and differentiated product sales. In the Women's and Misses' sector, for example, average after-tax rates of return on equity were 19 percent during the 1980s; The Limited, a private label sportswear retailer that contracts for its own exclusive production, had just over 29 percent average after-tax returns for the same period (Scott and Lee, 1991: 14). Using their market power to demand price concessions from suppliers (Dertouzos et al., 1989), large retailers also realize economies of scale in distribution systems and when they coordinate deliveries through EDI systems (Friedman, 1988: 19).

Apparel Manufacturers

Because of protection, domestic apparel production has flourished more than one might have expected. But domestic manufacturers have not been able to ignore the import threat and much of the restructuring since the late 1970s has been in response to it. Despite labor displacement and a secular decline in the number of apparel establishments, industry restructuring has been uneven. Since the late 1970s, employment decline has been more dramatic in the standardized chain, especially in Men's and Boys' clothing where rationalization programs involving capitalization and work reorganization have seen output stabilize but with fewer employees working. This contrasts with the fashion-oriented chain, primarily Women's and Misses' clothing where employment losses in large and medium-sized firms are somewhat compensated by far smaller losses (and some gains) in small firms (less than 20 workers).

As firms restructure production in ways that retain the higher economic value-added tasks, they do so in a competitive environment where speed of delivery can be as important as cost. Although competitive strategies remain rooted in transaction cost lowering methods, managing product flow is now seen as being as important as price competition. This is especially the case in the fashion-oriented chain. Short production runs keep inventory costs low, but fluctuating demand for differentiated products requires fast response times. Domestic contracting arrangements are ideal for such a situation. They provide geographically proximate production flexibility, plus the displacement of fixed labor costs to the contractor reduces operating overheads.

Item 807 and Far East contracting is more feasible for firms operating in mass markets with less fashionable products that are price sensitive *or* for private label firms (again The Gap is a good example) whose high volume sales in sportswear permit mass production of differentiated products. Long lead times are less problematic because planned product obsolescence eliminates many re-stocking needs.

The standardized, mass market that characterizes Men's and Boys' wear lends itself to both overseas and domestic production. Again long lead times are not problematic because the item is standardized and shipments regularized. Because it is price sensitive, labor costs and quality are pre-eminent production concerns. Securing reliable production sites, often through direct ownership of overseas factories of through subsidiary relationships, permits high levels of plant investment which can lead to productivity gains and better coordination of the manufacturing process. Major domestic firms such as Levi Strauss and VF Corporation (makers of Wrangler and Lee jeans) use directly owned overseas factories plus domestic sites to juggle quota, cost, and productivity criteria with global marketing strategies that are designed to increase market share and move their products' image up-market (*Wall Street Journal*, March 7, 1991).

Forced to compete with the dramatically lower labor costs of overseas firms, some larger U.S. companies have attempted to rationalize and automate production. What automation has occurred can be found in high-volume standard designs (such as men's shirts) that require fewer than 20 operations (*New York Times*, September 9, 1990). Restructured work, meanwhile, affords productivity levels that surpass overseas manufacturers and, when made part of electronic supply interchanges with retailers, can provide better coordinated production. Even in this standardized segment, firms are finding quality and timely delivery to be important attributes.

Contractors

Contractors, who are near the beginning of the fashion-oriented chain, retain a periphery-like status even though they may be located in the United States. Like their overseas counterparts, domestic contractors capitalize upon large pools of low-wage labor, extracting value via wage-depressing tactics. It is difficult to determine actual profits in this sector because most of the firms are privately held. But if their proliferation in the fashion-oriented regions is anything to go by, retained earnings must be attractive even by immigrant entrepreneurial standards for them to persist and flourish (Light and Bonacich, 1987).

Textile Firms

The final node in apparel commodity chains, the textile companies, use their oligopoly power to influence purchasing and distribution but nevertheless remain somewhat dependent upon the domestic apparel industry for customers. Productivity increases associated with mechanization have rationalized the industry, allowing firms to cut labor costs. Together, such changes have depressed fabric costs relative to inflation but enabled textile companies to retain high profit levels. Although textile companies impose constraints upon small apparel firms, sometimes forcing the latter to source fabric supply overseas and thus reconfiguring that part of the chain, relatively low textile costs and supply efficiencies have aided larger U.S. manufacturers in the standardized market.

CONCLUSION

Exploring the developments and strategic responses outlined above is likely to yield further insights into the commodity chain concept. It also clarifies the outcome of the current managerial pre-occupation with restructuring around flexible production systems.

Three forces may be viewed as compelling change in clothing manufacture. First, changing consumer demand leading to market segmentation rendered much of the mass production system in clothing inappropriate. Second, import penetration from the NICs introduced greater cost competition. As a result of these two developments, major retailers have exploited the diversity and competitive costs of imported apparel, using these as a lever vis-à-vis the indigenous clothing manufacturers. The third force derives from textile manufacturers, themselves under pressure from imported fabric, who have used superior economic power over clothing manufacturers to maintain profit margins. The clothing manufacturers now are sandwiched between the oligopsony of the major retailers and the oligopoly of the textile giants.

In assessing these trends from a commodity chain perspective, the following pattern emerges. Production is fragmented *between* firms domestically, *between* firms globally, or *within* firms domestically, depending upon the respective commodity chain. Each level reflect's further stratification of the production process as the apparel commodity chains have been reconfigured. At the respective production sites, standardized mass market firms rely upon technological innovation (introduction of design, production and processing technology) and labor intensification, whereas fashion-oriented firms are more likely to use decentralized production techniques (subcontractors and related wage-depressing tactics). Both procedures imply forms of flexible accumulation that remain decidedly Fordist in character.

Because of the complex interplay of constraining variables, such as the MFA, segmented consumer demand and institutional regulation, simple labor-cost differences are insufficient to explain production strategies at the various nodes in the chain. Instead, upgrading the unit value of products, thereby enhancing the relative economic value-added, or capturing a larger market share and increasing the volume of sales, also become central ways firms secure a more core-like position in the commodity chain.

NOTES

I would like to thank Gary Gereffi, Miguel Korzeniewicz, and Jonathan Winterton for helpful comments and suggestions on an earlier draft of this chapter.

1. From interviews with small men's wear manufacturers conducted in 1988, it was apparent that piece-goods supply problems were their worst headache. Three of the four firms interviewed had abandoned domestic manufacture, and acquired factories for product assembly in the sites where they purchased fabric (India and Bangladesh). Despite some quality problems they appeared generally satisfied with these new relationships.

2. For example, Bangladesh exported $3.7 million (at current exchange rates) of garment products in 1981 compared with $750 million a decade later (*Wall Street Journal*, August 6, 1991). Most of this growth has been in garment assembly under contract with Western firms.

3. In conversations with managers at a large men's shirt manufacturer that used several Central American sites outside of Mexico, corruption among and bribery of local government officials were cited as problematic. Particularly troublesome are the accounting headaches of "costing" such erratic and irregular procedures.

4. Recent estimates claim more than 35 percent of sewing shop workers in Los Angeles are paid less than the minimum wage, the majority are not properly compensated for overtime work, and 7 percent of apparel contractors use illegal child labor (*Los Angeles Times*, August 5, 1992).

REFERENCES

AAMA. 1986. *Planning and Implementing an Apparel Sourcing Strategy*. Report of the Technical Advisor's Committee, American Apparel Manufacturers Association, Washington D.C.

————. 1988. *Flexible Apparel Manufacturing*. Report of the Technical Advisory Committee, American Apparel Manufacturers Association, Washington D.C.

Blumenberg, Evelyn, and Ong, Paul. 1992. "Regional Strategies and Gender Differences in the U.S. Apparel Industries." Paper presented at the conference The Globalization of the Apparel Industry in the Pacific Rim, UCLA.

Bonacich, Edna. 1990. "Asian Immigrants in the Los Angeles Garment Industry." Unpublished manuscript.

Cline, William. 1987. *The Future of World Trade in Apparel*. Washington, D.C.: Institute for International Economics.

de la Torre, Jose, 1986. *Clothing Industry Adjustment in Developed Countries*. New York: St. Martin's Press.

Dertouzos, Michael; Lester, Richard; and Solow, R. 1989. *Made in America*. New York: Harper Books.

Deyo, Fred, ed. 1987. *The Political Economy of the New Asian Industrialism*. Ithaca, NY: Cornell University Press.

Dicken, P. 1992. *Global Shift*. New York: The Guilford Press.

Evans, Peter. 1987. "Class, State, and Dependence in East Asia." In F. Deyo, op. cit.

Falk, William, and Lyson, Thomas. 1988. *High Tech, Low Tech, No Tech*. Albany: State University of New York Press.

Friedman, Brian. 1988. "Productivity Trends in Department Stores, 1967–86." *Monthly Labor Review* 33:17–21.

Gereffi, Gary, and Korzeniewicz, Miguel. 1990. "Commodity Chains and Footwear Exports in the Semiperiphery." In *Semiperipheral States in the World-Economy*, edited by William G. Martin. Westport, CT: Greenwood Press.

Hoffman, Kurt, and Rush, Howard. 1988. *Micro-Electronics and Clothing*. New York: Praeger.

ILGWU. 1985. *The U.S. Apparel Industry, 1960–1985, with Special Emphasis on Women's and Children's Apparel*. New York. International Ladies Garment Workers Union.

Kolko, Joyce. 1988. *Restructuring the World Economy*. New York: Pantheon Books.

Laslett, John, and Tyler, Mary. 1989. *The ILGWU in Los Angeles 1907–1988*. Inglewood: Ten Star Press.

Light, Ivan, and Bonacich, Edna. 1987. *Immigrant Entrepreneurs*. Berkeley: University of California Press.

Lin, J. 1989. "The Social Geography of Garment Production in Lower Manhattan." REALM Working Paper Series. New York: New School for Social Research.

Nehmer, Stanley, and Love, Mark. 1985. "Textiles and Apparel: A Negotiated Approach to International Competition." In *U.S. Competitiveness in the World Economy*, edited by B. R. Scott and G. C. Lodge. Boston: Harvard Business School.

OTA. 1987. *The U.S. Textile and Apparel Industry: A Revolution in Progress*. Washington D.C.: Office of Technology Assessment.

Ross, Robert, Trachte, Kent. 1990. *Global Capitalism*. Albany: State University of New York Press.

Scott, Robert, and Lee, Thea. 1991. "Reconsidering the Benefits and Costs of Trade Protection: The Case of Textiles and Apparel." Working Paper No. 105. Economic Policy Institute, Washington D.C.

Shepherd, Jacob. 1987. "Mechanizing the Sewing Room." *Bobbin*. May, pp. 93–96.

Sieling, Mark Scott, and Curtin, Daniel. 1988. "Patterns of Productivity Change in Men's and Boys' Suits and Coats." *Monthly Labor Review*, 3, 2:25–31.

Sprinkle, Stephen; Charles, Paula; and Chepaitis, Jerry. 1992. "Computing New Solutions." *Bobbin*, July, pp. 43–48.

Stern, Aimee. 1986. "Retailers Restructure." *Dun's Business Month*, February, pp. 28–31.

U.S. Department of Commerce. 1990. *1990 U.S. Industrial Outlook: Apparel*. Washington, D.C.

Waldinger, Roger. 1986. *Through the Eye of the Needle*. New York: New York University Press.

11

Automobile Commodity Chains in the NICs: A Comparison of South Korea, Mexico, and Brazil

Naeyoung Lee and Jeffrey Cason

INTRODUCTION

A number of countries in the so-called semiperiphery have advanced significantly in recent years and moved up in the world-system. In this process, they have climbed up the technological ladder to produce more high-value-added goods. One of the many industries that clearly indicates upward mobility in the world system is the automobile industry. The auto industry is a capital- and technology-intensive industry that has high barriers to entry, and it is often assumed that lower-income countries with plentiful labor supplies do not have a comparative advantage in such industries. However, several semiperipheral countries have aggressively begun exporting in these industries. As Table 11.1 indicates, several countries have been particularly successful in their penetration of international markets in the auto industry. It is interesting to note that the "success stories," in terms of international market penetration, are not simply in East Asian countries, as is commonly assumed. Some Latin American countries have come to play an important role in the international auto industry.

This chapter is concerned with three of the most successful cases of auto export expansion. We find it especially useful to make this a cross-regional comparison, since both Latin American and East Asian countries have moved aggressively into auto export markets. We focus on the automobile industries in South Korea, Mexico, and Brazil. As Figure 11.1 shows, each of these countries has experienced rapid export growth in the auto industry in the last decade. In all three countries, exports from the auto sector represent a significant portion

Table 11.1
Production and Export of Motor Vehicles from Selected NICs (Thousands of Units)

Country	1970 Production	1970 Export	1980 Production	1980 Export	1988 Production	1988 Export	1990 Production	1990 Export
Brazil	416	0	1,165	157	1,069	320	914	254[a]
Argentina	220	1	289	4	164	2	100	2[a]
Mexico	193	0	490	18	510	173	821	279
South Korea	19	0	123	15	1,084	576	1,321	339
Taiwan	9	0	133	73	250	N.A.	339	NA
India	63	4	114	12	312	0	364	NA
TOTAL (A)	901	5	2,307	279	3,389	1,071	3,859	[b]
WORLD TOTAL (B)	29,667	8,661	38,495	15,161	46,713	19,323	48,113	19,499[a]
A/B (percent)	3.0		5.9	2.0	7.2	6.8	8.0	[b]

Sources: MVMA--World Motor Vehicle Data. Various Years; MVMA--Facts and Figures (1991); Automotive News (May 27, 1992).
[a] 1989 data
[b] Cannot be calculated because of lack of data

Figure 11.1
Auto Sector Exports, 1979–1989—Brazil, Mexico, and South Korea (Includes Finished Vehicles, Engines, and Parts)

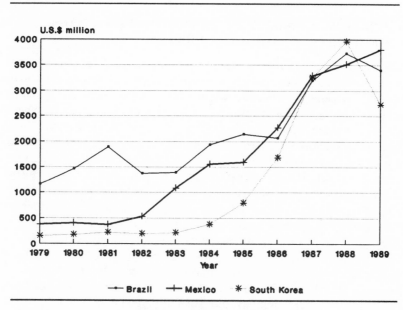

Sources: Brazil: ANFAVEA (1989) and Banco do Brasil (1990)
Mexico: INEGI (1990)
South Korea: KAMA (1991)

of total exports—11.1 percent of total Brazilian exports, 17.1 percent of total Mexican exports, and 6.5 percent of total exports in South Korea in 1988.

What is most revealing is how the same industries are associated with strikingly different development patterns in each country. The Latin American cases exhibit nearly complete transnational corporation (TNC) domination of the industry, while the South Korean auto industry is under the control of local capital. The export profile is strikingly different as well: South Korea, and to a lesser extent Brazil, have emphasized finished-vehicle exports. Mexico, on the other hand, has largely filled the niche of a parts exporter. Another striking difference between these countries is the destination of their exports. Mexico and South Korea send the vast majority of their exports to the North American market, while Brazil has a much wider range of customers for its auto industry, with significant quantities of exports to Europe and the Middle East.

To explain these different development patterns, we propose to use some of the insights that can be obtained by looking at the commodity chain of the auto industry. We conclude that by looking at the networks of the commodity chain, we can include such explanatory factors as state policy, business strategy, and geography that significantly affect patterns of internationalization in the auto industry. We demonstrate that the commodity chain can be a powerful analytical tool in the analysis of the development trajectories and the upward mobility of semiperipheral countries.

THEORETICAL CONSIDERATIONS: COMMODITY CHAINS IN THE WORLD AUTOMOBILE INDUSTRY

The world-systems literature, while offering substantial insights into the structure of the world-economy, is sometimes less enlightening about the development trajectories of particular countries within the system. The concern of much of this literature is on structural position rather than individual difference, and this emphasis often downplays the significance of individual differences. On the other hand, some recent state-centric theorizing has made the opposite mistake. Much of this literature (which often takes as its point of departure the world-systems literature) plays up the role of the state in determining the *uniqueness* of particular countries. While certainly every country has its own distinctive historical trajectory, it is often counterproductive to emphasize these differences while ignoring the systemic forces at work that influence this trajectory.

In the end, the problems associated with both of these approaches boil down to their level of analysis. While a world-systems approach takes into account international factors—world market trends or global political alliances—that influence development trajectories, a statist approach relies on domestic variables, such as class, coalition formation, and institutional development. Neither of these sets of variables is entirely satisfactory on its own, and each emphasis is vulnerable to the criticisms of the other.

We propose to bridge some of these differences by focusing on the auto commodity chain in several countries. The advantages of using the commodity chain concept are several. It is a useful framework in which to understand particular industries and their relationship to the international economy. In looking at a commodity chain, we can disaggregate an industry into its substages, and this helps in our understanding of what factors are most important in influencing an industry's trajectory. Concentrating on a commodity chain also emphasizes dynamism, in that it directs our attention to the possibilities of industrial upgrading. Industrial upgrading generally implies more control over some parts of the production process, and conceivably the ability to generate technical knowledge that can help in later efforts at upgrading. This approach also stresses the importance of the concept of market niche, which implies different types of integration with the international market. The particular niche occupied by an individual country within a commodity chain reflects domestic institutional, economic, and social configurations in individual countries; at the same time, the niche and the concomitant integration into the international economy reflects back on the domestic political economy.

Before getting into the analysis of the commodity chain in the auto industry, we must first clarify how we will apply the concept to the auto industry. A commodity chain, as defined by Hopkins and Wallerstein, is "a network of labor and production processes whose end result is a finished commodity" (1986: 159). The automobile is probably one of the most complex commodities that can be analyzed. The production of an automobile is the result of an extremely intricate industrial process that links suppliers and producers in many parts of the globe. We do not, however, pretend to analyze the entire chain in the auto industry. Nor do we propose to undertake a detailed analysis of auto parts production; instead, we will focus on the networks between autoparts producers and auto assemblers.

As further elaborated by Gereffi and Korzeniewicz, the commodity chain is made up of four segments: raw material supply, production, exporting, and marketing and retailing (1990: 51). Our approach is a bit different because we are analyzing an industry as complex as the auto industry. Instead of raw material supply, we focus on parts supply networks. And instead of making exporting a separate segment of the commodity chain, it is included in both the parts supply networks and the marketing networks. This is necessary since export linkages can take place either through the export of parts or through the export of finished vehicles. In other words, integration into the global commodity chain can occur at different places.

Our analysis of the automobile commodity chain must be careful to distinguish between different levels of analysis. In general, the commodity chain approach aims to be international in its level of analysis, but it is easy to slip back to a domestic level. The problem is identified by Newfarmer, who points out that when considering industries that are internationalized, the "analyst now must consider not only market structures in several countries but the links among them" (1985: 5). This problem can be dealt with by analyzing both internal and external markets, as well as the impact of the growth (or contraction) of one of the markets on the other.

The automobile industry has developed to supply both domestic and international markets. In most developing countries, the auto industry has been set up under the strategy of import-substituting industrialization (ISI). When these countries embark on ISI in the auto industry, their goal has often been to bring as much of the commodity chain *within* the country as possible. In this way they have attempted to *limit* the links to the international chain as much as possible. Thus, even when these industries eventually turn toward the international market, a still isolated domestic commodity chain can coexist with integration into the global commodity chain.

We now turn to our analysis of the commodity chain in the automobile industry in Brazil, Mexico, and South Korea. We focus on how the automobile industries in these three countries have undertaken distinct strategies of integration in the global auto commodity chain. We concentrate, in turn, on parts supply networks, assembly networks, and marketing networks. We then turn to an analysis of the outcome of these types of integration into the global auto commodity chain, with a consideration of the market niche occupied by the auto industries in each of these countries.

THE COMMODITY CHAINS OF THE AUTOMOBILE INDUSTRIES IN SOUTH KOREA, MEXICO AND BRAZIL

Parts Supply Networks

The production and supply of autoparts are critical in the commodity chain of the auto industry, since the cost and quality of autoparts determine the competitiveness of finished vehicles. Building effective supplier networks that produce a wide variety of auto parts is one of the most challenging tasks for the terminal firms in the auto industry, since a single vehicle is made up of more than 15,000 auto parts. While some important auto parts—such as engines—are produced by assemblers in house, a large proportion of auto parts are produced by separate auto parts firms and subsidiaries. Parts suppliers are made up of various tiers and differ in size and in terms of their linkage to assemblers. Usually, one assembler needs to organize several hundred auto parts firms, which have many more employees than the terminal firms.[1] Some large part firms produce key and sophisticated auto parts for the assemblers, while small firms produce minor parts that later become part of more sophisticated autoparts.

The three industries that we are considering have very different organizational configurations in the parts industry and in their assembler-supplier networks. To begin with, the three industries have had different types of linkages to foreign capital. The Korean parts industry is mainly controlled by local firms, while foreign capital has played the major role in the Mexican parts industry.[2] The Brazilian case occupies an intermediate position between Mexico and South Korea. In Brazil, local firms dominate the parts industry, even though there is substantial foreign participation.[3]

Second, the local content ratio differs in the three countries. Korea and Brazil reached substantially higher levels of local content than Mexico, as shown in Table 11.2. The different local content ratios are a result of bargaining between auto firms and the state. After an assembly stage that was based on imported autoparts, the three nations tried to develop an integrated auto industry by imposing obligatory local content levels to help the development of the local parts industry. TNCs did not like such requirements, since a high local content ratio increased production costs. A high ratio also reduced the cost advantages of foreign firms vis-à-vis local firms, since the TNCs were unable to use their access to parts suppliers in their home countries.

The local content ratio for export vehicles is generally much lower in all three countries than the ratio for vehicles sold domestically. This is mainly because some autoparts produced locally do not reach the quality required at the international level. Even when minimum quality and technical levels can be reached,

Table 11.2
Estimated Local Content Rates in the Auto Industry in South Korea, Brazil, and Mexico, 1988 (in Percent)

	South Korea	Brazil	Mexico
Vehicles for the Domestic market	90- 95	90	55-65
Vehicles for the Export market	80- 85	60-70	30- 55

Source: Authors's estimates based on statistics from business association publications

Note: Estimates are not always directly comparable, since measures of local content vary in different countries.

the cost of the domestically produced parts is much higher. In Brazil and Mexico the share of domestic components is one of the main bargaining issues in export agreements negotiated between the auto TNCs and the state.

Third, the level of auto parts exports differs significantly. The export of auto parts indicates the extent to which the locally produced parts are supplied to the auto commodity chain of other countries. Mexico has had the highest level of auto parts exports, while Korea has had a negligible amount of parts exports. Brazil again has occupied an intermediate position. The different level of auto parts exports is influenced by a number of factors, including firm strategy, state policies, and geographical location.

Because the Korean parts industry has been relatively insulated from the influence of foreign firms, the quality and productivity of locally produced auto parts have been below international standards. In addition, local parts firms have been unable to obtain access to the foreign market. As assembly firms increased their exports, they realized that the quality and technological level of the Korean parts industry was one of the most serious obstacles to their success in world markets. To overcome this problem, the Korean assemblers have assisted the parts firms and tried to build stable and long-term relationships with their suppliers. Partly as an outcome of state policies, in-house production by assemblers has been reduced and the proportion of auto parts obtained from subcontractors has increased. Assemblers have also attempted to build effective network links to parts suppliers. Assembly firms have provided financial support and technical assistance to the parts firms (Amsden, 1989: 179–88). In addition, assembly firms helped parts suppliers acquire advanced technologies through licensing or joint ventures with foreign firms. Finally, in the case of auto parts that require sophisticated technologies, terminal firms directly entered the joint-venture operation with the foreign parts firms. As a consequence of these efforts, exports of the Korean parts industry have increased significantly (from US$67 million in 1982 to US$398 million in 1989), and some parts that previously had been imported have been substituted by locally produced parts.

In Mexico, auto parts exports have increased significantly since the late 1970s. When the Big Three pursued their out-sourcing strategy with their "world cars," Mexico was chosen as a supplier of auto parts because of its proximity to the U.S. market and its preexisting connection to the U.S. firms. Since 1982, the *maquiladora* sector has grown impressively and has played a larger role in the auto sector. In fact, the auto parts sector was the most dynamically growing sector among the *maquiladora* industries in the 1980s (Gonzales, 1989; Arjona, 1990). Between 1979 and 1985, the number of plants in the transport equipment sector grew from 38 to 63. Employment in auto-industry-related *maquiladoras* grew from 5,035 in 1979 to 40,145 in 1985 (INEGI, 1989).

Although Brazilian auto parts exports have increased substantially in recent years, the general tendency has been to sell to the terminal firms in Brazil, who then export the finished vehicles or engines. Some of the larger Brazilian parts firms have developed sophisticated technological abilities—Metal Leve, a Brazilian firm, has set up its own research and design facility outside of Detroit—but for the most part the firms have exported via terminal firms. For example, in 1984, though parts firms claimed U.S. $1 billion in exports, only 34 percent of those exports were actually carried out independently (*Gazeta Mercantil*, February 26, 1985).

Assembly Production Networks

The assembly production network of the auto industry is the most complex part of the auto industry commodity chain. In order to produce a vehicle, several discrete stages are involved: the design of products, the building of facilities, the acquisition of technologies, and the operation of the production process. In addition, the production process itself is made up of different stages, such as engine production, pressing, stamping, soldering, painting, and final assembling. In the traditional mass production system, these various production processes on the assembly line are linked by conveyer belts. In the flexible production system, the different production processes are coordinated in a computerized central control room.

In the three auto industries that we are considering, the organizational characteristics of assembly firms differ significantly, as do the organization of production and relations of production. Table 11.3 summarizes some of the main characteristics of the assembly production networks. A crucial difference among the three cases is the ownership structure and the size and number of auto firms. The Korean assembly firms are owned by local big business, while TNC subsidiaries are the main assemblers in Mexico and Brazil. Yet there is an important difference between Mexico and Brazil: the main exporters in the Mexican auto industry have been the U.S. Big Three, while the European firms Volkswagen and Fiat have been the dominant exporters in Brazil. In South Korea, the lack

Table 11.3
Characteristics of Assembly Networks in South Korea, Mexico, and Brazil

	South Korea	Mexico	Brazil
Main Exporting Firms	Local Private Firms	U.S. Big Three	European TNCs (VW, Fiat)
Timing of Transition to Export Stage	Early 1980s	Late 1970s	Early 1970s
Export Strategy	Small Passenger Car Exports to North American Market	Rapid and Extensive Integration into Global Strategies of U.S. Big Three	Regional Exporter and Exporter to Other Developing Country Markets

of TNC dominance in the industry is the result of the interaction among the TNCs, local firms, and the state during the import substitution stage from the 1960s to the late 1970s. During this period the TNCs were not particularly interested in expanding their operations to South Korea, which combined with the efforts of the Korean state and big business to keep the industry national (Back, 1990; Lee, 1993).

This different ownership structure has an important impact on the business strategies of firms. The Korean local assembly firms have aggressively pursued an export strategy concentrating on finished vehicles. Hyundai has been the most successful in its penetration of the North American market. The export success of the Korean assemblers is influenced by several factors. First, the local Korean assemblers belong to large and powerful economic conglomerates and have a substantial degree of organizational strength. Two of the three large assembly firms, Hyundai and Daewoo, are members of the first and third largest economic conglomerates. With their organizational and financial strength, the Korean firms have been able to build new plants and to innovate in the production process and invest in research and development.

The main competitive strategy of the Korean assemblers has taken advantage of their cost competitiveness in producing small passenger cars by effectively using the Fordist mass production system. This cost advantage of the Korean assemblers is also helped by other institutional and market conditions, including the limited number of firms, the rapid expansion of the domestic market, and a cheap labor force.[4] A crucial factor contributing to the competitiveness of the Korean auto firms is their industry structure, which consists of a limited number of firms. In South Korea the number of firms has not exceeded four throughout the 1980s, and in passenger vehicle production, after the merger policy adopted

Table 11.4
Wages and Productivity Levels in the World Auto Industry, 1989

Country	Hourly Wage[a] (in US$)	Productivity (Hours per unit)	Labor Cost (US$ per unit)	Relative Labor Cost (US = 100)
Brazil	1	48.1	48.1	12.8
Mexico	2	40.1	80.2	21.3
South Korea	4	25.6[b]	102.4	27.2
Japan	10	16.8	168.0	44.6
United States	15	25.1	376.5	100.0

Source: Krafcik(1989)
[a] In hourly wage, various bonuses and fringe benefits are not included.
[b]Korean productivity data is based on Hyundai.

in 1981, only two firms remained.[5] This industry structure is one of the most crucial differences between the Korean case and the auto sectors of Mexico, Brazil, and Taiwan, where the limited market was fragmented by too many firms. This industry structure has allowed the Korean firms to achieve economies of scale and subsequent international competitiveness.

In addition, the internationalization of the Korean auto industry has taken place concurrently with the expansion of the domestic market. This is clearly contrasted to the Latin American cases, where export growth has occurred with the rapid decline of the domestic market, which is a result of the debt crisis and subsequent austerity policies. In the Korean case the expansion of the domestic market contributed to export success in two ways. First, auto firms invested profits from domestic sales in the development of new models and technological improvement. Second, rising domestic sales allowed firms to increase production volumes to the level at which economies of scale for the mass production system could be reached.

Furthermore, a relatively cheap but disciplined and productive labor force was an important factor contributing to the competitiveness of the Korean auto industry. Because the auto workers are poorly organized, management has greater flexibility.[6] Table 11.4 shows the wage and productivity levels of the three nations' industries, along with Japanese and U.S. auto industries. While hourly wages in South Korea are higher than in Mexico and Brazil, the productivity of the Korean auto industry is much higher than the two other cases. However, with the recent new union movement since 1987, labor unions have been organized and the average wage of auto workers has increased rapidly (see Ogle, 1990; Rogers, 1990). This contrasts with the Mexican case, where the labor force experienced drastic declines in average wages and bargaining power.

Finally, the South Korean firms have overcome their production and marketing limitations by entering into strategic alliances with TNCs. From foreign partners, the Korean firms have obtained advanced technologies and some key components that they lacked. In addition, Korean firms could rely on the marketing networks of the global firms to enter the world market (Dyer et al., 1987: 171–75; Terukito, 1986: 37–41; Cho, 1992; Lee, 1992).

In Mexico the TNCs concentrated on the export of engines until the mid-1980s, after which the export volume of finished vehicles has increased significantly. Engine exports more than quadrupled between 1982 and 1987, to a total of 1,367,000 units (AMIA, 1988). The TNCs needed new engine plants because of the restructuring of the world auto industry, which demanded more fuel-efficient engines. Since building new engine plants in North America would be far more costly, geographical proximity proved very advantageous for Mexico. This was especially true once the U.S. Big Three began to adopt the just-in-time delivery system. Finally, state policy also influenced this pattern of inter-nationalization when policymakers in Mexico began to demand that half of the exports come from locally produced parts, forcing TNCs to use their Mexican operations for export.

Among TNCs, the Big Three have pursued a more active export strategy than Volkswagen and Nissan. The U.S. Big Three have accounted for more than 70 percent of total exports since 1985, while Nissan and Volkswagen have been oriented toward the domestic market. There are several reasons why the Big Three and Nissan and Volkswagen chose different strategies. First, the two groups of firms have different market niches within the Mexican auto commodity chain. The U.S. Big Three had concentrated on the luxury and sports car segment, which was devastated after the 1982 economic crisis. Volkswagen and Nissan, with more emphasis on small cars, did not see their domestic market position damaged in the same way by the economic crisis, since with the crisis came a shift in consumer demand to compact and subcompact cars.

Geographic proximity to the U.S. market has also played a role in the dom-inance of the U.S. Big Three in Mexican auto exports. The Big Three have built state-of-the-art export engine and assembly plants in northern Mexico, where they have adopted advanced technologies and new production systems (Shaiken, 1987; Sandoval, 1987; Arteaga et al., 1989). In Volkswagen's case, it had such a small share of the U.S. market (2 percent in 1987) that it could not expect to engage in significant exports from Mexico. Nissan had already made the strategic decision to build transplants in the United States, and thus it did not need to use its Mexican operations to supply the U.S. market.

Another important dimension of the auto firms' strategies to restructure the Mexican auto industry as a dynamic export sector was an effort to maximize management's flexibility vis-à-vis workers and unions. Management has adopted several interrelated strategies, which have focused on changing employment policy and collective contracts, as well as the reorganization of union affiliations and the weakening of union power. Young, inexperienced, but more educated workers have been hired in the new export plants. In addition, the average wage in the auto industry has dropped almost 40 percent between 1982 and 1989. Furthermore, labor contracts at the new export plants have been written to allow a much more limited role for the union in the organization of the production process. In the northern export plants, management has far greater flexibility in hiring and promotion, the use of temporary workers, the organization of the production process, and the movement of employees between different production areas (Middlebrook, 1991, 286–89; Arteaga et al., 1989).

Brazilian terminal firms began their exports much earlier than either South Korea or Mexico. As early as 1972, the Brazilian state began to encourage the auto firms to export, since, as in Mexico, they were a constant drain on foreign exchange, primarily because of their import of machinery. Unlike Mexico, the state in Brazil was much more effective in the 1970s in achieving export commitments from the terminal firms, using both carrots and sticks to push the firms to export. The sticks included a threatened denial of access to foreign exchange as well as higher duties on imports for firms that did not formulate an export program. The carrots, however, were much more important: the Brazilian state set up a new program, called BEFIEX (Special Fiscal Benefits for Exports), which guaranteed federal and state tax credits, subsidized credit, and a tax credit bonus (an outright export subsidy) to firms willing to sign long-term (eight- to ten-year) export commitments. This made exporting very lucrative to these TNCs, and exports increased dramatically, from under U.S. $100 million in 1973 to U.S. $1.57 billion by 1981 (ANFAVEA, 1989). In effect, these auto TNCs were being induced to integrate what previously had been primarily a local commodity chain into the global commodity chain.

The firms integrated their operations into the global chain in very different ways. The main determining factor seems to have been the national origin of TNC capital, which determined the level of integration of the TNCs into the U.S. market. Ford and General Motors (GM) (Chrysler was out of the Brazilian market by the late 1970s) concentrated their export efforts primarily in engines and other parts exports. By far the biggest exporters of finished vehicles have been the two European firms involved in the Brazilian market, Volkswagen and Fiat. Because of their geographical distance from Brazil, European firms did not see much advantage in utilizing their Brazilian operations to supply engines and auto parts to their parent firms. Thus they tried to export finished vehicles to North America and South America.

Brazil has experienced slower and more erratic export growth in the 1980s, which can largely be attributed to the negative effects of state policy and conflictual labor relations. The Brazilian state has repeatedly frustrated TNC auto exporters with an erratic exchange rate policy. This was a consequence of the repeated efforts of the Brazilian state to carry out heterodox shocks to combat inflation without provoking recession. All of these stabilization plans (the Cruzado Plan in 1986, the Bresser Plan in 1987, and the Summer Plan in 1989) have frozen prices, wages, and the exchange rate. However, since these plans ultimately failed to slow inflation for very long, exporters, and in particular auto exporters, complained bitterly about the overvaluation of the Brazilian currency when each of these stabilization plans collapsed and the minidevaluations resumed. Auto exporters even went so far as to propose a special exchange rate for their industry to make Brazilian auto exports more lucrative in 1988 (*O Estado de São Paulo*, August 23, 1987; *Jornal do Brasil*, May 5, 1988). This contrasts with the Mexican case where the state has consistently adopted a radical economic stabilization program.

In addition, the Brazilian auto industry became a center of militant labor unionism beginning in the late 1970s. Again this contrasts with the Mexican case, where the auto firms have successfully introduced post-Fordist labor relations and weakened the bargaining power of organized labor. With these institutional conditions, the Brazilian auto firms failed to introduce advanced technologies and reorganize the production process. One of the principal reasons for the lack of application of more modern technology in the Brazilian auto industry, according to the TNCs, is the existence of Brazil's computer market reserve policy, which shuts out TNCs in some key aspects of the computer industry and excludes many high-technology imports as well.[7]

Marketing Networks

Marketing networks are the final stage of the auto commodity chain. Complex marketing networks incorporate various kinds of services, including the shipment of cars, the building of dealer networks, advertising and promotion, the development of financing firms, as well as the management of spare parts and repair services. The importance of marketing networks has increased with the globalization of the world auto industry since the 1970s. As the automobile market became increasingly global, competition intensified, forcing auto firms to strengthen their marketing networks. In addition, they had to adjust flexibly to changing market conditions and consumer preferences. Auto firms now try to incorporate feedback from consumers, sales divisions, and dealers into their product planning. The logic behind the new production system—flexible manufacturing or lean production, as it is known—is to increase adaptability to rapidly changing market conditions and consumer preferences. Thus we can conceptualize lean production as a consumer-centered production system, while the mass production system is a firm-centered system.[8]

The features of marketing networks are closely related to ownership structure and product specialization. Building market networks in the foreign market is especially demanding because it requires huge financial resources, experience, and expertise in foreign markets. This is especially true for the local firms in the Korean auto industry. For the Korean auto industry, the establishment of independent marketing networks abroad was the most difficult barrier for a latecomer to confront in the oligopolistic auto industry. Even after building a marketing network, advertising expenses and operating expenses for the maintenance of these networks were a tremendous burden for the latecomer. To confront these problems, the Korean auto firms chose different marketing strategies, depending on their organizational strength and management philosophy (see Lee, 1993).

Hyundai has entered the export market by building an independent marketing network, while Kia and Daewoo have exported to the North American market through Ford's and GM's marketing networks, respectively. Hyundai's decision to build an independent marketing network reflects the risk-taking attitude and strength of Hyundai. Having adopted this strategy, Hyundai has been vulnerable to the threat of trade barriers by the global firms. Kia and Daewoo could avoid these difficulties by relying on the marketing networks of Ford and GM, respectively. Such a strategy was obviously less risky. For example, while Hyundai's dealers in the U.S. market numbered only 183 in 1987, Ford had 5,700 dealers and GM's Pontiac Division had 3,000 dealers in the same year (Hyundai, 1988). But this more dependent strategy had its disadvantages as well, since the two firms could not obtain profits from the marketing process. For example, by exporting vehicles to the U.S. market, Hyundai obtained a 3 percent profit margin from production and a 7 percent margin from the Hyundai marketing subsidiary. Daewoo took a 3.6 percent profit margin, while GM appropriated a 8–9 percent margin from the marketing process (Hanguk Sanup Yeonkuhoi, 1989: 267–70). As Gereffi and Korzeniewicz (1990) found in the footwear industry, the marketing of the final product is often more profitable than its production.

In addition, Kia and Daewoo's export performance has been constrained by the global strategy of their foreign partners. GM and Ford have other foreign partners or subsidiaries, and the outsourcing of finished vehicles from the Korean firms is only one option among many. As the North American trade bloc emerges, for example, it is expected that the Big Three will reduce their outsourcing relations with East Asian partners and consolidate their relationship with Mexico.

In Mexico and Brazil, because the TNCs' global marketing networks can be utilized, these industries have advantages in terms of market access compared to the Korean auto firms. But the export performance of these TNC subsidiaries depends on whether the subsidiaries are selected as export locations within the global strategies of the auto TNCs. For example, GM and Ford have actively integrated their Mexican operations into their global strategies, while their Brazilian operations still focus mainly on the domestic market.

In addition, the marketing capacities of TNCs differ by firm and export destination. Certainly global firms have huge advantages when they export to their country or region of origin or to a region where they have a large market share. When they try to export to regions or countries where they have not established marketing networks, however, even the global firms have confronted obstacles. For example, Volkswagen and Fiat have very small market shares and poor marketing networks in North America. These poor marketing networks seem to be a crucial reason their Brazilian subsidiaries had little success in penetrating the U.S. market (Volkswagen) or did not even attempt to do so (Fiat). Further-

Figure 11.2
Export Destinations of Finished Vehicles from Brazil, Mexico, and South Korea, 1983–1989 (Cumulative Data)

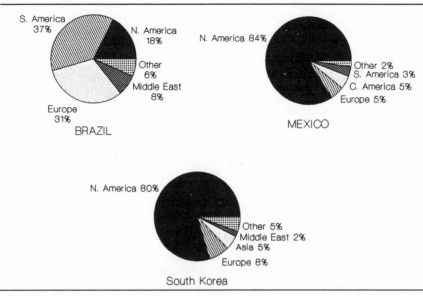

Source: MVMA. Various Years.
Note: Brazilian Data for 1983 and 1985 not included.

more, even when auto TNCs export to their countries of origin, they are constrained in their outsourcing strategies. Increasing the supply of finished vehicles or engines from foreign subsidiaries requires a reduction in domestic production, which often implies plant closings and confrontation with labor unions unless they can somehow manage to increase their current market share. Such increases have been very rare for the European and American firms, especially given the gains made by Japanese firms.

EXPORT NICHES AND INDUSTRIAL UPGRADING

As a combined result of their different types of integration into the global commodity chain, the three auto industries have created different export niches. An export niche refers to the segments of world markets captured by the different countries within an industrial sector. We consider export niche both in terms of export destination and product niche.

As can be seen in Figure 11.2, Mexico and South Korea have sent more than 80 percent of their exports to the North American market. Brazil, in contrast, has a much wider range of customers for its auto industry. The high proportion of the North American market in Korean auto exports is the result of the successful penetration by the Korean auto firms (especially Hyundai), and of the changing market situation and trade policy in the United States. After the first oil crisis, Japanese firms virtually dominated the small car market (Altshuler et al., 1984). In order to slow the growth of Japanese auto imports, the U.S. government pressed the Japanese government to impose voluntary export restraints in 1982 (Destler, 1986). This reduction in Japanese car imports made the U.S. small car market available to Korean auto firms. This situation provided Hyundai with a timely opportunity to become a major exporter to the small car market in North America.

The different export destinations of Mexico and Brazil are a result of the global strategies of the main exporters and their marketing capacity. The dominant position of the U.S. market in the Mexican case is a result of the global strategies of the Big Three as the dominant exporters. In Brazil the two main exporters, Volkswagen and Fiat, have exported finished vehicles to Europe and South America. The trend of regional integration of the auto sector between Brazil and Argentina also aided Brazil's role as a regional exporter. Finally, the auto industry in Brazil (and in particular Volkswagen) has been involved in state-negotiated barter trade in the Middle East, with the exchange of oil for manufactured goods from Brazil. VW's main customer in these arrangements was Iraq (*Jornal do Brasil*, July 22, 1987; *Gazeta Mercantil*, August 9, 1988).

Despite variations by firms within the countries, the three auto industries have developed distinctive product niches (see Figure 11.3). Mexican exports are much more concentrated in the parts and engine sector (more than 70 percent of the total), while South Korean firms export more than 80 percent in the finished vehicle sector. Of all three countries, Brazil has the most diversified product mix for exports, with significant export levels in parts, engines, and finished vehicles.

Recently the three auto industries have attempted to upgrade their export niches. The Korean auto firms wanted to upgrade their export items from subcompact cars to compact cars. This industrial upgrading is driven by several factors. First, the rapid appreciation of the Korean currency and the emergence of organized labor (which led to wage increases) have undermined the cost advantages in the small passenger car segment. Because of declining cost advantages, export volume has declined from the peak year of 1988. Second, in order to compete in the advanced country markets, it is critical to diversify products and to change models frequently. Yet these efforts at industrial upgrading have not been successful so far. In this market segment, competition is much more intense and the cost advantage of Korean cars is not large enough to compensate its mediocre quality. Moreover, the emergence of regional trade blocs in North America and Europe makes it difficult for the Korean firms to obtain access to the major auto markets. In addition, it is unclear how well South Korean firms can adapt to the radical technological changes in the auto industry. Finally, South Korean firms have been affected by especially conflictual relations between labor and capital.

The Mexican auto industry has experienced substantial industrial upgrading.

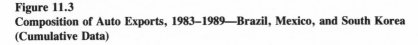

Figure 11.3
Composition of Auto Exports, 1983–1989—Brazil, Mexico, and South Korea
(Cumulative Data)

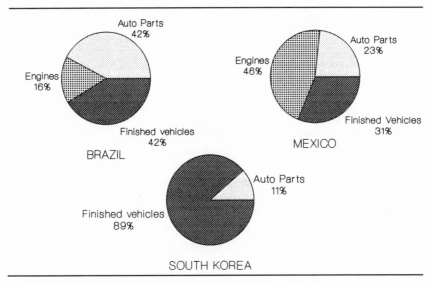

Sources: Brazil: ANFAVEA (1989) and Banco do Brasil (1990)
Mexico: INEGI (Various Years)
South Korea: KAMA (1991) and Korean Trade Association (1991)

During the second half of the 1980s, the Big Three increased their exports of finished vehicles; the proportion of finished vehicles in total exports reached 42 percent of total auto sector exports in 1989. This was related to the change in the global strategies of the Big Three. Another notable recent shift is that Nissan and Volkswagen have begun to use their Mexican operations as strategic locations to penetrate the U.S. market. In 1990 Nissan began to build a new assembly plant in Aguascalientes that will produce 100,000 passenger cars annually from 1993. Nissan plans to export vehicles produced in this plant to the United States. Volkswagen also has tried since 1987 to transform its Mexican operation toward exports to the United States. The recently negotiated North American Free Trade Agreement (NAFTA) will likely encourage these trends toward more auto sector investments in Mexico.

In this context of rapidly expanding exports and industrial upgrading, Brazil is something of an exception. The TNCs operating in Brazil attempted to diversify export destinations after the domestic Brazilian market collapsed in the 1980s and traditional export markets (especially the rest of Latin America) suffered economic contraction as well. But because of the already mentioned computer market reserve and the unwillingness of the TNCs to invest in an uncertain Brazilian economy, upgrading has been far less extensive than in the other two countries. Investments, in fact, have declined dramatically in recent years.

Whereas annual auto sector investments by TNCs averaged U.S. $132 million between 1972 and 1978 and U.S. $328 million in the 1979–1982 period, this annual figure had dropped precipitously to only U.S. $54 million between 1983 and 1988 (ANFAVEA, 1989). Reduced export subsidies have also dampened auto sector enthusiasm for increased export-oriented investments (*Exame*, May 31, 1989).

CONCLUSIONS AND IMPLICATIONS

The global commodity chain in the auto industry illustrates the different integration paths that have been taken by upwardly mobile semiperipheral countries within the same industry. The differences among South Korea, Mexico, and Brazil are striking. To begin with, the degree of integration of the local commodity chain into the global commodity chain differs significantly. The South Korean auto industry has managed to integrate with a significant degree of local capital control. The Mexican auto industry, on the other hand, is most clearly controlled by the TNCs, which dominate both terminal and parts firms. The Brazilian auto industry occupies an intermediate position, with TNCs controlling the terminal firms alongside substantial local capital participation in the parts industry.

Regional generalizations that lump Latin American countries together and East Asian countries together cannot, in an industry such as the automobile industry, stand up to close analysis. In fact, in some aspects (such as export destination and rapid internationalization) there are more similarities between South Korea and Mexico than between Mexico and Brazil. As for the composition of exports, Brazil looks more like South Korea than it does like Mexico (for a similar point, see Gereffi, 1990: 102–106). The experiences of the three auto industries also reveal that there is no single pattern that characterizes the incorporation of the NICs' industries into the world-market. Whereas Mexico has become a supplier of parts and engines in the global auto industry, South Korea has emerged as an exporter of compact cars. The Brazilian auto industry has been integrated into the global commodity chain with both exports of finished vehicles and parts and engines. There are many paths to upward mobility in the semiperiphery and many factors that influence such upward (or, as the case may be, downward) movement. State policy can certainly affect a nation's development trajectory, but an approach that emphasizes the evolution and connections of the commodity chain points to other explanatory factors, including world-market conditions, geography, and business strategy.

NOTES

The authors would like to thank Gary Gereff, Miguel Korzeniswicz, Roger Kittleson, and Roberto Korzeniewicz for their comments and suggestions on an earlier version of this chapter.

1. In Mexico, for example, the number of employees in the parts industry was 95,900 in 1988, while the number employed in the terminal industry was 51,200 (CIEMEX-WEFA, 1990: 61).

2. The importance of foreign capital in the Mexican parts industry is closely related to the dominance of the terminal industry by the TNCs (see Bennett, 1986 and Arjona, 1990).

3. In the Brazilian parts industry, domestic capital has consistently accounted for more than two-thirds of sales, though usually the foreign firms in the sector have been more profitable. In 1982 domestic firms accounted for 76.4 percent of sales and 62.8 percent of profits in the parts sector. *Visão*, August 31, 1983.

4. More recently the Korean firms have tried to adopt elements of the flexible specialization production system. In doing so, however, they have confronted a number of obstacles, including a lack of technological capacity and conflictual labor-management relations. See Cho (1992).

5. The state has played a crucial role in shaping this industry structure. From the beginning of the assembly stage, the South Korean state has consistently encouraged the merger of small firms and restricted the entry of firms into the auto sector. See Lee (1993).

6. On industrial relations in the Korean auto industry, see Hanguk Nodong Yeonguwon (1989) and Lee (1993).

7. Interview with an auto industry executive, São Paulo, November 28, 1990, and *Gazeta Mercantil*, May 15, 1985.

8. See Womack et al. (1990: 171–91). Despite these changes in the nature of the auto industry, the auto industry remains a producer-driven commodity chain, since TNCs still essentially control the production system. See Gereffi (chapter 5, this volume) for more on the distinction between producer-driven and buyer-driven commodity chains.

REFERENCES

Altshuler, Alan, et al. 1984. *The Future of the Automobile: The Report of MIT's International Automobile Program*. Boston: MIT Press.

AMIA (Asociación Mexicana de la Industria Automotriz). 1988. *La Industria Automotriz de México en Cifras*. Mexico: AMIA.

Amsden, Alice. 1989. *Asia's Next Giant*. Oxford: Oxford University Press.

ANFAVEA (Associação Nacional dos Fabricantes de Veículos Automotores). 1989. *Anuário Estatístico da Indústria Automobilística Brasileira*. São Paulo: ANFAVEA.

Arjona, Luis Enrique. 1990. "La Industria Mexicana de Autopartes Durante el Auge Exportador de los Años Ochenta." In *La Nueva Era de la Industria Automotriz en México*, edited by Jorge Carrillo, pp. 115–150. Tijuana: El Colegio de la Frontera Norte.

Arteaga, Arnulfo; Carillo, Jorge; and Michelli, Jordy. 1989. *Transformaciones Technológicas y Relaciones Laborales en la Industria Automotriz*. Mexico City: Fundación Friedrich.

Back, Jong-Gook. 1990. "Politics of Late Industrialization: The Origins and Processes of Automobile Industry Policies in Mexico and South Korea." Ph.D. dissertation, University of California, Los Angeles.

Banco do Brasil. 1990. *Exportação e Importação; Balança Comercial Brasileira, Janeiro/ Dezembro 1989.* Rio de Janeiro: Banco do Brasil–CACEX.

Bennett, Mark. 1986. *Public Policy and Industrial Development: The Case of the Mexican Auto Parts Industry.* Boulder, CO: Westview Press.

Cho, Hyung-Je. 1992. "Hanguk Jadongcha Sanupui Saengsan Bangsike Kwanhan Yeonku [A Study of the Production System of the Korean Automobile Industry]." Ph.D. dissertation, Seoul National University.

CIEMEX-WEFA (Centro de Investigación Econométrica de México–The WEFA Group). 1990. *Proyecto Automotriz de CIEMEX-WEFA.* Mexico: CIEMEX-WEFA.

Destler, I. M. 1986. *American Trade Politics: System Under Stress.* Washington, D.C.: Institute for International Economics.

Dyer, Davis; Salter, Malcolm; and Webber, Alan, eds. 1987. *Changing Alliances.* Boston: Harvard Business School Press.

Gereffi, Gary. 1990. "Big Business and the State." In *Manufacturing Miracles: Paths of Industrialization in Latin America and East Asia,* edited by Gary Gereffi and Donald L. Wyman, pp. 90-109. Princeton, NJ: Princeton University Press.

Gereffi, Gary, and Korzeniewicz, Miguel. 1990. "Commodity Chains and Footwear Exports in the Semiperiphery." In *Semiperipheral States in the World Economy,* edited by William G. Martin, pp. 45–68. Westport, CT: Greenwood Press.

Gonzales, Bernardo, ed. 1989. *La Industria Maquiladora Mexicana en los Setores Electrónica y de Autopartes.* Mexico City: Fundación Fredrich Ebert.

Hanguk Nodong Yeonguwon. 1989. *Jadongcha Gongup wi Nosa Kwankye* [Industrial Relations in the Auto Industry]. Seoul: Hanguk Nodong Yeonguwon.

Hanguk Sanup Yeonkuhoi. 1989. *Hanguk Jabonjuoui wa Jadongcha Sanup* [Korean Capitalism and the Auto Industry]. Seoul: Pulbit Press.

Hopkins, Terence K., and Wallerstein, Immanuel. 1986. "Commodity Chains in the World-Economy Prior to 1800." *Review* 10, 1: 157-70.

Hyundai Motor Company. 1988. *Hyundai Jadongcha Ishipnyunsa* [Twenty Years of the Hyundai Motor Company]. Seoul: Hyundai Motor Company.

INEGI (Instituto Nacional de Estadística Geográfica e Informática). 1989. *Estadística de la Industria Maquiladora de Exportación.* Mexico City: INEGI.

————. Various Years. *Estadística de Comercio Exterior de México.* Mexico City: INEGI.

KAMA (Korean Auto Manufacturers Association). 1991. *Hanguk wi Jadongcha Sanup* [The Auto Industry in Korea]. Seoul: KAMA.

Korean Trade Association. Various Years. *Suchul Tonkye* [Export Statistics]. Seoul: Korean Trade Association.

Krafcik, John. 1989. "A First Look at Performance Levels at New Entrant Assembly Plants." MIT MIVP Forum, manuscript.

Lee, Naeyoung. 1993. "The Politics of Industrial Restructuring: A Comparison of the Mexican and South Korean Auto Industries." Ph.D. dissertation, University of Wisconsin-Madison.

Middlebrook, Kevin. 1991. "The Politics of Industrial Restructuring: Transnational Firms' Search for Flexible Production in the Mexican Auto Industry." *Comparative Politics* 23, 3:275-97.

MVMA (Motor Vehicle Manufacturers Association). Various Years. *World Motor Vehicle Data.* Detroit: MVMA.

Newfarmer, Richard S. 1985. "An Introduction to the Issue." In *Profits, Progress, and*

Poverty: Case Studies of International Industries in Latin America, edited by Richard S. Newfarmer, pp. 1-12. Notre Dame, IN: University of Notre Dame Press.

Ogle, George. 1990. *South Korea: Dissent Within the Economic Miracle*. London: Zed Books Ltd.

Rogers, Ronald. 1990. "An Exclusionary Labor Regime Under Pressure: The Changes in Labor Relations in the Republic of Korea Since Mid-1987." *UCLA Pacific Basin Law Journal* 8, 1:91-162.

Sandoval, Sergio. 1987. "Los Enlaces Económicos y Políticos de la Ford Motor Company en Hermosillo." Master's thesis, Universidad de Sonora.

Shaiken, Harley. 1987. *Automation and Global Production*. La Jolla: Center for U.S.-Mexican Studies, University of California, San Diego.

Terukito, Hashimoto. 1986. *Kokusaikano Nakano Jidoshasangyo* [The Auto Industry's Trend of Internationalization]. Tokyo: Aokishoten.

Womack, James; Jones, Daniel; and Roos, Daniel. 1990. *The Machine that Changed the World*. New York: Rawson Associates.

Periodical Publications Cited

Automotive News. Detroit, USA
Exame. São Paulo, Brazil
Gazeta Mercantil. São Paulo, Brazil
Jornal do Brasil. Rio de Janiero, Brazil
O Estado de São Paulo. São Paulo, Brazil
Visão. São Paulo, Brazil.

PART IV

Consumption and Commodity Chains

12

Commodity Chains and Marketing Strategies: Nike and the Global Athletic Footwear Industry

Miguel Korzeniewicz

The world-economic trends and cycles of the past two decades have made it increasingly apparent that the production and distribution of goods take place in complex global networks that tie together groups, organizations, and regions. The concept of commodity chains is helpful in mapping these emerging forms of capitalist organization (Hopkins and Wallerstein, 1986; Gereffi and Korzeniewicz, 1990). Most often, analysts depict global commodity chains (GCCs) by focusing primarily on production processes and their immediate backward and forward linkages. Less attention has been paid to the crucial role played by the design, distribution, and marketing nodes within a GCC. These nodes are important because they often constitute the epicenter of innovative strategies that allow enterprises to capture greater shares of wealth within a chain. Furthermore, a GCC perspective helps us understand how marketing and consumption patterns in core areas of the world shape production patterns in peripheral and semiperipheral countries. Thus an analysis of the design, distribution, and marketing segments within a commodity chain can provide unique insights into the processes through which core-like activities are created, and competitive pressures are transferred elsewhere in the world-economy.[1]

To provide such an analysis, this chapter focuses on the distribution segment of a particular commodity chain: athletic footwear. In particular, this chapter examines the marketing strategy of one corporation within the global athletic shoe industry (Nike) to refine our understanding of the dynamic nature of global commodity chains. The example of athletic footwear is useful in exploring how commodity chains are embedded in cultural trends. The social organization of advertising, fashion, and consumption shapes the networks and nodes of global commodity chains. The athletic footwear case shows that the organization of culture itself is an innovative process that unevenly shapes patterns of production and consumption in core, semiperipheral, and peripheral areas of the world-economy.

The first section of the chapter highlights the phenomenal growth of the athletic shoe industry, and its economic and cultural importance in our society. Athletic footwear has experienced explosive growth over the past two decades. The meteoric popularity and success of athletic shoes as a consumer good is explained by a complex interaction of cultural and organizational innovations. The analysis of these innovations within a commodity chain's framework can help produce a more refined theoretical understanding of the relationship between economics and culture.

The second section examines the historical trajectory and organizational strategies of Nike Corporation. Nike provides a particularly clear example of how successful growth strategies by core enterprises generally entail constant upgrading, or a shift within the commodity chain toward control over more sophisticated and value-added service activities. This process of upgrading or innovation can best be appreciated by examining three periods that reflect different environmental constraints and response strategies on the part of Nike Corporation. This section examines each of these periods.

TRENDS IN THE U.S. ATHLETIC SHOE MARKET

The athletic footwear market in the United States has been characterized over the past two decades by phenomenal rates of growth. As indicated by Table 12.1 and Figure 12.1, wholesale revenues of athletic shoes in the United States tripled between 1980 and 1990 (NSGA, 1990). In the past six years, consumers in the United States more than doubled their expenditures on athletic shoes: In 1985 they spent $5 billion and bought 250 million pairs of shoes, whereas by the end of 1991 retail sales totaled $12 billion for nearly 400 million pairs of shoes (FMI, 1988; Fairchild Fact File, 1989; Freeman, 1991). Three-fourths of all Americans bought athletic shoes in 1991, compared with two-thirds in 1988 (AFA, 1992). In 1990, athletic shoes accounted for about a third of all shoes sold (NSGA, 1990). The athletic footwear industry today generates $12 billion in retail sales, with at least twenty-five companies earning $20 million or more in annual sales (Hsu, 1990). From the point of view of Schumpeterian innovations, the trajectory of the athletic footwear commodity chain over recent times provides valuable insights into the creation of a modern consumer market.

Retail markets for athletic shoes are highly segmented according to consumer age groups. Teen-agers are the most important consumers of athletic shoes. A study sponsored by the Athletic Footwear Association found that the average American over twelve years of age owns at least two pairs of athletic shoes, worn for both athletic and casual purposes (Fairchild Fact File, 1989). As ex-

Table 12.1
Wholesale Revenues in the U.S. Athletic Footwear Market, 1981–1990 (In Millions of U.S. Dollars)

	All firms	Nike	Reebok
1981	1785	458	1
1982	1900	694	4
1983	2189	867	13
1984	2381	920	66
1985	2989	946	307
1986	3128	1069	919
1987	3524	877	1389
1988	3772	1203	1785
1989	5763	1711	1822
1990	6437	2235	2159

Source: NSGA, 1990.

perienced by many parents and youngsters during the 1980s and 1990s, athletic shoes have been constructed and often promoted among teen-agers as an important and visible symbol of social status and identity.

The products in this commodity chain also are highly differentiated according to models and the particular sport for which they are purportedly designed. By 1989, Nike was producing shoes in 24 footwear categories, encompassing 300 models and 900 styles. Reebok sold 175 models of shoes in 450 colors, and planned to add 250 new designs. Adidas and L.A. Gear sell 500 different styles each (Arthur, 1990; NSGA, 1990). The two fastest-growing segments of athletic shoes in the late 1980s were basketball shoes and walking shoes, while the volume of sales for tennis and running shoes declined (Fairchild Fact File, 1989). In 1991, basketball shoes accounted for 22 percent of sales, and cross trainers for 14 percent of sales (Rifkin, 1992). Product differentiation provides an important vehicle both for competition among enterprises and price stratification.

Finally, the sports footwear market is highly segmented according to price. Indicative of this segmentation, the price distribution of athletic shoes has a very wide range. In 1989 the average cost of basketball, walking, and running shoes was between $40 and $47, while top-of-the-line shoes cost about $175 (Hsu, 1990). The bulk of production is oriented toward sales of the lower-priced shoes, while the market for the higher-priced commodities is substantially smaller. In 1990, more than 80 percent of athletic shoe purchases were priced under $35, with only 1.4 percent of shoes bought costing more than $65 (Kalette, 1991). Price rather than appearance or functionality often constitutes the primary matrix differentiating athletic shoes as status symbols.

Since displacing Adidas in the early 1980s, and after falling behind Reebok in the mid-1980s (see Tables 12.1 and 12.2), Nike Corporation has become the largest and most important athletic shoe company in the United States. Nike's sales have grown from $2 million in 1972 to $270 million in 1980, and to over $3 billion in 1991 (Rudolph, 1989; *The Economist*, 1989; *Value Line*). Reebok,

Figure 12.1
Total Wholesale Revenues of Athletic Footwear and Nike's and Reebok's Shares, 1981–1990

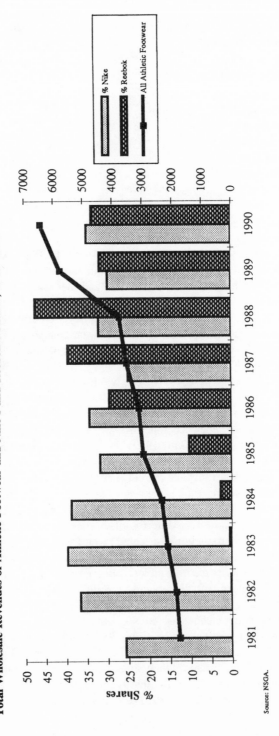

Source: NSGA.

the number-two brand in the United States today, experienced similar rates of growth—in fact, Reebok has been the fastest-growing company in the history of American business. Between 1981 and 1987, Reebok's sales grew from $1.5 million to $1.4 billion, experiencing an average annual growth rate of 155 percent (Sedgewick, 1989). Similarly, L.A. Gear grew at a dazzling rate, from $11 million in 1985 to $535 million in 1989 (Hsu, 1990). Between 1985 and 1990, Nike's share of the athletic footwear market in the United States declined from 30 to 25 percent, Reebok's rose from 14 to 24 percent; L.A. Gear's increased from a minimal share to 11 percent, and Converse's share declined from 9 to 5 percent (Hsu, 1990; *Business Week*, August 3, 1987). These data suggest that a limited number of large firms compete within the athletic footwear market in the United States, but also that the organization of the market provides considerable permeability for successful entry and competition by new enterprises.

What are the factors that explain the enormous growth of the athletic shoe industry? The evidence suggests, in part, that the most important enterprises within this commodity chain have grown by increasing their control over the nodes involved in the material production of athletic shoes. The most fundamental innovation of these enterprises, however, has been the *creation* of a market, and this has entailed the construction of a convincing world of symbols, ideas, and values harnessing the desires of individuals to the consumption of athletic shoes. By focusing on the marketing and circulation nodes of a commodity chain, greater analytical precision can be gained in identifying the crucial features of these innovations.

Rather than analyzing the athletic footwear chain as a whole, the next section focuses on a single enterprise, Nike Corporation. Although a comparative analysis of other enterprises would yield greater insights into possible differences in organizational trajectories, the focus on a single firm allows a more detailed exploration of the innovative strategies that have characterized the athletic footwear commodity chain. This approach also highlights the relevance of world-systems theory, and the concept of commodity chains, to the study of economic and social processes at a microlevel of observation. Nike's rise to prominence has been based on its ability to capture a succession of nodes along the commodity chain, increasing its expertise and control over the critical areas of design, distribution, marketing, and advertising. This strategy also involved a fundamental reshaping of production and consumption, hence contributing to the recent transformation of the athletic footwear commodity chain.

NIKE CORPORATION: COMPETITION, UPGRADING AND INNOVATION IN A COMMODITY CHAIN

The activities of Nike Corporation created a quintessential American product that has captured a large share of the giant U.S. athletic footwear market. Nike Corporation increased its revenues tenfold in the past ten years, from $270 million in 1980 to an estimated $3 billion in 1991 (Rudolph, 1989; Kalette, 1991). Nike sells tens of millions of athletic shoes in the United States every year, yet all of the firm's manufacturing operations are conducted overseas, making the company an archetype of a global sourcing strategy. Nike Corporation never relocated domestic production abroad, as many American companies have done, because the firm actually originated by importing shoes from Japan. It has subcontracted nearly all of its production overseas ever since: currently, "all but 1 percent of the millions of shoes Nike makes each year are manufactured in Asia" (Clifford, 1992: 56). In the United States, Nike has developed essentially as a design, distribution, and marketing enterprise.

Nike's successful implementation of its overseas sourcing strategy can best be understood as part of the firm's effort to retain control over highly profitable nodes in the athletic footwear commodity chain, while avoiding the rigidity and pressures that characterize the more competitive nodes of the chain. "We don't know the first thing about manufacturing," says Neal Lauridsen, Nike's vice-president for Asia-Pacific. "We are marketers and designers" (in Clifford, 1992: 56). Nike's practice of overseas sourcing provides strategic and geographical mobility to the firm by developing a complex division of labor among the components of a global subcontracting network. The way these characteristics are linked to consumer demand and marketing strategies helps explain the tremendous growth and success of Nike.

Imports and Distribution as a Competitive Strategy (1962–1975)

Nike Corporation originated in an enterprise called Blue Ribbon Sports. A founding member of the company was Philip Knight, who visited Japan in 1962 and claimed to represent an American distribution network for shoes that didn't really exist. In Japan, Philip Knight contacted the Onitsuka Company, manufacturers of a brand of athletic shoes (Tiger) whose image had been enhanced by the 1964 Tokyo Olympics. The timing of Knight's travel to Japan was fortunate because executives at the Onitsuka Company were beginning to realize the enormous potential of the U.S. market. After preliminary contacts, and upon returning to the United States, Phil Knight and Bill Bowerman (an Oregon track and field coach) contributed $500 each to start a new enterprise, the Blue Ribbon Sports Company (BRS). In February of 1964, Phil Knight placed his first order for BRS, totaling $1,107, and a few months later they sold their first pairs of Tiger shoes at a state high school track meet (Strasser and Becklund, 1991: 16–59). By the end of 1967, the total revenues of Blue Ribbon Sports were $300,000 (Center for Advertising History, 1990: 7). The company successfully developed a competitive market niche by targeting a small market of dedicated athletes, runners, and sports enthusiasts.

Tiger's marketing advantage in this early stage was based first and foremost on price competitiveness. The retail price of the very first shipment of Tiger shoes sold was $9.95, a few dollars below the price of the shoes made by Adidas.

Later, when BRS began to market Nike shoes, the company's target once again was to undercut their main competitors (Adidas and now Tiger) by a few dollars (Strasser and Becklund, 1991: 41, 135). The distribution network of these early years centered mostly on a few BRS outlet stores and a painstakingly constructed network of contacts with independent sporting goods retailers. Shoes were promoted primarily at track meets and marathons through word of mouth and very elementary forms of athletic endorsements.

Through the 1960s and early 1970s, Blue Ribbon Sports remained a distribution company in charge of importing and distributing Tiger shoes. During the first few years of the partnership between Onitsuka Company and BRS, the Japanese firm clearly held the upper hand because it was able to negotiate and bargain among several athletic footwear distributors in the United States. Trying to enhance its own bargaining position, BRS struggled to attain a contract granting it exclusive rights to distribute Tiger shoes in thirteen western states (Strasser and Becklund, 1991: 40). Over time, a successful distribution strategy allowed BRS to enhance its leverage, and in 1966 Onitsuka Company granted BRS exclusive rights for the distribution of Tiger shoes in the United States (Strasser and Becklund, 1991: 62–63). Already in this partnership, BRS began to contribute design and performance innovations to Tiger's basic models. Within this arrangement, BRS remained vulnerable because of its financial dependence on Onitsuka Company. But until the late 1960s, the partnership worked as originally conceived: Onitsuka Company manufactured and delivered Tiger shoes, and BRS distributed them in the United States.

By 1968, as the market for athletic shoes underwent rapid growth, strains began to develop in the partnership between BRS and Onitsuka Company. Each of the two firms sought to enhance its share of profits by affirming greater control over new nodes in the commodity chain. Seeking to exploit new market opportunities, Onitsuka Company expanded its volume of shoe production, and apparently began to explore alternative distribution networks. BRS, doubting Onitsuka's commitment to maintaining exclusive arrangements, began identifying alternative supply sources. For this latter purpose, Phil Knight enlisted the services of Nissho Iwai, one of the largest Japanese trading companies, which offered to finance shipments of shoes for a 2 percent commission. Eventually Nissho Iwai became the importer of record, receiving a commission on all shipments, and BRS enjoyed financial backing. As tensions between Onitsuka and BRS simmered, the former attempted to take over BRS in 1971 by extending an ultimatum proposal that would in effect give Onitsuka control over 51 percent of the company (Center for Advertising History, 1990: 7; also Donaghu and Barff, 1990: 541).

In 1971 Knight went to Japan and placed his first independent order for 20,000 shoes, which included 6,000 pairs with the Nike "swoosh" pattern. Eventually, BRS entered into a longstanding relationship with two Japanese shoe manufacturers: Nippon Rubber and Nihon-Koyo. In 1971, BRS split with Onitsuka (Center for Advertising History, 1990: 10). In 1972 Onitsuka decided to stop shipments of shoes to BRS after finding shoes with Nike brands in one of BRS's stockrooms (Strasser and Becklund, 1991: 138). Soon thereafter, both parties began lawsuits against each other. Onitsuka Company sued BRS in Japan for breach of contract. BRS sued for breach of contract, unfair competition, trademark infringement, and violation of the antitrust Clayton Act. In July of 1975, Phil Knight agreed to receive an out-of-court settlement of $400,000 after Onitsuka finally succumbed to pressure from the Tiger distributors to settle (Strasser and Becklund, 1991: 175, 180, 227). By making a decision to design its own logo and produce its own brand of shoes, Nike Corporation emerged out of this conflict with greater control vis-à-vis its overseas suppliers in Japan. Its corporate image was enhanced as well, so that by the end of the 1970s the Nike Corporation had superseded BRS.

During this initial period in the history of BRS/Nike, the company also began to delineate an innovative strategy regarding product design and promotion. Perhaps the one promotional idea that had the longest-lasting effect on the future of Nike Corporation was the choice of both the company's name (Nike is the name of the winged goddess of victory in Greek mythology) and the distinctive "swoosh" design on the side of the shoes. Although they later became promotional, the distinctive three stripes in the athletic shoes made by Adidas had primarily a functional purpose (additional bond between the upper and the sole). Nike's "swoosh," on the other hand, was designed solely on the basis of aesthetics. From that point on, anybody wearing Nike products was also advertising Nike shoes. Marketing and product design, in this sense, were closely related from the very beginning.

The Eugene, Oregon track and field Olympic trials in 1968 became the first major event where Nike developed its promotional efforts. Through its association with some of the best track and field athletes, who wore the company's newest models, Nike began to build a reputation as a new, specialized firm that focused on high-performance athletic shoes. The event convinced Nike that associating product promotion with athletes was a very effective form of advertising athletic shoes. For this reason, Blue Ribbon Sports initiated and maintained a program of subsidies for athletes and sponsorship of track meets throughout the 1970s. Later, Nike's strategy of associating its name with track and field athletes allowed the company's products to be viewed by consumers as associated with the development of first-class competitors for the 1980 Olympics, providing high visibility for Nike shoes.

Marketing as an Upgrading Strategy (1976–1984)

During this second period, Nike Corporation introduced major innovations in marketing, distribution, and subcontracting for the production of athletic footwear. First, between 1976 and 1984, Nike was shaped by (and helped to shape) the "fitness boom"—the phenomenal growth of jogging, running, and exercise as a common activity by millions of Americans. Nike was part of this phenomenon by implementing a marketing strategy that involved the development of a vast and visible network of endorsement contracts with basketball, baseball, and football players and coaches. Second, Nike's distribution network was enhanced by the establishment of a strategic alliance with Foot Locker, a rapidly growing chain of retail stores marketing athletic products. Finally, Nike Corporation sought to further enhance its control over subcontractors and lower production costs by shifting most manufacturing activities from Japan to South Korea and (to a lesser extent) Taiwan. Combined, these innovations provided a significant competitive edge to Nike Corporation.

Beginning in the mid-1970s, running, jogging, and exercise in general became part of mainstream American culture. Nike Corporation was in the right place at the right time to capitalize on this phenomenon by outperforming competing brands and becoming the most important athletic shoe company in the United States. But the ability to gain from this phenomenon required a major reorientation in the marketing of the company's products: Nike Corporation's main customer base had to shift, as one observer puts it, from "running geeks to yuppies" (Strasser and Becklund, 1991: 267–68). To achieve this shift, Nike's promotional efforts in the 1970s moved slowly but consistently away from amateur sports to professional sports, and from lesser-known track and field runners to highly visible sports figures. In 1977 and 1978 Nike developed a strategy to sign visible college basketball coaches; by 1979 it had signed over fifty college coaches. One measure of Nike's promotional success was the cover of *Sports Illustrated* of March 26, 1979, which showed Larry Bird (at the time a player in the NCAA tournament) wearing Nike shoes. In the late 1970s, Nike also began to promote heavily in baseball, and by 1980 a Nike representative had signed over fifty players in different baseball teams—as well as eight players in the Tampa Bay team that made it to the 1980 Super Bowl (Strasser and Becklund, 1991: 288–303). This new marketing strategy enhanced Nike's image in its new market niche.

Nike's rise as the largest athletic shoe company in the United States also involved creating a more effective distribution network. Foot Locker, an emerging chain of sport equipment retailers, became the most important distributor of Nike shoes. As a way to solve inventory and financial bottlenecks, Nike people devised an advance-order purchase system they called "futures." The system required major distributors to commit themselves to large orders six months in advance, in return for a 5–7 percent discount and a guaranteed delivery schedule. Foot Locker was one of the first dealers to try the futures contracts, and to benefit from them, eventually becoming Nike's most important retailer (Strasser and Becklund, 1991: 199–202). Another reason for Foot Locker's close relationship with Nike was the latter's flexibility, and its willingness to change design specifications on request from dealers. This responsiveness of Nike contrasted with Adidas' generally inflexible approach to their supply of shoes, and further extended the company's competitive edge.

Finally, the phenomenal growth in the demand for athletic shoes changed

Nike's subcontracting patterns. Nike now needed larger outputs, lower labor prices, and more control over the manufacturing process. In 1974 the great bulk of BRS's $4.8 million in sales was still coming from Japan. Phil Knight, aware of rising labor costs in Japan, began to look for sourcing alternatives. One of these alternatives was the United States. In early 1974, BRS rented space in an empty old factory in Exeter, New Hampshire, and later opened a second factory in Saco, New Hampshire. Domestic facilities also fulfilled a critical R&D function that Nike would later use to gain greater control over production processes abroad (Donaghu and Barff, 1990: 541). However, by 1984 imported shoes (mostly from Korea and Taiwan) rose to 72 percent of the U.S. shoe market, and U.S.-based factories were forced to close. The collapse of the U.S. production base was due primarily to its limited manufacturing capacity and its economic implausibility. Product timelines lagged and American-based manufacturing found itself unable to compete with lower Asian labor costs (Strasser and Becklund, 1991: 559).

While Nippon Rubber (Nike's Japanese supplier) reportedly made the decision to relocate part of its production to South Korea and Taiwan (Donaghu and Barff, 1990: 541), Nike also began to look for new sources of its own. In October 1975, Phil Knight flew to Asia to search for alternative supply sources to lessen his dependency on both Nissho Iwai and Nippon Rubber without losing either company. In Japan, Knight met a Chinese trader who agreed to set up a Nike-controlled corporation called Athena Corporation that established production facilities in Taiwan. In South Korea the Sam Hwa factory of Pusan became the main partner, which began 1977 making 10,000 pairs of Nike shoes a month, and ending the year by making about 100,000 pairs a month. By 1980, nearly 90 percent of Nike's shoe production was located in Korea and Taiwan (Strasser and Becklund, 1991: 229–32, 251–54, 324).

The consolidation of South Korea and Taiwan as the main geographical centers of manufacturing also involved the emergence of a complex system of stratification among Nike's suppliers. Donaghu and Barff (1990) identify three main classes of factories supplying Nike: developed partners, volume producers, and developing sources. "Developed partners" are the upper tier of Nike suppliers, responsible for the most innovative and sophisticated shoes. "Volume producers" are those that manufacture a specific type of product in large quantities. These factories are typically less flexible than developed partners in their manufacturing organization. Finally, "developing sources" are the newer factories that attracted Nike because of their low labor costs, entering into a series of tutelary arrangements both with Nike and the more experienced Nike suppliers.

The geographical dynamism of Nike's shifts in subcontracting arrangements interacted with this complex stratification system in interesting ways. As labor costs in Japan rose in the 1970s, Nike Corporation shifted production to emerging semiperipheral countries such as South Korea and Taiwan. As labor costs in the established semiperipheral supply locations began to rise in the 1980s, Nike tried to shift some of the labor-intensive, technologically less advanced segments of its production to new locations in peripheral areas (such as China). It is interesting to note, however, that linkages with developed partners remained critical for two reasons. First, several of Nike's more sophisticated models required the expertise and flexibility of older, more reliable partners. Second, the technological expertise and capital of the older partners was often necessary to bring newer production facilities up to Nike standards, leading to joint ventures between the older, more established sources and the newer ones. From this point of view, centralization and decentralization of subcontracting arrangements were constrained by marketing requirements.

Design, Advertising, and the Return to the Semiperiphery (post-1985)

After 1985, Nike entered into another period of high growth, based on innovations in product design (the creation of the "Air Nike" models, which quickly became immensely popular) and advertising strategies (signing its most popular endorser, Michael Jordan). Also, Nike Corporation continued to target new market niches, entering the aerobics segment of the market, where Reebok had become increasingly dominant, and the growing and profitable athletic apparel markets. Finally, Nike Corporation altered its subcontracting arrangements, shifting important segments in the manufacture of Nike's athletic shoes to the People's Republic of China, Thailand, and Indonesia.[2] However, the need for specialized and sophisticated production runs once again forced Nike to return to more experienced manufacturers in South Korea and Taiwan.

The ability to produce high-performance, sophisticated footwear models became critical to Nike because the company was able to pull out of its early 1980s stagnation through its "Nike Air" technological innovation. By 1984 the phenomenal growth of a mass market for jogging shoes began to stabilize, particularly in the men's segment of the market. Other companies, like Reebok and L.A. Gear, were becoming more effective in selling to the female and aerobics segments of the market. Nike Corporation, accustomed to years of high growth, was in crisis. Many endorsement contracts were canceled, the Athletics West program cut down its sponsored athletes from 88 to 50, and by the end of 1984, Nike had laid off 10 percent of its 4,000-person work force (Strasser and Becklund, 1991: 529–62). Another indication of Nike's bad fortunes was its declining influence among sports coaches and agents. To reverse this decline, Nike Corporation once again turned toward introducing a drastic product innovation.

Nike's declining fortunes in the mid-1980s (see Tables 12.1 and 12.2) were reversed by the introduction of Air Nike (a new technology that allowed a type of gas to be compressed and stored within the sole) and by the phenomenal success of its "Air Jordan" line of basketball shoes, as well as the success of the endorser they were named after, Michael Jordan. In Nike's Los Angeles store, the first two shipments of Air Jordans sold out in three days. By 1985 it was clear that Air Jordan shoes were a huge success. Nike sold in three months what had been projected for the entire year (Strasser and Becklund, 1991: 572). The first contract between Nike Corporation and Michael Jordan was worth $2.5 million over five years, and it included (among other things) a royalty to the athlete on all Air Jordan models sold by the company (Strasser and Becklund, 1991: 543).

The several advertising campaigns featuring Michael Jordan highlight Nike's capacity to influence market demand for its shoes. Nike's video and print advertisements have been among the most innovative and controversial in recent years, adding to Nike's visibility and undoubtedly contributing to its phenomenal growth. Part of the appeal of Nike advertising is its success in tapping and communicating a consistent set of values that many people in the 1970s and 1980s identified with: hipness, irreverence, individualism, narcissism, self-improvement, gender equality, racial equality, competitiveness, and health.

But there also have been several allegations made that by targeting inner-city youths in its advertising and marketing campaigns, Nike has profited substantially from sales directly related to drug and gang money, showing little concern for the social and financial stability of the predominantly black, poor communities, where sales account for 20 percent of the total athletic footwear market (Aurback, 1990). The relationship between the athletic footwear industry and drug money has become increasingly evident by the alarming rate of robberies and killings over expensive sports shoes. Some store owners claim that Nike is not only aware that drug money contributes heavily to its sales, but that Nike representatives adamantly encourage distributors in the inner cities to specifically target and cater to this market (Telander, 1990: 43).[3]

Nike commercials tend to be subtle. The trademark "swoosh" logo is often far more prominent than dialogue or a straightforward pitch. They are also controversial. Nike's use of the Beatles' song "Revolution" to advertise its new "Nike Air" was startling, and so has been its very recent use of John Lennon's song "Instant Karma." Some of the most distinctive Nike advertisements contain themes that can best be described as postmodern: the rapid succession of images, image self-consciousness, and "ads-within-ads" themes. The "Heritage" Nike commercial, showing a white adult runner training in an urban downtown area while images of sports heroes are projected on the sides of buildings, is particularly striking because it seeks to identify the viewer with an idealized figure (the runner) who is in turn identifying with idealized figures (the sports heroes). This ninety-second advertisement cost over $800,000 to run once in its entirety during the 1991 Superbowl. Though there is no dialogue, the product is identifiable (it is seen almost subliminally several times), and the message of the commercial is clear. Postmodern theory, given its sensitivity to new cultural phenomena, can be helpful in understanding advertising as a crucial element in the athletic footwear global commodity chain (Korzeniewicz, 1992). An understanding of consumption must be based on commodity aesthetics because consumption is increasingly the consumption of signs (Slater, 1987). Similarly, Featherstone (1990) has noted the increasing importance of the production of symbolic goods and images. In a sense, Nike represents an archetype of a firm selling to emerging postmodern consumer markets that rest on segmented, specialized, and dynamic features (Warde, 1990).

As in the previous periods, these drastic changes in marketing and distribution strategies were accompanied by shifts in the firm's subcontracting strategy. In 1980 Nike began a process of relocation to the periphery (particularly China, Indonesia, and Thailand) that most other companies would gradually follow in the course of the decade. This relocation was driven by cost advantages: "a mid-priced shoe made in South Korea which costs Nike U.S. $20 when it leaves the docks of Pusan will only cost about U.S. $15 to make in Indonesia or China" (Clifford, 1992: 59; see also Baker, 1992: E1). Nike Corporation was one of the very first companies to enter the People's Republic of China. In 1980, Phil Knight began to set up a manufacturing base in China. Soon an agreement between Nike Corporation and the Chinese government was finalized, and shoes began to be produced in the PRC (Harvard Business School, 1985: 1). This rapid success can be explained by the fact that Nike used a Chinese-born representative (David Chang) who was thoroughly familiar with the local environment, which meant that proposals were quickly translated into Chinese and attuned to the negotiating style and objectives of the Chinese government. Also, Nike's objectives were long-term and the volumes of production being negotiated were significant, which coincided with the development priorities of the Chinese government at the time (Harvard Business School, 1987: 2).

Just as Nike led the trend of entry into China, later in the mid-1980s it led a reevaluation of the benefits and disadvantages of associating directly with developing partners. By late 1984, production in Chinese factories totaled 150,000 pairs a month, one-seventh of the originally projected 1 million pairs a month (Harvard Business School, 1985: 2). The early 1980s also signaled a slowdown in the rapid growth of conventional athletic footwear markets at a time when competition from other athletic footwear firms (L.A. Gear, Reebok) was increasing. By 1983 Nike terminated its subcontracting arrangement with the Shanghai factory, and in 1984 negotiated an early termination of its contract with the Tianjin factory.[4]

In the mid-1980s Nike briefly considered shifting production back to established manufacturing sources in South Korea and Taiwan. The advantages of lower labor costs in the developing manufacturing areas had to be weighed against disadvantages in production flexibility, quality, raw material sourcing, and transportation. The development of a new shoe model from technical specifications to shoe production was four months in South Korea, compared to eight months in China. The ratio of perfect-quality (A-grade) shoes to aesthetically flawed, but structurally sound (B-grade) shoes was 99:1 in Korea, 98:2 in Taiwan, and 80:20 in China. While Taiwan and South Korea sourced 100 percent of the raw materials needed for production, China was only able to source 30 percent. Finally, shipping from Taiwan and South Korea was 20–25 days; from Shanghai it was 35–40 days (Harvard Business School, 1985: 11).

The mid-1980s also marked the introduction of the "Nike Air" technology and especially the "Air Jordan" model. Being more sophisticated, secretive, and expensive, this model required more experienced and trustworthy suppliers of the "developed partners" type that had been developed in South Korea over the years (Donaghu and Barff, 1990). One Reebok executive argued that "as the complexity of our product increases, it continues to go to [South Korea]. The primary reason is that product development out of Korean factories is quick and accurate for athletic footwear, better than any place in the world" (Gittelsohn, 1990: 13). An observer concluded in the mid-1980s that after the trend of relocation to low-wage locations like Thailand, Indonesia, and China, "buyers are starting to return [to Pusan] after finding that the extra cost of doing business in South Korea is offset by reliability and the large capacity of its factories" (Gittelsohn, 1990). This need for more established suppliers coincided with the adjustments that the Korean shoe producers themselves made in an effort to adapt to rising labor costs and the migration of many firms to other countries. Many Pusan firms shrunk in size but also increased the unit value of their production.

However, the relative importance of South Korean firms has continued to decline. Thus, "at least one-third of the lines in Pusan have shut down in the past three years. Only a handful of South Korean companies are expected to remain significant shoe exporters in a couple of years" (Clifford, 1992: 59). Similar changes have affected shoe-producing firms in Taiwan, where "since 1988, the number of footwear companies has fallen from 1,245 to 745. Athletic shoe exports slipped from US$ 1.5 billion in 1988 to US$ 1 billion (in 1991)" (Clifford, 1992: 60). Taiwanese and South Korean–based firms, on the other hand, are used for managing and mediating the relocation of production facilities to the periphery.

The shift of Nike's production to the periphery has become significant. "In the fiscal year to 31 May 1988, Nike bought 68% of its shoes from South Korea but only 42% in 1991–92. China, Indonesia and Thailand produced 44% of Nike's shoes last fiscal year; against less than 10% in 1987–88" (Clifford, 1992: 57). This same trend is expected to continue in the future: "now, Vietnam looks like the next country on the list. Two major Taiwanese suppliers, Feng Tay and Adi Corporation, are interested in starting production in Vietnam if and when the U.S. trade embargo of its old adversary is lifted" (Clifford, 1992: 57).

The advantages of Nike Corporation that have enabled it to become a powerful and profitable link in the athletic footwear commodity chain are the expertise of its designers in finding technological advances in shoe comfort and performance, the distribution networks built over the past twenty-five years, and the effectiveness of its marketing, promotion and advertising campaigns.

Overall Assessment

To summarize the arguments made in this section, Nike's development of its twin strategies of overseas subcontracting and domestic marketing can best be understood as involving three distinct periods, each corresponding to different patterns of market demand, geographical locus of production, and marketing strategies. In the first period, between 1962 and 1975, Nike Corporation emphasized control over the import and distribution nodes of its commodity chain. Between 1976 and 1984, Nike Corporation enhanced its relative competitive position by extending control to marketing, and by redesigning its subcontracting strategy to take advantage of new opportunities in Southeast Asia (in South Korea and Taiwan initially, later in China, Thailand, and Indonesia). Finally, beginning in the mid-1980s, Nike Corporation successfully extended control to product design and advertising, further upgrading the firm's organizational structure (see Figure 12.2). As a whole, these three periods suggest that Nike Corporation has sustained and enhanced its competitive edge through the implementation of frequent innovations in the nodes and networks of its commodity chain.

CONCLUSIONS

This chapter has examined the organizational strategies of Nike Corporation within the global athletic shoe industry. Nike's uncommon success and growth is due in part to social and cultural trends that have made leisure and fitness more important in our contemporary society. It is also the outcome of Nike's strategy of responding to these trends by accumulating expertise and control over the increasingly important service nodes of the athletic footwear commodity chain: import, distribution, marketing, and advertising.

Nike Corporation (and the athletic footwear industry in general) are excellent case studies of how goods emerge from complex, transnational linkages at different stages of production and distribution. Nike Corporation was born a globalized company. The study confirms a division of labor between core or postindustrial societies (that will presumably specialize in services over time) and noncore societies at different levels of industrialization (that will increasingly specialize in manufacturing) (Fiala, 1992). While Korean and Chinese firms are producing the actual shoe, U.S.-based Nike promotes the symbolic nature of the shoe and appropriates the greater share of the value resulting from its sales.

Nike and the athletic shoe industry show that there are emerging patterns of consumption that have enormous consequences for social and economic organization. Linkages between consumption and production must be explored in greater detail.[5] While a consensus has been building for some time that there are new patterns in the organization of production (alternatively called flexible specialization, flexible production, or post-Fordist production), we also need a better understanding of what may be called "post-Fordist consumption"—that is, the emerging patterns of consumption and distribution that are the counterpart to transformations in the realm of production (Abu-Lughod, 1991).

In looking at Nike, this chapter has highlighted the dynamic dimension of commodity chains and has analyzed how commodity chains are set in motion

Figure 12.2
Nike Corporation's Changing Spheres of Control Within the Athletic Footwear Commodity Chain[a]

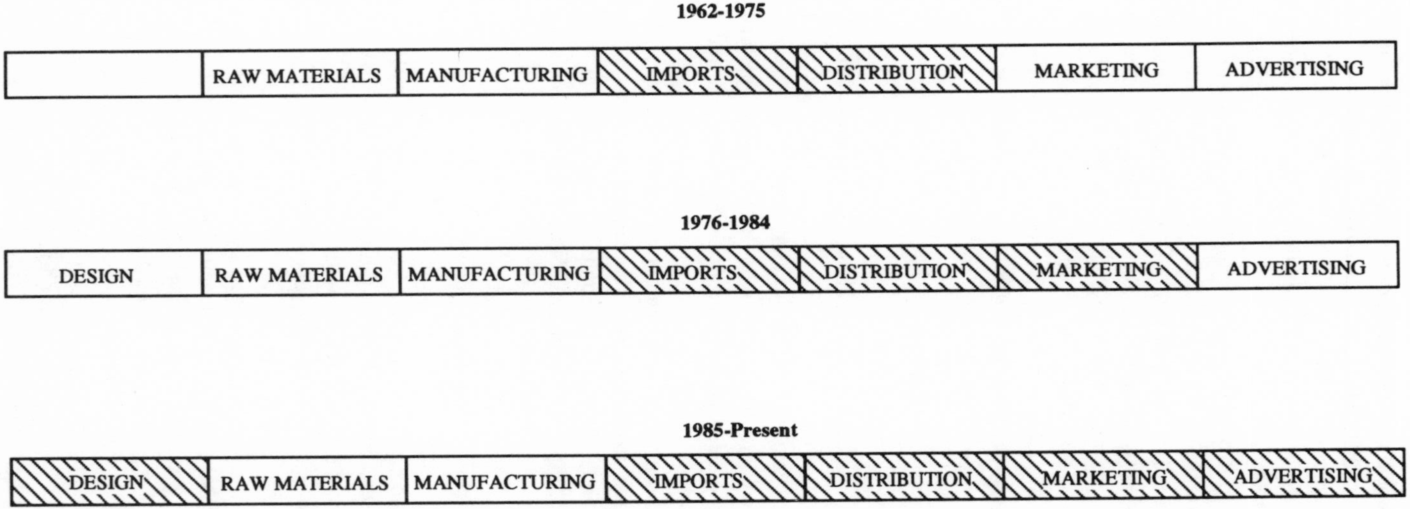

1962-1975

	RAW MATERIALS	MANUFACTURING	IMPORTS	DISTRIBUTION	MARKETING	ADVERTISING

1976-1984

DESIGN	RAW MATERIALS	MANUFACTURING	IMPORTS	DISTRIBUTION	MARKETING	ADVERTISING

1985-Present

DESIGN	RAW MATERIALS	MANUFACTURING	IMPORTS	DISTRIBUTION	MARKETING	ADVERTISING

[a]Striped areas represent nodes directly controlled by Nike Corporation.

and sustain growth. In the case of Nike Corporation, marketing and advertising have driven the rest of the commodity chain. Marketing, advertising, and consumption trends dictate what will be manufactured, how it will be manufactured, and where it will be manufactured. In explaining Nike Corporation's success, manufacturing processes are secondary to the control over the symbolic nature and status of athletic shoes. A more refined breakdown of the service activities involved in the commodity chain improves the understanding of the different economic rewards accrued by core, semiperiphery, and periphery organizations and groups.

NOTES

I am grateful to Victoria Carty for her invaluable research assistance, and to Robert Fiala and Gary Gereffi for their very helpful comments and insights.

1. For more on the notion of transfer of competitive pressures, see Arrighi and Drangel (1986).

2. This pattern of geographical relocation generally confirms what Gereffi and Korzeniewicz (1990) outlined in their study of the global footwear industry: that shoe production as a whole, over the past twenty-five years, has tended to gravitate from core production to locations in emerging core countries (Italy, Japan), then to semiperipheral, newly industrializing countries (South Korea and Taiwan), and finally to lower-wage peripheral countries (PRC and Thailand).

3. The organization PUSH (People United to Save Humanity) has publicly challenged Nike's activities in the inner cities, questioning Nike's contribution to those profitable communities. In July 1990, PUSH called for a boycott of Nike products, and asked the company to donate more of its annual sales to African-American consumers (who represent 30 percent of all Nike sales), to hire more minorities (particularly at managerial or executive-level positions), and to do more business with African-American–owned firms and services (Brown, 1990). Although the boycott was not successful, PUSH did force Nike into a general commitment to hire more minorities, and the action served to publicly raise important issues concerning corporate responsibility.

4. In 1982, however, Nike began sourcing athletic shoes produced by the Quanzhou Rubber Shoe Factory, located in Fujian province. By 1987 this factory was producing about 800,000 pairs of Nike shoes a month (Shayou, 1988).

5. Mintz's (1985) study of the sugar industry is a good example to follow.

REFERENCES

Abu-Lughod, Janet. 1991. "Message from the New Chair." *PEWS Notes* (Fall).

AFA (Athletic Footwear Association). 1992. "Consumer Purchase Study of Athletic Footwear." North Palm Beach: AFA.

Arrighi, Giovanni, and Drangel, Jessica. 1986. "The Stratification of the World-Economy: An Exploration of the Semiperipheral Zone." *Review* 10, 1 (Summer): 9–74.

Arthur, Charles. 1990. "Fashion's Fancy Footwork." *Business*, July pp. 84–88.

Aurback, Stuart. 1990. "The Sneaker Steps Out." *Washington Post*, July 22, p. H1.

Baker, Nena. 1992. "Sweating for Nike: Indonesians 'Just Do It.' " *San Francisco Examiner*, August 30, pp. E1, E4.

Brown, Frank. 1990. "It's More Than Just the Shoes." *Black Enterprise*, November 21, p. 17.

Center for Advertising History. 1990. *Nike Advertising: An Oral History and Documentary Project*. Washington, D.C.: Smithsonian Institute.

Clifford, Mark. 1992. "Nike Roars: All American, Made in Asia." *Far Eastern Economic Review*, November 5, pp. 56–60.

Donaghu, Michael, and Barff, Richard. 1990. "Nike Just Did It: International Subcontracting and Flexibility in Athletic Footwear Production" *Regional Studies* 24, 6: 537–52.

Doyle, Thomas. 1990. "The Athletic Phenomenon." Illinois: Bata Distributors.

The Economist, 1989. "Winged Victory." December 2, pp. 83–84.

Fairchild Fact File: Footwear. 1989. "Athletic Footwear." North Palm Beach: AFA.

Featherstone, Mike. 1990. "Perspectives on Consumer Culture." *Sociology* (Special Issue: The Sociology of Consumption) 24, 1 (Feb.): 5–22.

Fiala, Robert. 1992. "Postindustrial Society." In *Encyclopedia of Sociology,* edited by Edgar Borgatta and Marie Borgatta, pp. 1512–22 New York: Macmillan.

FMI (*Footwear Marketing Insights*). 1988. Nashville, TN.

Footwear News (various issues). New York: Fairchild Publications.

Freeman, Laurie. 1991. "Flat Footed: Ad Campaigns Try to Spark Sales as Sports Shoes Hit Plateau." *Stores* 73, 8 (August): 67–82.

Gereffi, Gary, and Korzeniewicz, Miguel. 1990. "Commodity Chains and Footwear Exports in the Semiperiphery." In *Semiperipheral States in the World Economy*, edited by William G. Martin, pp. 45–68. Westport, CT: Greenwood Press.

Gittelsohn, John. 1990. "Light on Their Feet." *Far Eastern Economic Review* 148 (June 14): 53–54.

Harvard Business School. 1985. "Nike in China." HBS Case No. 9-386-065. Cambridge: Harvard Business School.

―――. 1987. "Nike in China: Teaching Note." HBS Case No. 5-388-010. Cambridge, MA: Harvard Business School.

Hopkins, Terence K., and Wallerstein, Immanuel. 1986. "Commodity Chains in the World-Economy Prior to 1800." *Review* 10, 1: 157–70.

Hsu, Spencer. 1990. "The Sneaker Steps Out." *The Washington Post*, July 22, p. PH1.

Kalette, Denise. 1991. "Buyers Kicking Pricey Shoe Habit." *USA Today*, July 9, p. 4B.

Korzeniewicz, Miguel. 1992. "Global Commodity Networks and the Leather Footwear Industry: Emerging Forms of Economic Organization in the Postmodern World." *Sociological Perspectives*, 35.

Mintz, Sidney W. 1985. *Sweetness and Power. The Place of Sugar in Modern History.* New York: Viking.

NSGA (National Sporting Goods Association). 1990. "The Sporting Goods Market in 1990." Illinois: NSGA.

Rifkin, Glenn. 1992. "High Tops: High Style, High Tech, High Cost." *New York Times*, January 5, p. 10.

Rudolph, Barbara. 1989. "Foot Paradise." *Time*, August 28, pp 54–55.

Sedgewick, John. 1989. "Treading on Air" *Business Month* 133–4 (Jan.): 29–34.

Slater, Don. 1987. "On the Wings of the Sign: Commodity Culture and Social Practice." *Media, Culture and Society* 9: 457–80.

Shaoyu, Chen. 1988. "China-Made Nikes: 'We Proved We Could Make It.' " *Beijing Review* 31 (March 21–27): 38–39.

Strasser, J. B., and Becklund, Laurie. 1991. *SWOOSH: The Story of Nike and the Men Who Played There*. New York: Harcourt Brace Jovanovich.

Telander, Rick. 1990. "Senseless." *Sports Illustrated* 72 (May 14): 36.

Value Line (various issues). New York: Value Line Publishing, Inc.

Warde, Alan. 1990. "Introduction to the Sociology of Consumption." *Sociology* 24, 1 (Feb.): 1–4.

13

Fresh Demand: The Consumption of Chilean Produce in the United States

Walter L. Goldfrank

When J. Alfred Prufrock, T. S. Eliot's bewildered and alienated modern Everyman, wondered if he dared to eat a peach as he walked along the beach, surely he focused neither on pesticide residues, nor vitamins and minerals, nor his middle-age spread, nor his food budget, nor the political morality of supporting dictators, nor yet the proprieties or status meanings of consuming relatively expensive counterseasonal produce. Presumably we have come a long way from the confused indecisiveness of poor Prufrock, because we spend millions of dollars to eat peaches year round, and not only peaches but grapes, nectarines, plums, cherries, raspberries, kiwis, and many more. A growing number of social scientists has in fact turned increasing attention to the internationalization of the fresh produce business, not long ago limited to local, regional, and national channels with the exception of a few items like bananas and coconuts.

For understandable reasons—above all, the economic importance of this business to the producing zones in the periphery and semiperiphery—virtually all of this attention has gone to the growing, packing, and transportation end of these commodity chains, and virtually none to their distribution, marketing, and consumption. It is this imbalance I mean to help correct in the following exploration of the consumption of Chilean produce in the United States.

BACKGROUND

Cultural changes in the core are the driving force of this commodity chain, namely, the changing diet of affluent and middle-income consumers, abetted by the produce wholesalers and distributors who otherwise would have sharply reduced sales volumes in the winter months. But before exploring this process, two background conditions need mentioning: (1) the rise in produce exports as part of Chile's neoliberal economic reorientation, and (2) the aforementioned internationalization of the fresh produce business itself.

Starting with the latter, we can refer to Friedland's (1991) provisional summary of what researchers studying produce internationalization have learned to date. First, with the exception of one product (bananas) and one very small market segment (the "carriage trade," i.e., the ultra-rich, those who once rode in carriages), internationalization is a phenomenon of the last twenty years. The tables presented by Friedland reveal a worldwide quadrupling of fresh fruit and vegetable exports between the early 1970s and the mid-1980s, and growth of at least another 50 percent from that point to the end of the decade. (These tables do not, unfortunately, separate out the intracore and core-periphery dimensions; we know that intra-European commerce comprises an important proportion, much of it intracore rather than involving semiperipheral Portugal or Greece.)

Second, the social usage of the term "fresh" has come to mean "not ostensibly processed," or made into something visibly different, although many human hands have touched the commodities themselves before they reach the consumer. "Sell it or smell it" is the industry watchword, and governmental regulatory agencies police the use of the term "fresh," recently banning its use, for example, to describe reconstituted frozen orange juice. So the cachet of "fresh" may be claimed for produce picked weeks or even months in advance, cooled, stored, and/or shipped with the aid of spoilage-retardant chemicals, handled by workers at multiple job sites. Freshness, then, inheres in the pristine appearance of the foodstuff, not in its space-time proximity to the consumer.

Third, four innovations are driving expansion in this sector: the availability of counterseasonal produce thanks to the development of long-distance cool chains; the growth of a mass clientele for fresh as opposed to canned or frozen produce; further differentiation of the produce market with niches for new varieties as well as new products (so-called exotics); and the possibilities for value-adding at the retail level, increasing ease of preparation as with prewashed and cut salads, precored and peeled pineapples, and microwaveable trays of mushrooms. These last are now available, thanks to a Santa Cruz firm, with a choice of four sauces including an "Oriental" and a "Mexican" option that supermarkets are encouraged to feature in their Chinese New Year and 5 de Mayo promotions.

Taking a step beyond Friedland, one could assert that the internationalization of the fresh produce business implies a large-scale move toward the wholesalers' and retailers' dream of supplying affluent consumers everywhere with a complete line of temperate and tropical commodities throughout the calendar year, yet another triumph of capitalism over nature. As Dole has recently advertised in *The Packer* (November 7, 1992, p. C3), weekly newspaper of the U.S. produce business, "Dole delivers variety . . . all year long" (ellipsis in the original).

The second necessary context for my subject is the neoliberal reorientation of the Chilean economy, in which fresh opposite-season produce exports have come to account for a significant proportion of both foreign exchange (about 10 percent in 1989) and waged employment (perhaps as much as 15 percent). In Goldfrank's previous papers (1990, 1991) and in collaborative work with Gomez (1991)—not to mention his and others' publications (e.g., Gomez and Echenique 1988)—many aspects of the Chilean produce boom have been analyzed. In terms of commodity chains (see Figure 13.1), these include such upstream activities as research and development, technological transfer, input sourcing, infrastructural investments, and labor supply. They also include the organization of production itself among large, sometimes multinational corporations as well as medium and small growers, and their relations with packers and shippers. We have discussed as well some downstream activities, especially pertaining to transportation. Finally, we have analyzed the changes in Chile's rural class structure that facilitated the emergence of both a dynamic market in land and a desperate low-wage labor force. But the marketing and consumption of Chilean fruit, which supplies the northern hemisphere during its winter months, have received only passing mention, enumeration of some aspects, no more.

DIET FOR A SMALL SEGMENT

In the prior work cited above, we have insisted, as has Friedland in his appraisal of internationalization, that a major factor causing the produce boom is dietary change among the core countries' upper and middle strata. Gomez (1991: 10) went so far as to call this change "*the* essential new fact" accounting for the Chilean agroexport boom, as if to remind his Chilean audience of their dependence on the possibly capricious preferences of distant strangers. There are many ways to characterize this shift in the upper third or so of the income hierarchy. As Mintz (1985: ch. 5) pointed out in his pioneering study of the promotion and consumption of sugar, the meat-and-potatoes habit of the wealthier Euro-Americans in the modern era represented an historical and cross-civilizational departure from the standard dietary pattern of "grain-plus," in which a core carbohydrate such as wheat or rice is "fringed" by other foods such as vegetables or fish, with (presumably scarce) meat reserved for festive occasions. The current shift, however, encompasses more than a departure from a carnicentric diet, and differs from a return to the cross-civilizational norm that preceded that diet: it includes variations on an entire complex of such value themes as nutrition, health, fitness, convenience, and cosmopolitanism. And this shift is happening very fast: the Harvard health letter reported last year that whereas, in 1982, 56 percent of faculty at the Medical School ate red meat four or more times a week, in 1991 that proportion had dropped to 11 percent (*Nutrition Action* 19, April 3, 1992, p. 2).

The following is another example, this one from the mass media: advice columnist Abigail Van Buren, "Dear Abby," recently printed a letter from a

Figure 13.1
The Commodity Chain in Chilean Fruit

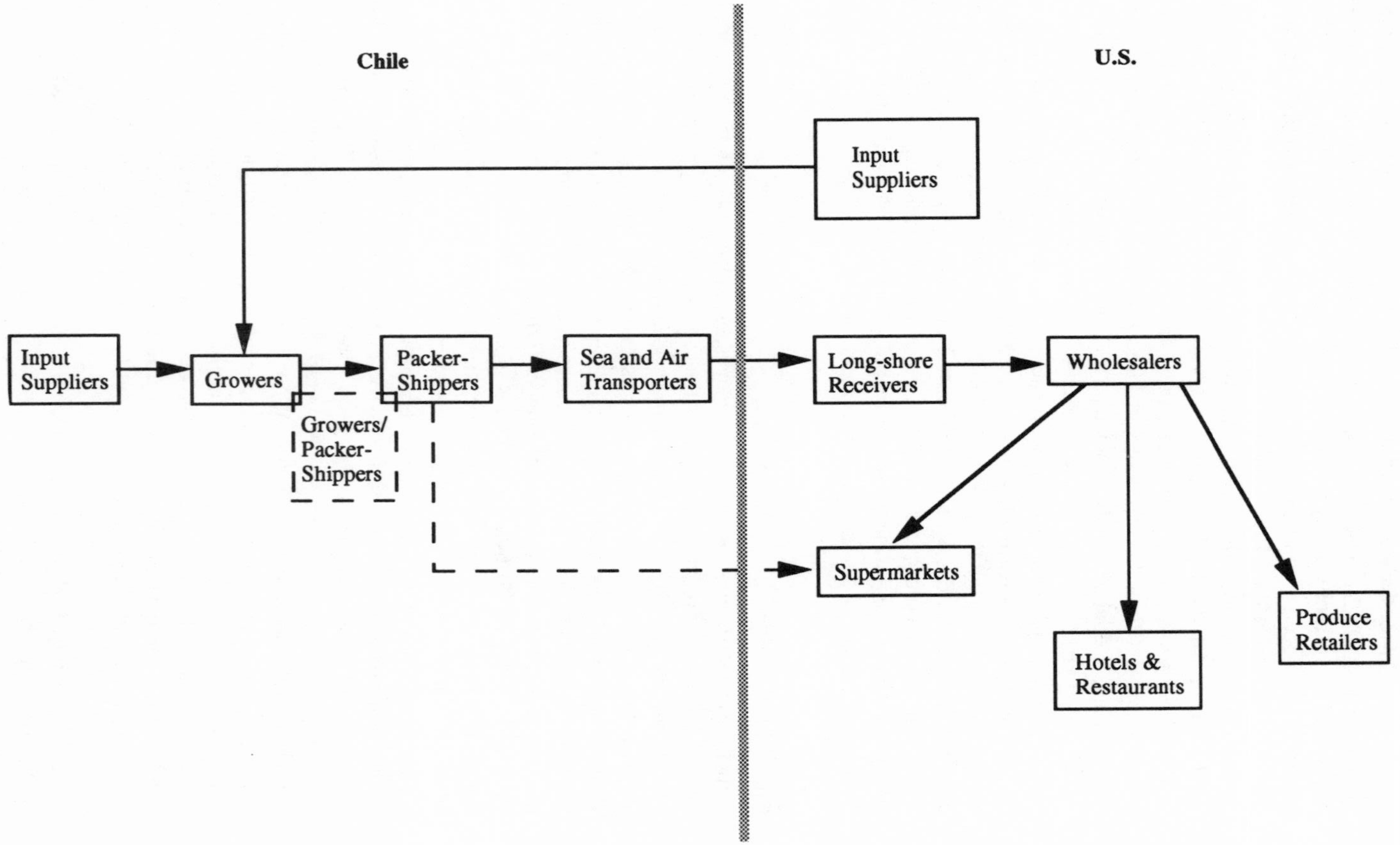

Minnesota woman (*San Francisco Chronicle*, March 27, 1992) outlining a contemporary version of the Jack Sprat problem. She and her fiancé are compatible in all but their eating habits. She loves fruits and vegetables and ethnic foods, while he is a meat-and-potatoes man who won't try anything new or different. She worries that after marriage, this incompatibility will cause serious problems.

In response, Ms. Van Buren recommends seeing a dietician or the prospective family physician, tells her huge readership that the traditional U.S. diet is worse than unhealthy, and predicts that unless the man wises up, the couple "will disagree three times a day for as long as [the] marriage (or [the] husband) lasts." Are we witnessing the emergence of a "produce-stand" ethic?

One measure of how important fresh produce has become is the volume of market research and economic analysis it has generated. Relying on much of this research, Roberta L. Cook (1990: 67–70) tells us the following about contemporary trends in the demand for produce. New product development in food accelerated in the 1980s, with 12,055 innovations in 1989 alone; the average supermarket produce department sold 65 items in 1975 but 210 in 1988. The changing age structure of the U.S. population augurs well for produce sellers: those 55–64-years-old buy 39 percent more fresh fruit and 34 percent more fresh vegetables than the national average. Aging baby boomers will want higher quality as well as larger quantities as they move into their peak earning years. Cook documents the increasingly clear division into "upscale and downscale markets," citing a Food Institute finding that households above the $40,000 income mark spend over 25 percent more on fresh produce than those earning between $20,000 and $30,000. She cites data showing an inverse correlation between household size and produce expenditure and indicating the preference of working women for convenience foods. She documents the trend toward fresh ("1988 was the first year that fresh vegetable consumption equalled processed" [p. 69]) and suggests that sometimes increasing health and nutrition awareness conflicts with the desire for convenience. What she fails to say, however, is that this is precisely where fresh fruit comes in, as it requires virtually no preparation beyond washing (apples or stone fruit, such as peaches) or peeling (bananas) or cutting (melon). In this sense fresh fruit is no less inconvenient than canned or frozen, unlike most vegetables, which require cooking and often seasoning. Table grapes, by far the single most important Chilean agricultural product shipped to the United States, have yet another advantage: they lend themselves to perfectly calibrated portion control.

PORTS OF ENTRY

Looking again at Figure 13.1, one sees first off that this is a particular type of buyer-driven commodity chain, in which the importer/wholesalers, some of whom are vertically integrated into exporting transnationals like Dole, are the key enterprises. Second, one notes that a considerable portion of the inputs to the primary production process in Chile comes from sources in the United States (research and development, chemicals) and Europe (chemicals). Third, it is clear that the wholesale and retail end of the chain has importance as a locus of profits, as Gereffi and Korzeniewicz (1990) show for semiperipheral footwear exports.

Selected inputs aside, the first U.S. link in the commodity chain is at harborside, principally greater Philadelphia for markets east of the Rockies, and Los Angeles/Long Beach for the west coast. Although both Chile and California face the Pacific Ocean, shipping from Valparaiso is about a day shorter and ten cents a box cheaper to the *eastern* United States—due north via the Panama Canal. Consumption of Chilean fruit is greater in both the East and West than in the Midwest and South by 40–50 percent, partly because of differences in class composition, partly because of lags in cultural trends, and partly ease of transportation from these ports of entry, which have major advantages in cooled warehousing capacity and refrigerated trucking services. The port of Houston has failed to make much of a mark in the receiving business, and with the Chapter 11 reorganization of International Cargo Network, its major importer, it appears that for 1992 and 1993 at least, Philadelphia and Los Angeles/Long Beach will handle virtually all of the deal. But Gulfport, Mississippi, and Tampa, Florida, are bidding to compete in the southern sector of the eastern market; the former already handles large volumes of Central American fruit and offers two fewer days and hence $40,000 to $50,000 lower costs per ship than Philadelphia. And other cities are bidding to compete with the established centers: Seattle, Tacoma, San Francisco, and San Diego on the Pacific; New Bedford, Wilmington, Baltimore, Norfolk, and Miami on the Atlantic.

Initial inquiry into the port activities of unloading, inspecting, warehousing, and trucking Chilean fruit led me to a paper presented by LaRue and Heinzelmann (1990) at the 2nd International Fruit Congress held in Santiago in late November 1990. Its authors are Executive Director of the Philadelphia Regional Port Authority and Director of Port Operations of the Delaware River Port Authority (DRPA); the DRPA has an office in Santiago to facilitate its dealings with Chilean shippers and growers. The major impression derived from this paper is the strength of the transnational sectoral alliance between Chileans and North Americans. The paper describes how over the previous three years the latter used the ideology of free trade to lobby Congress and the federal bureaucracy to remove the restrictions of U.S. marketing orders limiting imports that might compete with California produce. It recounts multimillion-dollar public investments on both banks of the Delaware, investments in warehouse modernization and refurbishing, cooling, and heating facilities. It boasts of Philadelphia's having dispatched 25,000 truckloads of Chilean fruit during the previous (1989–1990) season, 1,500 a week at the peak, via its excellent freeway system and its enormous fleet of "reefer" (i.e., refrigerated) trucks. It mentions that within a 300-mile radius of Philadelphia live 60 million consumers, or 25 percent of the U.S. market; within 500 miles, 36 percent; within 1,000 miles, sixty-four percent. It describes an industry-wide conference at which (1) the ILA assured that not even a strike would interfere with the unloading operations, (2) the federal government assured that inspection would be routine and speedy, and (3) the port assured that it could manage increasing volumes of fumigation. In addition, stevedores were to receive increased training in how to handle delicate produce so as to minimize damage, and newspapers' food editors were to attend another round of workshops to further publicize the commodity. Then comes perhaps their most revealing datum: Chilean fruit represents about 700,000 man-hours of dockwork alone, more than one-third of the port's annual total. No wonder, then, that the DRPA and the Philadelphians are eager to please their commercial allies in Chile.

WHOLESALING PRODUCE

To the observer first encountering the wholesale produce business, it appears as a motley array of firms, in terms of both size and degree of specialization. Local, regional, national, and international markets are variously serviced by everything from transnational integrated packer-shippers with brand-name goods to single-commodity specialists. Some firms operate in spatially concrete terminal markets in large metropolitan areas; others bypass this step by delivering directly to supermarket chains' central warehouses (for a detailed description, see How, 1991). In terms of handling Chilean produce, the giant multinationals Dole and Chiquita-Frupac deal directly with giant retail merchants, including their Chilean imports along with all the other fresh commodities they sell. Before its acquisition by Chiquita, Frupac had worked through independent jobbers in California, but in 1991 achieved vertical integration. David Del Curto, the largest of all the Chilean grower-shippers and the only one of the largest firms wholly owned by Chileans, sells to retailers and local wholesalers through Jac Vandenberg on the east coast and David Oppenheimer on the west coast. Another large Chilean firm, with significant participation by Dutch capital, is Frutas Naturales, which markets its fruit under the brand name "Clee." Before the 1991–1992 season began, it linked up with Florida-based DNE World Fruit Sales, the largest independent shipper of Florida citrus. This kind of integration appears to be growing in produce distribution, and independents such as Sbrocco International find themselves wholesaling internationalized lines that include along with Chilean grapes and stone fruits such items as Italian chestnuts, Spanish clementines, and Caribbean melons.

Yet another type of player in this market is Pandol, the Delano, California, firm specializing in table grapes, a firm that early on became involved in importing Chilean grapes. In the past few years, in partnership with the Chilean firm Andina, Pandol has started growing grapes in Chile's northernmost producing zone near Copiapo, which yields a harvest in November before the principal zones to the south begin theirs. This privileged temporal niche is similar to that enjoyed by California's Coachella Valley, where the grape harvest begins in early April; the overlap with the end of the Chilean season has caused friction regulated by the marketing orders.

PROMOTION

Advertising and promotion are essential to the commercial success of new products, and the Chileans have been quick to understand their value. To be sure, nothing in the produce business approaches the megabucks spent by Nike or Reebok to sell athletic shoes. For years the Chileans have concentrated on inexpensive radio spots and in-store displays, but recently the advertising agency representing the Winter Fruit Association and the public relations firm working with the Chilean Exporters Association have been branching out in new directions. For example, video recordings depicting growing, harvesting, and packing are now available for in-store viewing. For the 1991–1992 season a Chilean tour was organized for food writers and editors from six major "women's" magazines (e.g., *Ladies' Home Journal*), four major newspapers, and two television food shows. According to the public relations executive, the editors will, among other things, visit Chilean families "so they can learn first-hand that Chilean society is a current counterpart to that in the United States" (*The Packer*, January 11, 1992, p. 4D). In 1992–1993, one-third of the $3 million advertising budget will go to radio spots in sixteen major metropolitan markets and another one-fourth to store displays.

Newspaper advertising by supermarket chains and independent grocers is another vehicle of promotion. In the course of the 1991–1992 season, Chilean fruit was featured or mentioned almost weekly, sometimes as simply available, sometimes as one of several special bargains of the week, occasionally even as a "loss leader," that is, an item sold at or below cost to attract customers to the store generally or to its produce department specifically. Having followed this sort of promotion for the last few years, my distinct impression is that the newspaper treatment has helped to normalize Chilean fruit, to make it a routinely expectable and affordable item among others. Sometimes the advertisements label it as "Chilean," sometimes as "South American," sometimes as merely "imported." But its treatment is no different from Washington apples, or Texas onions, or other featured products, although it is different from Mexican produce, whose country of origin rarely receives mention in advertisements.

RETAILING

Supermarket chains, independents, and greengrocers account for most produce retailing, although restaurants and hotels provide an alternate route to the final consumer. In the latter connection several aspects deserve mention, among them the boundary between the upscale mass market and the carriage trade, and the competitive struggle for preference as a garnish among grapes, parsley, strawberries, and pickles. The presentation of entrees, as shown in photographed spreads in glossy magazines, may include small bunches of grape varieties such as Perlette or Flame or Thompson seedless, for color and for a suggestion of Roman luxury. Restaurant and hotel purveyors tend to be more interested in such air-shipped luxury items as raspberries and asparagus than in table grapes and stone fruit: the whole point of "dining out" (as opposed to fast food or "middle mass" convenience eating outside the home) is to escape from the quotidian and to assert—if only for one evening—one's difference from and superiority to the hoi polloi.

But direct retailing to the public accounts for by far the largest proportion of produce sales, and within this category, chain supermarkets have the largest market share—and it is growing. In Great Britain, nine chains now do 70 percent of the produce retailing, and as Ian Cook (1991) describes, the leaders among them have made significant efforts to increase consumer knowledge and purchases of imports, including exotics he calls "vanity" foods. In the United States, supermarkets have in the last decade increased the size and attractiveness of their produce departments. These are now estimated to account for 15 percent of profits on only 9 percent of sales, and with the exception of milk, shoppers are more likely to make a produce purchase than any other single acquisition, whether they have come to the supermarket on "stock-up," "routine," or "fill-in" trips.

THE PRODUCE-STAND ETHIC

Here I present fragmentary data from two sources, a professional national sample survey[1] and home-grown semi-structured interviews. Nineteen ninety-two was the first year in which the national produce survey included questions on fresh fruit imports, a fact that itself is a significant indicator of their rising importance. Consumers were asked if they saw or purchased (% saw/% purchased) New Zealand kiwis (59%/43%), Chilean table grapes (37%/29%), Chilean tree fruit (30%/21%), and Central American melons (26%/16%). Males were significantly more likely to report having seen and bought Chilean fruit than females (49% to 35% seeing grapes, 40% to 28% seeing tree fruit; 36% to 27% buying grapes, 28% to 19% buying tree fruit).

The data on age are more intriguing, with noticing and buying both more likely in the older generation, but a significantly greater proportion of those who notice also purchasing among the younger age groups. Thus 26% of the 18–29-year-olds saw Chilean grapes in the market, compared to 47% of those over 60; but 20% of the 18–29 group bought them as compared to 33% of the older group. For tree fruit the difference is more pronounced: 22% of the young noticed and 18% bought, whereas among the older consumers 40% saw but only 22% bought. These findings strongly suggest that younger consumers, if sufficiently attuned to currently fashionable theories about the importance of eating fresh produce, are more likely than older ones to buy it from whatever suppliers make it available.

Not surprisingly, residents of the Northeast and West were more likely to see and to buy Chilean fruit than those of the North Central United States or the South. But there were no differences among the regions in the purchasing behavior of those who recall seeing Chilean fruit in their markets. As for income, households with more than $50,000 led the lower brackets in likelihood of seeing and purchasing, although the relationship between income and consumer behavior is not monotonic—the $35K–50K group trails both the $12.5K–22.5K and $22.5K–35K groups. Unfortunately, the data do not say anything about the volume or frequency of these purchases. But they do reveal judgements about quality. Chilean grapes were rated as excellent by 15%, good by 62%, fair by 18%, poor by 1%, and inconsistent by 3%. For tree fruit, the proportions are: excellent, 11%; good, 54%; fair, 23%; poor, 5%; and inconsistent, 6%.

These quantitative data reinforce the hope among Chilean producers that U.S. sales have considerable potential for augmentation in the future. United States winter grape consumption is less than half that of summer, when California supplies the fruit; there clearly exist produce consumers who eat grapes in the summer but have not yet discovered or who cannot afford the Chilean product during the northern hemisphere winter.

As for more qualitative data, in the winter of 1992, I tried to go behind the numbers to discern some of the cultural meanings and attitudes surrounding Chilean winter fruit in the U.S. market. I conducted twenty-eight focused interviews with a nonrandom sample of shoppers and consumers, eleven chosen from my own national circle of acquaintances, the rest accosted in and around local supermarkets. Some excerpts from my respondents' answers deserve quotation (my questions are in brackets).

Norma T. buys Chilean grapes from her New York neighborhood greengrocer and also from a street vendor's cart near her midtown office. At twenty-five, she is a college graduate who scuba dives, jogs, and bicycles; she describes herself as "addicted" to sushi and to highly spiced Asian and Mexican foods. She reports: "I love Chilean grapes, especially the red ones. They're so crunchy, they taste so fresh. [Does price matter?] Not at all, unless it's out of sight. I usually pay a dollar and a half for a nice bunch from the cart on the corner. I used to eat pretzels or bagels or even sometimes a hot dog. No more. No way."

Sarah S. described her discovery of Chilean nectarines as a revelation. Approaching fifty, she works as a middle manager in a Bay Area county's statistical service. With her attorney husband (they are so-called DINKs, double income, no kids), she enjoys a comfortable six-figure household income that allows for frequent dining out, strenuous world travel to eco-tourist hot spots, and more scuba diving. Since she often jogs at lunch hour, she prefers to eat at her desk, typically a meal of nonfat cottage cheese and sliced nectarines.

The flavor's as good or better than the summer ones from California. I have them almost every day. . . . They don't cost too much, especially compared to eating out. They make me feel healthy. [Do you worry about pesticide residues or other chemicals?] Not really. Not from Chile. I just associate that country with cleanliness, high standards. Not like Mexico, I'm a little afraid of Mexican cantaloupes and veggies. [You seem to know a lot about produce.] Oh yeah, I have my own vegetable garden and some fruit trees. Some weeks that's all I eat, well, with grains or something. [Do you want to live forever?] Not really. But I can't stand the idea of being inactive or feeble or chronically ill. I mean, when it happens I just want to drop or die in my sleep as healthy as I am right now.

Polly M. gives the appearance of middle-class prosperity as she watches the checker total her grocery bill one February morning. I notice a sizable number of Chilean plums in her cart. [Do you like those Chilean plums?] "Oh. They're from Chile? I didn't know that. Yeah, this time of year you can't get a decent tomato. I buy these for my salads."

Andrea M. is a middle-aged staff worker in a university office. Armed with Chilean grapes, she battles her tendency to gain weight. "It's a treat, you know, something a little special that's better for me than cookies or pastry. I need treats, sometimes more than once a day. Coming from the far North [she is a native of Saskatchewan], I can't believe I'm eating grapes in January. They just help keep me going."

William and Laura H. are Californian political progressives and professional educators with adult children and a substantial income. They admit to obsessing about their food consumption and their budget; they buy Chilean fruit throughout the winter. They explain this seeming extravagance with reference to their overall shopping basket:

We used to buy a lot of meat, good meat, expensive lean cuts. Now we don't see meat unless it shows up in something Thai or Chinese. Even over a dollar a pound it's [fruit] a lot cheaper than beef or lamb. And there's no cholesterol, zero. [Ever boycott grapes?] Oh, sure, even picketed at the Safeway. For years I would never buy grapes except at a farmers' market. But I got into the Chilean stuff a couple of winters ago, right around when they got rid of the dictator, you know, what's his name, Pinochet. Now I'm hooked. [How's the quality?] Great, really good, except, um, sometimes the peaches. Well, the California peaches can be pretty mediocre too, you know, they're not like in France or Italy.

What are these respondents telling us about themselves and this commodity? Foremost seems to be a concern with health, part narcissism, part dread. To be overweight, or to show "symptoms" of aging, frightens them. It perhaps defies analysis to disentangle the status-marking and social-acceptability aspects of so-called healthy eating from the rational effort to avoid illness, but for this middle to upper-middle end of the stratification hierarchy, red meat approaches tobacco as a taboo. Strong moral overtones accompany the emphasis on healthy eating, as if the working class and the poor deserve to be sicker because they do not take good enough care of themselves. A privatized form of prayerful communion with produce—combined with the ardent pursuit of exercise—has replaced reading the Bible as the individual's path to salvation. But this new "produce-stand" ethic is simultaneously a hedonistic one: both the food consumption and the physical exercise bring sensual pleasure even as they represent self-discipline and self-denial.

CONCLUSION

It is perhaps worth recalling the original meaning that Karl Marx gave to the concept of the fetishism of commodities, that is, the way the appearance of things conceals relationships of social and economic power. This chapter has attempted to convey the final steps in a long chain of such relationships, which are routinely hidden from the consciousness of health- and status-seeking consumers. In our contemporary conquest of nature, we have come to take for granted the availability of many goods that were once produced by our own or our neighbors' quite visible hands, in plain view, displayed and sold at local produce stands, farmers' markets, or greengrocers. Now the livelihoods of thousands of workers and commercial intermediaries depend on the changing and partially manipulated consumer preferences of a global upper stratum disproportionately located in North America, Western Europe, and Japan. Too much knowledge of the exploitation of human beings and/or the spoliation of nature required to satisfy those preferences could leave a bad taste in their mouths.

NOTE

1. Market research on imported fresh fruit was kindly made available to me by Vance Research Services, which conducts the national sample survey reported annually in *Fresh Trends*, a glossy publication of *The Packer*, the weekly newspaper of the produce business.

REFERENCES

Cook, Ian. 1991. "New Fruits and Vanity: Highlighting the Role of Symbolic Production in the Global Food Economy." Paper presented at the International Multidisciplinary Conference on the Globalization of the Agricultural and Food Order, June 2–6, Columbia. MO.

Cook, Roberta L. 1990. "Challenges and Opportunities in the U.S. Fresh Produce Industry." *Journal of Food Distribution Research*, February, pp. 67–74.

Friedland, William H. 1991. "The New Globalization: The Case of Fresh Produce." Paper presented at the International Multidisciplinary Conference on the Globalization of the Agricultural and Food Order, June 2–6, Columbia, MO.

Gereffi, Gary, and Korzeniewicz, Miguel. 1990. "Commodity Chains and Footwear Exports in the Semiperiphery." In *Semiperipheral States in the World-Economy*, edited by William G. Martin, pp. 45–68. Westport, CT: Greenwood Press.

Goldfrank, W. L. 1990. "Harvesting Counterrevolution: Agricultural Exports in Pinochet's Chile." In *Revolution in the World-System*, edited by T. Boswell, pp. 189–98. Westport, CT: Greenwood Press.

———. 1991. "State, Market, and Agriculture in Pinochet's Chile." In *Semiperipheral States in the World-Economy*, edited by William G. Martin, p. 69–77. Westport, CT: Greenwood Press.

Gomez, Sergio. 1991. "La Uva Chilena en el Mercado de los Estados Unidos." Paper delivered to the Workshop on The Globalization of the Fresh Fruit and Vegetable System, December 6–9, Santa Cruz, CA.

Gomez, Sergio, and Echenique, Jorge. 1988. *La Agricultura Chilena*. Santiago: FLACSO.

Gomez, Sergio, and Goldfrank, W. L. 1991. "Evolución del mercado agrario mundial: el caso del Chile neoliberal." *Agricultura y Sociedad* 60 (July–Sept.): 13–28.

How, R. Brian. 1991. *Marketing Fresh Fruits and Vegetables*. New York: Van Nostrand, Reinhardt.

LaRue, John, and Heinzelmann, Ray. 1990. "En Preparación para la Temporada 1990/1991 en Estados Unidos." Paper presented at the 2nd International Fruit Congress, November 26–29, Santiago.

Mintz, Sidney. 1985. *Sweetness and Power*. New York: Viking.

14

Commodity Chains and the Korean Automobile Industry

Hyung Kook Kim and Su-Hoon Lee

Over the last two decades the automobile industry of South Korea has developed and expanded with remarkable speed. Characterized by sustainable product quality, the industry has succeeded in carving a niche in the highly competitive world auto market. For this reason, the Korean automobile industry presents a useful case to address some key issues raised by the world-system perspective in general, and by a commodity chains analysis in particular. Utilizing the "commodity chains" framework originally proposed by Hopkins and Wallerstein (1986), and later extended by Gereffi and Korzeniewicz (1990), we analyze automobile production and marketing as core processes.

We focus on the origins of crucial auto components and sales strategies promoted in the overseas market to examine how large Korean automakers were able to establish forward linkages in production in the early stages of massive exports to North America during the mid-1980s. We also seek to provide insights into the mechanisms through which Korean firms successfully sold their products in the U.S. and Canadian markets and diversified their exports to the European market in the 1990s when they faced the "relative decline" of the North American market (Cho, 1992). The first section of this chapter uses production statistics to briefly depict the remarkable growth of the Korean auto industry. Next, we analyze the developmental strategy of the Korean auto industry within the comparative context of other NICs. Third, we carry out a commodity chains analysis of automobiles, focusing on four segments of this chain. Finally, we discuss market concentration in the Korean auto industry, as well as issues related to the opening of the Korean auto market to U.S. and Japanese cars.

Table 14.1
Automobile Production in Selected Newly Industrializing Countries

	1950	1960	1970	1980	1990
Mexico	21,575	49,807	192,841	490,006	820,558
Brazil	0	133,041	416,089	1,165,174	914,684
Argentina	0	89,338	219,599	288,917	99,649
Yugoslavia	0	15,921	130,563	283,744	319,116
India	14,688	51,136	82,766	113,326	364,181
Korea	0	0	28,819	123,135	1,321,630
Sub total	36,263	337,243	1,070,677	2,464,302	3,839,808
World total	10,577,426	16,488,340	29,403,479	38,513,645	49,697,761
Ratio %	0.3	2.0	3.6	6.4	7.7

Source: Korean Auto Industries Cooperative Association (KAICA), *World Automobile Industry Statistics*, 1992, pp. 12–15.

TRANS-PACIFIC DIVISION OF LABOR IN TRADE

The South Korean automobile industry has emerged as one of the most competitive industries in the world automobile market. This remarkable achievement has been largely due to external factors, such as technological dependence on Japan and market concentration in North America, pointing to the existence of a geographical international division of labor that encompasses at least South Korea, Japan, and the United States. This division of labor is organized around the Pacific Ocean, so it could well be called a regional division of labor. The dynamic Korean auto industry, like many other leading sectors of the twentieth century, has been characterized by the prevalence of domestic industrial conglomerates (or *chaebol*). Korea's large, diversified automobile firms have taken advantage of regional competition between Japan and the United States during the 1970s (Cumings, 1984: 48–51).

Table 14.1 shows automobile production in major newly industrialized countries during the 1950–1990 period. In 1960 the total production of these nations represented merely 2.0 percent of total world production. Their share increased modestly to 3.6 percent in 1970. But during the 1980s they achieved considerable growth, recording a 6.4 percent share of world production in 1980 and a 7.7 percent share in 1990. Among these latecomers, the growth of the South Korean

Table 14.2
Korean Automobile Firms' Sales, 1991

	Hyundai	Kia	Daewoo	Asia	Ssangyong	Others*	Total
Total sales							
1991	767,487	430,210	202,647	27,60	24,161	42,432	1,494,546
Domestic sales							
1991	512,932	350,190	151,394	24,493	22,982	40,844	1,102,835
	(66.8%)	(81.4%)	(74.7%)	(88.7%)	(95.1%)	(96.3%)	(73.8%)
Export sales							
1991	254,555	80,020	51,253	3,116	1,179	1,588	391,711
	(33.2%)	(18.6%)	(25.3%)	(11.3%)	(4.9%)	(3.7%)	(26.2%)
Passenger car sales							
1991	641,574	259,773	189,181	0	0	31,783	1,122,311
	(83.6%)	(60.4%)	(93.4%)	(0.0%)	(0.0%)	(74.9%)	(75.1%)

Source: KAMA, *Monthly Automobile Statistics*, 1991 December, pp. 1–9.
*Others include Daewoo Shipbuilding, Hyundai Mechanics, Jindo.

automobile industry has been the most spectacular. According to Table 14.1, South Korea possessed little capacity to produce automobiles until 1960, but emerged into the top echelon of new producers by 1990. With more than 1.3 million units produced in 1990, the Korean industry increased its output by a factor of more than 10 in the past decade.

The nation's performance is even more remarkable regarding exports. Until 1983, Hyundai together with Daewoo exported no more than 20,000 cars. Beginning in 1984, exports of Korean automobiles began to increase rapidly. Korean automakers exported 564,000 passenger cars in 1984, a figure 40 times greater than the 14,000 cars exported in 1980. In 1991 the Korean auto industry produced almost 1.5 million assembled automobiles, and exported 390,000 passenger cars (see Table 14.2). By the year 2000, according to a recent government publication (*Hanguk Kyeongje Shinmoon*, March 7, 1992), South Korea is expected to produce 4.2 million cars and to export 2.5 million, accounting for 11.9 percent of the country's total production, 7 percent of total employment, and 25.6 percent of total exports, thus making it the world's fifth-largest automobile producer.

Hyundai was highly successful in its initial entry into the Canadian market in 1984. The major models exported to Canada were the Pony and the Stellar. These models were soon followed by the Pony Excel (Hyundai) in 1986, and the Kia Pride and the Daewoo LeMans in 1987. These models entered the U.S. market as well. In 1986, after entry of the Pony Excel to the United States, the North American market accounted for 90 percent of total Korean automobile exports; the United States alone accounted for a 68 percent share (KAMA, 1991, p.17). Adding Pride and LeMans, Korea directed 91 percent of its automobile exports to the United States in 1988. South Korean automobiles accounted for 10 percent of U.S. compact car imports in 1988, second to Japan but outpacing both Mexico and Brazil. Although South Korea's export volume fell to 217,000 units in 1989 (representing a 38 percent decline from 1988) and experienced a further 2.4 percent decline in 1990, South Korean automobile exports have remained concentrated in the North American market. Exports to the United States, for example, have represented 66 percent of total Korean automobile exports in 1989 and 57 percent in 1990.

STRATEGY OF THE KOREAN AUTOMOBILE INDUSTRY FROM A COMPARATIVE PERSPECTIVE

One of the best ways to explain the development pattern of the South Korean auto industry is through a comparative discussion of industrialization in Asian and Latin American countries (Gereffi and Wyman, 1987). Overall, the growth of the automobile industry in developing countries has been affected by its level of concentration, the degree of multinationality, the maturity of technology, and local labor skills. When Latin American countries encountered the deadlock of import-substituting industrialization (ISI) and the shortage of foreign currency in the 1950s and 1960s, they were receptive to foreign capital inducement for heavy and intermediate industries, including the automobile sector. The foreign investment flows from technologically advanced countries were largely attributable to potential sales in the domestic market rather than export-oriented incentives.

In other words, Latin American automobile development was the outcome of both TNC strategies and domestic policy changes. One important outcome of this policy was the fact that major TNCs took on local firms (which were previously protected by domestic legislation) as subcontractors. By 1971, foreign-owned firms controlled almost 100 percent of Brazilian production, 97 percent of Argentine production, and 84 percent of Mexican production. Coupling significant increases in industrial output with continued foreign domination, the development of the Latin American motor vehicle industry represents a seemingly successful illustration of what some have called "dependent industrialization'' (Kronisch and Mericle, 1984: 263). The world car strategy by TNCs, which was adopted in the late 1970s in Latin America, can also be interpreted in this context.

Although foreign capital inflow in Asia responded to ISI saturation and shortages of foreign currency, just like the Latin American cases, automobile production in the Asian countries differed from the Latin American pattern. South Korea, along with India and Taiwan, allowed direct foreign investment, but they limited foreign ownership to 50 percent shares. India was especially concerned with protecting its domestic market and limiting foreign capital participation to exclude the possibility of foreign domination of its industry. TNCs were less attracted to the East Asian countries, and they did not penetrate actively into the region. As a result, South Korea's firms remained controlled largely by local capital (as in the case of Taiwan), but found it more difficult to receive foreign technologies. The fact that Asian countries, with less integration, had to develop their own technologies more than in Latin America contributed to the former's automobile development in the 1980s.

Besides the degree of denationalization, competition by the world's leading automobile firms from the United States and Japan helped to promote automobile industrialization in the East Asian region. In addition to producing the ''world car,'' U.S. companies initiated a new transnational strategy when they recognized that protectionism against Japanese firms would not in itself solve the basic problems in the automobile industry, particularly given the fact that quotas sharply increased the profitability of Japanese firms. As David Yoffie (1983) indicates, quotas, including voluntary export restraints, usually increase prices because of forced or anticipated reductions in supply. Captive imports, which is the strategy for the major car producers to import cars from their offshore affiliates, penetrated into Japan first and later expanded into the other Asian countries. General Motors (which owned 35 percent of Isuzu and 5 percent of Suzuki Motor) and Chrysler (which owned 15 percent of Mitsubishi) imported cars from their affiliates and marketed them under their own names. This captive import strategy expanded immediately to other East Asian countries, including South Korea. GM (which shared 50 percent ownership with Daewoo) and Ford (which in turn owned 10 percent of Kia) have pursued the same strategies.

Japanese firms responded to trade frictions and voluntary export restraints (VER) by undertaking joint ventures, including Japanese transplant investments in the United States. In 1982 Honda launched its production of Accords in Ohio, and in 1983 Nissan built a truck factory in Tennessee. Perhaps the most innovative case was Toyota's joint venture with GM to produce 250,000 subcompact units at its plant in Fremont, California. With Japanese transplants in the United States, Mitsubishi along with Mazda and Isuzu shifted their production sites to South Korea for two reasons. First, they needed low-end plants to produce front-wheel-drive engines to supply Japanese transplants in the United States (for example, Mitsubishi engaged in a 10 percent equity partnership with Hyundai to provide front-wheel engine-related technology, and eventually increased its share to 14.7

percent). Second, Japanese firms had to upgrade their products to circumvent quantitative limitations to the U.S. market via VER regulation. These offshore investments greatly changed the structure of the South Korean automobile industry.

Availability of low-cost labor, productivity, and a good geographical location were the major reasons for Japan's investments in South Korea. In 1982 wages in Mexico and Brazil were $3.53 and $3.66 respectively (roughly half of those prevailing in Japan, and one-fifth of those in the United States), while Korean wages were $1.95. In addition to low wages, the productivity of labor in the Asian countries was substantially higher than that of other low-labor-cost countries. In South Korea, average productivity was lower than Japan but almost 80 percent of the U.S. level. Caporaso (1981: 367) summarizes the impact of these conditions for East Asian industrialization by indicating that "the lower the gap in productivity between two countries, and the higher the difference in costs, the greater the flow of capital and accompanying technology from the higher-cost to lower-cost areas." For Japanese companies, following Vernon's (1966) product cycle, geographical proximity to South Korea facilitated these investment shifts.

THE KOREAN AUTOMOBILE INDUSTRY: A COMMODITY CHAINS ANALYSIS

The selection and implementation of development strategies in the NICs has been influenced by various types of exchange networks within the domestic and international economies. Network variations among the NICs appear in the forms of subcontracting, technology transfer, and marketing links. This section examines these networks by focusing on automobiles as a commodity chain.

Gereffi and Korzeniewicz (1990) extended the "commodity chains" framework of Hopkins and Wallerstein (1986) to apply it to a comparative analysis of the footwear industry, an industry that exemplifies export-oriented manufacturing in the NICs during the late twentieth century. The authors pay attention to exports to core countries and argue for the need to include forward (e.g., marketing) as well as backward linkages, indicating that the major source of economic surplus in light manufacturing industries lies not at the production stage but generally at the last stage of the chain (Gereffi and Korzeniewicz, 1990: 50–51). They propose a model composed of four major segments: (1) raw material supply; (2) production; (3) exporting; and (4) marketing and retailing. Our automobile commodity chain shares many characteristics with Gereffi and Korzeniewicz's footwear case (e.g., NICs as production loci, the importance of export penetration of the core market, and diverse marketing strategies), so their four segments are relevant to our analysis of automobile manufacturing in South Korea (see Figure 14.1).

Figure 14.1
Korean Automobile Commodity Chain

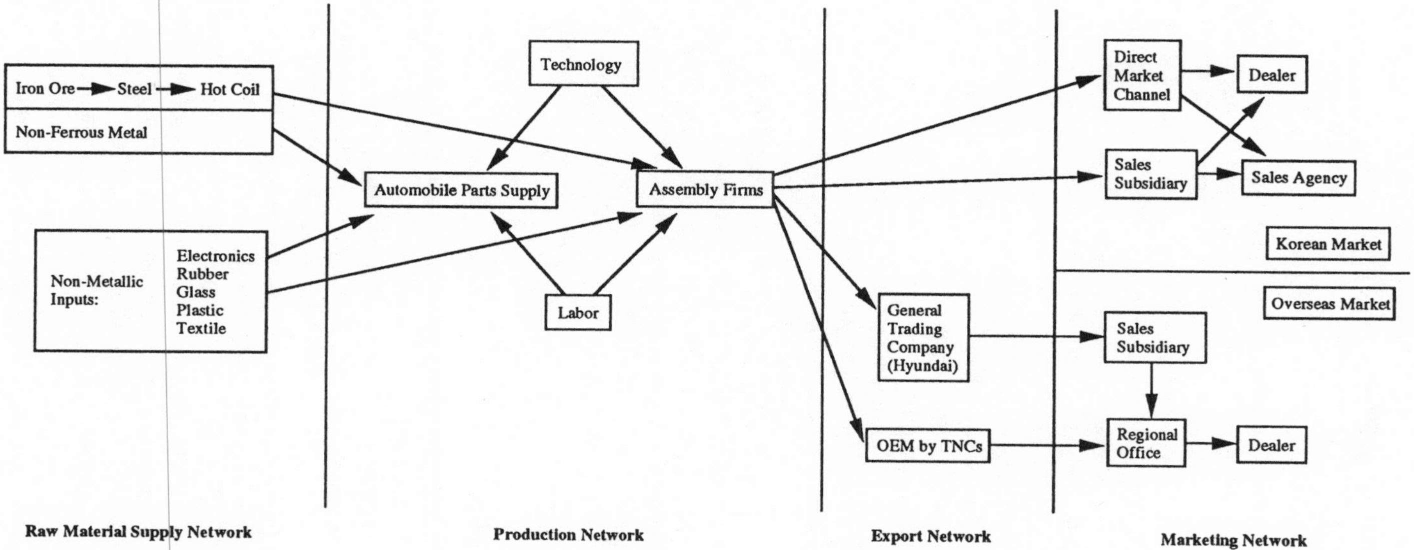

Raw Material Supply Network | Production Network | Export Network | Marketing Network

Raw Material Supply

Automobile manufacturing is not an integrated process industry, but a discrete parts industry. It needs various raw materials, including more than 15,000 component parts. Steel, electronics, plastic, rubber, glass, textile, and mechanical materials are all related to automobile manufacturing. The major drawback for South Korea has been the industry's dependence on imports, in particular regarding machinery from Japan. Nevertheless, the most important strength of Korean automobile production resides in its vertical integration. Korean automobile producers like Hyundai and Daewoo, for example, run diverse business links with the electronics and aluminum sectors.

Steel is the most important backward-linkage sector for automobile production, although aluminum and plastic have recently substituted steel products. During the early stage of Korean automobile manufacturing, steel contributed almost 81 percent of the total raw materials. This figure was slightly higher than the international standard of 76 percent (KISRG, 1990: 26). The Pohang Steel Corporation (POSCO), initiating production in 1973, constituted an organizational imperative for the automobile producers to create not only a stable supply network, but also lower costs. The domestic price of Korean steel in 1982 was 32 percent lower than imported steel. POSCO also succeeded in establishing stable procurement networks for imported iron ore (Kim, 1988: 256–69). This was significant because roughly 95 percent of all the iron ore consumed in South Korea has been imported. The purchase price of imported iron ore was $24.43 in 1983, considerably lower than the domestic iron ore purchase price ($33.00) (Marcus and Kirsis, 1985: 5–7). The major source for imported iron ore has been Australia. POSCO and heavy chemical industrialization during the 1970s provided a key intersectoral linkage for automobile manufacturers.

Production Networks

The automobile production network is defined in terms of three key variables relevant to organizational characteristics and relations of production: size of firms, technology influx, and labor pattern. The relative importance of these variables is affected by the sequencing of production trajectories.

The development of the automobile industry in South Korea has changed sequentially from assembly-related factories, to integrated domestic production, to design-oriented technology development. Each stage has been a response to external factors. These stages suggest that technology inflow constitutes the key variable for automobile production in developing countries, where the level of technology is low and the major source of comparative advantages involves cheap labor.

The period from 1962 to 1973 represented a major thrust in the Korean automobile assembly. Automobile production was initiated via import substitution and domestic firms concentrated on assembling knocked-down kits. This assembly required the use of low-level skills. Ownership remained primarily under local control and firms were characterized by strong competition. Korean automobile companies relied not on direct foreign investment, but on technology infusion. Under the government's "Long-Term Automobile Promotion Policies" plan, domestic firms tried to produce Korean-type small compact cars. The initial outcome (until 1975) was an annual production of 50,000 units. The Pony model resulted from this effort.

Korean automobile firms are controlled by *chaebol*, giving them access to the huge financial resources of these large enterprises. While imitating U.S. and Japanese TNCs, they possess their own production capacity. The size of firms, in particular, seems to have important consequences for capturing and consolidating export niches. The Korean automakers' concentrated industrial structure has been enormously helpful in developing mass production. But economies of scope, which need to be responsive to design changes in core country consumer markets, are not sufficiently developed in terms of labor skills and innovative R&D investment. It is reasonable to assume that the relative concentration and productive rigidity of Korean automobile producers may have prevented South Korea from breaking effectively and successfully into other segments of the world automobile market.

Korean automobile firms possess economies of scale. The big three, Hyundai, Kia, and Daewoo, have been an interesting mixture in terms of ownership, particularly when compared to the Latin American auto industry. Since the government does not allow exclusive foreign control, General Motors participates in Daewoo with a 50 percent equity holding. Daewoo's technology licensings are from Adam Opel of Germany, and from Isuzu and Nissan of Japan. Hyundai is owned primarily by domestic sources, with Mitsubishi holding a 15 percent equity, and some licenses from Ford and Mitsubishi. Kia is mainly owned by domestic capital in a tripartite alliance with Mazda and Ford (Ford shares 10 percent equity, while Mazda holds 8 percent and C. Itoh—Mazda's trading company—2 percent).

Hyundai and Kia show little integration, and Daewoo has an intermediate level of integration with GM. As a result, management styles are different. Hyundai, which grew out of the domestic market by producing the Pony model locally, is concerned not with annual model changes or the global strategy of a TNC, but with developing its own technology and its own market, both domestically and internationally. Daewoo's strategy is similar to GM's, with annual model changes, global licensing of parts, world cars, and original equipment manufacturing for GM, all of which are exemplified by the production of the LeMans model under a Pontiac brand.

The most interesting aspect of this mixture is Kia's supremacy over Daewoo. Until 1987 Kia was not allowed to enter passenger car production. Kia enhanced its mobility after the entry embargo was lifted in 1987. A flexible specialization system (or lean production) was adopted. NC (numerical control) and CNC (computerized numerical control) have been highly utilized at the Sohari plant.

In fact, Kia has been the only automobile-related *chaebol* group in Korea. Kia owned the Asia Automobile Co., which specializes in producing commercial cars. Six other companies, including Kia Machinery and TRW, have made strong backward linkages to provide parts and supplies for Kia. More than anything else, Kia has adopted an unusual management strategy for specialization. Kia's board of trustees decided to promote a management specialist to the firm's top executive position. Following successful sales of the Bongo model, the Concord and Capital models were developed from old-fashioned Mazda models, but with economies of scale. These successes enabled Kia to overtake Daewoo, which had a management conflict with GM and encountered serious labor disputes during 1987–1989.

On the parts supply side, the Korean auto industry has had a significant technological dependence on Japan. Almost 90 percent of parts supply firms (such as those in emissions) have relied on joint ventures with Japan. Joint-venture firms had fewer linkages with major assembly firms. Thus parts supply firms have paid 17–18 percent of their 20 percent annual profits to Japan in the form of royalties.

Automobile production and exports hinge on the availability of skilled labor. There is a sharp contrast in labor skills between automobile industries in core and semiperipheral countries. In 1990 the average hourly skill productivity in the Japanese automobile industry was 1.5 times higher than that of Korea. At the same time, labor costs in Korea rose sharply because of militant labor disputes. The competitiveness of the Korean automobile industry lost its momentum after late 1987. From 1987 to 1989, Korean automobile workers increased their wages by almost 100 percent, substantially higher than the wage increases in Korea's other industrial sectors.

Export Networks

Automobile exports from technology-receiving countries are classified into two categories: foreign-company-led and domestic-company-led. This difference among major export actors involves heterogeneous forms of export intermediation between producers in the manufacturing location and the distribution networks in the consumer markets. Captive imports from TNCs are usually designed to take advantage of cheap labor costs and productivity differentials. In the U.S. market, Korean automobile imports are distributed by two major kinds of organization: Hyundai's regional office (via Hyundai Motor America) and original equipment manufacturing (OEM). OEM has been the major strategy for TNCs to re-export to core countries automobiles assembled at offshore plants. Ford signed a contract with Kia through which the latter exported the Pride model under the Festiva brand. GM had a similar contract with Daewoo, which exported the LeMans model to the U.S. market under the Pontiac brand.

Hyundai's strategy has been an exemplary case of how a domestic company from a technology-receiving country promoted exports to a core country such as the United States. Hyundai's strategy was to create the initial impulse for an export network by utilizing its conglomerate business organization. More than 99.7 percent of its exports were channeled through its own subsidiary (Hyundai Motor America, or HMA) in the United States. The firm's marketing strategy revolved around low product prices (around \$5,000–\$6,000 per car, or \$600–\$1,000 less than Japanese subcompacts of similar quality) targeting customers whose annual income was around \$30,000. Sales were conducted through single-point dealerships specializing in Hyundai's car, and these dealerships were organized around a strategic sales network concentrated in three regional offices (Los Angeles, New York, and Atlanta—which was switched to Chicago in 1989).

The shape of export networks in the NICs is closely associated with their industrial structures and patterns of product specialization. The South Korean automobile industry has relied on a concentrated structure of export networks. The relatively small number of traders reflects three features that are peculiar to the South Korean auto industry: the firm size of the Korean automobile industry is itself more concentrated; large and diversified General Trading Companies are very active; and South Korea has specialized in the production of compact and medium-sized cars, which have a more direct route from production to marketing.

Marketing Networks

Automobile products reach consumers through distinct marketing channels, which are the end-point of our automobile commodity chain. As previously indicated, Hyundai built its own marketing strategy based on the HMA, while Kia and Daewoo relied on the OEM networks of TNCs (i.e., the Korean automakers produced TNC car models that were marketed and sold by the foreign companies). These initial strategies changed when they encountered sales bottlenecks in America. Such shifts in marketing and retailing strategies must be analyzed to show how a "producer-driven" commodity chain like the automobile sector (Gereffi, 1993) developed in Korea.

Hyundai changed its system from single-point (or exclusive) dealerships to dual-point dealerships (i.e., dealers could sell other brands), and simultaneously launched an export diversification strategy by entering European markets. Hyundai, as a latecomer, encountered difficulties in building a sales network and meeting consumer tastes. Despite these hardships, 263,000 Pony Excels were sold in the American market during the first year of operation. Single-point dealerships turned out to be one of the key factors for this initial success. Dealers were able to yield almost 15 percent sales margins in the case of the Presto AMX model, while HMA secured a 7 percent profit. The discriminate price for export markets by the South Korean firm contributed to this success (KISRG, 1990: 186, 275). In addition to comparatively high margins, dealer efficiency could be doubled because Hyundai made exclusive contracts with a limited number of dealers (p. 183). The single-point system worked very well during the early stage of penetration because most dealers were aware of the success of the subcompact cars supplied by Japanese automakers.

But Hyundai's sales were also successful because of the appreciation of the Japanese yen following the 1985 Plaza agreement. In selling the Pony Excel, a model similar to the Honda Civic, Hyundai did not encounter serious price competition from Japanese cars because the yen-U.S. dollar exchange rate was almost twice as high as before. Furthermore, Hyundai also benefited from export restraint arrangements and other U.S. restrictions against Japanese cars. These conditions affected Japanese imports in the United States and produced greater demand for subcompacts between 1986 and 1988. Introduction of the Pony Excel model allowed Hyundai to take advantage of this situation.

After this initial stage, on the other hand, Hyundai faced grater obstacles. Its export of the Sonata model in September 1988 was not as successful as its earlier models, suggesting that its medium-sized cars were not competitive in the U.S. market. In addition, there was a heightening trade conflict between the United States and South Korea, and the appreciation of the Korean won negatively affected Sonata exports. But the most important reason for the Sonata's lack of success was that the model could not capitalize on U.S.-Japanese trade competition. Facing these difficulties, Hyundai considered changing its initial policy to make a contract with Chrysler establishing an OEM arrangement.

Hyundai's loss of its competitive edge should be understood within broader trends. The problem in fact is not solely Hyundai's, but a general reduction in demand for South Korean cars in the U.S. market. In part, this could be attributed to the U.S. economic recession. The U.S. automobile market of 10.5 million units in 1988 shrank by 7.2 percent to 9.7 million in 1989, and again by 4.8 percent to 9.3 million in 1990. Subcompact cars, which were targeted toward low-income consumers, were most sensitive to such market reductions. But this explanation cannot fully account for the sales reduction of South Korean cars in the United States. Japanese cars were able to maintain stable sales levels during the economic recession. A more comprehensive explanation is needed.

First, Japanese automakers responded effectively to the American customer taste by changing their models in a four-year cycle. Korean automakers were unable to meet this rate of change, affecting consumer perceptions of their models (KERI, 1991a: 62–63). According to *Consumer Reports*, Hyundai receives the lowest grade in categories such as brakes, styling, and suspension. J. D. Power Associates gives the lowest ranking to Hyundai and Daewoo for quality evaluations. Only Festiva of Kia ranks over average (Park, 1991: 32–34). Moreover, there were problems in the after-service system. In the case of Hyundai, because all parts were supplied via three regional offices, long delays resulted in after-service complaints. These perceptions negatively affected Hyundai autos in terms of consumer competitiveness. Purchase incentives for customers were also weak. Hyundai's 13 percent interest rates constituted unattractive financing terms compared with those available through U.S. and Japanese companies. The reason for these high rates was that the low-income echelon of Hyundai customers increased the risks of repayment.

From the point of view of production, costs rose because of the appreciation of the Korean won and wage increases. Wages rose but productivity did not improve. Productivity in Hyundai and Kia's was about 17 cars per worker in 1989, while Toyota and Nissan had productivity levels of 40 to 60 cars per worker in 1988. Thus, although wages in the Korean auto sector are half of comparable Japanese wages, Hyundai's wage efficiency equals only 61 percent of Toyota's (KERI, 1990: 15-17). The small price advantage that Korean cars had obtained over competitors was therefore erased by productivity problems.

Finally, we must consider changing external environments. In the late 1980s, Japanese firms circumvented U.S. import quota restrictions by producing their cars in America. For example, the Saturn project was established to produce compact cars with American workers. But competition in the American market is not limited to the two leading world auto producers. Anticipating the establishment of a North American Free Trade Agreement in 1993, TNCs have invested heavily in Mexico, from where they will be allowed to export directly to the American market without any tariffs. Already in 1990, Mexico manufactured 242,000 cars or 42 percent more cars than those produced in 1989 (KAMA, 1991: 167).

The decline in the U.S. market provided South Korean automobile firms an incentive to diversify their exports. Hyundai produced models (Elantra and Scoupe) aimed at enhancing market shares. The sports-car-shaped Scoupe sold 32,000 units, accounting for a 13.5 percent share of Hyundai's total sales in the U.S. market in 1990. In 1991 the Elantra model sold 117,600 units, second only to the Pony Excel. This product-specific strategy was followed by an expansion of Hyundai's dealership network to more than 500 outlets, and by an abandonment of the single-point dealership system to allowed dealers to sell other brands.

Daewoo and Kia have also experimented with alternative marketing strategies. The strategy initially followed by Hyundai differed substantially from the OEM model. Daewoo's LeMans was sold in the Pontiac division, and Kia's Pride was sold as Festiva by Ford. GM and Ford dominated the sales margin. Within their sales network, dealers did not give preferential treatment to the Daewoo or Kia models. As a result, Kia and Daewoo made lower profits than Hyundai from this export market. Following a similar approach as the one developed by Hyundai, and responding to the 9.8 percent reduction of the U.S. market in 1991, Kia is introducing new models to the U.S. market and trying to build a sales subsidiary independently of Ford. Kia's Sepia compact car is scheduled to be shown to American customers in 1993. Kia has signed contracts with fifty dealerships. Kia's new strategy is possible because the Sepia model was developed largely in cooperation with Isuzu technology.

In spite of these efforts, however, South Korean automobile sales in the North American market have kept declining. In the first semester of 1992, Korean firms sold only 58,000 cars (including 45,000 in the United States), a 42 percent reduction over the same period in 1991. To respond to this downturn, South Korean automakers have sought to diversify their export markets to Europe. Hyundai has been most successful in the European market, accounting for 93 percent of Korea's total exports to Europe in 1991. This strategy has been successful for two reasons. First, the establishment of diplomatic relationships with East European countries helped Hyundai carve a niche in newly growing European markets. Second, Japanese cars are regulated by EEC import restrictions initiated by France, Italy, and Spain. As a latecomer, Hyundai was able to sidestep much of this protection.

INDUSTRIAL DIVERSIFICATION AND MARKETING NEXUS IN A TRIANGULAR RELATIONSHIP

Korean automobile firms have maintained their strategy of industrial diversification. The major reason that the Korean automobile firms were able to maintain high rates of car production is domestic market expansion; the latter has countered the current reduction of the North American market. Thus the proportion of exports fell sharply to 32 percent in 1989 from 53 percent in 1988. The importance of the domestic market as a share of total production increased from 47 percent in 1988, to 68 percent in 1989, and 73 percent by 1990.

A strategy to diversify models reflects the fact that automakers are sensitive to customer tastes. This can be seen in the shifting characteristics of cars sold. If we classify passenger cars into three categories (small, small-medium, and medium-large), South Korean consumers tend to prefer the larger cars. Accordingly, the share of small-sized cars declined from 62 percent of total sales in 1989 to 53 percent in 1990. The share of small-medium cars rose from 13 to 16 percent during the same period, and the share of medium-large cars increased from 25 to 31 percent. This preference for large-size cars also manifests itself in increased demand for imported cars (such as Ford's Sable).

The automobile distribution and marketing networks in South Korea are becoming more differentiated because of model diversification. Most firms are setting up direct marketing channels: Hyundai has established the Hyundai Automobile Service Co. to control marketing and the after-service system. Kia and Daewoo have taken similar steps. One of the important reasons for these marketing strategies is to react to consumer demands for better service. But a more crucial consideration underlying this change is to prepare for the future opening of the South Korean automobile market to foreign imports (KERI, 1991b: 7–32).

After a limited opening of their market to foreign cars in 1987, major South Korean automobile producers are serving as importers for the products made by their TNC partners (for example, Kia imports the Ford Sable, while Daewoo had the same relationship to GM). Until now, TNCs have not built their own sales subsidiaries in South Korea. Rather, they utilized their local partners in the Korean market, similarly to the way they sell Kia's or Daewoo's exports in the United States. But these reciprocal relationships are now changing. Kia wants independence from Ford in selling the Sepia model in the United States. Sales of Ford's Sable has been one of the trade conflict issues between Korea and the United States (the U.S. government claimed that the price of the Sable was intentionally high). Organizational conflicts also have emerged between Daewoo and GM on a variety of issues (including production of the Tico model by Daewoo Shipbuilding with no capital participation by GM).

Preparation for a market opening is not limited to the prospective entry of American automobiles. Korean automobile producers also have to prepare for imports from Japan. Given the higher quality of Japanese cars of similar size, Korean automobile producers (as well as the government) are expressing great concern. Up to now, the Korean government prohibited direct Japanese car imports under the rationale of import diversification. However, Kia exports the Pride model using Mazda's network. Hyundai as the largest producer, worrying about potential demands for reciprocal market opening, has been cautious enough not to export its products to Japan (Kim, 1991: 404-406). Regardless, the South Korean automobile market is likely to open in the near future. If investment in R&D offers one possible strategy for protecting the domestic market, promotion of local marketing channels provides another.

CONCLUSION

One of the unique elements of the South Korean automobile industry is its trans-Pacific division of labor. Therefore an analysis of the South Korean auto industry needs to look at the networks linking Japanese technology, Korean national capital, North American markets, and so forth. A careful examination of the Korean automobile industry shows its dependence on foreign technology, distribution, and service. But in terms of ownership, South Korea shows a significantly lower degree of foreign integration compared to firms in Latin America. The strength of the Korean automobile industry is based on the fact that the automobile sector is owned and managed by national capital, in particular the *chaebol*. In Korea, producers possess the strength to limit the degree of TNC penetration. On the marketing end, automobile producers are orchestrating the purchases of consumers.

Nevertheless, Korean automobile producers have to meet consumer preferences and tastes in order to enhance their marketing network for international competitiveness. When automobile firms are able to develop effective marketing networks and an after-service system in the domestic market, this experience should be extended to the external market. In this vein, even in producer-driven commodity chains like automobiles, the marketing nexus should be given an analytical focus along with industrial upgrading of the production side.

REFERENCES

Caporaso, James A. 1981. "Industrialization in the Periphery: The Evolving Global Division of Labor." *International Studies Quarterly*, 25, 3.

Cho, Hyung Je. 1992. "The Korean Automobile Industry and Structure of the International Division of Labor" (in Korean). Ph.D. dissertation, Seoul National University.

Cumings, Bruce. 1984. "The Origins and Development of the Northeast Asian Political Economy: Industrial Sectors, Product Cycles, and Political Consequences." *International Organization* 38, 1.

Gereffi, Gary. 1993. "The Organization of Buyer-Driven Global Commodity Chains: How U.S. Retailers Shape Overseas Production Networks," chapter 5 in this volume.

Gereffi, Gary, and Korzeniewicz, Miguel. 1990. "Commodity Chains and Footwear Exports in the Semiperiphery." In *Semiperipheral States in the World-Economy*, edited by William G. Martin. Westport, CT: Greenwood Press.

Gereffi, Gary, and Wyman, Donald. 1987. "Determinants of Development Strategies in Latin America and East Asia." *Pacific Focus* 2, 1.

Hopkins, Terence K., and Wallerstein, Immanuel. 1986. "Commodity Chains in the World-Economy Prior to 1800." *Review* 10, 1.

KAMA (Korean Automobile Manufacturers Association). 1991. *Monthly Automobile Statistics* (in Korean). Seoul: KAMA.

———. 1991. World Automobile Industry Trend (in Korean). Seoul: KAMA.

KERI (Kia Economic Research Institute). 1990. "Mid and Long-Term Prospects for Automobile Demand" (*KERI research report 7*) (in Korean). Seoul: Kia Economic Research Institute.

———. 1991a. "The National Economy and the Automobile Industry" (*KERI research report 8*) (in Korean). Seoul: Kia Economic Research Institute.

———. 1991b. "Market Openness and Automobile Industry" (*KERI special report*) (in Korean). Seoul: Kia Economic Research Institute.

Kim, Hyung Kook. 1988. "The Political Economy of Industrial Adjustment Strategies in South Korea: A Comparative Study of the Textile, Steel, and Semiconductor Industries," Ph.D. dissertation, Duke University.

———. 1991. "Automobile Industry and State capacity." In *State and Public Policies*, edited by Kang Min (in Korean), Seoul: Bummunsa.

KISRG (Korean Industrial Society Research Group). 1990. *Korean Capitalism and the Automobile Industry* (in Korean). Seoul: Pulish.

Kronisch, Rich, and Mericle, Kenneth S., eds. 1984. *The Political Economy of the Latin American Motor Vehicle Industry*. Cambridge, MA: MIT Press.

Marcus, Peter F., and Kirsis, Karlis M. 1985. *Posco: Korea's Emerging Steel Giant*. Paine Webber.

Park, Sung-Jo. 1991. "Prospects of the World Automotive Industry in the 1990s." In *Technology and Labor in the Automotive Industry*, edited by Sung Jo Park. Frankfurt: Campus Vertag.

Vernon, Raymond. 1966. "International Investment and International Trade in the Product Cycle." *Quarterly Journal of Economics* 80.

Yoffie, David B. 1983. *Power and Protectionism*. New York: Columbia University Press.

15

Cocaine, Commodity Chains, and Drug Politics: A Transnational Approach

Suzanne Wilson and Marta Zambrano

Most works on the cocaine trade take either the local or national level as their unit of analysis. Scholars such as Morales (1989) and Molano (1987) have written about coca production at the local level in Perú and Colombia. The few studies about drug distribution in the United States such as Adler (1985) and Williams (1989) also focus on the local level. On the national level in Latin America, several books have systematically examined the cocaine trade (e.g., Arrieta et al., 1991), but few studies have looked at the region's role as a whole (e.g., Lee, 1989). The few works taking a transnational perspective have focused on one part of the trade, such as money laundering (e.g., Lernoux, 1984), excluding other segments such as the chemical industry. While some scholars, such as McCoy (1991), recognize the utility of studying cocaine as a global commodity, no study to date has systematically analyzed the trade from this perspective.

In this chapter we analyze cocaine not only as a transnational commodity but as an end product of a global commodity chain. The commodity chain framework has several advantages. It allows for an examination of both "forward and backward linkages in the production process" in a comparative and historical manner (see Gereffi, chapter 5 in this volume), raising different questions from those normally present in the literature on the cocaine trade. How does each segment of the production process relate and link to the other segments? What is the dispersion of production and distribution processes across core/semiperiphery/periphery zones? Is cocaine, an "illegal" commodity, different from "legal" commodities?

This chapter's purpose is to explore these questions and thereby address the gap in the literature by analyzing cocaine as a transnational commodity chain. The chapter has two main parts. After a brief discussion of our sources, we examine the historical origins and current structure of the cocaine commodity chain. In the second section we compare cocaine with other transnational commodities, showing that despite obvious differences—the fact that cocaine is illegal—cocaine shares similarities with other commodities.

Constructing the cocaine commodity chain required multiple sources of data. U.S. government reports and statistics and congressional reports were major sources. Like others who study the cocaine trade (e.g., Arrieta et al., 1991 and Gómez, 1990), we drew on statistics from the National Narcotics Intelligence Consumers Committee (NNICC) and the Drug Enforcement Administration (DEA). Studies by historians and social scientists also provided valuable information on segments of the trade such as coca cultivation and cocaine distribution within consumer countries. We also drew on reliable periodical publications (e.g., the Colombian weekly, Semana). Among the various data sources available, we systematically selected the most conservative estimates.[1] Hence our arguments, if anything, underestimate the extent and the profitability of the trade.

COCAINE'S HISTORY

Coca, a South American plant, has been cultivated in Perú, Bolivia, and Colombia for over a millennium. Coca leaves have played, and still play, key social, medicinal, and ritual purposes in millions of indigenous peoples' lives in the Central and North Andes and Amazonia. Lee (1989:24) estimates that 10,000 metric tons of coca are still used legally in Perú and Bolivia for chewing or as medicine.

Coca, a mild stimulant, has been demonized and equated with cocaine, a concentrated derivative from coca leaves.[2] Cocaine is a laboratory-produced alkaloid first separated from coca in Germany in 1855, during a period when European researchers and scientists studied and processed a number of "exotic" plants.[3] Research on coca not only produced cocaine but the first modern industry based on coca when Angelo Mariani, a Corsican chemist, created a tonic-stimulant by steeping whole coca leaves into Bordeaux wine. By the 1880s the wine had realized its greatest popularity in Europe and the United States. In the United States, Mariani's wine was so successful that it "inspired a host of coca products to appear on the market" (Kennedy, 1985:86). In 1885, copying Mariani, J. S. Pemberton used coca leaves to brew a tonic beverage named French Wine Cola. One year later, Pemberton substituted carbonated water for wine, added sugar, and renamed it Coca-Cola. Coca leaves continue to be an ingredient in Coca-Cola, although the company currently removes the cocaine alkaloid. During the late nineteenth century, coca leaves also enjoyed great popularity in the United States and Europe as a medicine. Physicians customarily prescribed coca syrups, tonics, and beverages for the treatment of diseases including cardiac irregularities, asthma, hay fever, and depression (Kennedy, 1985:65).

Further research on cocaine's properties (among which Freud's contribution was prominent), a burgeoning patent-medicine market, and the drive for higher efficiency and profits led to the replacement of coca leaves by cocaine.[4] These catalysts prompted companies involved in the importation and manufacturing of coca and cocaine to reorganize their production processes. The U.S. company, Parke-Davis was among the first companies to determine that it was cheaper to convert coca leaves into crude cocaine in Latin America rather than in the United States. Compared to the bulky and perishable coca leaves, crude cocaine was lighter, more compact, and safer to send, and thus cut transportation costs. By 1891 several foreign-owned factories were producing crude cocaine in Perú and Bolivia (Kennedy, 1985:74). Over a century ago, cocaine was already a transnational commodity in its production and consumption.

At the turn of the century, cocaine popularity surged and the U.S. government engaged in its first war on cocaine. As a result of this war, the U.S. government banned cocaine and coca from free consumption and classified them as illegal narcotics in 1915, which resulted in soaring numbers of illegal dealers and skyrocketing cocaine prices (Courtwright, 1982; Musto, 1987). By the 1920s, lower-priced heroin had largely replaced cocaine in the market and in drug-control officials' concerns.

Two significant legacies from this first war persist in today's war on cocaine. On the domestic front, dominant discourses on drug abuse viewed cocaine use as a criminal activity, employing racist imagery to purport that the majority of users were blacks, despite the fact that studies at the time showed that they were white, a pattern similar to today's (Courtwright et al., 1989). In the international arena, the U.S. government started advocating international drug policies to control coca production at source countries (Taylor, 1969; Walker, 1989).

The Current Cocaine Boom

The contemporary war on cocaine, which built on Nixon's preexisting war against heroin and marijuana, gained force with cocaine's comeback as a recreational drug in the 1970s. Not only was cocaine compatible with the general pattern of consuming drug commodities (both legal and illegal) for entertainment and pleasure, but as Waldorf et al. (1991:281–82) point out, "in a competitive, achievement-addicted, 'Type-A society,' cocaine's ability to make us feel empowered, euphoric, energetic, and ebullient fits our culture like a glove." While social scientists have debated the current boom's causes, cocaine's image of glamour and status (the "champagne" drug); the media's publicity of its use by entertainers, sports stars, and the rich; and its reputation as an innocuous drug, all probably contributed to spreading and sustaining cocaine's popularity among affluent and middle-class users in the 1970s.[5]

During this period, the United States quickly became and still remains the world's largest cocaine-consumer market. According to John Lawn, former DEA head, U.S citizens, 6 percent of the world's population, consume 60 percent of the "illegal" drugs in the world.[6] The National Institute on Drug Abuse's (NIDA) observed estimates on cocaine usage indicate the extent of the U.S. market and trends in the numbers of consumers.[7] The NIDA (1977) estimated that 6,490,000 persons in 1974 and 11,460,000 in 1977 either currently used cocaine or had consumed it in their lifetimes.[8] Reflecting the boom of the late 1970s and early 1980s, the number of past and present users rose to 37,640,000 in 1982 (NIDA, 1982). These numbers peaked in 1985 at 40,190,000 (NIDA, 1985). In 1990, 34,667,000 persons admitted to being either current or past consumers of crack or cocaine, revealing a huge past and current market for cocaine (NIDA 1990b).[9]

The cocaine-consuming population also switched from being predominantly well-off, middle-class, and white in the 1970s to being more heterogeneous in terms of race, ethnicity, and income by the 1990s (Waldorf et al., 1991: 4–5). In the 1970s and early 1980s, NIDA surveys showed not only that larger absolute numbers of whites used cocaine but that higher current usage rates existed among whites than blacks (Miller et al., 1982). In 1990, however, 11.7 percent of whites, 11.5 percent of Hispanics, and 10 percent of blacks claimed to have used cocaine in their lifetimes, but Hispanics and blacks had higher percentages (but smaller absolute numbers) claiming current usage (NIDA, 1990a: 51).

Crack

Crack's appearance in the mid-1980s expanded the availability of cocaine-based products to lower-income groups. Crack's roots lie in smoking freebase, a "purer, more solid form" of cocaine (Waldorf et al., 1991: 103). Although freebase's reputation of a concentrated rush and intense high was known among various groups of cocaine consumers, freebase's consumption was restricted to the well-off and its production was circumscribed because of cost (considerable amounts of powdered cocaine are required to produce freebase) and limitations of its production (e.g., the use of expensive and highly flammable solvents such as ether) (Inciardi, 1987; Waldorf et al., 1991). Crack production was able to overcome the constraints of freebase production, thus allowing for cheaper, easier, and more efficient production of smokable cocaine. Unlike freebase, crack can be made from highly adulterated cocaine powder, and uses readily available baking soda and water instead of expensive solvents such as ether (Inciardi, 1987:468).

While the media have greatly exaggerated the extent of the crack "crisis" (Reinarman and Levine, 1989), crack use did spread through major urban areas in 1985 and 1986, fueled by cocaine's popularity, smokable cocaine's renown as a good high, an astute mass marketing strategy by dealers, and the availability of a cocaine product at a low per-unit cost. Building on crack's crystalline appearance, dealers at first promoted crack as purified cocaine leading users to believe that they were getting a cheap and fantastic high (Fagan and Chin, 1989: 580, 1991: 317). Instead of selling crack by weight like cocaine, dealers retailed crack in units ("rocks") costing only a fraction of the smallest measure of cocaine sold (one gram). These "rocks" could sell for as low as $5–$10 compared to $100 and up for a gram for cocaine (Williams, 1989; Fagan and Chin, 1989, 1991).

Crack's mass marketing in urban areas increased the heterogeneity of cocaine consumers by making a low per-unit cost form of cocaine ingestion available to nonaffluent populations in white and African-American communities (Waldorf et al., 1991). While crack use did grow in poor African-American, urban neighborhoods previously having few cocaine consumers (Johnson et al., 1990), rural crack use has also flourished and larger absolute numbers of whites consume crack (NIDA, 1988, 1990b). Nevertheless, the media's widespread coverage of crack as an inner-city problem continues to fuel the perception of crack as a predominantly inner-city and African-American social problem, thus reinforcing preexisting, racist assumptions about African-Americans and drug usage.

In brief, crack consumption in the mid-1980s had several effects. First, it opened a previously restricted market of cocaine consumers. Second, crack also changed the cocaine commodity chain in that value could be added to powdered cocaine at the chain's bottom ends. Finally, a point that will be discussed later, the crack trade offered jobs in inner-city neighborhoods decimated by job loss and cuts in social spending.

COCAINE AS A TRANSNATIONAL COMMODITY CHAIN

Using Hopkins and Wallerstein's (1986: 159) definition of a commodity chain as "a network of labor and production processes whose end result is a finished commodity," we can depict cocaine as a five-part transnational commodity chain: coca cultivation, coca paste production, refining coca paste into cocaine, cocaine export to consumer markets, and distribution within cocaine-importing countries. The global financial system that allows for the laundering of illegally earned money back into the formal economy ties the whole chain together. Figure 15.1 presents the chain in schematic form.

Coca Cultivation

Increasing U.S. demand for cocaine in the 1970s triggered a coca production boom in South America. Starting in the late 1970s and increasing in the 1980s and 1990s, expanding numbers of Andean migrant farmers incorporated the cultivation of coca as a cash crop in rain forest territories. Strug (1986: 78) estimates that in the Peruvian Tingo Maria region cultivation expanded from 1,600 hectares in 1972 to 20,000 hectares in 1985. Between 1977 and 1982, coca cultivation increased from 275 to 30,000 hectares in the Peruvian *Departamento* of San Martin.[10] The NNICC (1991) estimates that Perú had 121,300 hectares, Bolivia 50,300 hectares, and Colombia 40,100 hectares in coca cultivation in 1990, having the potential to produce 771 to 980 tons of cocaine.

Coca is grown basically in small plots, interspersed in upper Amazonian rain

Figure 15.1
The Cocaine Commodity Chain

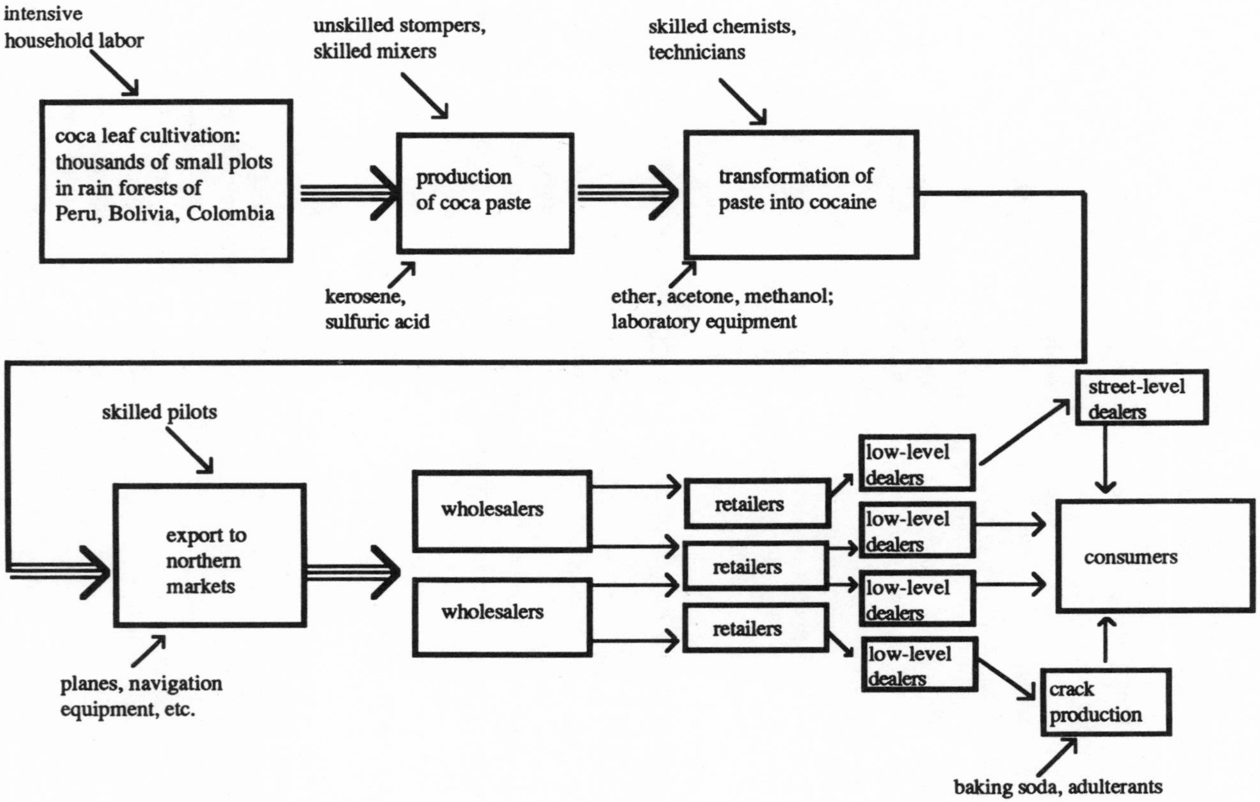

forests. While the best-quality coca is cultivated in Perú and Bolivia, the world's largest suppliers, Colombia also produces some lower-quality coca. According to Lee (1989:21), 99 percent of the world's coca production is in these countries. Coca constitutes an ideal cash crop for farmers in sparsely populated areas because: (1) unremunerated household labor used in coca cultivation fits closely with the preexisting, labor-intensive practices employed in other crops, and (2) it uses readily available indigenous technology, developed locally during coca's longtime cultivation. In addition, coca is one of the most adaptable crops in the rain forest ecology. First, it grows where other cash crops do not. Second, coca grows in depleted soils and does not require major purchases of technological inputs (e.g., fertilizers or specialized machinery). Third, coca produces three to six harvests a year and, once planted, a field can produce for as long as twenty years (Lee, 1989: 26). Last, but not least, it has higher market prices than other cash crops such as coffee or cacao, which, in turn, require larger capital investments and higher costs for transporting the crops to markets.

Coca Paste Production

After the coca leaves are harvested, skilled mixers convert the leaves into coca paste. This process usually takes place in rain forest areas near where coca is harvested. In order to produce coca paste, the mixers first add kerosene and sulfuric acid to the coca leaves. Stompers, called *pisadores*, then pound the mixture to form the coca paste. Like coca cultivation, this procedure is very labor-intensive and does not require sophisticated equipment. Processing the leaves into coca paste, however, requires key chemicals and skilled mixers.

Cocaine Refining

From these local sites, middlemen employed by Colombian drug-trafficking organizations transport raw coca leaves or coca paste to laboratories where the paste is transformed into cocaine. Although found in many South American countries, the majority of cocaine-refining laboratories are in Colombia, usually located in "marginal" areas, little-populated regions characterized by an absence of infrastructure (e.g., good roads) and state services. Regardless of geographic location, Colombian organizations generally own and control these laboratories.[11] In these laboratories, chemists or similarly trained technicians refine the paste into cocaine by combining it with imported chemicals—ether, acetone, and methanol—and then drying the resultant mixture. Basic laboratory equipment such as glass or pyrex bowls is necessary for cocaine processing as well as drying equipment (e.g., lightbulbs or microwave ovens) (Morales, 1989: 85). Unlike coca cultivation and coca paste production, refining cocaine requires major capital investment. For example, while the chemicals used for transforming coca leaves into paste are relatively cheap, domestically produced, and widely available, those necessary for transforming coca paste into cocaine are very expensive, imported from core countries (i.e., the United States and Germany), and difficult to obtain (ether and acetone are controlled substances).

Transportation and Export

Transportation and export methods adapted and devised by Colombian organizations transformed the cocaine trade. In the early 1970s the cocaine business was a small cottage industry run mainly by Bolivian and Peruvian nationals. By the early 1980s, it had become a far-reaching multinational predominantly run by Colombian organizations. These organizations benefited from Colombia's strategic geographic location—mainly its Caribbean coastline near important U.S. cities, especially Miami, and its Amazonian rain forest bordering on Perú and Bolivia (major coca cultivation regions). More importantly, Colombian traffickers achieved control of the trade by adapting methods developed during the earlier Colombian marijuana boom. Key among these methods was air transportation, devised to export marijuana from Colombia to the United States. Building on the know-how of experienced pilots and using already available clandestine airstrips, Colombian entrepreneurs effectively gained control of the cocaine trade, a dominance they continue today.

The NNICC (1991) reports that Colombian organizations control the production and transportation of 75–80 percent of the cocaine entering the United States. Because of the long distances involved, cocaine's transportation requires large airstrips, navigation equipment, and airplanes with the capacity to fly long distances. Like the processing stage, the export stage involves employing skilled professionals and substantial capital investment. Both stages also necessitate substantial investment in security (e.g., guns, guards, and bribes).

Distribution and Consumption

While Colombian organizations have managed in some cities to participate at the wholesale dealer level, U.S. organizations control most of the distribution networks, the most profitable stages in the cocaine commodity chain. The research literature has clearly shown that U.S. citizens control distribution at the low and middle levels. At the wholesale levels, the evidence is more mixed. Williams (1989) found that in New York Colombians participated in the wholesale distribution of cocaine. In Southern California, however, U.S. citizens monopolized the wholesale distribution of cocaine (Adler, 1985). Lee (1989) concludes that Colombians worked with U.S. residents in the major entry points (e.g., Miami) but U.S. citizens controlled the wholesale level in other cities (e.g., Atlanta).[12] While Colombians may have built some wholesale distribution organizations, two points are clear. First, many U.S. citizens participate in the trade and receive the profits. Second, the bulk of the profits remain in the United States.

Although regional and local variation exists, research on drug distribution within the United States describes three basic levels—wholesale distributors, retail sellers, and low-level distributors (Johnson et al., 1990: 19; Adler, 1985; Lee, 1989).[13] Additionally, street-level dealers in many cases can be differentiated from other low-level dealers who sell to acquaintances and well-known contacts in the privacy and relative safety of homes or at prearranged meeting places. At each level, the price of cocaine increases, generating enormous profits, one reason why most of the profits from the trade (87 percent) remain in drug-consuming countries (Wilson and Zambrano, 1990). The markup can be seen in the differences in price between production costs and final retail prices. Morales (1989: 92–93) estimates that the total cost (seeds, rent, electricity, fuel, etc.) of producing one kilogram of cocaine is $5,000. This kilogram's value after adulteration is $35,000 at the wholesale level in New York City and can be as high as $200,000 at the final retail level.

Crack's introduction allowed value to be added easily in the commodity chain's later parts. Above and beyond adulteration, crack production involves transforming cocaine into a new product with low costs for inputs (e.g., baking soda). Crack's low unit selling price and its rapid market expansion also offered opportunities for individuals and organizations to participate in the informal drug economy in inner-city neighborhoods (Fagan and Chin, 1991:318). Additionally, the crack industry arrived as spending on social services and infrastructure (e.g., education) in these neighborhoods was declining, industrial jobs were being lost, and the informal economy was growing (Sassen-Koob, 1989; Johnson et al., 1990; Fagan and Chin, 1989, 1991). An interesting parallel exists between informal-economy growth and commodity prices' decline in Latin America and the growth of the informal economy and the loss of jobs in the cities of the United States. Just as coca cultivation is more economically rewarding than other crops, so does participation in the informal drug economy earn more money than lowly paid jobs in the formal sector or unemployment.

Core Countries' Role

The United States is not only the world's largest cocaine market and home to a majority of the trade's profits, but industries based in the country also supply the necessary manufactured inputs such as airplanes, navigation equipment, arms, and key chemicals (e.g., ether and acetone) required for producing coca paste and cocaine. According to the DEA, 70 percent of the acetone used in cocaine processing comes from U.S. companies.[14] Thirty-three percent of the ether originates in the United States, with the remainder being supplied by West Germany.[15]

Although precise figures on the volume of chemicals employed in cocaine production are unavailable, existing evidence suggests that it is huge. Media reports on laboratory seizures provide illustrative clues. In August 1989 the Colombian police seized a large cocaine plant that contained, in addition to 1,200 kilograms of pure cocaine, a half-million gallons of chemicals.[16] Our estimates of the chemicals required to produce cocaine also imply a huge volume. According to Morales (1989: 85–86), one kilogram of cocaine requires 3.75 kilograms of coca paste, 300 milliliters of hydrochloric acid, eight gallons of acetone, and one gallon of ether. Using the NNICC's (1991) minimum estimates (771 tons) for cocaine produced in South America in 1990, we calculated that 783,382 gallons of ether and 6,267,056 gallons of acetone were needed for this volume of cocaine.

Besides chemicals, the United States is also a major source of guns, other security apparatuses (e.g., walkie-talkies), and transportation equipment. According to a 1989 study by the Bureau of Alcohol, Tobacco and Firearms, more than two-thirds of the weapons recently seized from drug traffickers in Colombia were manufactured in the United States (Majority Staffs of Senate Judiciary Committee and International Narcotics Control Caucus, 1991: 32). Much of the sophisticated transportation supplies—airplanes and radar equipment—used by drug traffickers is also made in the U.S.A.

Money Laundering

Tying the whole commodity chain in cocaine together at all levels is money laundering, the process by which drug-related profits are deposited in bank accounts or legitimate businesses and then withdrawn or transferred into other accounts as clean money. By means of money laundering, drug traffickers can turn $20 or $100 bills into money-market deposits and business or property investments. Money laundering, a key component of the trade, thus ties the illegal economy with the legal economy by recycling drug money into the legal financial system.

The money-laundering process is complex, global in scope, and difficult to track. Many methods drug traffickers use to launder money, such as offshore bank accounts, are also widely used by legal corporations as tax shelters. According to Anthony S. Ginsberg, a Los Angeles–based financial consultant, offshore centers are now integral to the global economy, with as much as half of the world's money residing or passing through them.[17]

In brief, the cocaine trade binds Peruvians and Bolivians, who cultivate coca and process the coca paste, with Colombian drug organizations, which refine, transport, and distribute cocaine to the United States, where U.S. wholesalers, middlemen, and peddlers sell it to the world's largest market of cocaine consumers. While Colombian nationals control the chain's early segments, the United States and other core countries participate in the primary, transport, and export stages by providing key components (chemicals, airplanes, equipment) and, most importantly, in the chain's end portions by controlling the profitable distribution networks. Last but not least, the international financial system provides the means for the trade's profits to be laundered and invested in the legal economy.

THE COCAINE COMMODITY CHAIN:
A COMPARATIVE PERSPECTIVE

Despite cocaine's peculiarities stemming from its illegal status, cocaine production and the distribution of its profits closely resemble those of other transnational commodities. First, we discuss the differences and then examine the similarities.

Differences Between Cocaine and Other Commodities

The most obvious difference between cocaine and other commodities is that the United States and other states agree on defining cocaine as an "illegal" commodity. This social and political definition of "illegality" has several implications for the cocaine trade. First, the risks, violence, and profitability of its production and commercialization increase enormously. While the trade's illegality and U.S. drug policy have raised processing costs by necessitating the purchase of costly protection equipment and hiring of security personnel, the very same illegality, plus the absence of regulations, fully compensates for these costs (McCoy, 1991: 3). Hence its illegality gives cocaine high market prices and high rates of return.[18]

Second, cocaine is not regulated in the same manner as other commodities. There are no state policies, no taxation, or no tariffs to promote the trade and cocaine manufacturing such as Gereffi and Korzeniewicz (1990) describe for shoe manufacturing in Brazil and South Korea. This point, however, should not be pushed too far, since cocaine also mirrors current global tendencies toward the informalization of the world economy and the decline of state intervention in the production of an increasing number of commodities. In a global context in which unregulated economic activities expand within, and at the expense of, a framework of regulated activities, cocaine resembles many legal commodities that are produced and/or exchanged outside labor, tax, and safety regulations (Castells and Portes, 1989; Sassen-Koob, 1989). Although the trade is outside of state regulation in many respects, state policies do shape the cocaine trade both in what *they do* and what *they overlook*. Foremost, among the state policies shaping the trade is U.S. drug policy. The U.S. government not only has devoted resources for combating the cocaine trade but has pressured Latin American governments to engage in this "war" and has given foreign aid and tactical support to that task. In this next section, we argue that this policy is very selective and distributes the risks of participation in the trade unequally throughout the cocaine commodity chain.

For many years, the U.S. government has pursued a war on illegal drugs. Currently, most funding for the "drug war" is domestic but the overall strategy is internationally oriented (Collett, 1989). These two fronts share a common law enforcement approach. On the domestic front, the main thrust of narcotics policy is directed toward arresting low-level street dealers and most domestic funding

(70 percent) goes toward law enforcement (Majority Staffs of Senate Judiciary Committee and International Narcotics Control Caucus, 1991). On the international front, most narcotics aid has been given to the military, resulting in "de facto" aid for counterinsurgency programs and repression of local populations. In recent years, under the Bush administration, the trend toward increased militarization has accelerated (Youngers, 1990). Both in 1989 and 1990, most narcotics assitance given to Bolivia, Perú, and Colombia was for either military or law enforcement purposes (Youngers, 1990:27).[19] Even programs with an economic rationale such as eradication have been implemented in a militaristic fashion. These trends have resulted in persons at the chain's tail ends (i.e., coca farmers and street-level dealers) having greater probabilities of being harassed, persecuted, and/or imprisoned.

Other components of the international "drug war" have also influenced the cocaine commodity chain. Policies directed at the chain's middle stages have consistently favored those with large amounts of money over smaller entrepreneurs. Border interdiction has made the transportation or smuggling stage more capital-intensive. Adler (1985) reported that, as border interdiction increased in the late 1970s, many smaller smugglers dropped out of the business because they could no longer easily cross the border or fly on commercial airlines to Colombia to buy cocaine. Ironically, border interdiction ended up favoring larger drug dealers, who had enough capital either to buy in bulk from the Colombian organizations and/or to purchase the equipment (e.g., boats and airplanes) to smuggle cocaine into the country from offshore. The other major policy component directed at the chain's middle stages, extradition, has not only been unsuccessful but also favors individuals and organizations with large amounts of capital for bribes and protection money. U.S. drug policy, then, has added to the preexisting capital-intensity of the chain's middle stages.

It is important to examine not only what U.S. policy does but what it disregards. These policies' selective character is also present in their supply-side approach, which not only ignores that cocaine is a transnational commodity (McCoy, 1991) but downplays the formal sector's and United States' key roles (e.g., supplying chemicals and the financial system's role in money laundering). For example, the DEA estimates that 98 percent of the ether entering Colombia goes to cocaine processing.[20] Yet, Congress and drug enforcement agencies have done little to stop the illegal flow of chemicals to cocaine-producing areas. The U.S. Congress only passed a Chemical Diversion and Trafficking Act in 1988, and one year later the DEA had not obtained one indictment for illegal exports of chemicals (Majority Staffs of Senate Judiciary Committee and International Narcotics Control Caucus, 1991: 41). Additionally, this law has many loopholes, including specifying that only new customers of chemicals can be investigated for selling chemicals for cocaine manufacturing and that, once cleared, a customer cannot be investigated again.[21] Also, programs that target formal sector segments of the trade lack sufficient amounts of money and agents.

In summary, U.S. drug policy has been directed toward increased law enforcement and military efforts against the illegal, informal components of the trade while generally ignoring the more formal components located mainly in the United States and other core countries. Furthermore, policies directed at the chain's export and transportation segments (e.g., border interdiction) favor traffickers with larger amounts of capital rather than disrupting the trade at these stages. Hence these policies distribute the hazards unequally throughout the commodity chain with the participants at the chain's tail ends (cultivation and low-level street dealers) disproportionately assuming the risks.

In addition to its illegality, cocaine differs from other Latin American exports in other respects. Cocaine is one of the few regional agricultural exports, such as oranges, processed in the region, and it is, perhaps, the only case where a "local elite" controls the transportation routes and the majority of the international trade. Unlike with other Latin American products, this cocaine elite manages the entire production process—purchasing coca leaves or coca paste, supervising the two processing stages, financing the production costs, transporting the cocaine to importing countries, and controlling the wholesale commercialization to the foreign markets. Former Peruvian president Alan García captured the distinctive trait of the cocaine trade when he described it as "Latin America's only successful multinational."[22]

Similarities Between Cocaine and Other Commodities

Cocaine's emergence, however, closely resembles that of other Latin American agricultural products. During successive periods of boom and bust, the global market has launched the production of different legal "drugs" (e.g., coffee) and illegal "drugs" (e.g., marijuana). Changes in the global economy (e.g., trends toward less state intervention and the informal economy growth) have affected cocaine like other commodities. Not only has the cocaine trade benefited from the decline in formal labor arrangements, drawing from the flexible reserves of labor thereby created, but it has been able to provide better-paying jobs to the unskilled and skilled (Blanes, 1989; Salazar, 1990). Changes in the international financial system such as globalization, computerized banking, and the rise in offshore banking have also shaped the cocaine trade by making money laundering easier and facilitating the transfer of money across national borders.

Another important similarity springs from the distribution of profits. Like other commodities, most of the profits remain in core countries. Although we do not have estimates for the European and Japanese markets, using NNICC figures, we have shown that 87 percent of the trade's profits stay in the United States, with only 13 percent remaining in Colombia, Perú, and Bolivia in 1988 (Wilson and Zambrano, 1990). Using DEA 1988–1990 data published in *Intelligence Trends*, we confirm our earlier findings. In 1988, one kilogram of cocaine sold for $14,000 at the wholesale level in Miami but yielded $160,000 in sales to consumers. For this year then, 95 percent of the profits were made between wholesaling and consumer sales, points in the chain which were all located in the United States. The 1989 estimates show a kilogram of cocaine sold for $13,000 at the wholesale level to generate $80,000 at the consumer level; thus United States' profits for 1989 were 84 percent. The 1990 figures indicate that one kilogram selling for $16,000 at the wholesale level produced $70,000 in retail sales, with 77 percent of the profits staying in the United States.

Although the estimates vary by year and source, in all cases high percentages of the profits stay in the United States. The fact that cocaine prices are even higher in Europe and Japan (NNICC, 1991) indicates that a similar pattern occurs in these countries. Despite the fact that Colombian drug organizations control the exportation of processed cocaine into core countries, the distribution of profits reflects and reproduces the distinction among core, semiperipheral, and peripheral countries.

Even though the global division of labor varies from commodity to commodity, an important similarity among commodities (including cocaine) is that organizations within core countries control the distribution within the major and most profitable markets (i.e., core-country markets). While there are obvious differences between commodities exported in an unprocessed or semiprocessed form and those exported in a manufactured form, in both cases, organizations in core countries control the products' distribution. It is at this stage that the majority of the profits are generated and the greatest additions in value are added. Gereffi and Korzeniewicz (1990) show this to be the case for shoes even when South Korea and Brazil have managed to capture significant portions of core countries' markets. Our analysis confirms this pattern for cocaine.

These findings go against what Chase-Dunn (1989: 204) has labeled the "level of processing" approach for the distinction between core and periphery. This approach argues that the distinction between core and periphery is based on the production of raw versus manufactured goods. Cocaine's case shows that even when a regional elite controls the commodity's production and transportation, the majority of profits remain within core countries, thus reproducing the stratification among core, semiperiphery, and periphery. Our findings do, however, concur with Arrighi and Drangel (1986), who suggest that the distinction between core and periphery is at the level of profits and high returns regardless of the type of activity—agricultural or manufacturing, legal or illegal. Chase-Dunn (1989: 206) points out that Arrighi and Drangel's approach suggests that core countries receive larger percentages of profits because of their abilities to control prices, thus enabling them to generate "surplus profits" at the stages where the most value is added (e.g., distribution).

How core countries manage to control prices, to receive higher profits, and to maintain an unequal distribution of rewards in the cocaine commodity chain remain unanswered questions, along with how these mechanisms are historically structured. Our search through the social science literature, congressional hearings, and U.S. government data yielded little information on the details of cocaine distribution networks within core countries, who exactly controls these networks at the top levels, the concentration of profits, and how the profits are distributed.

CONCLUSIONS

In this chapter we have briefly described cocaine's historical origins and its transnational commodity chain. Unlike other analyses, we have not only described and analyzed the informal, illegal segments of the trade but the formal ones and the transnational linkages between the informal and formal segments. Our analysis has also shown that despite the fact that cocaine is an illegal commodity and that a regional, Latin American elite controls production, it still shares similarities with other transnational commodities—profits remain within core countries and the trade is tied to the global economy by links to legal industries such as chemical and arms manufacturing and the world's financial system. We have attempted to point out how these linkages occur at all stages of cocaine production—processing of coca paste, refining the paste into cocaine, exportation, and distribution.

Looking at cocaine from this perspective then raises issues about the cocaine trade ignored by other analyses, including: (a) how trends in the global economy interact with the cocaine commodity chain; and (b) how and by what means core countries manage to maintain high percentages of profits across a range of commodities. Most important, examining cocaine as a commodity chain allows for a critical scrutiny of the selective nature of U.S. drug policy. By overlooking the formal sector's and core countries' roles and focusing on law enforcement and militarization directed against the trade's illegal and informal components, U.S. policy mainly attacks the chain's tail ends, with cultivators and low-level street dealers disproportionately taking on the risks.

NOTES

We would like to thank Bill Martin for his encouragement, support, and suggestions. We are also grateful to Gary Gereffi, Miguel Korzeniewicz, Ann Reisner, and the conference participants for their comments and insights.

1. Although the cocaine trade is difficult to study, it is not always easy studying "legal" commodities either. For example, very few sources on the chemical industry exist and the extant sources consistently note the difficulties and problems studying this particular industry.

2. An extensive anthropological and interdisciplinary literature stresses the cultural, historical, and chemical distinctions between coca and cocaine. See, for example, Instituto Indigenista Interamericano (1986) and Kennedy (1985).

3. In 1804, Wilhelm Seturner separated morphine from crude opium; and in 1820 quinine was separated from chinchona.

4. This process was more complex. Other factors that influenced the replacement of coca with cocaine included the discovery that cocaine was the long-searched-for local anesthetic.

5. Much disagreement and little concrete research exists on the causes of the 1970s cocaine boom. Musto (1987) argues that drug consumption goes through historical cycles of usage and decline. Buchanan (1992) presents a variant of this argument, asserting that

such cycles appear after major national crises (e.g., the Civil War, the 1960s). Others suggest that the 1960s, with a more tolerant and relaxed view toward drugs (e.g., Wisotsky, 1986) and/or a breakdown of societal values, helped cause the current cocaine boom. Kennedy (1985) reviews contentions that media in those years with movies such as *Easy Rider* helped glamorized the drug culture.

Another set of explanations looks at specific factors. Wisotsky (1986) and Waldorf et al. (1991) point to legislation restricting the production and supply of amphetamines that passed shortly before the second cocaine boom, and led users of amphetamines to switch to cocaine. Inciardi (1987) notes that legislation restricting sedative use accompanied the passage of the amphetamine legislation, and that both could have contributed to the current boom. Inciardi (1987: 464) also points to the fact that transportation routes to coca-growing areas (e.g., the Huallaga River Valley) had been recently opened up (e.g., the building of the Pan American Highway). Wisotsky (1986) claims that the Cuban immigration to the United States during those years may have facilitated easier access and better connections to cocaine supplies in Latin America.

6. See an interview with John Lawn in *USA Today*, February 28, 1990, p. 9A.

7. We do not discuss the numbers of tons of cocaine entering the United States because the existing data in that area are unreliable and inconsistent (Wisotsky, 1986). Although all sources agree that the United States is by far the world's largest cocaine market and the number of users began declining around 1985, the exact number of cocaine users has been controversial. We use figures from the *National Household Survey on Drug Abuse* because it is the only annual national survey on cocaine usage for persons of all ages. The survey's main source of bias is an underestimation of the number of users because respondents may not wish to report socially undesirable drug usage, and the survey excludes prison inmates, students, military personnel, and the homeless (NIDA, 1990a). Even the harshest critics of this survey (e.g., Senate Committee of the Judiciary, 1990), however, do *not* dispute our major claims: (a) that the United States is the world's largest cocaine market; (b) that cocaine usage has declined since 1985; and (c) that characteristics of cocaine users over time have become more heterogeneous over time.

8. Prior to 1982, the NIDA categorized current cocaine users as either having consumed cocaine in the past month or in their lifetime. After 1982, the NIDA added a category, usage in the past year. Hence, the pre-1982 figures are the totals of the NIDA's observed estimates for past month and lifetime usage. The post-1982 totals include NIDA's new category, usage in the last year. Reflecting crack's appearance, the 1990 totals also contain crack usage in the past month, year, and lifetime.

9. One possible explanation for lowered cocaine consumption is that respondents are less likely to reply positively to cocaine or crack usage in a survey. Also, beginning in the early 1980s, the media switched from portraying cocaine as a glamour drug to demonizing it (Wisotsky, 1986). Another explanation is that teen-agers and young adults use illicit drugs more often and the number of young persons has decreased with the passing of the baby boom (Erickson et al., 1987).

10. See *Semana*, April 4, 1988.

11. As law enforcement efforts crack down on these laboratories in one region or country, drug-trafficking organizations tend to move them to other regions or countries (the "balloon" or "mercury ball" effect).

12. A problem that these scholars overlook is how to distinguish Colombians from Latinos or "Colombian-Americans." This is especially problematic for cities such as New York and Miami with large populations of Colombians. Also, these studies only

provide clues about whether the distribution networks are centralized or decentralized. Our suspicion is that the networks are centralized at the top and decentralized at the bottom. We would like to thank Jonathan Hartlyn for bringing this point about centralization to our attention.

13. Johnson et al. (1990) group importers and wholesale dealers together as traffickers. The literature also varies on the number of levels within each of the three levels.

14. See *Semana*, March 5, 1990.

15. See *Semana*, November 17, 1984, p. 36.

16. See *U.S. News and World Report*, October 11, 1989, p. 20.

17. See *New York Times Magazine*, March 29, 1992, p. 28.

18. The emphasis on militarization over other methods (e.g., economic ones) only disrupts the trade at selective local sites (e.g., eradication of coca cultivation); it does not remove any of the economic incentives, such as the higher prices for coca as compared to other crops, that make participation in the trade so profitable at all levels.

19. Figures from the Congressional Information Service (1991) also show the increased militarization of drug funding.

20. See *Semana*, November 17, 1984, p. 36.

21. Although we only discuss the chemical industry here, the same pattern of neglect can easily be documented for money laundering and the arms industry.

22. See *The Economist* (October 8, 1988, p. 22) for Alan García's quote.

REFERENCES

Adler, Patricia A. 1985. *Wheeling and Dealing: An Ethnography of Upper-Level Drug Dealing and Smuggling Communities*. New York: Columbia University Press.

Arrieta, Carlos G.; Orjuela, Luis J.; Sarmiento P., Eduardo; and Tokatlian, Juan G. 1991. *Narcotráfico en Colombia: Dimensiones políticas, económicas, jurídicas e internacionales*. Bogotá: Tercer Mundo Editores.

Arrighi, Giovanni, and Drangel, Jessica. 1986. "The Stratification of the World-Economy: An Explanation of the Semiperipheral Zone." *Review* 10, 1:9–74.

Blanes Jiménez, José. 1989. "Cocaine, Informality, and the Urban Economy in La Paz, Bolivia." In *The Informal Economy: Studies in Advanced and Less Developed Countries*, edited by Alejandro Portes, Manuel Castells, and Lauren Benton, pp. 150–70. Baltimore: Johns Hopkins University Press.

Buchanan, David R. 1992. "A Social History of American Drug Use." *The Journal of Drug Issues* 22, 1:31–52.

Castells, Manuel, and Portes, Alejandro. 1989. "World Underneath: The Origins, Dynamics, and Effects of the Informal Economy." In *The Informal Economy: Studies in Advanced and Less Developed Countries*, edited by Alejandro Portes, Manuel Castells, and Lauren Benton, pp. 11–37. Baltimore: Johns Hopkins University Press.

Chase-Dunn, Christopher. 1989. *Global Formation: Structures of the World Economy*. Oxford: Basil Blackwell.

Collett, Merrill. 1989. *The Cocaine Connection: Drug Trafficking and Inter-American Relations*. New York: Foreign Policy Association.

Courtwright, David T. 1982. *Dark Paradise: Opiate Addiction in America before 1940*. Cambridge, MA: Harvard University Press.

Courtwright, David; Joseph, Herman; and Des Jarlais, Don. 1989. *Addicts Who Survived:*

An Oral History of Narcotic Use in America, 1923–1965. Knoxville: The University of Tennessee Press.

Erickson, Patricia G.; Adalf, Edward M.; Murray, Glenn F.; and Smart, Reginald G. 1987. *The Steel Drug: Cocaine in Perspective*. Lexington, MA: Lexington Books.

Fagan, Jeffrey, and Chin, Ko-lin. 1989. "Initiation into Crack and Cocaine: A Tale of Two Epidemics." *Contemporary Drug Problems* 16, 4 (Winter):579–618.

———. 1991. "Social Processes of Initiation into Crack." *The Journal of Drug Issues* 21, 2:313–43.

Gereffi, Gary, and Korzeniewicz, Miguel. 1990. "Commodity Chains and Footwear Exports in the Semiperiphery." In *Semiperipheral States in the World-Economy*, edited by William G. Martin. Westport, CT: Greenwood Press.

Gómez, Hernando José. 1990. "El tamaño del narcotráfico y su impacto económico." *Economía Colombiana* 226–27 (Feb.-March): 8–17.

Hopkins, Terence K., and Wallerstein, Immanuel. 1986. "Commodity Chains in the World-Economy Prior to 1800." *Review* 10, 1:157–70.

Inciardi, James A. 1987. "Beyond Cocaine: Basuco, Crack, and Other Coca Products." *Contemporary Drug Problems* 14, 3 (Fall): 461–92.

Instituto Indigenista Interamericano. 1986. *La Coca Andina. Visión de una planta satanizada*. México: Boldó i Clemente Editores.

Johnson, Bruce D.; Williams, Terry; Dei, Kojo A.; and Sanabria, Harry. 1990. "Drug Abuse in the Inner City: Impact on Hard-Drug Users and the Community." In *Drugs and Crime*, edited by Michael Tonry and James Q. Wilson, pp. 9–68. Chicago: University of Chicago Press.

Kennedy, Joseph. 1985. *Coca Exotica: The Illustrated Story of Cocaine*. New York: Cornwall Books.

Lee, Rensselaer W. III. 1989. *The White Labyrinth: Cocaine and Political Power*. New Brunswick, NJ: Transaction Books.

Lernoux, Penny. 1984. *In Banks We Trust*. New York: Anchor Press/Doubleday.

McCoy, Alfred W. 1991. *The Politics of Heroin: CIA Complicity in the Global Drug Trade*. New York: Lawrence Hill Books.

Miller, Judith Droitcour; Cisin, Ira H.; Gardner-Keaton, Hilary; Harrell, Adele V.; Wirtz, Philip W.; Abelson, Herbert I.; and Fishburne, Patricia, M. 1982. *National Survey on Drug Abuse: Main Findings 1982*. Rockville, MD: National Institute on Drug Abuse.

Molano, Alfredo. 1987. *Selva adentro: Una historia oral de la colonización del Guaviare*. Bogotá: Ancora.

Morales, Edmundo. 1989. *Cocaine: White Gold Rush in Peru*. Tucson: University of Arizona Press.

Musto, David. 1987. *The American Disease: Origins of Narcotic Control*. Expanded ed. New York: Oxford University Press.

Reinarman, Craig, and Levine, Harry G. 1989. "Crack in Context: Politics and Media in the Making of a Drug Scare." *Contemporary Drug Problems* 16, 4 (Winter): 535–79.

Salazar, Alonso J. 1990. *No nacimos pa' semilla. La cultura de las bandas juveniles de Medellín*. Bogotá: CINEP.

Sassen-Koob, Saskia. 1989. "New York City's Informal Sector." In *The Informal Economy: Studies in Advanced and Less Developed Countries*, edited by Alejandro

Portes, Manuel Castells, and Lauren Benton. pp. 60–77. Baltimore: Johns Hopkins University Press.

Strug, David L. 1986. "The Foreign Politics of Cocaine: Comments on a Plan to Eradicate the Coca Leaf in Peru." In *Coca and Cocaine: Effects on People and Policy in Latin America*, edited by Deborah Pacini and Christine Franquemont, pp. 73–88. *Cultural Survival Report* No. 23.

Taylor, Arnold H. 1969. *American Diplomacy and the Narcotics Traffic, 1900–1939*. Durham, NC: Duke University Press.

Waldorf, Dan; Reinarman, Craig; and Murphy, Sheigla. 1991. *Cocaine Changes: The Experience of Using and Quitting*. Philadelphia: Temple University Press.

Walker, William O. 1989. *Drug Control in the Americas*. Albuquerque: University of New Mexico Press.

Williams, Terry. 1989. *The Cocaine Kids*. New York: Addison-Wesley.

Wilson, Suzanne, and Zambrano, Marta. 1990. "Warlords and Druglords: The U.S. Role in the Drug Trade." Paper Presented at the Illinois Conference of Latin Americanists, November 16–17, Champaign, IL.

Wisotsky, Steven. 1986. *Breaking the Impasse in the War on Drugs*. Westport, CT: Greenwood Press.

Youngers, Coletta. 1990. *The War in the Andes: The Military Role in the U.S. International Drug Policy. WOLA Briefing Series: Issues in International Drug Policy*. Washington D.C.: Washington Office on Latin America.

U.S. Government Publications

Congressional Information Service. 1991. *U.S. Overseas Loans and Grants and Assistance from International Organizations, Annual Report 1991*.

Drug Enforcement Administration. 1987–1991, various issues. *Intelligence Trends*.

Majority Staffs of Senate Judiciary Committee and International Narcotics Control Caucus. 1991. *Fighting Drug Abuse: New Directions for Our National Strategy*.

NIDA (National Institute on Drug Abuse). 1977. *Supplemental Tables. Population Projections based on The National Survey of Drug Abuse: 1977*.

———. 1982. *Population Projections: Based on the National Survey of Drug Abuse, 1982*.

———. 1985. *National Household Survey of Drug Abuse: Population Estimates 1985*.

———. 1990a. *National Household Survey of Drug Abuse: Main Findings 1990*.

———. 1990b. *National Household Survey of Drug Abuse: Population Estimates 1990*.

NNICC (The National Narcotics Intelligence Consumers Committee). 1991. *The NNICC Report: The Supply of Illicit Drugs to the United States 1989–90*.

Senate Committee of the Judiciary, United States Senate. 1990. *Drug Abuse in America: Is the Epidemic Really Over? Summary of Findings of a Majority Staff Study*. One Hundred and First Congress, Second Session.

Bibliography

Alba, Richard D. 1982. "Taking Stock of Network Analysis: A Decade's Results." *Research in the Sociology of Organizations* 1: 39–74.

Appelbaum, Richard P., and Henderson, Jeffrey, eds. 1992. *States and Development in the Asian Pacific Rim.* Newbury Park, CA: Sage Publications.

Arrighi, Giovanni. 1990. "The Developmentalist Illusion: A Reconceptualization of the Semiperiphery." In *Semiperipheral States in the World-Economy,* edited by William G. Martin, pp. 11–42. Westport, CT: Greenwood Press.

Arrighi, Giovanni, and Drangel, Jessica. 1986. "The Stratification of the World-Economy: An Exploration of the Semiperipheral Zone." *Review* 10, 1 (Summer): 9–74.

Arrighi, Giovanni, Korzeniewicz, Roberto P., and Martin, William. 1986. "Three Crises, Three Zones: Core-Periphery Relations in the Long Twentieth Century." *Cahier du GIS Economie Mondiale, Tiers Monde, Développement* 6 (Mar.): 125–62.

Block, Fred. 1990. *Postindustrial Possibilities: A Critique of Economic Discourse.* Berkeley: University of California Press.

Chandler, Alfred D., Jr. 1977. *The Visible Hand.* Cambridge, MA: Harvard University Press.

Chase-Dunn, Christopher. 1990. *Global Formation.* Cambridge, MA: Basil Blackwell.

Cohen, Stephen S., and Zysman, John. 1987. *Manufacturing Matters: The Myth of the Post-Industrial Economy.* New York: Basic Books.

Dicken, Peter. 1992. *Global Shift: The Internationalization of Economic Activity.* 2d. ed. New York: The Guilford Press.

Donaghu, Michael T., and Barff, Richard. 1990. "Nike Just Did It: International Subcontracting and Flexibility in Athletic Footwear Production." *Regional Studies* 24, 6: 537–52.

Doner, Richard F. 1991. *Driving a Bargain: Automobile Industrialization and Japanese Firms in Southeast Asia*. Berkeley: University of California Press.

Fajnzylber, Fernando. 1990. *Unavoidable Industrial Restructuring in Latin America*. Durham, NC: Duke University Press.

Fishlow, Albert. 1989. "Latin American Failure against the Background of Asian Success." *The Annals* 505 (Sept.): 117–28.

Freeman, Christopher, ed. 1990. *The Economics of Innovation*. Hants., England: Edward Elgar.

Gereffi, Gary. 1989a. "Rethinking Development Theory: Insights from East Asia and Latin America." *Sociological Forum* 4, 4 (Fall): 505–33.

———. 1989b. "Development Strategies and the Global Factory." *The Annals* 505 (Sept.): 92–104.

Gereffi, Gary, and Korzeniewicz, Miguel. 1990. "Commodity Chains and Footwear Exports in the Semiperiphery." In *Semiperipheral States in the World-Economy*, edited by William G. Martin, pp. 45–68. Westport, CT: Greenwood Press.

Gereffi, Gary, and Wyman, Donald, eds. 1990. *Manufacturing Miracles: Paths of Industrialization in Latin America and East Asia*. Princeton, NJ: Princeton University Press.

Hamilton, Gary, and Biggart, Nicole. 1988. "Market, Culture and Authority: A Comparative Analysis of Management and Organization in the Far East." *American Journal of Sociology* 94 (supplement): S52–S94.

Harris, Nigel. 1987. *The End of the Third World*. New York: Penguin Books.

Henderson, Jeffrey. 1989. *The Globalisation of High Technology Production: Society, Space and Semiconductors in the Restructuring of the Modern World*. New York: Routledge.

Hill, Richard C. 1989. "Comparing Transnational Production Systems: The Automobile Industry in the USA and Japan." *International Journal of Urban and Regional Research* 13, 3 (Sept.): 462–80.

Hopkins, Terence K., and Wallerstein, Immanuel. 1986. "Commodity Chains in the World-Economy Prior to 1800." *Review* 10, 1: 157–70.

Keesing, Donald B. 1983. "Linking Up to Distant Markets: South to North Exports of Manufactured Consumer Goods." *American Economic Review* 73: 338–42.

Korzeniewicz, Miguel E. 1990. "The Social Foundations of International Competitiveness: Footwear Exports in Argentina and Brazil, 1970–1990." Ph.D. dissertation, Duke University.

———. 1992. "Global Commodity Networks and the Leather Footwear Industry: Emerging Forms of Economic Organization in the Postmodern World." *Sociological Perspectives* 35.

Lardner, James. 1988. "The Sweater Trade—I and II." *The New Yorker*, Jan. 11, pp. 39–73, and Jan. 18, pp. 57–73.

Law, Christopher M. 1991. *Restructuring the Global Automobile Industry*. London: Routledge.

Mody, Ashoka, and Wheeler, David. 1987. "Towards a Vanishing Middle: Competition in the Garment Industry." *World Development* 15, 10/11: 1269–84.

Morawetz, David. 1977. *Why the Emperor's New Clothes Are Not Made in Colombia*. New York: Oxford University Press.

Nemeth, Roger, and Smith, David. 1985. "International Trade and World-system Structure: A Multiple Network Analysis." *Review* 8: 517–60.

Nolan, Patrick. 1983. "Status in the World System, Income Inequality, and Economic Growth." *American Journal of Sociology* 89: 410–409.

Pfeffer, Jeffrey. 1987. "Bringing the Environment Back In: The Social Context of Business Strategy." In *The Competitive Challenge: Strategies for Industrial Innovation and Renewal*, edited by David J. Teece, pp. 119–35. Cambridge, MA: Ballinger.

Piore, Michael J., and Sabel, Charles F. 1984. *The Second Industrial Divide*. New York: Basic Books.

Porter, Michael. 1985. *Competitive Advantage: Creating and Sustaining Superior Performance*. New York: The Free Press.

———. 1987. "Changing Patterns of International Competition." In *The Competitive Challenge: Strategies for Industrial Innovation and Renewal*, edited by David J. Teece, pp. 27–57. Cambridge, MA: Ballinger.

———. 1990. *The Competitive Advantage of Nations*. New York: Free Press.

Reich, Robert B. 1991. *The Work of Nations: Preparing Ourselves for 21st-Century Capitalism*. New York: Alfred A. Knopf.

Ross, Robert J. S., and Trachte, Kent C. 1990. *Global Capitalism: The New Leviathan*. Albany: State University of New York Press.

Rueschemeyer, Dietrich, and Evans, Peter. 1985. "The State and Economic Transformation: Toward an Analysis of the Conditions Underlying Effective Intervention." In *Bringing the State Back In*, edited by Peter Evans, Dietrich Rueschemeyer, and Theda Skocpol, pp. 44–77. Cambridge, England: Cambridge University Press.

Sayer, Andrew, and Walker, Richard. 1992. *The New Social Economy: Reworking the Division of Labor*. Cambridge, MA: Basil Blackwell.

Schwartz, Hugh H. 1991. *Supply and Marketing Constraints on Latin American Manufacturing Exports*. Washington, D.C.: Interamerican Development Bank.

Scott, Allen J., and Storper, Michael. eds. 1986. *Production, Work, and Territory: The Geographical Anatomy of Industrial Capitalism*. Boston: Allen & Unwin.

Scott, W. Richard. 1983. "The Organization of Environments: Network, Cultural and Historical Elements." In *Organizational Environments: Ritual and Rationality*, edited by John W. Meyer and W. Richard Scott, pp. 155–75. Beverly Hills, CA: Sage Publications.

Snyder, D., and Kick, E. 1979. "Structural Position in the World-System and Economic Growth, 1955–1970." *American Journal of Sociology* 84, 5 (Oct.): 1096–1126.

Storper, Michael, and Harrison, Bennett. 1991. "Flexibility, Hierarchy and Regional Development: The Changing Structure of Industrial Production Systems and Their Forms of Governance in the 1990s." *Research Policy* 20, 5 (Oct.): 407–22.

Taylor, Peter J. 1988. "Alternative Geography, A Supportive Note on Arrighi and Drangel." *Review*, 11, 4 (Fall): 569–79.

Wallerstein, Immanuel. 1979. *The Capitalist World-Economy*. New York: Cambridge University Press.

Wellman, Barry, and Berkowitz, S. D. 1988. *Social Structures: A Network Approach*. Cambridge, England: Cambridge University Press.

Whitehead, Laurence. 1989. "Tigers in Latin America?" *The Annals* 505 (Sept.): 142–51.

Index

Adam Opel, 289
Adidas, 249, 252, 254
Advertising campaigns, 54–55, 125, 157, 274
Aetna Insurance Company, 135
Afghanistan, 88
Afterthoughts, 118 n.13
Agriculture: Coca. (*See* Cocaine); diagram of cocaine GCC, 302; diagram of produce GCC, 150; exports, traditional and nontraditional, 143, 147–48, 152–54, 156; flexible specialization in, 155–58; Fordist and post-Fordist models, 144–46, 155–58; global commodity chain in, 148–49; marketing of fresh produce, 154–55; ownership patterns in fresh produce exporting, 148; processing, 152–54; production, 144; quality control, 149; raw materials, 149–54
Albania, 88
Algeria, 88
American Airlines Sabre CRS, 134
Andina, 273
Angola, 88

A-phases, 5, 31, 41–42, 44, 73
Apparel industry: backward and forward linkages in, 103–4, 117; computer-aided design systems, 216; computer-controlled cutters, 216; contract manufacturing in, 210–11, 215–16, 219–20; diagram of apparel GCC, 207; distribution of, 206; domestic sourcing, 215–16; 807 programs, 214–15; export networks in, 106, 113–15, 189–91, 193–95, 202; government policies, 190–91, 210–11, 215, 234; high-value vs. low-value nodes, 191; import networks, 110–13, 194–98, 210; labor costs, 205, 208–9, 211, 213–16; linkages in, 187; manufacturing, 218–20; marketing networks, 106; Men's and Boys', 208, 217, 218–19; men's wool suits, 191–95; merchandising of, 99; mergers in, 103; overseas sourcing, 102–3, 110–13, 116, 211, 214–15; Pacific Rim, 190–91, 193–98, 201–2; production, 193–96, 198, 201–2; production costs, 206; protectionism in, 190–91; quotas in, 116; raw

227; parts exports, 225, 229–30, 233;
transnational domination of, 225, 284
—*maquiladora* industries, 117 n.4, 120
n.29, 230
Mitsubishi, 285, 289–90
Mitsubishi/CITC, 119 n.23
Mongolia, 88, 190
Montgomery Ward, 115, 118 n.11, 119
n.22
Morawetz, David, 85
Morse Shoe, 118 n.12
Motor vehicles, 74–76, 82, 88
Mozambique, 88
Multifiber Arrangement, 190–91, 210
Myanmar, 110

NAFTA. *See* North American Free Trade
Agreement
Namibia, 88
National Institute on Drug Abuse, 300
National Narcotics Intelligence
Consumers Committee, 298, 310
Navigation Acts, 27–28
Netherlands, 25, 28, 38, 41, 42, 48, 87,
198
New England, 25, 27
Newfarmer, Richard S., 227
Newly industrializing countries (NICs),
73, 84, 95, 100, 110, 113–17, 120
nn.30, 31, 130, 177–78, 187, 205,
208, 212, 220, 281, 286, 291
New Zealand, 87, 193–94
Nicaragua, 88
Niger, 88
Nigeria, 88
Nihon-Koyo, 253
Nike Corporation, 12, 99, 119 n.21, 120
n.26, 129, 137, 176, 247–61, 274
Nippon Rubber, 253, 255
Nissan, 233, 239, 289, 293
Nissho Iwai, 253, 255
Nordstrom, 118 n.9
North Africa, 40, 43
North American Free Trade Agreement,
183, 239, 293
North Korea, 88, 115, 190
Norway, 26, 28, 87

OEM. *See* Original equipment
manufacturing
Onitsuka Company, 252–54
Oppenheimer, David, 273
Original equipment manufacturing, 290–
92
Otis Elevator Corporation, 135
Özveren, Eyüp, 3, 5

PACE Membership Warehouse, 119 n.15
Pagoda Trading Co., 119 nn.19, 24
Pakistan, 88
Panama, 88
Pandol, 273
Paraguay, 88
Parke-Davis, 299
Pay Less Drug Stores, 119 n.15
Payless Shoe Source, 118 n.12, 119
nn.19, 24
PDC. *See* Producer-driven commodity
chains
Pelizzon, Sheila, 3
Peru, 88, 301–2, 304, 306, 308
Philippines, 88, 110
Phillips-Van-Heusen, 111
Pic'n Pay, 118 n.12
Piore, Michael J., 99, 145
Pohang Steel Corporation, 288
Poland, 36, 37, 38–40, 44, 45, 88, 195,
198
Polo/Ralph Lauren, 120 n.26
Porter, Michael E., 1, 6, 102, 188–89,
201
Post-Fordism, 144–45, 155–58; definition
of, 145
Processing of fruits and vegetables, 152–
54
Produce, Chilean: advertising of, 274; as
BDC, 271; cultural influences on
consumption, 267–78; demographic
changes in consumption, 271–72, 275–
76; diagram of produce GCC, 270;
exports, growth of, 268–70; freshness,
268, 271; government policies, 272;
growing season, 268, 273; input
sourcing, 268; market demand for,
268–72; produce-stand ethic, 275–77;
retailing, 274–75; transportation of,

About the Contributors

RICHARD P. APPELBAUM is professor of sociology at the University of California, Santa Barbara, where he is director of the Community and Organization Research Institute and the Center for Global Studies. His most recent books include *States and Development in the Asian Pacific Rim*, *Karl Marx*, and *Rethinking Rental Housing*. His research focuses on the globalization of production, with case studies of the apparel industry. He is co-editor of the journal, *Global Competition and Change*.

JEFFREY CASON is a postdoctoral research associate with the Global Studies Research Program at the University of Wisconsin-Madison, where he received his Ph.D. in political science. His research focuses on the political economy of trade and industrial policies in Brazil.

XIANGMING CHEN is assistant professor of sociology at the University of Illinois at Chicago. His recent research focuses on the interface between urban and economic development from a comparative perspective with a central focus on China. He has published articles in *Social Problems*, *Urban Affairs Quarterly*, *Urban Studies*, *Asia-Pacific Population Journal*, and *Journal of Marriage and the Family*.

BRAD CHRISTERSON is a Ph.D. candidate in sociology at the University of California, Santa Barbara. His dissertation research involves modeling global economic processes using geographic information systems and spatial statistics.

GARY GEREFFI is associate professor of sociology at Duke University. He is the author of *The Pharmaceutical Industry and Dependency in the Third World* and co-editor of *Manufacturing Miracles: Paths of Industrialization in Latin America and East Asia*. His research interests deal with business organizations, export networks, and the social bases of international competitiveness in East Asia and Latin America, with an emphasis on the implications of recent trends for development and organizational theories. He currently is studying the garment, footwear, automobile, and computer industries in South Korea, Taiwan, Hong Kong, China, Mexico, the Caribbean Basin, and the United States.

WALTER L. GOLDFRANK is professor of sociology and provost of College Eight at the University of California, Santa Cruz. He edited the second volume in this PEWS series, *The World-System of Capitalism: Past and Present*, and is currently working on Chilean export agriculture.

TERENCE K. HOPKINS is professor of sociology and member of the executive board of the Fernand Braudel Center for the Study of Economies, Historical Systems, and Civilization, Binghamton University. He is co-author of *Antisystemic Movements* and *Processes of the World-System*.

EUN MEE KIM is associate professor of sociology at the University of Southern California. She is the author of *Big Business, Strong State: Collusion and Conflict in South Korean Development, 1960–1990*. Her research interests include economic development, economic liberalization, and democratization in East Asia.

HYUNG KOOK KIM is associate professor of international realtions at Chung Ang University in the Republic of Korea. He is the author of *Between State and Market: Industrial Adjustment Strategy in Korea*. His research interests include government-business relations, industrial and trade policy, and economic relations between North and South Korea.

MIGUEL KORZENIEWICZ is assistant professor of sociology at the University of New Mexico. His areas of interest are political economy, organizations, and Latin America. Recent publications include "Global Commodity Networks and the Leather Footwear Industry: Emerging Forms of Economic Organization in a Postmodern World" in *Sociological Perspectives*, and "Commodity Chains and Footwear Exports in the Semiperiphery."

ROBERTO P. KORZENIEWICZ is assistant professor of sociology at the University of Maryland. He has published several articles on the labor movement in Argentina, and he has worked on labor unrest, democracy, and development in the semiperiphery. His current research focuses on innovation, international competitiveness, and export growth in Latin America.

NAEYOUNG LEE is a recent Ph.D. in political science at the University of Wisconsin-Madison. His research interests include comparative political economy and the relationship between the state and business in Latin America and East Asia.

SU-HOON LEE is associate professor of sociology at Kyungnam University, where he also directs its Institute for Far Eastern Studies in Seoul. He is the author of *State-Building in the Contemporary Third World* and *The Capitalist World-Economy*. His articles on Korean politics include "Moving Toward Democracy? South Korean Political Change in the 1990s" and "Transitional Politics: Activation for Civil Society."

WILLIAM MARTIN teaches sociology and African studies courses at the University of Illinois at Urbana-Champaign. He is co-author of *How Far the Wind? Southern Africa 1975–2000*, editor of *Semiperipheral States in the World-Economy*, and author of numerous articles on regional and world-economic relationships. His most recent work includes research on transnational relationships in the production of knowledge, including "Fifteen Years of World-Systems Analysis: Assessing the Attempt to Move Beyond Euro-North American Conceptions" in *Review*.

EYÜP ÖZVEREN is assistant professor of economics at the Middle East Technical University, Ankara, Turkey and research associate of the Fernand Braudel Center for the Study of Economies, Historical Systems, and Civilizations, Binghamton University. He teaches political economy and economic history. He is the author of "International Political Economy in the Making: Parameters of Turkey's Changing Regional Role."

SHEILA PELIZZON is research associate, Fernand Braudel Center for the Study of Economies, Historical Systems, and Civilizations, Binghamton University. She currently is finishing her dissertation on "Gender and the Transition from Feudalism to Capitalism," and is the co-author of "Hegemonic Cities in the Modern World-System."

EILEEN RABACH is a Ph.D. candidate in the Political Economy and Public Policy Program at the University of Southern California. She is currently completing her dissertation.

LAURA T. RAYNOLDS is a visiting assistant professor of sociology at Binghamton University. Her research focuses on current processes of restructuring in Latin America and the Caribbean, linking global transformations, shifting state policies, patterns of firm reorganization, and the changing livelihoods of local populations. Recent publications include "Women and Agriculture in the Third

World: A Review and Critique'' and ''The Restructuring of Export Agriculture in the Dominican Republic: Changing Agrarian Production Relations and the State.''

ERICA SCHOENBERGER is associate professor in the Department of Geography and Environmental Engineering of The Johns Hopkins University with a joint appointment in the Department of Anthropology. She has written on the investment strategies of multinational corporations, problems of adjustment in the automobile, electronics and aerospace industries, and the transition to a regime of flexible accumulation.

DAVID SMITH is associate professor of sociology at the University of California, Irvine. He recently has published articles on comparative urbanization and development, technology in the world-system, and network analysis of the global economy in *Urban Affairs Quarterly, Science, Technology, and Human Values*, and *Social Forces*. Among his on-going research interests are studies mapping the world city system, tracing raw material commodity chains, and examining Los Angeles as a global city.

IAN M. TAPLIN is associate professor of sociology at Wake Forest University. His recent publications include ''Rising from the Ashes: The Deskilling Debate and Tobacco Processing'' in *Social Science Journal*, and ''Segmentation and the Organization of Work in the Italian Clothing Industry'' in *Social Sciences Quarterly*. Currently he is researching restructuring, employment practices, and technological changes in the U.S. clothing industry.

IMMANUEL WALLERSTEIN is distinguished professor of sociology and director, Fernand Braudel Center for the Study of Economies, Historical Systems, and Civilizations, Binghamton University. He is the author of *The Modern World-System* (3 vols.), *Historical Capitalism*, and *Unthinking Social Science: The Limits of Nineteenth-Century Paradigms*.

SUZANNE WILSON is a doctoral candidate in sociology at the University of Illinois at Urbana-Champaign. She is completing a dissertation on the middle class and politics in Colombia and has collaborated for four years with Marta Zambrano in an interdisciplinary study of the cocaine trade.

MARTA ZAMBRANO is a Colombian scholar and a doctoral candidate in anthropology at the University of Illinois at Urbana-Champaign. In addition to her ongoing study of the cocaine trade, she is currently completing a dissertation on early colonial relations, culture, and power in Colombia.

Studies in the Political Economy of the World-System
(Formerly published as Political Economy of the World-System Annuals)

Numbers 1–6 published by Sage Publications.